DATE DUE

SPIES
OF THE
CONFEDERACY

BY
JOHN BAKELESS

DOVER PUBLICATIONS, INC.
Mineola, New York

ns
Master of the Historian's Art

Copyright

Published in Canada by General Publishing Company, Ltd., 30 Lesmill Road, Don Mills, Toronto, Ontario.
Published in the United Kingdom by Constable and Company, Ltd., 3 The Lanchesters, 162–164 Fulham Palace Road, London W6 9ER.

Bibliographical Note

This Dover edition, first published in 1997, is an unabridged republication of the work originally published in 1970 by J. B. Lippincott Company, Philadelphia & New York.

Library of Congress Cataloging-in-Publication Data

Bakeless, John Edwin, 1894–
    Spies of the Confederacy / by John Bakeless.
        p.   cm.
    Includes bibliographical references (p.   ) and index.
    ISBN 0-486-29865-5 (pbk.)
    1. Spies—Confederate States of America. 2. United States—History—Civil War, 1861–1865—Secret service. I. Title.
    [E806.B13   1997]
    973.7'86—dc21   97-23084
                                                            CIP

Manufactured in the United States of America
Dover Publications, Inc., 31 East 2nd Street, Mineola, N.Y. 11501

PREFACE

When, some twenty years ago, I began studies in the history of American military intelligence in the American Revolution, I was warned by a well-meaning editor that it would be quite impossible to find adequate sources. As I had studied the sources and the editor hadn't, I was not unduly discouraged. I continued the study anyhow—with another editor—and speedily discovered that there were so many documents, largely unknown, that it would be quite impossible to treat the subject in a single volume. In the end, it was possible to limit the subject to the British and American intelligence services in the main theater of operations, ignoring some very lively doings on the frontiers, in Canada, in England, and in Europe.

The same plethora of information—which, it is astonishing to note, no one has hitherto discovered—appears in Civil War intelligence. This book began as an effort to study both the Confederate and the Union services. It soon became apparent that there would have to be two books, one on Confederate spies, one on their Union rivals. Eventually, the mass of undiscovered material turned out to be so great that it was necessary to ignore Confederate saboteurs, secret couriers, and secret recruiting agents. They were, of course, technically spies, but they were not primarily concerned with collecting military information. Thus it is impossible to discuss here such gallant figures as Walter Bowie, who was mainly seeking recruits; the two agents who died so gallantly at Fort Granger, who seem to have been part of a secret transatlantic courier service; or Acting Master John Y. Beall, Confederate States Navy, who was engaged mainly in sabotage.

This abundance of unused material is all the more surprising in view of the destruction, before the fall of Richmond, of all espionage documents in the Confederate War Department.

Sources for the present study, as the Notes will show, are found in manuscript materials in national and state archives; small and highly local historical journals; obscure locally published books and pamphlets, sometimes surviving in unique copies only; personal narratives in the *Confederate Veteran*; official G-2 reports in the *Official Records*; and personal records published by such agents as Belle Boyd, Captain Conrad, and Mrs. Greenhow.

Evaluating sources is more difficult in a book such as this than it is in most historical studies. The materials were largely secret to begin with. A secret agent is perhaps more inclined to exaggerate his achievements than other mortals; and—while it is surprising how often confirmation does appear—it is sometimes necessary simply to accept data, though with suitable reservations.

The names of as many as possible of the colleagues who have aided me are listed in a special section. A few obligations are so great, however, that they must be mentioned here. A generous grant from the Huntington Library enabled me to work in its unrivaled collections for six months, during which Dr. James Thorpe, the director; Dr. Allan Nevins; Dr. Ray A. Billington; Miss Mary Isabel Fry; and other staff members gave me every possible assistance. The Yale University Library has again—as for the last thirty years— placed its immense resources and admirably efficient staff at my disposal.

Professor William Matthews, of the University of California at Los Angeles, let me draw upon his astonishing knowledge of American diaries. Mrs. Matthews, by a *tour de force* unique in historical research, was able to locate a long-lost Civil War "diary" which was supposed to exist, but which no one had ever been able to find. It was, as it turned out, not a diary at all, but a lady's club paper—not, however, an ordinary club paper, for in it a diplomat's wife recorded the stern warning on espionage given to her personally by Secretary Seward!

My wife having announced that she is weary of being acknowledged in prefaces, I make no mention whatever of many years of assistance, endless typing, proofreading, and revision, or many thousands of miles as a chauffeuse.

JOHN BAKELESS

Elbowroom Farm, Great Hill
Seymour, Connecticut
February, 1970

CONTENTS

1

THE REBEL SPIES
IN WASHINGTON

The Confederate states entered the Civil War with certain marked advantages over their Federal opponents. One great advantage lay in the fact that, to win the war, the Confederates had only to defend themselves. They were not trying to conquer the North. All they wanted was to get out of the Union. The Yankees, on the other hand, were trying to make the South stay in the Union; they had first to conquer, then to occupy, the entire territory of all eleven Southern states.

The Confederates had the further military advantage of interior lines. They could shift troops and supplies back and forth across a relatively short distance, behind the great defensive curve of their northern boundaries. The Federals had to operate over much longer distances, along the outer rim of that huge arc.

The Confederates had still another advantage. They were a hardy outdoor breed, primarily rural, accustomed to horses, to firearms, and to an outdoor life. Federal soldiers, largely town and city bred, often had to be taught to shoot, stay on a horse, march, camp, and live in the open.

The Confederates were also fortunate in discovering, at the very

beginning of the war, a group of superb generals, three of whom—
Lee, Jackson, and Stuart—rank among the great captains of all time.
More than half the Civil War was over before President Lincoln
could find leaders able to cope with them.

But the Confederates had one other and even greater advantage.
They began the war with an espionage system already organized and
highly efficient, with tentacles reaching into the vital secrets of the
Federal government, especially the War Department. Often the
rebels knew what the Yankees were going to do almost as soon as
the decision was reached—and long before the Union troops began
to move.

The Federals, on the other hand, had nothing of the sort when
war began. Even when it was clear war was approaching, there was
no way to work Yankee spies into the Confederate government.
There *was* no Confederate government. No one knew exactly what
that government would be, which states would join it, where it
would place its capital, how strong its army would be, which generals would take command.

Eventually, as the war went on, the Union intelligence services
came to equal their Confederate rivals. But they never succeeded
in protecting their secrets from the Confederate spies, who continued to penetrate the highest Federal headquarters and government offices until the very end. One rebel spy continued placidly
at work in the office of General Lafayette C. Baker, chief of Union
counterintelligence, all through the war. Even today, only his name
is known—and that is probably a pseudonym. Confederate secret
agents were so frequently in Washington that one hotel kept a room
permanently reserved for their use.

I

Before the war began, while the secession movement was growing,
Southern sympathizers in Washington were in an ideal position for
secret service. They had only to remain in their Washington homes
and offices—and spy as much as they pleased. Border states, like
Delaware, Maryland, and Kentucky, were the homes of innumerable
Confederate sympathizers. The younger men slipped off to join the
rebel army. The older men and all the women could be useful as

secret agents, as messengers, and as smugglers of medical supplies, recruits, arms, uniforms, and ammunition. All this was assisted by a widespread and well-organized secret society, the Knights of the Golden Circle, which had Northern and Southern branches, closely cooperating with each other.

The North had few such opportunities. It had no friends in high position in Jefferson Davis's government. It could not rely on many sympathizers beyond the Mason and Dixon line. Even men like Robert E. Lee, personally opposed to secession and devoted to the Union, felt it a duty to "go with their states." It took a long time for the Northern army to find Southerners still loyal to the Union and willing to risk their lives as Yankee spies. Even in a state like Tennessee, where sympathies were almost equally divided, there was for a long time no Union intelligence service at all, while rebel espionage was rampant.

All this made it difficult at first for the North to find out what the Confederates were doing and what strength their armies had—while the Confederates knew all about the Yankees. Allan Pinkerton had been called to Washington in April, 1861, to guard against spies; but he found such confusion that he could accomplish nothing, and went back to Ohio as Chief Detective on General McClellan's staff.

When McClellan took command in Washington in November, 1861, he brought his Chief Detective to the capital in charge of military intelligence. Long used to catching criminals, Pinkerton and his operatives found spy catching very much the same thing; but they totally failed to secure adequate intelligence of the rebel army. They had no idea what information an army needed, where and how to find it, least of all how to evaluate it. They were still floundering when McClellan was relieved in November, 1862. After that, Pinkerton gave up military intelligence altogether, to investigate frauds against the government, a task for which his experience with criminals well fitted him. Lecturers in staff colleges to this day hold him up as a horrible example of what an intelligence officer ought not to be.

As it became apparent, long before secession was an accomplished fact, that hostilities between the states were inevitable, various devoted Southern volunteers set to work, far in advance, to establish an elaborate Confederate system of secret intelligence and secret communication. They had ample opportunity to learn everything the Federals were doing, since there were practically no security precautions in Washington at all. Moreover, practically all the higher Confederate civilian officials had formerly been Federal officials and, as such, had known all about the operations of the Federal government from the inside. The leading Confederate Army officers were former U.S. Regulars, graduates of West Point. President Jefferson Davis was not only a West Point graduate, he had rejected a brigadier general's commission in the Regular Army, preferring to enter the Senate. He had been Secretary of War under President Franklin Pierce (1853–1857) and was again Senator from Mississippi when his state seceded. General John B. Floyd had already entertained in his Washington home Belle Boyd—not yet a Confederate spy. He had been President James Buchanan's Secretary of War until December 29, 1860—about seven months before Bull Run. Secretary Floyd may not, as Federals alleged, have ordered munitions stored in Southern arsenals to make sure Confederates could seize them easily; but he certainly knew all about the U.S. Army when he began to lead Confederate troops against it.

During the months before hostilities began, while the Southern states were one by one seceding, Confederate espionage in Washington operated in an almost friendly atmosphere. Army and Navy officers from the South, who had resigned from the United States services and were on their way to join the Confederates, were allowed to pass freely through Washington, observing anything they wished. Southern Senators, Congressmen, and government officials departed gradually, some of them at surprisingly late dates. They traveled without any restriction, and they carried much valuable information with them. The voyage of the Federal steamer *Star of the West* to supply Fort Sumter was betrayed to the Confederates by Jacob Thompson, who had been Secretary of the Interior in Buchanan's cabinet.

When civilian officials and Army and Navy officers from the Confederate states had all gone home, a host of Southerners still remained in Washington. Some, though their homes were in Dixie, put their loyalty to the Union above their loyalty to their states—men like the Virginian commander-in-chief of the U.S. Army, General Winfield Scott, or the future "Rock of Chickamauga," General

George H. Thomas. But many others were intensely loyal to the South. Some were social leaders from Southern families, long domiciled in Washington. Others were from border states. Still others were minor officials, safely ensconced in various Federal departments, ideally situated for treason. Some of these agents operated throughout the war, never suspected, never discovered, never confessing, unknown even today—save by the information they transmitted. Others, outside the government, were ready to provide shelter, emergency funds, or transportation to the rebel spies.

Charming Southern ladies who had long made their homes in the nation's capital remained in those homes and continued to charm Northern officers—to the great benefit of the Confederacy. Many of these women came from border states which never formally seceded but in which Confederate sympathies were strong.

Colonel E. D. Keyes, military secretary to General Scott, later remarked that, while on duty in Washington, he "found great delight with the Southern damsels, and even with some of the matrons, notwithstanding the incandescence of their treason." Among these Dixieland sirens, he notes, Mrs. Rose O'Neal Greenhow, an astute, wealthy, and highly placed Washington hostess of fanatically rebel sympathies, was "reputed to be the most persuasive woman that was ever known in Washington." That lady, as head of an important Confederate spy ring, must have found the colonel a useful acquaintance, for General Scott was at that time busy making war plans, and his secretary knew all about them.

Southern surveillance entered the domestic circle of the White House itself. Shortly after the inauguration, Mrs. Lincoln, a Kentuckian with a brother, three half brothers, and three brothers-in-law in the Confederate Army, found that one of her White House guests was "in the habit of listening about the Cabinet room doors" and then "retailing all the information he could thus gather to those only too willing to make use of it." When President Lincoln gave his sister-in-law a pass through the lines, the lady carried south "her weight almost, in quinine," a drug the Confederates badly needed.

Such incidents make it easy to believe the statement, sometimes made, that every decision of Lincoln's Cabinet during the first months of the war was known in Richmond within twenty-four hours. There was one bad Cabinet leak under President Buchanan.

Jacob Thompson, his Secretary of the Interior, later admitted that he had given the Confederacy advance warning that the steamer *Star of the West* was bringing relief to Sumter, so that the Confederates knew about when she was coming and "she received a warm welcome from booming cannon."

Many other leaks were made possible by individuals like Mrs. Lincoln's eavesdropping guest, by careless talk, and by numerous disloyal postmasters in Maryland towns, who helped speed treasonable messages on their way.

II

At least three Confederate spy rings, independent of each other, existed in Washington at various periods of the Civil War. The first was directed by Mrs. Greenhow; the second by Captain Thomas Nelson Conrad, 3rd Virginia Cavalry, an amazingly successful intelligence officer operating for J. E. B. Stuart; and a third (much later) system by Private Frank Stringfellow, 4th Virginia Cavalry, another of Stuart's star secret agents. The last two had some connection with the Confederate Signal Service under Major William Norris, which did, indeed, operate flag, torch, and telegraphic signals but which was essentially an espionage service. The Signal Corps was not established until 1862, however. Before that there seems to have been no centralized intelligence.

Still another spy, the Shakespearean actor James Harrison, a Confederate officer of unknown rank, was operating in Washington and perhaps elsewhere, certainly by 1863, probably much earlier.*

It is doubtful if any of these spy rings were connected. Both Mrs. Greenhow and Captain Conrad published accounts of their adventures, but neither mentions the other, though both are surprisingly frank. Harrison's identity was a mystery for a hundred years. If he ever was part of a spy ring, the secret is now lost. Such operation of several intelligence organizations in complete independence of each other is, of course, the soundest kind of intelligence practice.

There were also numerous Confederate sympathizers, connected with no networks at all, who gathered up such information as they could find in Washington and the Army's outpost lines along the

---

* See Chapter 17, Secrets of Gettysburg.

Potomac, sending it on to Confederate intelligence officers as best they could by methods of their own devising. One learns of them mostly from records of arrest and trial or from the reports of indignant pro-Union informants. But as to the really clever ones, who never did attract attention, the rest is silence.

Captain Thomas Jordan, U.S. Army, established the first Confederate spy net—which he turned over to Mrs. Greenhow's management—sometime in 1860 or perhaps in the first weeks of 1861. Jordan, who had served in the 3rd and 5th U.S. Infantry regiments, was soon to become a lieutenant colonel and later a brigadier general in the Confederate Army. He retained his Regular Army commission and stayed in Washington until he had fully organized his spies and was ready to hand them over to Mrs. Greenhow. Under her management, the ring worked undisturbed until August, 1861, when she and others were arrested. Even then, its flow of information to Richmond continued for months.

Captain Jordan had graduated from West Point, where he had been Sherman's roommate, in 1840. He had made a good record in the Seminole Indian wars and in the Mexican War. When hostilities ended in Mexico, he had shown special logistical talent as a staff officer, assisting the homeward movement of General Winfield Scott's troops.

Scott, though a Virginian, was General-in-Chief of the Army, combining the modern duties of the chief of staff and a commanding general. As such, Scott was in charge of war plans. Captain Jordan's former association with the general who now commanded the whole Army must have been a great help in his Confederate espionage— of which the general knew nothing.

By the time Jordan did resign from the Union Army, he had done his work so well that the espionage he had initiated could go on without him. Mrs. Greenhow continued to receive reports from the various spies they had together selected. She could send their information on in cipher, through a secret courier system, running directly to Jordan's new post at Beauregard's headquarters and thence on to Richmond. Either the Confederate War Department or General Beauregard could send back queries requesting special information with equal ease.

It is amazing how boldly Confederate officers hung about Washington, in the general perplexity and confusion of early '61. Jordan himself did not resign till May 21, more than a month after Beauregard—whose staff he joined immediately—had opened fire on Fort Sumter (April 12, 1861). In her diary for June 29, 1861, a Union officer's widow noted that a certain Captain Heyward was still in the capital. "He is General Beauregard's aide and goes to Manassas tomorrow." This was less than a month before Bull Run. It was no secret where Captain Heyward was going. But nobody stopped him.

To some degree this appalling Northern carelessness about casually wandering Confederates lasted all through the war. In 1863, when the Union Army occupied Nashville, paroled Confederate officers were allowed to move about the city as they pleased. One of them taught a Sunday school class that included Union soldiers! In the closing months of the war—when the Northerners should long since have learned their lesson—Captain W. H. Webb, a North Carolina officer who had escaped from Battery Park Prison, strolled about New York City in a faded Confederate uniform, as long as he wished. When questioned, he invariably stated the exact truth: He was a Confederate prisoner, escaped from the Battery. People broke into merry laughter and passed on! No wonder there was lax security in the first months of '61!

A proper regard for security was never really achieved on either side. A Confederate spy just returned from Washington was, at least once, introduced as such, with pride, in Jefferson Davis's White House. Stuart rashly let a Virginia political leader know what two of his best spies were doing, thereby horrifying Robert E. Lee when the politician let their names appear in the press. As late as 1863 a telegraph messenger, John Lancaster, with a father and a brother in the Confederate Army, was caught reading U.S. War Department telegrams while delivering them to the telegraph office. Sapiently describing this enterprising lad as "a very improper person to be employed by the Telegraph Company," the Federal authorities finally sent him to prison in the Old Capitol Building.

III

Captain Jordan could not have found a better leader for his spy ring than Mrs. Greenhow. Maryland born and an ardent secessionist, she had grown up as a "pampered Washington belle" in the capital's inevitably political atmosphere. Her girlhood mentor had been that arch-politico, John C. Calhoun. Inevitably, she had been widely acquainted in governmental circles since girlhood and had acquired a surprising degree of influence—which she was quite willing to use in the service of the Confederates.

"Major E. J. Allen"—that is, Allan Pinkerton, head of the secret service—reported officially that she had "secret and insidious agents in all parts of this city [i.e., Washington] and scattered over a large extent of country." (This last statement explains why papers in the ciphers used by the Rebel Rose eventually turned up hundreds of miles from Washington.) These reports supplied "the most valuable information," including statistics available "nowhere but in the national archives." Much of this information, he was sure, "must have been obtained from employees and agents in the various Departments of the Government"—a surmise which is now known to have been correct.

Through her late husband, Dr. Robert Greenhow, a State Department official, Mrs. Greenhow had long since become well acquainted with the diplomatic corps. After Dr. Greenhow's death, his wealthy widow had continued to live in Washington, becoming a recognized power in a city where petticoat influence has always been powerful. The political pull she had long possessed increased during President James Buchanan's administration, since Mrs. Greenhow and the bachelor President had always been close friends, corresponding on political affairs, even while Buchanan was abroad as Minister to the Court of St. James's. When he entered the White House, Buchanan remained a frequent caller at Mrs. Greenhow's, in spite of the tradition that the President of the United States does not call at private homes.

Nor was President Buchanan the Confederate spy's only close friend in high official stations. The Secretary of State, William H. Seward (until very recently a particularly powerful Senator from New York), dined at her beautifully appointed table with other officials and almost equally distinguished guests. The lady's most ardent admirer can undoubtedly be identified as Senator Henry Wilson of Massachusetts—later Vice President of the United States—though he signed the flaming love letters that he wrote her only with an "H." His was a very useful friendship for a Confederate spy, for Wilson was chairman of the Military Affairs Committee of the United States Senate.

Another of the lady's senatorial admirers was Joseph E. Lane of Oregon. Though there are no flaming protestations of his affection, Senator Lane was another useful man to know, for he was also on the Military Affairs Committee.

There seems to be little doubt that Senator Wilson did write the "H" letters. They are on Senate stationery. They show that the writer was much interested in the Pacific Railroad bill—as Wilson was. They are in a hand that exactly resembles his and that resembles the hand of no other Senator of the period, so far as can be discovered.

How far the intimacy between the captivating lady and the enraptured legislator may have gone, no one can now determine. The impassioned tone of the "H" letters—seized when Mrs. Greenhow was arrested and now in the National Archives—does not sound Platonic and is not at all what one expects in normal senatorial correspondence. Indeed, it suggests that "H" and Mrs. Greenhow were very close friends indeed. Or rather, it suggests that Mrs. Greenhow found it desirable to keep "H" thinking so. If the letters were not Senator Wilson's, they still prove that some other prominent Union leader was madly devoted to this dangerous lady and was, at best, not very discreet.

"You well know that I love you—and will sacrifice anything," said one flaming note, only "I have feared to bring you into trouble." After this, a few less romantic words about the Pacific Railroad bill. Then: "You know that I *do love* you. I am suffering this morning, in fact I am sick physically and mentally, and know that nothing would soothe me so much as an hour with you. And tonight, at whatever cost I will see you. . . . I will be with you tonight, and then I will tell you again and again that I love you."

In such a mood, even the most sedate of statesmen is not likely to set rigorous guard upon his tongue. The ardor of the letters suggests that Mrs. Greenhow had little difficulty in getting whatever information she wanted from this particular admirer.

When the war was over, Jordan admitted that he was partly responsible for all this. He had learned of an "intimacy" between the charming widow and the susceptible Senator. After he learned that, said Jordan, he himself cultivated Mrs. Greenhow's acquaintance and then "induced her to get from Wilson all the information she could."

Mrs. Greenhow secured some startling information, which—no matter from whom Mrs. Greenhow secured it—had certainly at some time or other been in Wilson's hands, though she does not name her source. The lady herself says she was able to report what General Scott was writing to Senator Wilson. Correspondence between the General-in-Chief of the U.S. Army and the chairman of the Military Affairs Committee of the U.S. Senate was just the sort of thing to interest the Confederates. And who but Senator Wilson could have told Mrs. Greenhow about it? Certainly not General Scott!

She also learned exactly what General McClellan had said to Senator Wilson. And where did the general and the Senator converse? In President Lincoln's own reception room in the White House!

The omniscient Confederate lady likewise knew, almost as soon as the orders came out, the names of three officers newly appointed to McClellan's staff. Worse still, she discovered what McClellan meant to do, just as she learned what General Irvin McDowell meant to do. "She knew my plans," wrote McClellan himself, bitterly, "and has four times compelled me to change them." She learned McClellan's scheme for army reorganization, which should never have gone beyond the inner circles of the War Department.

This wasn't all that Mrs. Greenhow knew. She knew the exact place where President Lincoln's guard was stationed. She knew about speculations in the War Department when Simon Cameron was still Secretary of War, before the scandal was revealed to the public. All this was information available to Senator Wilson as chairman of the Military Affairs Committee.

Mrs. Greenhow, who had known Secretary of State Seward for many years, had had abundant opportunity on innumerable glittering social occasions to note an amiable weakness in that stern man's character. Although the Secretary was coldly efficient by day, "after supper and under the influence of the generous gifts the gods provide" he was likely to become what Mrs. Greenhow called "properly attuned." That is how the Confederates on one occasion secured some useful naval intelligence. While "properly attuned"—that is, mildly squiffy—the Secretary of State, in chatting with a diplomat, let slip a few useful facts about the U.S. Navy's strength and plans. The Rebel Rose, who had plenty of diplomatic contacts, secured the information while it was timely enough to be useful, enciphered it, and sent it on to Beauregard. The general—to whom strictly naval information was no use at all—sped it on to Jefferson Davis, who could make very good use of it, indeed.

Soldiers as well as politicians succumbed to Rose's artful wiles. "She has not used her powers in vain among the officers of the army, not a few of whom she has robbed of patriotic hearts," said a disgusted Federal when the truth began to come out, much too late.

Government clerks could also be useful. A young Washington clerk named Doolittle, said to have been a relative of Senator James R. Doolittle of Wisconsin, was another well-informed individual with access to high official levels, who, according to Mrs. Greenhow, was "an occasional and useful visitor to my house." Mrs. Greenhow says this youth was "clerk of the military committee." If so, he would certainly have been a useful acquaintance for any rebel spy. There were, however, two clerks named Doolittle in government service at the time, and both were assisting the Committee on Indian (not Military) Affairs. Possibly Mrs. Greenhow was thinking of the Senator's son, Anson O. Doolittle.

In this case, however, Mrs. Greenhow may not have been quite so astute as she imagined. The younger Doolittle—whichever one it was—may have been playing a much deeper game than he admitted. He may have been a well-covered Federal counterintelligence agent throughout his whole acquaintance with her.

Mrs. Greenhow became suspicious when the young clerk brought a letter, asking her to forward it to a certain Colonel Corcoran in Richmond. Instead of denying she was in touch with Richmond at all (something her young friend would never have believed anyhow), the guileful matron accepted the missive, carefully explaining it would probably be impossible to send it to Richmond, because General McClellan's counterintelligence measures were so strict. After that she simply kept it and, to all the young man's inquiries, replied only that she had had no chance to forward it. This was probably meant to suggest that she had no communication with the

Confederates at all and that, if she had ever done any espionage, she had given it up. She was, in fact, still in almost daily contact with Beauregard's headquarters, whence Jordan could, with the utmost ease, forward to Richmond anything she sent him.

2

THE SPIES WHO
WON BULL RUN

The two remarkable Confederate triumphs with which the Civil War began—the capture of the Harpers Ferry arsenal and the victory at Bull Run—were both the results of early and correct military intelligence. They were also the results of the speed with which the Confederate leaders recognized the accuracy of the information— and acted upon it.

By a queer sort of irony, however, the seizure of Harpers Ferry (April 18, 1861), with several million dollars' worth of ordnance supplies, had no connection whatever with the elaborate intelligence network Captain Jordan and Mrs. Greenhow had labored so assiduously to establish. Neither the captain nor the lady secured a single scrap of the intelligence that made the raid successful; and this is especially odd because Captain Jordan, still on duty in the War Department, should have known for months that this important post had only a skeleton garrison which could not possibly defend it.

As Virginia approached secession, the U.S. Army prepared to strengthen the Harpers Ferry garrison. Captain Jordan should have known all about that, too, but not a word from him or Mrs.

Greenhow reached the rebel leaders. The Confederates would not have captured the arsenal at all—at least, not in 1861—had it not been for the swift intervention of two Confederate volunteer spies, complete amateurs, having no connection with any network.

I

Harpers Ferry was guarded by a young Regular Army officer, Lieutenant Roger Jones, with a small detachment, originally sixty soldiers, now only forty-eight. These troops had been sent in January, 1861, when Alfred M. Barbour, superintendent of the arsenal, had warned Washington there was danger of attack. Barbour, though a Virginian, felt "the duty of protecting the property of the Federal Government now under my charge," especially as Virginia had not yet seceded. It was typical of the tragic confusion of the times that Barbour, when he resigned his post, felt it equally his duty to help Virginia state troops to seize that same "property of the Federal Government" which hitherto he had so zealously safeguarded. Virginia's ordinance of secession was passed April 17; Barbour helped capture the arsenal on the eighteenth.

Lieutenant Jones, who knew his little guard was totally inadequate, had sent a secret messenger to Washington, asking for reinforcements. But the messenger lost courage. He didn't go to Washington at all. He simply went home.

On April 15, 1861, as it became evident that Virginia was going to secede (the State Legislature voted the ordinance of secession only two days later), ex-Governor Henry A. Wise, a future Confederate general, authorized Captain John D. Imboden, another future Confederate general, to have a force of state militia standing by, ready to seize the arsenal as soon as the state formally left the Union.

Imboden's son-in-law, Dr. Alex Y. Garnett, lived in Washington. Though he is not known to have been part of any Confederate undercover organization, the doctor in some way discovered that the Federal government was about to send a Massachusetts regiment, 1,000 strong, to reinforce Lieutenant Jones at Harpers Ferry. He telegraphed the news to his father-in-law. With the assistance of various Virginia military officers, including Turner Ashby—soon to distinguish himself as a cavalry leader and intelligence agent—Imboden loaded ammunition on a passenger train, put some state troops aboard, and started off to seize the arsenal before the Union reinforcements could arrive. Additional militia companies had orders to stand by, at various stations along the line, waiting for Imboden to pick them up. Barbour, former superintendent of the arsenal, traveled with him.

Just before the train pulled out, Barbour made an incautious remark which roused the suspicion of a Northern passenger. The Yankee promptly wrote out a telegraphic warning to President Lincoln but, as the train was ready to start, could not send it himself. Instead, he gave it to a Negro, with instructions to take it to the nearest telegraph office, at the same time handing the man a dollar.

The Southern conspirators had already learned to fear telegraphic leaks, suspecting that Union spies might be quietly listening to the clatter of the keys. In this they were entirely correct. At least one Union agent, who was also a telegraph operator, had persuaded General Beauregard himself to introduce him at the Manassas railroad station as "a railroad man willing to undertake any work you may have for him to do." He was already busy sweeping out the telegraph station and listening to every message that came in.

If the telegram sent by the suspicious Yankee passenger had ever reached Washington, Harpers Ferry might have been reinforced in time and the arsenal saved to equip the Union forces. But an equally observant Southern passenger had noticed what the Yankee was doing. The Southerner could not leave the train either, but he sent a friend to follow the Negro, stop him before he could reach the telegraph office, and take away the message.

This, says Imboden, "perhaps prevented more troops being sent to head us off." At any rate, no Union reinforcements ever did reach Harpers Ferry.

The driver of the locomotive was, however, a Union sympathizer, too. Northern engineers were common in the South, for, in that agricultural society, skill with machinery was rare; and many a clever Yankee mechanic crossed the Mason and Dixon line to drive a railroad engine. The man at the throttle of Imboden's locomotive on April 17 was one of these; and he, too, had no difficulty guessing the mission of the armed men in the cars behind him. Letting his fires go out, as if by accident, he managed to stop the train; but the Confederates forced him, at pistol point, to fire up again and get the train moving with no great loss of time. Imboden rode in the cab with him the rest of the way, to make sure there would be no more accidents.

At Harpers Ferry Lieutenant Jones, seeing his danger in time, set fire to the arsenal, destroying between 17,000 and 20,000 muskets or rifles, which both Union and Confederate armies badly needed. But the shops themselves, with many unassembled parts for small arms, were saved. Most important of all, the fire did not damage the machinery for making U.S. Rifle Model 1841 (the "Mississippi Rifle") and U.S. Rifle Musket Model 1855. All this equipment the Confederates seized and sent south to arsenals of their own.

II

This achievement was followed in July by the overwhelming victory at Bull Run, made possible by essential information supplied by the Jordan-Greenhow organization. However brief the existence of their spy net, this one success fully justified all the work and danger involved in establishing it; and, if the victorious Confederates had attempted an advance on Washington, the additional information collected for that purpose would have been equally valuable.

General Beauregard soon found that he could trust the "arrangements" made "through the foresight of Colonel Thomas Jordan." These arrangements, he said after the war, enabled him "to receive regularly, from private persons at the Federal capital, most accurate information, of which politicians high in council, as well as War Department clerks, were the unconscious ducts." (Some of the sources were, however, not quite so "unconscious" of what they were doing as the general supposed.)

Though the Rebel Rose had been supplying intelligence long before Bull Run and continued to supply it for some months afterward, her greatest service of the entire war was the advance information she sent immediately before the battle. This told Beauregard exactly what McDowell was going to do, long before the poor man had a chance to do it.

Though there are no surviving records to show how much information Jordan sent before resigning from the Regular Army, with regard to the strength of the growing Union forces, the information was available to him as a staff officer in the War Department, and it is inconceivable that he failed to supply it. Beauregard himself says only that he had full-strength reports from "Washington agencies."

On July 4, 1861, a little more than two weeks before the battle, Beauregard secured additional authentic information confirming the reports he had already received. By a great stroke of luck, his outposts caught a Union soldier who was on duty in the office of McDowell's adjutant general, compiling strength returns to about July 1. The prisoner was perfectly willing to talk.

Prisoners or deserters eager to provide intelligence about their own army have to be handled with care, since they are very likely to be enemy "plants." Using them was a favorite Confederate trick, which the Federals also were quite capable of employing. This man, however, seemed to be genuine—though what an enlisted man from the commanding general's headquarters was doing in front of enemy outposts is a question nobody has ever answered. According to Beauregard himself, this deserter's figures on McDowell's strength "tallied so closely with that which had been acquired through my Washington agencies," that the Confederate general "could not doubt them."

Further confirmation of these Union strength reports was supplied by Northern newspapers, "regular files of which were also transmitted to my headquarters from the Federal capital." However reckless the press may have been, it was hardly publishing official Union strength reports, but it certainly *was* publishing reports of troop movements. Such reports identified individual regiments; and, given a list of regiments known to exist, it was not difficult to get a fairly clear idea what forces the Union had raised and where these forces were.

III

Valuable as this exact knowledge of Union strength was, Beauregard still needed to know what McDowell was going to do with that strength. In most tactical situations, it is dangerous to try to guess the enemy's intentions, for he may change his mind at any moment. The only safe thing for a general to do is to list enemy capabilities—not what the enemy *will* do but what the enemy *can* do. Thanks to his Washington spies, however, Beauregard was lucky enough to know in advance what McDowell meant to do and exactly—to the very day—when he was going to do it.

Mrs. Greenhow supplied this precious information in three messages, sent July 10, 16, and 17, after which McDowell obligingly did all that was anticipated, until the battle began July 21, 1861. By this time, Captain Jordan—now a Confederate lieutenant colonel—was with Beauregard. He was the ideal man to evaluate the intelligence Mrs. Greenhow was sending. Never before or since in military history has an intelligence officer dealt with secret information from the enemy's War Department staff only three weeks after having himself been a member of that staff.

It was evident that General McDowell would soon have to march south and attack Beauregard's Confederates at Bull Run. Otherwise, most of his army would go home without having done anything at all. President Lincoln had issued a call on April 15, 1861, for three-month volunteers, though most of these men could not be mustered into service until some weeks later. Their periods of enlistment ran from the date on which they had been mustered in, and by mid-July, 1861, these enlistments were beginning to expire. Some Union troops actually marched off the Bull Run battlefield, because their time was up!

Though he had at first planned to attack Washington, Beauregard eventually decided to stand on the defensive at Manassas, in a good position, close to his bases but far enough north to defend Virginia, and with the army of General Joseph E. Johnston, in the Shenandoah Valley, close enough to give support. He now hoped the Yankees would take the offensive. "If I could only get the enemy to attack me, as I am trying to have him do," he wrote Richmond, "I would stake my reputation on the handsomest victory that could be hoped for." Mrs. Greenhow's news showed that McDowell was going to do exactly that.

The first of her three crucial messages preceded the Union advance by six days. Mrs. Greenhow sent it in cipher on July 10, McDowell's march began on the sixteenth, there was a Union reconnoissance in force by one division on the eighteenth, and battle was joined on the twenty-first. The lady herself says that she had seen the march order, which was, or should have been, the most carefully guarded secret the government possessed. Though no copy can now be found in the National Archives, McDowell must have issued some kind of written order, and of this actual text Mrs. Greenhow says she had a transcript.

Probably it had been smuggled to her by one of her numerous admirers officially connected with military affairs. Senator Wilson's name has inevitably been suggested. Jordan himself says that the clerk, John F. Callan, was an informant for the Washington spy ring, with close military contacts, well acquainted with Mrs. Greenhow. If he was a genuine Confederate sympathizer, which is by no means certain, he, too, might have betrayed the secret of McDowell's march. Mrs. Greenhow says only that she "received a copy of the order to McDowell," but she gives no hint where she got it.

Her messenger was Betty Duvall, the young and very pretty daughter of a Maryland couple whose home was in Washington. Coming from a long line of Marylanders, Betty knew the country and the people on both sides of the Potomac thoroughly and, like most Southern girls of the period, was experienced with horses. After enciphering her message, Mrs. Greenhow folded it into a tiny packet, which she sewed up in silk. This she fastened into Betty's luxuriant black hair, where it was held in place by a "tucking comb" —a small, semicircular comb then worn to support a knot of hair at the top of the head.

The Confederates had evidently used this method of concealment before. Mrs. Chesnut's *Diary from Dixie*, on July 13, refers to spies "from Washington, galloping in with the exact number of the enemy done up in their hair."

Very plainly dressed, to look like a farmer's daughter, Betty boldly drove an ordinary farm cart out of Washington and across the Chain Bridge, about noon on July 10, 1861. Beauregard himself

says she brought "the first message from Greenhow" to General
M. L. Bonham, at Fairfax Court House, "about" July 10. Bonham,
formerly a South Carolina Congressman, was now a newly hatched
Confederate brigadier.

With McDowell's whole army about to advance, any remotely sensible counterintelligence service would have clamped an iron security ring around the capital—a control such as was clamped
around Britain immediately before D Day, 1944. Everyone in
Washington could see what was going to happen, for it is impossible
to conceal preparations for the movement of a large force. Mrs.
Greenhow herself describes the indications perfectly: "Officers and
orderlies on horse were seen flying from place to place; the tramp
of armed men was heard on every side—martial music filled the
air." Field trains were being prepared. Quartermasters were busy.
Transport and combat wagons were being loaded. Confederate spies
merely had to stroll about the streets to see that an advance was
imminent. But the Union Army had, as yet, very few intelligence
agents of its own and no idea how to stop the enemy's.

Betty Duvall was thus able to drive peacefully out of the city,
encountering nothing more dangerous than admiring male glances
(to which she was fully accustomed). Unmolested, she proceeded to
the Virginia home of Lieutenant Catesby ap R. Jones, late U.S.N.,
now an officer in the new Confederate Navy and destined to become
executive officer of the *Merrimack*. The lieutenant was absent on
duty, but his family gave Mrs. Greenhow's messenger a warm welcome for the night.

In the morning, no longer disguised as a farm girl driving a produce wagon but trimly clad in a smart riding habit with a girl cousin
for companion, Betty rode toward Fairfax Court House. Somewhere
near there, a Confederate picket stopped her. She had run into
General Bonham's outpost line, and the pickets were at first
obdurate. General Bonham had just given orders that no more
women were to pass the rebel lines. He seems to have suspected
that Yankee female spies were slipping through, though, so far as
can now be ascertained, the only women agents then active were
Confederate.

After some argument, Betty persuaded the suspicious soldiers
to send her on. The provost marshal himself took her to General

Bonham, who already knew Betty, having probably made her acquaintance during his service as a Congressman. No man who had once seen Betty Duvall was ever likely to forget her. General Bonham hadn't.

Indeed, the susceptible general has left an account of the effect of the dashing young brunette's appearance at his astounded and delighted headquarters. The provost marshal, he says, brought in "a beautiful young lady, a brunette with sparkling black eyes, perfect features, glossy black hair." She had, according to the general, "a fine person of medium height," and he could see "the glow of patriotic devotion burning in her face."

Betty had evidently said nothing at the outpost except that she must see the general at once, with important information. To General Bonham she said that she had important information for General Beauregard. Would the general receive it and forward it immediately? If not, might she have permission to ride on herself?

Bonham replied that he "would have it faithfully forwarded at once."

Thus assured, Betty "took out her tucking comb and let fall the longest and most beautiful roll of hair that I have ever seen." (The general sounds like a connoisseur; he was at least appreciative.) With her raven locks flowing about her, Betty "took then from the back of her head, where it had been safely tied, a small package, not larger than a silver dollar, sewed up in silk." Probably without knowing what was in it, Bonham rushed the packet on to Beauregard, who later sent it by officer courier to Jefferson Davis.

The message was brief and very much to the point: "McDowell has certainly been ordered to advance on the sixteenth. R.O.G."

Events soon proved Mrs. Greenhow's complete accuracy. General McDowell's troops began to move toward Bull Run on July 16, exactly as she had predicted. Beauregard's army was waiting—already in position, with a line of outguards pushed well forward, beyond the stream.

As McDowell's superior Federal forces drew gradually closer to Beauregard's front line, the situation grew tense. More than ever, Beauregard needed constant information from sources inside Washington. This Lieutenant Colonel Jordan secured with commendable speed. A quiet civilian traveler presently appeared on the southern bank of the Potomac and crossed in a boat—which he seems to have had no difficulty finding, rowed by an oarsman who conveniently appeared from nowhere, at the right moment. Securing a horse and buggy with suspicious ease, he drove into Washington. It was all quite simple.

The silent traveler was George Donellan, surveyor and engineer, who had been an official in the Land Office until Lincoln's inauguration, when he hastily resigned. He arrived at Mrs. Greenhow's home on Sixteenth Street in the early morning of July 16, 1861. The maid who received him roused her sleeping mistress.

Either Mrs. Greenhow had not known Donellan when he was in the Department of the Interior or she thought it wise to pretend he was a stranger. From whom did he come? "Mr. Rayford, of Virginia." In other words, Lieutenant Colonel Jordan, whose intelligence pseudonym was "Thomas J. Rayford." But anyone could say that. Had he further identification? Donellan handed over a cipher message from Jordan.

"Trust bearer," it said. That was enough.

The Rebel Rose gave Donellan the second of her three vital messages. This showed the number of McDowell's troops and the route he would follow. The Federal commander would have 55,000 men—an exaggerated figure, but Jordan was probably able to correct it by comparison with the figures given by the prisoner captured July 4. Mrs. Greenhow confirmed her report about McDowell's march order. The Federals would "positively commence that day [July 16, 1861] to advance from Arlington Heights and Alexandria on to Manassas, via Fairfax Court House and Centreville."

Donellan left Washington with the message on July 16, 1861, as McDowell's advance began, and reached Beauregard's camp at eight o'clock that night. By that time the Confederate pickets had already been pushed back—partly confirming Mrs. Greenhow's news. To reach the Confederate lines at all, her courier had to force his way past the advancing Yankee columns. But none of McDowell's half-trained officers thought of halting an unexplained civilian, even if he *was* riding straight toward the enemy.

The speed of the Confederates' secret communication system is surprising. By noon of the seventeenth, Mrs. Greenhow had an answer from Jordan: "Yours was received at eight o'clock at night.

Let them come; we are ready for them. We rely upon you for precise
information. Be particular as to description and destination of forces,
quantity of artillery, etc."

On the night of the seventeenth, Mrs. Greenhow sent her third
vital message. She had just learned that the Federals hoped to cut
the railroad between Winchester and Manassas, thus delaying Johnston's march from the Shenandoah Valley to reinforce Beauregard at Manassas. This, however, the Union forces never succeeded
in doing, probably because of Mrs. Greenhow's warning. One Yankee
engineer tried to delay the movement of these troops by deliberately mishandling his locomotive—exactly what the engineer of
Imboden's train had tried to do, to delay the move on Harpers
Ferry. But neither man succeeded.

Even though Major General Robert Patterson, Union commander
in the Shenandoah, had failed to attack Johnston's rear and delay
his march, the Federals would still almost certainly have won the
day at Bull Run if they had cut that railroad. It was the sudden arrival of Johnston's army that turned Confederate defeat into victory.

Beauregard now had two additional bits of luck which enabled
him to verify the complete accuracy of Mrs. Greenhow's reports on
McDowell's march. One was an intelligence report from a spy with
a glass eye named John Burke, who, though a Texan in a Texan
regiment, had been born in the North and thus possessed a Northern accent that enabled him to move about among Yankees without rousing suspicion. The details of Burke's report are lost, but
there is no doubt that he gave general confirmation of what Mrs.
Greenhow had already reported.

The other bit of luck was an extremely pretty girl named Antonia Ford, daughter of E. R. Ford, a merchant of Fairfax Court
House. The Ford home was ideally situated for espionage, being
exactly midway between Washington and Manassas, so that the
whole Ford family could watch McDowell's troops and tell exactly
which roads they were taking.

On July 19, three days after Mrs. Greenhow's first crucial report
and two days before the battle, Miss Antonia appeared at Beauregard's camp. She had walked six miles from her father's house to her
grandfather's—no great matter for a sturdy country maiden of

1861; had there secured a horse; and had persuaded an aunt to go with her to warn the general.

Beauregard's advanced posts had been near the Ford home until the general pulled them back. When Federal troops appeared, the Fords' first thought was to inform their own side. Antonia's father—who had himself been suspected of espionage for the Confederates—may have sent the girl, thinking her more likely to pass unquestioned than a man. This was certainly her first secret mission, though not by any means her last.

Antonia Ford's news of the Federal advance was welcome confirmation of Mrs. Greenhow's earlier reports. But the Confederate staff members, who knew nothing about her, were at first suspicious. Was she a genuine Confederate sympathizer? Or was she a Federal plant? Giving the enemy a few accurate facts that he will soon discover anyway is an old, old game; every double agent in history has used it. Except as belated confirmation, the girl's information had no great value. Ordinary mounted reconnoissance would soon have provided the same facts. There was no use taking chances.

On general principles, Beauregard's staff arrested poor Antonia and sent her under guard to Brentsville, a small town south of Manassas, lest she carry information back to the Union forces. At about this time, however, one of J. E. B. Stuart's Washington spies —John Burke, the Confederate officer from Texas with the Northern accent and the glass eye—brought in further confirmation. And before long events fully confirmed the information Mrs. Greenhow, Antonia Ford, and Burke had jointly provided. There was no more doubt.

Released after twenty-four hours, Miss Antonia had to go home by a circuitous route, for the roads were swarming with bluecoats, whose coming she had predicted.

After this adventure, she continued to spy, though no one knows exactly what she did, except that she supplied information to Mosby. It took Federal counterintelligence nearly three years to get Antonia under lock and key. And what good did that do? Antonia simply married the Union major set to guard her a year after they locked her up.

Various other Confederate sympathizers—probably not regularly occupied in espionage, but amateurs eager to supply such information as came their way—sent bits of information, further supplementing what Beauregard and Jordan already knew.

At Dranesville, a hamlet north of Washington, dwelt a certain George Coleman, "very energetic in collecting information of the movements of the Federal Army, and carrying it to the rebels, both before and after the battle of Bull Run." He had the assistance of a Negro named Davy, who helped him gather facts. There was also Charles Follin, of Water's Hill, near Vienna, Virginia, directly west of Washington. When Follin was at last arrested on the Union front line, in December, 1861, he was charged with "communicating important information to the insurgent authorities." This, it was charged, had been going on for a long time. Presumably, then, he had begun spying before Bull Run.

At Manassas and at Richmond, things began to happen as soon as Rebel Rose's messages had been studied, certainly before all the confirmatory reports had been received from other agents. Beauregard had expected McDowell to have a strong force, but not the 55,000 men his most trustworthy secret agent was now reporting. (In fact, McDowell had only 34,000, but even 34,000 men were enough to outnumber Beauregard.) At least, however, the Confederate commander had his wish: McDowell was going to attack.

The High Command in Richmond had learned to trust Mrs. Greenhow. Orders went out at once to General Joseph E. Johnston, commanding in the Shenandoah. Johnston had 11,000 men, including an eccentric brigade commander of no particular reputation, named Thomas Jonathan Jackson, and a young cavalry officer, named J. E. B. Stuart, who, as yet, had still less reputation. Johnston had been sent there to contain much larger Federal forces threatening the Valley, under Major General Patterson, an elderly "dugout" from Philadelphia, who had had a good record in the Mexican War and no record at all, thereafter.

The new orders reached Johnston not long after midnight on July 18, 1861, a few hours after Mrs. Greenhow had sent her third message. The general's problem now was to take his own forces quickly to Manassas to support Beauregard and at the same time to keep Patterson where he was. Colonel J. E. B. Stuart—soon to be a general and the most renowned cavalry commander in either army—managed to bluff Patterson into staying where he was. At dusk, having held back 18,000 men with one regiment, Colonel Stuart withdrew his horsemen and followed Johnston to Manassas. After that, the rear of Johnston's 11,000-man army lay wide open to attack by Patterson's 18,000.

The Union commander could, with the greatest ease, have pursued Johnston and forced him to give battle. In that case, Johnston would probably have been defeated. He would certainly have been delayed. In either case, he could not possibly have come in upon the flank of the almost victorious McDowell at Bull Run, turning a Federal success into overwhelming Federal disaster. If Patterson had delayed Johnston, the Civil War might easily have been ended on that July afternoon in 1861!

The Union was defeated at Bull Run because the besotted Patterson would not believe the completely accurate and confirmed intelligence brought him. A few West Virginia loyalists in the Shenandoah Valley had been carefully watching the Confederate movements there. One devoted artist spy had even made sketching trips through the Confederate camps. When Johnston started to Bull Run, these Unionist civilians had hung, unobserved, upon his tracks. They even watched his soldiers crossing to the east bank of the Shenandoah, a move that left no doubt where he was going. Then two secret agents crept forward secretly from the Union Army and independently verified the civilians' reports.

All of this military information reached General Patterson· in plenty of time for action. But Patterson and most of his staff not only refused to believe these accurate and timely reports, they did not even send the news to Washington. (It is not altogether surprising that General Patterson found himself a civilian again, only a few days later.)

3

THE GREENHOW RING
AFTER BULL RUN

July 20, 1861, the day before the Battle of Bull Run, was a day with whose events Mrs. Greenhow and the Washington spies had no concern. There was nothing more they could do to influence the next day's fighting. They had done their part of the work. The soldiers would have to finish it.

Mrs. Greenhow did not even wait in Washington to learn the outcome of her plots. She started for New York on the twentieth and spent the next day, while the battle was raging, putting her second daughter, Leila, aboard ship for California, where she was to live with her older sister till the war was over. Mrs. Greenhow could easily foresee that the next few years of her own life would be stormy; but at least two of her daughters would be safely distant from the fighting, though she could not send away her youngest daughter, Rose, still a mere child.

During July 18–19, false rumors of a great Federal victory at Bull Run reached Washington, spreading to New York City on the twentieth, the day before the battle itself. These were presumably due to the fighting on the eighteenth, which was really only a reconnoissance in force, but which could be made to seem like a Union victory. Even when the real battle was fought on the twenty-first, McDowell himself believed, as late as three o'clock in the afternoon, that he had won the day. Then Johnston's troops from the Shenandoah appeared on the Union flank and rear—the troops that Mrs. Greenhow's intelligence had brought to the battlefield—and McDowell's army collapsed.

The Rebel Rose received the first false reports of Union victory with incredulity and dismay; but her spirits lifted as the later accurate reports of crushing Federal defeat poured in. She watched, with immense satisfaction, the panic in Manhattan on the twenty-second, as news of the defeat was "cried through the streets."

"The whole city," she wrote, "seemed paralysed by fear, and I verily believe that a thousand men could have marched from the Central Park to the Battery."

Reaching Washington at six o'clock on the morning of July 23, Mrs. Greenhow received a message from her friend Jordan at Manassas: "Our President and our General direct me to thank you. We rely on your further information. The Confederacy owes you a debt."

Mrs. Greenhow began to consider the question of "further information." The organization of her ring was by this time probably nearly complete, though it will never be possible to name all its members. George Donellan of the U.S. Land Office managed communications, with Colonel Michael Thompson, who used the code name "Colonel Empty," from his initials, as a substitute. Dr. Aaron Van Camp, a well-known Washington dentist, also carried messages and probably did espionage of his own. Lewis Linn McArthur, Colonel Thompson's clerk, apparently assisted with cipher; at least, a new cipher was found in his desk. William T. Smithson, an F Street banker, was in touch both with Mrs. Greenhow and the Confederate War Department. Betty Duvall, Mrs. F. A. Hassler (Bettie Hassler), and Lily Mackall were among the couriers. Various younger men had some kind of undefined relationship to the ring, and a certain Samuel Applegate, probably a Union soldier, may have been a double agent from the beginning. Doubtless there were many others.

I

It had already become apparent that something would have to be done to improve communication between Confederate headquarters and the Confederates in Washington. Federal counterintelligence was certain to become more alert. Betty Duvall had succeeded brilliantly—once. But so pretty a girl was certain to be noticed, especially in a city full of soldiers. She might continue as a resident lady spy, picking up information from her admirers among Union officers—as she certainly did; but she could not go back and forth on many future trips without causing suspicion. Frequent trips by Donellan himself would also grow more dangerous.

Realizing this, he began to set up a new courier line to Beauregard and Richmond on July 21, while the fighting was still in progress at Bull Run. The new men he found were so devoted, skillful, and discreet that the line itself and many of its couriers and letter drops escaped Federal detection throughout the war. On the twenty-first, the very day of the battle, he sent the mysterious Dr. Wyvill, Wivill, or Whyvill, who lived near the Washington Navy Yard, instructions for his service as a courier in the new line. It was, Donellan told him, to be established "next day." The doctor was to get in touch with one Grymes (either James or Benjamin) at Matthias Point. Later, an equally mysterious Dr. Kent is mentioned as another medical man serving as courier, and there was one more doctor, whose very name is unknown.

These physicians were particularly useful because, as medical men, they could go anywhere, at any hour, without rousing suspicion. Moreover, as every doctor of that day was a kind of traveling drugstore, carrying his medicines with him, his bulging pockets and large black bags excited no suspicion. Since they paid professional calls either on horseback or in buggies, each of the three physicians could carry documents to safe houses along the southern limit of his ordinary rural practice. Here the next doctor could pick them up, until they were far enough south for official Confederate secret couriers to take them. This was the beginning of the highly effective "Doctors' Line," which was to continue serving General J. E. B. Stuart's Washington secret agents long after Mrs. Greenhow had been arrested and her spy ring broken up.

The victory at Bull Run was so overwhelming that the obvious next step for the victors was the capture of Washington. Such a blow to the Union cause might easily force Lincoln's government to admit defeat and agree to secession. On the night after the battle, Stonewall Jackson declared that he could capture the Federal capital with 10,000 men. Beauregard, who had a good many more men than that, was not so sure, but he submitted to Jefferson Davis a "full plan of campaign for concentrating our forces, crushing successively McDowell and Patterson and capturing Washington."

The first request Donellan brought from the Confederate command after the battle was for information "regarding the movements of the two or three next successive days." Defeat had forced McDowell's army so far to the rear that the victors hardly knew what it was doing. It was easy enough for Mrs. Greenhow to get this information. The hopeless confusion of the Union Army was everywhere apparent; and, though Donellan himself had gone to Manassas with important information of his own, Colonel "Empty" Thompson could arrange emergency communications while the new line was being set up.

II

The spies' next great task was preparation for the capture of Washington. Mrs. Greenhow knew well enough the information Beauregard would need: What was the Federal system of alarm signals? What fortifications existed? Where? How strong? How fully manned? What artillery? Where emplaced? Troop movements?

The Federal alarm signal that was to herald a Confederate attack on Washington seems to have been one of her first discoveries— "three guns from the Provost-Marshal's office, followed by the tolling of the church bells at intervals of fifteen minutes."

The incredible Federal indifference to security still assisted the rebel spies. To investigate the alarm signals, Mrs. Greenhow simply "went round with the principal officer in charge of this duty, and took advantage of the situation." Her good luck in being able to do so she regarded as a direct intervention of Providence on behalf of General Beauregard and the Confederate intelligence service. "It would be wrong to ascribe these things to chance," she said piously. In other words, God may not have been "on the side of the big battalions" (the Union forces were much larger than the Confederate), but He was certainly on the side of Confederate spies who kept their eyes open.

Surviving intelligence reports of the Greenhow ring of this period exist only in ciphered documents which were torn to bits before the Federal detectives found them. Some were then pasted together and copied out in clear after the Confederate cipher had been broken. Naturally, there are a good many gaps. Many are not dated; but, since they deal with preparations for the proposed attack on Washington, they must obviously have been written between Mrs. Greenhow's return to the capital on July 23, 1861, after Bull Run, and her arrest on August 23. There is no doubt that she continued to collect and forward other intelligence even when a prisoner herself. But these reports were written after the earlier papers had been seized.

One report, written July 31, 1861, says that in Washington "the panic is great and the attack hourly expected. They believe that the attack will be simultaneous from Edward's Ferry.*** Baltimore.*** A troupe [sic] of Cavalry will start from here this morning to Harper's Ferry. Don't give time for re-organizing."

Another report of about this date gives Union troop locations: "There are 45,000 on the Va. side, 15,000 around the city, to wit, up the river above Chain Bridge, at Tenallytown, Bladensburg, across Anacostia Branch and Commanding every approach to the city. If McClellan can be permitted to prepare, he expects [to] surprise you but now is preparing *** Look out for mas[ked b]atteries wherever you go."

A report dated 7 p.m. August 10, 1861, says:

> McClellan is very active and very discreet. McDowell moved toward Fairfax yesterday at 9 A.M. with 20,000 men. Every order is being executed without attracting attention. Activity pervades McClellan's forces.—It is reliably stated that 45,000 occupy the Va. side and 15,000 the approaches from the District side of the City. An attack is apprehended by McClellan, Judging McClellan's movements indicate apprehension of an attack. Banks has 35,000 men more or less. So the reliable rumor says. It is doubt *** a combined force of 100,000***

Mrs. Greenhow's spies reported on shortage of blankets, guards at the approaches to Washington, the railroad to Baltimore, artillery at Tanallytown, McClellan's efforts to make the secret service more efficient, and the "works in the vicinity of Washington," with a list of forts that occupies a page and a half.

The spies had been especially careful to study troop movements. One report, supposed to be in Donellan's handwriting, says: "Every arrival and departure every movement in fact has been noted by Eye witnesses placed at the out and inlets for such purpose." Observation of this sort was evidence that "the papers do still chronicle the movements correctly," and that the Yankees were not concealing facts by false reporting. This was an important matter for Confederate staff officers, who diligently read enormous consignments of Northern newspapers all through the war.

Mrs. Greenhow was also establishing a fifth column to operate in Washington when the Confederates attacked: "We are endeavor*** to effect an organization here in order to take advantage of emergencies. If possible their telegraph wires will*** all be simultaneously cut, and their guns spiked along the Va. side." Another report is very similar: "At proper times an effort will be made here to cut their telegraph wires and if possible to spike their guns wherever they are left unmanned."

III

This kind of thing could not go on indefinitely without increasing the suspicions that had long existed—especially as Mrs. Greenhow had been a great deal too outspoken from the very beginning. Even before Lincoln's inauguration, there had been an embarrassing scene at one of her brilliant political dinners. Though ardently Southern herself, the hostess had been a little too broad-minded in selecting her guests. Dining formally with her that evening were Senator William H. Seward, Charles Francis Adams, and Colonel John Bankhead Magruder, U.S.A. It was an ill-assorted company. In a very short time, Senator Seward would be Abraham Lincoln's Secretary of State. Adams would be Lincoln's Minister to the Court of St. James's, desperately trying to keep the British from aiding the Confederacy. Colonel Magruder would be a Confederate general.

It was all due to Mrs. Adams. She insisted on discussing the recent hanging of John Brown, whom she described as a "holy saint and martyr." This was too much for their hostess.

"He was a traitor," she rejoined, "and met a traitor's death."

Legally, there was certainly something to be said for that point of view. Magruder, a Virginian, inevitably supported Mrs. Greenhow's arguments, after which it remained for Seward, ever the diplomat, to smooth matters over. He did—but episodes of that sort were widely whispered about in Washington.

Now, John Brown was hanged December 2, 1859. The somewhat acrimonious conversation at Mrs. Greenhow's table sounds as if it took place while feeling was still strong—in other words, not long after the execution. In that case, the dinner with its revealing conversation can hardly have been later than 1860. When, in March, 1861, Senator Seward became Secretary of State and for some months took over the additional duty of running down Confederate spies and other disloyal persons, he could have no doubt where Mrs. Greenhow stood. Once she had begun espionage, she should have disguised her Southern sympathies as much as possible, but instead she went right on expressing them, even after hostilities had opened.

A good many other Southern ladies were just as indiscreet. The amateur lady spies in Washington could not avoid boasting of their share in the rebel victory. One Federal agent reported that "fine ladies were secretly giving information to the enemy." And, he added, "it was openly boasted that the secret information given to the rebel generals had been mainly the cause of the defeat of our armies at Bull Run." Which was the literal truth.

The War Department was now convinced that Mrs. Greenhow was "corresponding with the rebel authorities and furnishing them with much valuable information." It also feared—correctly—"from her previous association with officers in the army, that she was using her talents in procuring information from them which would be immediately communicated to the rebel government." Nobody noticed that the charming Betty Duvall was doing the same thing. That beautiful young creature kept it up for years, until the military authorities at last made trouble—in spite of which she married a U.S. Army officer.

The man who eventually ended the dangerous Mrs. Greenhow's career in espionage was Allan Pinkerton, founder of the famous detective agency. Pinkerton had been in Washington briefly in 1861, after helping Lincoln get there in safety. When McClellan brought him back to Washington in 1862, the detective masqueraded as "Major E. J. Allen," a disguise so perfectly maintained that General Fitz-John Porter, who had known "Allen" all through the Civil War, was astonished to learn, years after the war was over, who he really was.

Soon after the detective's arrival in Washington, Assistant Secretary Scott at last decided to do something definite about Mrs. Greenhow. Pinkerton says he received orders "that a strict watch should be kept upon this house, and that every person entering or leaving the same should come under the close surveillance of my men."

For several days operatives hovered about Mrs. Greenhow and also around several of her friends and their homes. The agents were to identify "every person entering or leaving" and see whether they communicated with other suspicious persons. Any of these people who tried to go south were to be seized and searched. Anything found on them would be examined by the Secretary or Assistant Secretary of War.

At dusk one day in early August, 1861, three shadowy figures quietly closed in on the Greenhow residence. After looking the ground over, Pinkerton placed his two detectives where they would not be obvious and went off to get three more. The watchers were aided by darkness, rain, and a strong wind, which covered any noise they might make. In such weather, passers-by were few and were concerned mainly with getting home to shelter. None of them disturbed the lurking figures.

From their hiding place, the watchers could see lights in two rooms on the "parlor floor," the first floor above the basement; but, to Pinkerton's annoyance, the Venetian blinds were tightly closed. Determined to find some way of peering in, Pinkerton called two men, took off his shoes to spare their epidermis, and stood on their shoulders, while he silently slipped the sash up and turned the slats in the blind just enough to let him look inside. After all this trouble, he saw nothing whatever. The room was empty.

At this moment, someone approached along Sixteenth Street, and the three detectives scuttled for cover under "the stoop which led up to the front door." The pedestrian turned up the steps. As they huddled together there, the detectives could hear everything that was happening above their heads. Mrs. Greenhow's bell rang. The door opened. The visitor entered.

The slats of the Venetian blind were, fortunately, still open. Drenched to the skin by the driving rain, Pinkerton again mounted the shoulders of his long-suffering operatives and peered in. He could catch a glimpse of the visitor. Aha! An infantry captain of the Regular Army. Pinkerton knew the man, whom he had met that very morning. He commanded one of the stations of the provost guard of Washington, the equivalent of modern military police. An officer of the provost guard was the very last man in the world who ought to be paying secret visits to a suspected enemy spy.

The officer was alone, but, as Pinkerton watched, he saw Mrs. Greenhow enter the room. He had had time only to recognize her when his lookout gave warning: again someone was coming along the street. Again they hid.

When Pinkerton resumed his watch, he had another disappointment. The pair were talking in tones so low the howling wind nearly drowned their voices. Eventually, he heard enough to be sure the captain was giving information about troop dispositions. Presently, the man took a map from his pocket. Pinkerton thought he recognized it, even from a distance, as a plan of Washington fortifications. (In the book she wrote a few years later, Mrs. Greenhow boasted of sending military maps to Beauregard; and, though she was careful to protect her sources, it is likely enough she received some or all of her maps from the treacherous captain.)

Silently Pinkerton watched, while the pair went over the maps together, occasionally pointing out areas of special interest to each other.

More footsteps on the pavement. This time, several pedestrians were approaching. Again the detectives fled to cover. When Pinkerton dared peer in once more, the room was empty. For an hour he watched—nothing. Then, as the couple reappeared, there was another warning from the lookout. Someone was passing. Hastily concealing themselves under the stoop, the detectives heard the door opening above them, "a whispered good-night, and something that sounded very much like a kiss," after which the captain came down the steps and set off along the street.

Melodrama changed to slapstick farce. Pinkerton had slipped off his shoes to climb on the shoulders of the detectives. Though the streets were wet with rain, there was no time to put them on now, for the suspected traitor was rapidly disappearing into the night. Pinkerton padded off in pursuit in his stocking feet, through "blinding mist and pelting storms" and—what was worse still—on clammy pavements.

At a suitable distance, one of his detectives, William Ascot, followed. Experienced though he was, Pinkerton this time did not prove successful in shadowing. Success in that difficult art depends on remaining unsuspected by the subject, but the combined darkness, mist, and rain forced the detective to keep too close to his prey. Twice the officer seemed to feel he was being followed. They had gone only to the corner of Pennsylvania Avenue and Fifteenth Street when Pinkerton thought he saw a revolver in his quarry's hand. Then he lost him entirely. The officer had slipped swiftly into the doorway of a building, before which a sentry stood. His disappearance took the trailing detective by surprise, but he had been following so closely that he dared not now make himself conspicuous by turning around and starting the other way. Instead, he did the only thing he could do. He strolled on toward the sentry, stocking feet and all—very wet, very muddy, very suspicious, very uncomfortable, and very worried—trying to look like any other belated wayfarer.

It was no use. Four soldiers rushed out with bayonets fixed.

"Halt, or I fire!" yelled the officer of the guard. His men seized first Pinkerton, then Ascot.

Half an hour later, the disconsolate chief of the U.S. secret service was standing before the man he had been trailing, who played significantly with two revolvers while he interrogated his prisoner.

Pinkerton gave only his usual cover name, "E. J. Allen." When he declined further information, he soon found himself—still spattered with mud and dripping water—in a very cold guardhouse, with an excellent chance of developing a bad cold or pneumonia, amid a choice collection of drunks. Ascot met the same fate, but he at least had shoes.

A sympathetic guard finally brought Pinkerton a blanket and an overcoat and agreed to carry a note to the Assistant Secretary of War's home as soon as he himself went off duty. At 6 A.M., August 24, the servants, already awake when the soldier arrived, took the note to Scott's bedroom. By seven o'clock, he was back at Pinkerton's barred door. The Assistant Secretary had accepted the note but the soldier dared not say so. Instead they spoke in swiftly improvised code.

"How is the weather outside?" asked Pinkerton.

"All right, sir," answered his messenger, winking.

Pinkerton knew well enough what the wink meant. So did Ascot. But neither detective spoke to the other. They had carefully been behaving like strangers, from the moment of their arrest.

By half-past eight, a rescue party arrived from the War Department. The sergeant of the guard approached the barred door with a paper in his hand, calling for "E. J. Allen and William Ascot." Everyone knew now that these were no ordinary prisoners, but they might be prisoners of state so dangerous that the High Command wanted to deal with them itself. All the guard was allowed to know was that they were being taken to the War Department. The captain seems not yet to have realized how odd it was that senior War Department officials should suddenly show so much interest in two routine arrests which had not been officially reported to them— and show it after only a few hours. He went to the War Department with them.

Scott, when he beheld his bedraggled secret service chief—still shoeless, soaked, with soggy clothes and a hat that never would be much good for anything again—managed to retain his gravity till he could take him to a private room. Then he burst into roars of laughter. Orders went out for continued surveillance over the Rebel Rose and for her immediate arrest if she tried to escape from the city.

The captain had to be dealt with at once. Scott called in that erring officer and asked for details of Pinkerton's arrest. The captain had his story ready. Even now, he did not seem to realize who Pinkerton was or to guess that the detective had observed him with Mrs. Greenhow and the map. The room in which he had met the Confederate enchantress had seemed perfectly secure. Otherwise, he would certainly have told the Assistant Secretary a different tale. He had, he said, been visiting "friends" in the outskirts of Washington, returning late. He *had* noticed—as Pinkerton had feared—that he was being followed and had ordered the man tailing him arrested. Then Scott asked a critical question:

"Did you see anyone last evening who is inimical to the cause of the government?"

The captain denied it; Scott was stern. Was the captain sure of that? He was. Quite sure? The captain was quite sure. But these not very competently told lies were useless. He was ordered to hand over his sword and was placed under arrest.

Search of his possessions soon provided evidence that he was in communication with the enemy. Herself shockingly careless about keeping incriminating papers, Mrs. Greenhow had not properly trained her assistants either. The captain went to Fort McHenry in Chesapeake Bay, near Baltimore, but was for some reason released within a year. Pinkerton says only, "He died shortly afterward."

Pinkerton charitably veils the man's identity under what he himself says is a pseudonym, "Captain Ellison"—a wholly needless delicacy in the case of an army officer secretly communicating with the enemy in violation of his military oath. There have been efforts to identify him as Captain John Elwood, 5th Infantry, who was appointed provost marshal of Washington, May 1, 1861, arrested October 25, 1862, and sent to the Old Capitol Prison, where he died December 3; but there are discrepancies between the stories of Pinkerton's Captain "Ellison" and the real Captain Elwood. Elwood's arrest was a great deal later than the arrest Pinkerton reports. He was charged with financial irregularities, not espionage. He did not die a natural death but committed suicide. The whole thing is rather queer. Elwood's case is too close to "Ellison's" to be ignored, yet not close enough to prove that the pseudonymous "Ellison" stood for the real Elwood.

When Pinkerton splashed down Sixteenth Street in his stocking feet, followed by Ascot, the other detectives had stayed at Mrs. Greenhow's home and had, by this time, been there all night and well into the morning. As soon as the disloyal captain—whoever he was—had been disposed of, Pinkerton sent reliefs, and the watchers presently rejoined him. They had nothing in particular to report, but they had been thoughtful enough to bring back their chief's shoes.

Though she did not know that her interview with "Ellison" had been watched and may not for a while have learned what had happened to "Ellison" himself, Mrs. Greenhow soon realized that she was under serious official suspicion. One of General McClellan's officers let slip to a lady in Georgetown the news that Mrs. Greenhow and a prominent pro-Confederate man in Washington had been placed on a special list of dangerous persons. Either McClellan's officer was disloyal or he was the kind of person (not uncommon on hastily organized staffs) who simply cannot be discreet.

The Georgetown lady passed the word to Mrs. Greenhow, who, in spite of the warnings, had to stay at her post. The male suspect was William Preston, a Kentuckian who had lately returned from service as Minister to Spain. Perhaps warned by Mrs. Greenhow, he fled south in time to save himself.

Continuous surveillance soon showed who the charming widow's suspiciously frequent callers were. Since Mrs. Greenhow had always been deep in politics, some of them were Congressmen, though they seemed to be men whose loyalty was above suspicion. Pinkerton is even charitable enough to suggest that they "were, perhaps, in entire ignorance of the lady's true character." But his watchers soon found one man who called on Mrs. Greenhow almost every evening and invariably stayed a long time. Though Pinkerton does not name him, this was undoubtedly "Colonel Empty," Michael Thompson, a South Carolina attorney practicing in Washington. Placed under special surveillance, he was found to be combining espionage with his legal practice, assisted by his clerk, Lewis Linn MacArthur. Shadows soon found Thompson was also associated with Mrs. Greenhow's business friend, William T. Smithson (alias Charles R. Cables), and the dentist, Dr. Aaron Van Camp. Many of their letters were found aboard the captured Confederate schooner *Lucretia*. It was time to halt the lawyer's activities, and Pinkerton gathered him in.

IV

Mrs. Greenhow herself began to notice that queer things were happening. She had suddenly ceased to hear from her friend Captain "Ellison." She became aware that she was being followed "by those emissaries of the State Department, the detective police." (More experienced operatives would not have let themselves be noticed, but surveillance by Federal counterintelligence in those days was not by any means so adroit and unobtrusive as it ought to have been.)

Mrs. Greenhow's own technique, however, was not much better than that of the sleuths who sniffed along the beautiful lady's perfumed trail—and let themselves be caught doing it! She and her friend Lily Mackall found it rather amusing to be followed (it often is), but they made the mistake of letting their shadows see that they had been observed.

If Mrs. Greenhow had had a little more experience, she would have pretended she hadn't even noticed. But she and Lily Mackall could not always resist the temptation to have a little fun at the other side's expense. They liked to turn suddenly in the street. If someone else turned, too, they found it amusing to "follow those who we fancied were giving us an undue share of attention."

The two rather enjoyed the game, but it was far from discreet. It could not fail to warn the pursuing Federals that the rebel spy was aware of the surveillance and would certainly take steps of some kind to evade it. They would have to do something definite now.

4

LADIES IN JAIL

By late August, 1861, Pinkerton was ready to strike. It was a trifle more than a month since the rebel victory at Bull Run, in which Mrs. Greenhow had taken so large a part. Suspicion was growing apace. Pinkerton operatives had watched a steady stream of Confederate sympathizers, spies, and couriers knocking at her door—which a more experienced director of espionage would never have allowed them to approach.

Pinkerton, however, had orders to move cautiously. The lady still had friends in Congress; and everybody in Washington has always walked delicately before those fortunate mortals who have friends in Congress.

After months of success, Mrs. Greenhow was growing overbold. About this time she went calling on Mrs. Robert Hunt Morris. Mrs. Morris had a husband in the State Department. In spite of that, Mrs. Morris also had a brother-in-law on Beauregard's staff. Without admitting that she was Beauregard's leading spy (a fact which, by this time, half of Washington more or less took for granted), Mrs. Greenhow offered to transmit a letter. She did not, it is true, offer to transmit it to the rebel officer. Only to his wife. But, according to

Mrs. Morris, the Rebel Rose was rash enough to add, "I'm a personal friend of Beauregard, and if you will bring me a letter, I will see that your sister receives it."

Like a dutiful wife, Mrs. Morris reported this to her husband. State Department officials, however, are remarkable for their caution. Morris told his wife to drop Mrs. Greenhow's acquaintance instantly and entirely. Sometime later, Secretary of War Stanton asked Mrs. Morris to visit his office.

"My dear little woman," he said, when the lady appeared, "we wish to thank you for the great service you rendered your country." That may have been sincerely meant, or it may have been rather heavy irony. It was followed by a scarcely veiled warning, a gently interpolated remark about "the possible escape you had by not sending a letter to Richmond."

I

On August 23, Mrs. Greenhow went for a "promenade" with a "diplomat" not otherwise identified. As usual, a Pinkerton man went trailing after. On her way home, after parting from her diplomatic friend, the lady paused to inquire about a neighbor's children, who had been ill. While chatting with a group on the sidewalk, she was able to pick up "some valuable information"—perhaps oral, perhaps written—from one of her agents who had apparently been loitering there in the hope that she would pass. Probably Mrs. Greenhow had also been getting information from the unnamed diplomat with whom she had been walking, for she had in her possession at that moment "a very important note," not necessarily the information that had been slipped to her on the sidewalk. People do not ordinarily "promenade" merely for pleasure in the subtropical heat of a Washington August, and a long walk is the safest way in the world to make sure a conversation cannot be overheard. No operative, however skilled, can eavesdrop in an empty street. The "diplomat" may have given her papers, or she may have made her own note on oral information from him.

Someone in that little group on the sidewalk had been concerned with observations that had nothing to do with the health of Mrs. Greenhow's neighbor's children. This unknown individual now warned her that her house had been watched all night and that she had been followed during her walk with the diplomat. The two men who had followed her were still lingering near. Mrs. Greenhow had at times been able to spot other Pinkerton operatives, but this pair she now noticed for the first time.

Trying to look ostentatiously innocent, these men now walked past 398 Sixteenth Street, "with an air of conscious authority"—which is just the air no shadow should ever assume, but then, Mrs. Greenhow was prejudiced. When they reached "the end of the pavement" (apparently this means the corner), both stopped and stood watching her—another elementary blunder.

When she saw that the two men meant to continue hanging about, Mrs. Greenhow could guess what was coming. She must at once get rid of the incriminating papers she had with her, which luckily were not very bulky. Fortune favored her, for at that moment one of her spies passed—they seem to have been swarming on Sixteenth Street. Pretending not to notice the watchful Pinkerton men, she muttered to the agent as he passed, "Those men will probably arrest me. Wait at Corcoran's Corner, and see. If I raise my handkerchief to my face, give information."

The agent went whistling down the street with cheery nonchalance. Rose slipped her "very important note" into her mouth and "destroyed" it. Presumably, that means she chewed it up and swallowed it.

With the message safely disposed of, Rebel Rose crossed the street and, outwardly calm, started up the steps. Before she could get the door open, the detectives were behind her. One was Pinkerton himself, in a major's uniform.

"Is this Mrs. Greenhow?"

"Yes."

Both detectives hesitated—and who can blame them? They were about to arrest one of the leading ornaments of the capital's society, a warm personal friend of the last President, a hostess who had entertained the present Secretary of State and the Minister to the Court of St. James's, even after he became President.

Seeing their hesitation, the Rebel Rose boldly demanded, "Who are you, and what do you want?"

Pinkerton replied, "I come to arrest you."

"By what authority?"

"By sufficient authority."

"Let me see your warrant."

This was awkward. There was no warrant. Pinkerton could only say he had oral authority from both State and War departments.

The Rebel Rose—who, in spite of her later loud complaints, probably found it all delightfully exciting—was playing this little comedy for the benefit of her own spies, one of whom, she knew, was observing the scene. She raised her handkerchief to her lips, glancing to see if the watcher on the corner had understood the signal. Meantime, the two detectives had fallen in, one on each side of her. Thus guarded, the social leader entered her aristocratic home.

"I have no power to resist you," she told her captors. "But had I been inside of my house, I would have killed one of you before I had submitted to this illegal process."

"That would have been wrong," said a detective, primly.

Mrs. Greenhow thought they showed "evident trepidation"; but Pinkerton, who had spent his life chasing some of the most desperate criminals in North America, can hardly have been very much frightened, especially when supported by a second detective. Both men knew, however, that another Confederate lady spy, Belle Boyd, had shot a Union soldier dead at her door.

The detectives tried to pacify the furious widow.

"We only obey orders."

Other operatives now began to appear, seemingly from nowhere. The house was expertly isolated.

"What are you going to do?" demanded the lady.

"To search," replied Pinkerton, briefly.

Mrs. Greenhow made a show of being helpful. From a vase she took a letter Jordan had written at Manassas, two days after the battle. Its contents—what was left of them—were quite innocent. All it said was: "Lt.-Col. Jordan's compliments to Mrs. R. Greenhow. Well, but hard-worked." The rest had been torn off before reaching her through the mails. Was the post office interfering with her letters? She "suspected its delicate mission." Was this a trap of some kind? She had already been careful to show the note boldly to her friend Senator Wilson, two army officers, and several other people. Now she showed it to Pinkerton, too, apparently hoping she could disarm suspicion by pretending frankness. But that veteran was not easily deceived. His search continued.

The counterintelligence men examined beds, drawers, wardrobes, soiled laundry, harmless papers that had been stored for years, children's scribblings, books, scraps of paper, fragments in the fireplaces and "other receptacles" (presumably wastebaskets), and a stove. No matter how the lady sneered at all this in the book she later published, the search did turn up a vast deal of incriminating material, now preserved in the National Archives.

Pinkerton had been careful to leave no visible guard outside the door, lest he alarm other members of the spy ring who might drop in during the day. He hoped people in the street had noticed nothing unusual and might suppose that two ordinary visitors had entered the house with Mrs. Greenhow, on what might—from a sufficient distance—seem to be amicable terms. Pinkerton knew nothing about the rebel agent, waiting to catch Mrs. Greenhow's signal with her handkerchief, who had promptly rushed off to spread the news.

These efforts were greatly assisted by Mrs. Greenhow's little girl, who slipped outdoors and began chanting, "Mother's been arrested! Mother's been arrested!" Detectives dashed out to silence the child —but she climbed a tree before they were able to reach her, and continued her chant, until she could be hauled down from her perch.

One couple, allowed by a careless guard to approach the house during the evening, were warned off by Mrs. Greenhow herself. A detective, referred to as Captain Dennis, seized her by the arm "with the spring of a tiger," according to the lady herself. The prisoner was furious at this "brutal outrage"—which was the only way Dennis could stop her. As a matter of fact, the captain's spring wasn't nearly tigerish enough: Mrs. Greenhow had time to give her warning before he could reach her, and the pair escaped.

Trying to be conciliatory, the Federal men carefully took orders for her meals, hoping to persuade her to forget the incident— "as if," said she, "aught but the life's blood of the dastard could efface it." (Mrs. Greenhow often wrote like that, probably because, like many Southern gentry, she read too many novels by Sir Walter Scott.)

II

The arrest had taken place about 11 A.M., and the news spread swiftly. No Confederate agents appeared at the house until about three o'clock, when Lily Mackall and her sister arrived. These women knew they were walking into a hornets' nest but had decided to find out, at any cost, what was being done with their friend. A detective, standing behind the door as it opened, pushed them both forward into the room, so that they could not escape—"rudely," says Mrs. Greenhow; but it is hard to seize a prisoner politely.

When the raiders began their search, they at first found nothing very seriously incriminating; but Mrs. Greenhow knew there was a great deal more, which they were certain to find eventually. The note she had chewed up had not been the only paper she was carrying. She also had the cipher key Colonel Jordan had made for her and other papers of nearly the same importance. It had been the worst kind of folly to carry the cipher about with her at all; but the other papers were probably some she had collected during the morning and had not yet had time to secrete.

The heat of the day furnished a convenient pretext. She asked permission to go to her bedroom to change her dress. The Pinkerton men foolishly agreed, then had afterthoughts. One man rushed upstairs and rapped on the bedroom door with a cry of "Madam! Madam!" He opened the door, but, seeing the prisoner "legitimately employed"—in other words, changing or preparing to do so —he withdrew. When he closed the door, Rebel Rose, instead of shooting the unsuspecting intruder, as she had at first intended, quietly put away her pistol, which these very careless officers had failed to secure. One detective noted with amusement that she had failed to cock it.

Presently a Pinkerton woman operative arrived and made the lady strip to her linen, examining each garment as she took it off. This precaution came too late to secure the cipher Mrs. Greenhow had been carrying in her pocket. Somehow, she had concealed it elsewhere, but she knew that a second day's search would reveal many other dangerous papers. Characteristically, the Rebel Rose decided she would burn her whole house down, if she could not destroy these before morning.

Meantime, the Pinkerton men, on general principles, had been seizing everyone who knocked, but all these visitors seem to have been ordinary callers. Mrs. Mackall, Lily's mother, who came to see what had become of her daughter, was detained. A former servant and his sister, who merely happened to be passing at this unlucky moment, were also pounced upon.

Mrs. Greenhow found it was no use asking these temporarily detained callers to try to smuggle papers out of the house. Again the counterintelligence men missed a fine chance. They could easily have admitted the visitors, let them alone till they tried to smuggle papers out of the house, and then arrested them. They would thus have secured papers not discovered; and, if they had then followed the visitors, they might have been guided to some new spies. Instead, they carefully warned the visitors not to accept papers and eventually let them go.

About ten-thirty that night two more of Mrs. Greenhow's friends appeared. One was William J. Walker, who, after several years as post office messenger, had become agent for Southern railroads, giving up the work only when the rebellion destroyed his business. The other was a certain Frank Rennehan, for many years a Washington resident, so deeply implicated in rebel plots of some kind he did not even try to pretend loyalty. Why they wanted to see Mrs. Greenhow at 10:30 P.M. no one has ever found out, but they were not actuated by enthusiasm for President Lincoln's government. Obviously the warning that was being spread through the Greenhow spy ring had not yet reached them.

After Pinkerton himself left, discovery of abundant rum and brandy (Mrs. Greenhow's hospitality was famous) somewhat mellowed the detectives, as they had previously mellowed Secretary of State Seward. The lady herself says that Pinkerton's assistants were presently in such a "state of inebriation" that she was able to slip unobserved into her library "in the dark." Her papers were all in one folio volume on an upper shelf, so placed that she could find it easily, without a light. It must have been a very small folio, for she was able to hide it in the folds of her dress and return undisturbed.

Maliciously, Mrs. Greenhow did what she could to get the detectives quarreling among themselves and as tipsy as possible. She hoped that loud and wrangling male voices, coming from her sedate drawing room, would warn off any members of her ring who might call that night; and she learned later that her ruse had succeeded.

Lily Mackall and the other visitors were taken home under guard between three and four o'clock in the morning. Their homes were kept under surveillance for some days. Mrs. Greenhow herself finally got to bed after a "most trying day"—which was a remarkable understatement—with a guard at each of the two doors of her bedroom.

Lily Mackall, who soon moved into the house to live through the ordeal with her, was allowed to come and go as she pleased. It is fairly obvious that the government men hoped Lily would lead them to other members of the Greenhow group. But this seems to have been equally obvious to Lily. What precautions she took to break her trail, one can only guess. Somehow she did it. So far as is known, her shadows trailed after her in vain.

For several days, detectives ransacked the house. All books were taken from their shelves. There would, as the spy mistress remarks with sly satisfaction, "have been some wisdom in this the first day," but she had taken the most dangerous documents out of the folio; and when a government agent took Lily Mackall home, the documents went along in Lily's shoes. It is extraordinary that no one asked the lady to take them off; it is equally extraordinary that some time passed before anyone thought of taking away Mrs. Greenhow's pistol.

One Federal agent, remembering that, like many Marylanders, Mrs. Greenhow was a Roman Catholic, had an Irish detective begin to show signs of sympathy for a coreligionist, at the same time courting her maid, Lucy Fitzgerald, who was almost certainly a Catholic, too. Lucy cheerfully accepted entertainment on a government expense account, enjoying herself immensely, and, in her own demure words, "led Pat a dance."

Lucy was thus able to do some important errands for her mistress. Her ostensible admirer, as part of his show of sympathy, offered to smuggle letters past the guards. Mrs. Greenhow, not at all deceived by this rather obvious *agent provocateur*, learned through sources of her own that the provost marshal's office was receiving a daily report of everything she did. It was perfectly obvious where the helpful guard would deliver the letters.

Uncertain of the government's legal position—it was certainly lawful to arrest Mrs. Greenhow on suspicion of espionage, but was it legal to seize her real estate?—some official sent a quartermaster captain with an offer to buy the prisoner's house. This was on August 29, 1861, less than a week after her arrest. The officials wanted to take over the whole building as a place of detention for Mrs. Greenhow herself and various other prisoners.

When the captive owner refused this handsome offer, the authorities took over the house anyway and confined Mrs. Greenhow, her maid, her daughter, and Lily to a single room. Later, a small additional room was allotted the maid and the child, but Mrs. Greenhow was not allowed to enter it. The Federals had learned a thing or two about that resourceful lady. The second room had a window facing the street, and, given such a chance, there was no telling what Mrs. Greenhow might do. Later, she was allowed to use her library, too, but the rest of her house was prepared to receive the additional prisoners, who soon began to arrive.

III

Though Mrs. Greenhow, who loved a literary flourish, alludes to this period of detention as "my prison life," she was not actually jailed for nearly five months. Her home, however, became something very like a jail, when the government took it over and began to send in one prisoner after another. That many of these people—including Rebel Rose—probably deserved all they got does not alter the fact that Constitutional safeguards of liberty and property (though happily not of life) were being completely ignored by the government of a leading lawyer, Abraham Lincoln, and a Cabinet full of lawyers, who had gone to war to uphold the Constitution.

Among the first to arrive were the family of Philip Phillips, a Washington attorney, formerly Congressman from Alabama. Phillips himself was beyond the Federals' reach, but the Phillips house in Washington was taken over and searched, while Mrs. Phillips, a sister, and at least two of her daughters were marched off to confinement in Mrs. Greenhow's home. It is likely enough that Mrs. Phillips had been sending intelligence to Beauregard; but, whatever mischief she may have engaged in, powerful influences secured her release and she was soon sent south, only to get into more trouble with Ben Butler at New Orleans.

Next came Bettie Hassler (Mrs. F. A. Hassler), who had been one of Mrs. Greenhow's couriers, taking dispatches south. On the night of her own arrest, Mrs. Greenhow had tried to send a warning, but the messenger found soldiers already occupying the Hassler house when he arrived. The Rebel Rose had apparently dealt with her only through a "cut-out," so that Mrs. Hassler did not even know to whose house she was taken. Though Jordan himself had vouched for her trustworthiness, there was some fear the authorities might try to use her as a witness. Next morning the mistress of the house "diverted the attention of the guard"—the Rebel Rose had always understood men—while Lily Mackall slipped into Mrs. Hassler's room to apprise her of the situation.

To "Greenhow Prison," probably while Mrs. Greenhow was still confined there, came another woman agent, not one of the Washington spies but a Virginian. This was Miss Ella (or Ellie) M. Poole, who had been arrested at Wheeling, West Virginia, October 6, 1861. A search of the house showed no incriminating papers, for the very good reason that Ellie had sneaked them out in her guitar case and hidden them, just in time.

"The lady not being in good health," a good-natured U.S. marshal allowed her to live at home under guard. That night, the poor, suffering creature rose from her bed of pain, found a key that had been left lying about, unlocked the door, and made an exit through the basement. Learning, after she had taken refuge with a neighbor, that that house, too, would be searched, she left by the back door, just as the Federals reached the front one, and proceeded to still another refuge. When that was searched, she escaped again. In all, in spite of the ill health that Confederate lady spies were likely to develop when arrested or in danger of arrest, she did this four times before she found a skiff and floated forty miles down the Ohio to Martinsville, whence she made her way by steamboat to Cincinnati, going on to Louisville and making friends en route with a Union officer, who "talked rather freely to her about the affairs of the Government."

In Louisville, Ellie discovered she was being followed by Delos Thurmon Bligh, a Federal detective famous for relentless pursuit of his quarry. Bligh was acting on General Sherman's orders. When she started for Mitchell, Indiana, Bligh was on the same train, but he did not arrest her until they reached Vincennes. She had $7,500 of Confederate funds in her possession. Bligh took the lady back to Louisville, where he brought her before Sherman himself. The Federals knew by this time that she had made several trips to Richmond, and Sherman wanted her as far away as possible, since she was regarded as a "shrewd and dangerous spy." Bligh himself brought her to the "Greenhow Prison," and she seems to have been sent on to the Old Capitol about the same time as Mrs. Greenhow.

Ellie Poole is alleged to have changed sides, spied on Mrs. Greenhow, and thus received specially favorable treatment from the Federal authorities. She was, indeed, released from the Old Capitol a few weeks before Mrs. Greenhow and is said to have received $50 in gold. But there is no real evidence that she was ever anything but a devoted Confederate; and, in any case, there was no longer much need of Federal espionage to determine Mrs. Greenhow's guilt. It was well established—in fact, she gloried in it.

After a prolonged search of the Greenhow dwelling, Pinkerton's men withdrew, and a detail of twenty-one men from the Sturgis Rifles (McClellan's own bodyguard) took over. Among them may have been John C. Babcock, one of the regiment's early volunteers, soon to become one of the ablest secret agents the Union Army ever had.

IV

About this time, their chief prisoner began to display a sudden interest in tapestry making—a word which, as then used in Washington, may have meant simple embroidery. Although this seemed a natural and harmless occupation for an imprisoned gentlewoman with too much time on her hands, the provost marshal's men had learned to keep their eyes open when dealing with Mrs. Greenhow. They insisted that all her balls of "colors" must pass inspection before being sent into the house for her use—though at least once a ball of yarn, with a message inside, was tossed into her open window without discovery. The material the Federals did inspect seemed harmless enough and, after examination, was always turned over to the prisoner.

It *was* harmless enough when it came into the house. It was not harmless at all when it had been made into "tapestry." No one guessed that the Rebel Rose and her correspondents had worked out a "vocabulary of colors." This could not serve for many messages, but it helped.

What helped still more was the sudden inspiration of somebody in the War Department who was just a little too clever. Orders reached the guard that Mrs. Greenhow should be allowed to correspond freely. Who knew what secrets might be learned by reading her letters?

Who knew? Everybody who knew Mrs. Greenhow knew. Absolutely nothing! The Federal authorities had simply given their prisoner a fine chance to send letters in code. A cipher, with its queer characters, would have been seized immediately; code could be made to sound innocent, using the ordinary words of everyday life with special military meanings known only to Richmond and its spies.

To make matters easier for Mrs. Greenhow, the new and amateurish counterintelligence men watching her were hopelessly unimaginative. One of them remarked that for a "clever woman, Mrs. Greenhow wrote the greatest pack of trash that was ever read." He was perfectly correct, too. It isn't always easy to fill in the blanks between code words so as to make an apparently sensible message, and the effort to do so sometimes produces rather strained writing. The sudden oddity of the literary lady's epistolary style should have been a plain warning. When, in the intelligence service, an opponent of known ability suddenly begins doing or writing apparently senseless things, there is likely to be a catch somewhere. It is high time to look into the matter closely. It all may be a cunningly devised cover for some specially effective piece of deviltry.

After Mrs. Greenhow had been sent to the Old Capitol and newspaper men were allowed to explore her dwelling, they saw what they believed to be a phial of invisible ink and a phial of developer. It would have been natural for her to use this common method of secret writing, but government reports never mention it. Apparently no one had been bright enough to test her letters for anything of the sort.

Perhaps Mrs. Greenhow, when she knew arrest was imminent, had guessed she might need a code (which could be disguised) as well as her cipher (which could be instantly recognized for what it was) and had made arrangements with Jordan accordingly. Perhaps the code was smuggled in to her after she had been arrested. This would have been easy enough, since she continued to receive military intelligence and send it on to Jordan for a long time after her arrest—even from the Old Capitol Prison. She seems to have been able to smuggle cipher through the guards at times, for messages in the original cipher alphabet continued to reach Richmond as late as October, 1861, two months after the arrest; but Colonel Jordan feared some of them were plants contrived by the Federal officials.

It was indeed possible that the Federals had already broken the cipher. Certainly they eventually did so, for they had plenty of messages on which to work—an essential for breaking old-fashioned substitution ciphers, in which a count of the characters will soon reveal which cipher characters stand for "e," the most frequently used letter in English, "t," the next most frequent, and so on. They had made a rich haul of material in the stove, into which Mrs. Greenhow had thrown a mass of documents she had torn to bits but had failed to burn.

She had also failed to burn the most incriminating document she had, the blotter she had used on her July 16 message announcing McDowell's advance on Bull Run. In fact, she had not even torn it up. Anyone who knew how to read in reverse—or who could use a mirror—could read it with the utmost ease. Since Lily Mackall found it in time, the Federals never learned of its existence; but the torn bits of the ciphered documents went into the files of the U.S. government, where they still are. Many of them could be fitted together and made entirely legible.

This did not disturb Mrs. Greenhow, who was sure nobody could read them: "Champollion himself would have required a key."

Colonel Jordan, however, having made the cipher, knew a great deal better. He realized this had been his "first attempt and hastily devised." He knew that sooner or later it could "be deciphered by any expert." At any moment the Yankees might be sending him planted intelligence in his own cipher.

Breaking even a simple cipher takes time, however, and the inexperienced Union cryptanalysts probably had a good deal of difficulty. Both Jordan and Mrs. Greenhow heard that they were having so much trouble that "a reward is offered for the key." It was, according to Mrs. Greenhow, "a very large sum," indeed an "extraordinary sum." So far as can now be discovered, the government had not really made any such offer to anyone, though it had received an unsolicited offer from a Confederate sympathizer to sell a cipher key—which may or may not have been genuine.

Knowing that his cipher would be broken sooner or later, anyhow, Jordan began to wonder whether the Confederacy might not make a little money, which it badly needed, through an apparently treacherous secret intermediary. He suggested this, not to Beauregard but to the Confederate Secretary of War. "I am inclined to furnish it through a person in Washington and let the friend get the consideration," he wrote, "for I repeat the possession of the key can do no possible good now nor can it prejudice any one."

The Federals never found Mrs. Greenhow's own copy of the cipher key, which she took secretly to prison with her, used there for a time, and destroyed only after she had received authority to do so from Jefferson Davis himself. Little Rose probably helped smuggle these last ciphered reports from the prison, when allowed to go out for play.

Jordan's cheerful proposal to sell a now useless cipher to the enemy seems to have had no success. On the other hand, the Federals do not seem to have been able to plant any false intelligence after they had broken the cipher. (The complete destruction of Confederate secret intelligence records before the evacuation of Richmond in 1865 makes positive statements impossible.)

The secret couriers in Washington were still operating through cut-outs, so that Union investigators, even when they arrested a courier, could rarely find the next link in the chain of communications. Thus, Mrs. Greenhow could write a message to her "Aunt

Sally" (a pseudonym actually used). A courier, posing as a mere social visitor, could smuggle this out of the house for Mrs. Greenhow. The courier, in such a case, knew where to find "Aunt Sally"— and knew absolutely nothing else.

If the Federals found the letter, they could arrest the courier and harry their prisoner all they pleased. It did no good. The coded letters would *appear* innocent. The Federals knew very well they weren't. But the courier couldn't tell them what the real message in the letters meant, because the courier didn't know. Nor could the courier (who in Washington was likely to be a lady) be forced to identify Aunt Sally unless the Federals beat the information out of her; and, in this gentlemanly war, you didn't beat information out of ladies. In fact, no matter how much they deserved it, you didn't even hang them. (The Confederates did sentence the Federal actress spy, Pauline Cushman, to be hanged, but Union troops rescued her from the guardhouse. The Federals passed the same sentence on Jane Ferguson, a Tennessee girl in her teens, with a face "frank and simple as a child's," who dressed as a Union soldier and entered the Union lines for information; but that sentence was reversed.)

Mrs. Greenhow's code was fairly simple. One of her messages told "Aunt Sally" that she had "some old shoes for *the children*." She wanted Aunt Sally to send "some one *down town* to take them." She also inquired about a charitable person to help take care of them. Decoded, "old shoes" meant "important information." "Down town" meant "across the Potomac River." "Some one" was a courier. The rest of the message, describing an imaginary philanthropist, was pure padding to make the letter sound natural.

Mrs. Greenhow's home was now being described as "Greenhow Prison," but its walls did not a prison make for that enterprising lady. She continued to pour information south, because the Pinkertons had not yet succeeded in cutting her communications with Richmond through secret couriers. She seems by this time to have had two ways of reaching the Confederate capital, for she refers to her "other" line.

Jefferson Davis was at first concerned for the prisoner's safety. Later—knowing Washington as only a former Secretary of War and Senator could know it—he was much amused (as well as delighted) by her success in deluding the Yankees. He had good reason for his satisfaction, since Mrs. Greenhow continued to be nearly as useful as ever. There was a series of reports on Union war plans from October, 1861, onward. In that month an unknown A.M.H. reported the place where General Ambrose E. Burnside's "Annapolis Armada" would attack the North Carolina coast. On December 28, 1861, there was a second warning. One of these messages—or perhaps a third message—was sent by John F. Callan, supposedly clerk of the Senate Committee on Military Affairs, and was carried south by Mrs. Greenhow's dentist friend, Dr. Aaron Van Camp of Washington, whose wounded son had recently been made an orderly at Beauregard's headquarters.

The "Armada," which was based at Annapolis, was Burnside's expedition against the North Carolina coast. (It must not be confused with Admiral Samuel F. Du Pont's attack on Port Royal, South Carolina, in November, 1861, which sailed from Hampton Roads, nor with Burnside's 1864 concentration, also at Annapolis.) The information may have leaked when Seward—after dinner— talked a little too freely to a diplomat. A spy said the information came from one of McClellan's aides and "Fox of the Navy Department." This can only have been Gustavus Vasa Fox, former naval officer, now First Assistant Secretary of the Navy. There is no question of these men's loyalty to the Union, but someone may have been less than discreet. All that Mrs. Greenhow ever said was that "a little bird" told her.

Some of these messages were transmitted with astonishing speed. A report on McClellan and Burnside dated December 30, 1861, was received at Centreville next day, together with a similar report of the twenty-seventh.

One can hardly blame Major General John E. Wool for an explosive message from his headquarters at Fortress Monroe. He telegraphed Seward, January 7, 1862, that some Confederate agent in Washington was obtaining "all the information necessary for those who command in the rebel army. They know much better than I do what is doing at Washington. The expedition of General Burnside is perfectly known at Norfolk." The general also noted, somewhat superfluously, "You have any number of rebel spies in Washington."

Burnside's expedition sailed January 11, 1862, in such secrecy

that the naval captains opened their sealed orders only when
they were at sea. These Federal precautions were useless, but the
Confederates did not make very good use of their secret information, for Burnside won a small but resounding victory. Other
predicted Federal attacks do not seem to have occurred exactly
when and where predicted, but this may mean that the War Department changed its plans.

On November 18, 1861, Colonel Jordan, at Beauregard's headquarters, was able to read the news story on the capture of the Confederate diplomats, Mason and Slidell, that had been published in
the 3 P.M. edition of the *Washington Star* of November 16. Under
war conditions, with the necessity of secret communication by horse
and rowboat and almost certainly by night, this report arrived with
amazing speed. Jordan rushed it on to Richmond by telegraph.

For some time, the arrest of the two Confederate commissioners,
James Murray Mason and John Slidell, by Captain Charles Wilkes,
commanding U.S.S. *San Jacinto*—while the commissioners were
aboard the mail steamer *Trent*, under the British flag—seemed likely
to lead to an Anglo-American war. This would have meant an immediate Confederate victory. It was, therefore, vital to get the
news to President Davis with the utmost speed, though in the end
Seward's dextrous diplomacy avoided war.

Federal counterintelligence managed to persuade one Samuel
Applegate, said to have been a former member of the Greenhow
ring, to change sides. (Perhaps he had been a Federal double agent
from the beginning.) Pretending that he was still a Confederate
spy, Applegate got in touch with the courier, Mrs. Hassler, with
whom he may already have been acquainted. Into her ears he
poured a marvelous tale of ill treatment by the Federal authorities, exhibiting a torn hat to show how badly he had been mauled—
not really a very convincing bit of evidence, though it seems to
have worked. He now wanted Mrs. Hassler to put him in touch with
Mrs. Greenhow, as he had important information. Could Mrs. Hassler communicate with her? (It was an obvious effort to discover
Mrs. Greenhow's communication line.)

Mrs. Greenhow seems to have known in advance that the Federals would try this hoary stratagem. She had expected Applegate
to approach Mrs. Hassler, knew his story had been cooked up in

the provost marshal's office, knew even the name of the Union officer who had thought up that bit about the torn hat—a certain Captain William Woods Averell, who later, as a Union cavalry general, would operate a pretty good spy system himself.

Though he does not seem to have accomplished very much, Applegate did manage to secure and turn over to Secretary Seward a cipher dispatch and drawings of the capital's fortifications, emphasizing weak points. When broken, the cipher was found to contain information that would be useful if the proposed Confederate attack on Washington were ever carried out. Army officers described the ciphered report as "a very able production" and pronounced the drawings "equal to those of their best engineers."

"Well they might," said Rebel Rose when, a year later, she was in England, publishing an account of her exploits. In other words, these *were* drawings by U.S. Army Engineers, or exact copies.

Mrs. Greenhow did nothing whatever about Applegate's and Captain Averell's joint endeavors. The discovery of the documents was regrettable, but not fatal. Mrs. Hassler may have talked too much; but—and this was the advantage of using cut-outs—there was very little she could tell. She knew where she had delivered messages but not what was in them. All this probably went on between Mrs. Hassler's arrest, August 23, 1861, and her final release "on oath of allegiance and parole" in October. That the Federals were willing to release her on these lenient terms, months before they released Mrs. Greenhow and other state prisoners, suggests that she had, in some way, been useful to them.

V

On January 18, 1862, at 2 P.M., Mrs. Greenhow was suddenly told she was being moved and was given two hours to get ready. By four o'clock, she was in a carriage, complete with military guard, on her way to the Old Capitol Prison, where a room "comfortable, though not extravagant in style," awaited her. The windows of adjoining houses were crowded with curious onlookers, among them the Washington men of the leading New York and Philadelphia newspapers, as the Rebel Rose left her home forever.

Various major and minor Confederate secret agents were also in the Old Capitol about this time, some of whom had probably helped with Mrs. Greenhow's secret communication lines. They included Thomas A. Jones, who managed a rebel mail drop on the Potomac, near Port Tobacco, Maryland; George Dent, Jones's neighbor, who had also been active in the secret courier service that used the mail drop; and Dent's son, still a child, whose apparent innocence—which was not innocence at all—was very useful in moving Confederate secret mail without rousing suspicion.

There were also numerous other individuals, charged—probably correctly—with espionage. There were, for example, Josiah E. Bailey, a "rebel officer found in Washington in citizen's clothes," and William Eaton, "found within our lines with citizen's dress over a rebel uniform." Other prisoners included one Isaac G. Mask, whose mail the Federals had been reading for some time and always with increasing disapproval. When they were sure he was "giving information of expeditions in the course of preparation by the Government," they arrested him and persuaded him to admit his guilt, but he does not seem to have suffered any very dire fate.

Pinkerton was startled when John F. C. Offutt, a Baltimore policeman accused of encouraging the riots that had made it impossible early in the war to send troops through the city, was found in the capital. He was jailed as a spy and had to be held for some time because he had recognized a Pinkerton operative and his release would endanger other operatives then working as Federal spies in Richmond. The Federal authorities were by no means cheered when a second member of the Offutt family, James by name, was caught making nocturnal journeys between Georgetown and Rockville, "carrying letters and papers with him."

VI

In June, 1862, the government decided it might as well get rid of a large part of its prison population, and Mrs. Greenhow was released from the Old Capitol. Melodramatic to the end, she had a Confederate flag wrapped about her but concealed under a light shawl. She was taken to Fortress Monroe, where she signed a promise "not to return north of the Potomac River during the present hostilities without the permission of the Secretary of War of the U.S."

On June 13 Jefferson Davis wrote from Richmond to his wife, "Madam looks much changed, and has the air of one whose nerves are shaken by mental torture."

Imprisoning Mrs. Greenhow and her assistants, though it did not end her intelligence work, gravely hampered it. Nevertheless, important information from Washington continued to reach the Confederates. Some of this may have been forwarded directly, by Greenhow spies whom the Federals had failed to identify. Other information almost certainly came from enthusiastic Southern sympathizers who had access to information and who, whenever they learned anything of value, sent it on as best they could.

Someone of this sort probably provided the forecast of Federal intentions which, on December 3, 1861, Jordan reported to Secretary of War Benjamin in Richmond: "Our friends insist there will be an advance this season." Jordan thought this reliable because some of the facts came from "an undoubted source—a secret agent of theirs." It was a little naïve to suppose that a Federal secret agent was necessarily cognizant of Federal war plans; but Jordan's statement does show how deeply rebel espionage had penetrated the Federal government.

The report, dated November 25, 1861, indicated a Union attack on the Potomac, with "Hooker below; McCall, McDowell, and McClellan in the centre; and Banks above." "McClellan will certainly make a bolt at you next week," said another agent's report of November 30.

This last prediction turned out to be wrong. McClellan's plan was to move the main Federal force up the Rappahannock to Urbanna, Virginia, thus cutting neatly in behind the Confederate position at Bull Run. But this plan, too, the rebel spies discovered. One day after Lincoln set a time limit for the operation, General Joseph E. Johnston pulled his Confederates back to Culpeper, thus upsetting McClellan's entire scheme before he could move a man!

Antonia Ford and Betty Duvall were not the only sweet (and deadly) young things busily spying for the South in or near Washington. An unknown but youthful blonde girl spy in Fairfax Court House is mentioned by General J. E. B. Stuart's secret agent, George D. Shadburne, as having assisted him. This may have been

Antonia. Two portraits show that she was not a brunette, but had hair of a rather sandy color. A third, probably painted in her early youth, shows blond coloring. She certainly had two very blond daughters in later life. Shadburne, who was dealing with only one girl spy, may not have been observing with his usual care. There may, of course, have been a second girl spy in Fairfax Court House.

Not far away dwelt Miss Laura Ratcliffe, who, like Antonia, became a valued secret agent for Stuart and for his trusted subordinate, John S. Mosby. Stuart presented her with an album and several specimens of the execrably bad lyric verse he had been writing ever since he was a cadet.

Miss Laura lived at a crossroads, then called the "Frying-pan," near Floris, Virginia, about ten miles west of Washington. Thence the Ratcliffe family lands stretched eastward toward Herndon and west toward Chantilly. The estate was "within trotting distance" of both Washington and Bull Run—an ideal location for a volunteer secret agent.

Laura Ratcliffe was a rather striking brunette, quite as skilled as Betty Duvall in getting susceptible young Federals to talking carelessly. How much espionage she did before the war was over is an open question. She does not seem to have been collecting intelligence before Bull Run, but Stuart, who employed many secret agents, knew her well enough to call on his way back from his raid on Dumfries, in late December, 1862, and he introduced her to Mosby. Her help was of great value to Mosby, who at times used the Ratcliffe house as headquarters. On one occasion he trusted her with several thousand dollars in Federal greenbacks—always badly needed in the Confederate Army—which he had seized in one of his raids. The girl hid the money near her home, under "Mosby's Rock," which the guerrilla had long used as a letter drop and rendezvous. The Federals guessed where the money must be, but, search as they might, they could never find it.

Mosby himself believed that he owed his life to Laura Ratcliffe's success in worming information out of Federal soldiers. A certain Lieutenant Palmer of the 1st Virginia (one of the few Southern regiments in the Union Army) had hidden a considerable force in a pine woods, not far from the Ratcliffe home. He had been careful to leave a few soldiers on the edge of the woods, in sight from the road, where he knew (some Union spy had been busy) that Mosby was likely to pass.

The guerrilla leader would have been surprised and overwhelmed if one of Palmer's soldiers had not paused at the Ratcliffe kitchen to get some milk. He boasted of the ambush the Federals had laid.

"We will get Mosby this time," he said. "On his next raid he will certainly come by Frying-pan and it will not be possible for him to escape." The wretched fellow capped his already blazing indiscretion by adding, "I know you would give Mosby any information in your possession; but, as you have no horses and the mud is too deep for women folks to walk, you can't tell him; so the next you hear of your 'pal' he will be either dead or our prisoner."

Laura Ratcliffe set out, mud or no mud, the moment the man was out of sight. She had at first meant only to tell local sympathizers to watch for Mosby and warn him. But, by good luck, glancing through a friend's window, she caught sight of cavalry riding along the road. With one female companion, she dashed out, saw so many blue uniforms in the little column that, for an anxious moment, she thought they were Yankees, then recognized Mosby. (The blue uniforms meant nothing. As usual, Mosby's men were wearing captured Federal clothing.)

Laura had come just in time. Mosby had already detected the weak little post by the pine grove. The handful of troops visible to him looked like easy prey, and he was preparing to attack. Now, having been warned of the powerful reserve lurking within the woods, he turned aside, raided a Federal picket near Dranesville instead, and rode away in perfect safety with fifteen prisoners, plus horses and equipment.

Mosby was sure Laura and her friend had saved him. "But for meeting them, my life as a partisan would have closed that day."

5

J. E. B. STUART'S
SECRET AGENTS

PART 1.
The Reverend Captain Conrad's Spy Ring

The arrest and deportation of Mrs. Greenhow and the discovery of so many of her agents broke up her ring. But destroying Mrs. Greenhow's organization did the Union cause singularly little good, since it was soon replaced by two others, equally efficient and conducted with such skill that both were able to operate undiscovered till the war was over.

Many of Mrs. Greenhow's agents probably went right on spying for several years after the Rebel Rose had left Washington. Betty Duvall, at least, is known to have continued her espionage for a long time. She continued to live with her parents in Washington, she continued to charm young officers in blue uniforms, and no Federal official ever made any serious trouble for her. The charming Betty undoubtedly did not fail to use her natural advantages for the benefit of the Confederacy. There is, it is true, only a little documentary proof that she did—but a good spy doesn't leave much proof.

One ex-member of the Confederate secret service seems to have been referring to Betty when, in describing Confederate female spies, he noted that "almost all of them were successful, more than one well nigh invaluable for the information she brought sewed in her riding habit or coiled in her hair." But perhaps other Confederate ladies also used Betty's methods.

The rest of this account strongly suggests that a number of Southern women residing in the North continued to spy right through the war. They were

> petted belles in the society of Baltimore and Washington and of Virginia summer resorts of yore—who rode through night and peril alike, to carry tidings of cheer home and to bring back news women may best acquire. New York, Baltimore and Washington to-day boast of three beautiful and gifted women, high in their social rank, who could— if they would—recite tales of lonely race and perilous adventure to raise the hair of the budding beaux about them.

These enterprising ladies may have been independent operators, or they may have been members of the two formidable espionage organizations under Captain Thomas Nelson Conrad, 3rd Virginia Cavalry, and Private Frank Stringfellow, 4th Virginia Cavalry, which replaced the Greenhow ring. Both Conrad and Stringfellow operated primarily for Stuart.

From the beginning, Stuart had other agents, who may have been completely independent. Few of them can now be identified. During the war, their work was secret; and, when the war was over, secrecy remained essential for many of them. Those who were arrested can, of course, be identified—assuming that the Federal charges of espionage were correct.

One such was Francis A. Dickens, who lived near Annandale, Virginia. Federal agents laid Dickens low early in 1862, or perhaps late in 1861. A Negro who had, for a little while, been a camp servant of Stuart's, swore before the War Department Commission on State Prisoners that Dickens, supposedly a loyal Union man, came to the Confederate camp regularly two or three times a week. The Negro had often heard Confederate soldiers in the general's tent, reporting information obtained from Dickens. Northern sympathizers living near Annandale noted that, whenever a Confederate patrol went out, Dickens, in civilian clothing, was likely to be riding in the same direction—and far enough ahead to give instant warning of any possible danger.

I

The first of Stuart's spy nets in Washington was directed by Captain Thomas N. Conrad, regimental chaplain of the 3rd Virginia Cavalry. Though he did a chaplain's ordinary duties when he had time, this unusual spiritual director frequently rode into combat with the rest of the troops and spent most of the Civil War in field reconnoissance, spying in Washington itself, or lurking in a rebel secret service lair along the banks of the Potomac, not far from Washington. Besides directing his own subordinate secret agents— one of whom was ostensibly working for General Lafayette C. Baker in the Federal counterintelligence service!—he managed a courier line that was never broken; and he did a great deal of important espionage himself.

Though Conrad and Mrs. Greenhow may, for a time, have used the same line of communications, their networks were entirely separate. Though both published accounts of their exploits, neither shows the slightest awareness of what the other was doing. This was not due to reticence or military secrecy, for they mention some of their other associates freely. The wisdom of this complete separation of the networks was demonstrated after Mrs. Greenhow had been arrested and her network broken up. Conrad and his agents, entirely unaffected, spied cheerfully ahead, and his couriers continued their appointed rounds, undisturbed, till the war was over.

One of these arrests, in 1865, was a pure waste of the Federals' time. Conrad's espionage was over; and they were not arresting him for espionage anyhow, but on charges of being John Wilkes Booth, who had just assassinated Lincoln. Conrad, who habitually changed his appearance, especially his hair and beard, from time to time, had recently adopted a new tonsorial disguise and, by an odd misfortune, had chosen the exact haircut and mustache that Booth had long affected. Booth had shot Lincoln on April 14, 1865, and had fled south into Virginia at almost the exact moment when Conrad was crossing the Potomac northward into Maryland. On Sunday night, April 16, sailors from the U.S.S. *Jacob Bell*, patrolling the Potomac, caught him sleeping in a farmhouse and arrested him under the impression that they had caught the murderer.

Though Conrad had plotted the kidnaping of Lincoln, he knew

nothing whatever about the assassination plot. It might, however, have gone hard with him, had the Federals guessed that Booth had ridden up to the Garrett farm, where he was killed, on one of the three horses Conrad used in his secret journeys. Mortimer B. Ruggles, one of the spy's secret couriers, had borrowed Conrad's cherished mount, "Old Whitie," had met the injured Booth, and had charitably given him a lift, a fact which Conrad did not reveal until 1904. Booth's ride on "Old Whitie," however, was pure coincidence, about which Conrad knew nothing till long afterward.

Colonel William P. Wood, commanding the Old Capitol Prison, personally released Conrad when his identity was established, bought him a badly needed suit of clothes, and introduced him to Lafayette C. Baker, head of the Federal secret service. Baker, who had been trying to catch Conrad for months, was now very cordial, treated him like a distinguished opponent (which he certainly was!), and provided an official pass to help get him home to Virginia.

Returning to Virginia after all this, Conrad was arrested for the last time, apparently on vague general suspicion, tricked his guards by pretending to be asleep, and jumped off the train when the guards relaxed. He then went into hiding, part of the time in the Luray Cavern, now a major tourist attraction, but in those days blocked off with stone. When it was safe to do so, he married his childhood sweetheart, whose name was Minnie Ball—also the name of a particularly deadly Federal bullet—and resumed his educational career, which led to two college presidencies.

Though Virginian by birth, Conrad was a graduate of Dickinson College, Carlisle, Pennsylvania, which in those days had more Southern than Northern students. Indeed, it is said that, when Carlisle was shelled during the Gettysburg campaign, Dickinson alumni in the Confederate artillery carefully directed their fire so as to spare their alma mater. Conrad's roommate at Dickinson was another Virginian, Mountjoy Cloud, later a much-trusted associate in the spy ring. In 1860, just as the excitement preceding the Civil War was at its height, Conrad took a Dickinson M.A.—probably by private study *in absentia,* for soon after his graduation he had become head of a school in Georgetown, across Rock Creek from Washington.

The boys in the school, like most people in Georgetown, were enthusiastic Confederates who made no effort to conceal their sympathies. Indeed, a Federal spy reported that Conrad's pupils were passing secret messages across the Potomac from the school's windows. It may be doubted whether schoolboys had any information worth reporting, but it is entirely possible that the principal himself was already spying—rather more efficiently than his youthful charges; and he was also suspected of sending recruits to the Confederate Army.

Though the school's Southern sympathies had thus been known for a long time, not till Commencement day in June of 1861 did the patience of the Federal authorities at last wear thin. Principal Conrad had long been known as "too pronounced" in his secessionist views. Now, some of his boys' Commencement orations "smacked of the strongest Southern sentiment." That was bad enough. But when, at the close of the Commencement program, the band struck up "Dixie," the sedateness appropriate to academic solemnities vanished. "Cheer after cheer sounded through the hall." Ladies—Southern ladies—"stood upon chairs, frantically waving their handkerchiefs." The rebel yell was not, as yet, customary save in fox hunting, but there was a good deal of noise.

That evening a squad of Yankees gathered in Principal Conrad at his own school building, put him in irons, and marched that learned man to the Old Capitol Prison. Colonel William E. Doster, then commanding the prison, says Conrad was charged with communicating with the enemy and sending recruits to the Confederate Army.

The Federal authorities, not yet in a mood for their later severities, paroled the schoolmaster after a few days. He was allowed to wander about the capital for a month and a half, seeing all that went on and required only to report weekly to the authorities. Inevitably, as Conrad later remarked, he "proceeded to get into more mischief without delay."

It was rather serious mischief, too. Devoutly religious though he was, Conrad joined a plot to assassinate General Winfield Scott, Commander-in-Chief of the Union Army. The best weapon the spies could find was an old musket, which they loaded up and prepared for action—apparently believing that a stranger with a loaded musket would be able to hang around the War Department without arousing official curiosity. Luckily, somebody in the plot decided it would be well to consult the central Confederate government before embarking upon political assassination. Cooler heads in Richmond prevailed. Emphatic orders came back. There must be no murder.

Richmond's decision not to kill Scott left the murderous parson and his associates with a highly incriminating weapon on their hands. They solved this problem by flinging musket, gunpowder, bullet, and all down a well not far from the White House, where they probably still remain. Conrad was sent to Fortress Monroe soon afterward, and thence sent on to Richmond as an exchanged prisoner.

II

The Reverend Major Dabney Ball, chaplain of the Cavalry Corps, took Conrad to J. E. B. Stuart in July, 1861. Ball proposed Conrad be made a cavalry chaplain with the rank of captain, though he was not an ordained clergyman but only a "lay reader" in the Methodist Church—or, as modern Methodists would say, a "local preacher" or "lay preacher." Conrad may have begun his religious duties at once, but it was not until 1863 that the colonel of the 3rd Virginia Cavalry asked that he be made regimental chaplain.

Stuart agreed to Major Ball's proposal—and at once assigned the new spiritual director to "scouting duty"! This, at first, meant ordinary reconnoissance, then almost continual espionage. Until the end of hostilities, Conrad rode through the Virginia woods and swamps he had known from boyhood, hovering along the line of Union outguards, secretly entering the Union lines, or visiting the capital itself.

Immediately after Bull Run, when the front was static, he began to amuse himself by exchanging his Confederate uniform, that is, the "drab-colored English felt jacket and black velvet pants" which he wore while reconnoitering, for a sober "straight-breasted coat of black cloth" in which he could pose as a Federal chaplain. Thus arrayed, he had no difficulty in being accepted as such by Fed-

eral soldiers; and, since a chaplain's duties take him everywhere, he
had no trouble lingering in their camps and entering the headquarters of their commanders. He was so successful as a secret agent
that Stuart sent him again and again to the higher Union headquarters "to pick up any possible information about contemplated
movements or advances."

Though he himself remarks that "the chaplain's duties were not
my forte," it may be said for Captain Conrad that he did his best
to "edify, encourage, enliven, elevate and spiritualize" his regiment by discourse on uplifting themes. Among his subjects were
"The Christian Soldier," "The Power of Prayer," "Paul, a Great
Hero," "David, a Mighty Warrior," and "God in History."

According to Conrad, Stuart employed numerous other secret
agents, few of whom were ever detected by Union intelligence officers. Part of the success of these spies may have been due to
Stuart's habit of himself denouncing them as Confederate deserters.

Stuart's purpose was to make sure that no Confederate officer
could inadvertently expose the spies, if he himself were captured.
The brutal methods of eliciting information from prisoners of war
by torture employed in some armies in both World Wars were not
usual in the Civil War, though occasionally employed. Stuart did
not fear his officers would voluntarily reveal information. What he
did fear, as Captain Conrad remarked when the war was over, was
"a chance word, a glance even, from the captured officers within
the Yankee lines." Conrad himself was convinced that Stuart's fierce
denunciations of his own devoted secret agents saved many of
them from "a drum head court martial and an ignominious death."

Captain Conrad himself had barely departed on his first secret
mission when Stuart called in Major Ball.

"Well, Major," said Jeb, apparently much disturbed, "your man
Conrad was a fine specimen. He has deserted and there is no telling
what information he has carried to Washington."

"Impossible!" said Ball, and eventually Stuart had to admit that
he didn't really mean it. The veil of secrecy the general tried to
throw about the movements of this particular spy soon wore thin,
and many soldiers learned what their chaplain was really doing.
His return from one secret mission was greeted with "loud rejoicings

and fraternal exclamations." He himself was indiscreet enough to discuss one Washington visit with regimental officers. It was the height of folly, but no harm came of it.

Before long the chaplain was ordered to Richmond for special duty. Secretary of War Benjamin personally sent him to Washington to meet two commissioners, one French, the other British, secretly arriving to negotiate a $3,000,000 loan for the Confederacy. This, according to Conrad, was the direct result of the negotiations of Mason and Slidell in France and England.

The incident has escaped historians; but Conrad must in general be regarded as reliable, for, when his narrative can be tested by other sources, it is usually confirmed, except as to some of his dates. That the incident does not now appear in diplomatic documents proves only that sometimes secret missions really stay secret.

Whether such a loan was ever actually made, whether it was merely discussed, whether other similar schemes were being considered, will probably never be known. Conrad himself certainly knew nothing but what he was told, and one rarely tells a spy everything.

Since it was dangerous to run the Federal blockade into a Confederate port, the two foreign officials went first to Washington, posing as ordinary travelers. Conrad was ordered to approach them there, get them safely and secretly across the lines, and start them to Richmond. It was his first venture back into Washington as a secret agent.

Before his departure, the War Department in Richmond provided a pass, which Conrad himself dictated:

> War Department, Richmond, Va.
> The bearer, who may be known by a gash in his tongue and a scar upon the index finger of his left hand, has the confidence of this department.

That would take him through the Confederate lines and would identify him to the foreign emissaries as an authorized agent of the Confederacy. (It would also identify him to the Federals and would earn him a rope's end, if captured.)

Undisturbed by such reflections—and undisturbed, too, by the Federal counterintelligence agencies—Conrad proceeded at leisure to Washington. His beard, originally full, was now trimmed. His chin was shaven but surrounded with side whiskers, in the style already made familiar by General Burnside. (Later, when the spy feared he was becoming known by the striking architecture of these whiskers, he altered the trim to a heavy mustache and a long imperial.) He was also careful to buy Northern shoes, which differed from those worn in the South, a difference for which Northern detectives were always watching, and he exchanged the plug tobacco favored in the South for the "short cut" used by Northerners.

The Confederate signal service kept a secret station and a boat ready on the Potomac, some miles below Washington, so that traveling spies were always sure of a safe and easy crossing. Conrad took the precaution of waiting for low tide, before landing on the Maryland shore, and then walked through the mud, so that the next tide would obliterate his footprints.

He was also careful to go resolutely past his parents' house in Maryland, knowing that Union sympathizers were likely to watch the homes of Confederate sympathizers, to detect just such visits. Instead, he went to the tavern of John Harrison Surratt, whose wife was hanged a few years later for alleged participation in the Lincoln assassination plot. The tavern early became a rendezvous for passing rebel spies.

Hiring a horse from Surratt and dressing himself to look like a Maryland farmer, Conrad drove unchallenged into Washington, where he put up at a hotel on Pennsylvania Avenue much frequented by visiting countryfolk. By inspecting the register of one hotel after another, he soon found the foreign negotiators at Willard's, showed them his secret pass, exhibited his scarred finger, and stuck out his tongue.

Taking the foreigners' shoes and more important papers, Conrad visited a trustworthy cobbler, who hollowed out the heels, inserted the papers, and nailed the heels on again. Then, after buying a carriage and pair, he drove his charges past the White House and McClellan's headquarters, allowing himself "an anxious though quizzical smile" as he "peered into the mansion of 'Father Abraham.'"

Along the Potomac, near Poolesville, Maryland, a farmer with Confederate sympathies, who had already agreed to put the party across the river whenever Conrad wished, summoned a trusted slave. After his owner had provided "quite a clever lunch" about midnight, the Negro accepted a ten-dollar gold piece, then guided them to an unguarded ford, splashing ahead on his horse to show where the water was shallow.

The party met with unexpected difficulty at a culvert, where the Chesapeake & Ohio Canal passed over a mountain stream. Conrad dared not risk the ordinary bridges over the canal, and the carriage top turned out to be too high to go through the culvert. Waking a local Confederate sympathizer, the spy borrowed a hand saw and, with great difficulty, the travelers sawed off and lowered the top. Not till it was all over did it occur to Conrad how much easier it would have been to take off the wheels and carry the vehicle through!

About dawn, they met a Confederate vedette, who passed them to the rear. With an armed guard, the two financiers rode on to Leesburg, thence on the Valley Railroad to Richmond.

The chaplain spy says definitely that, as a result of these negotiations, the Confederacy actually did receive a secret loan a few weeks later. He also says that the British negotiator had authority from Lord Palmerston himself to make a binding agreement whereby the British fleet would fight to raise the Union blockade. In this, Conrad certainly exaggerates. No Foreign Office ever gave such power to a single secret negotiator, although the British agent may have begun tentative discussions. Obviously no such treaty was ever signed.

Conrad also says that Colonel William P. Wood went to Richmond as a spy, investigating this affair. Later he reported to Washington what was going on and—so Conrad believed—Lincoln himself knew what the British were planning. When six Russian men-of-war suddenly appeared in New York harbor, Conrad, like most Americans, believed that the State Department had persuaded Prince Gorchakov to offer naval support to the Federal government, in case Great Britain intervened on behalf of the Confederates.

This was mere guesswork on Conrad's part. He had no way of knowing what was going on in the higher levels of diplomacy. Recent discoveries of hitherto secret Russian official documents show, however, that the Russian naval authorities sailed their fleet out of the Baltic mainly to make sure the British could not bottle it up there, in the event of an Anglo-Russian war, which at that time seemed a distinct possibility.

III

After getting his French and British charges across the Potomac and starting them on their way to Richmond, Conrad took a stage at Poolesville, Maryland, and started back to Washington to attend to some unfinished Confederate business there. It did not take long to secure the additional information that Stuart wanted. "Trusted Southern sympathizers" were still working in the War Department, under Secretary Stanton's very nose, though to this day there is not the slightest clue to their identity. These spies assured Conrad (correctly) that McClellan was planning to advance up the Peninsula, between the York and James Rivers, against Richmond. The captain returned at once to report this important news to Stuart. (Since McClellan began this movement in March of 1862, Conrad's own account suggests that he was engaged in intelligence work for Stuart sometime before his arrest in August, 1862, perhaps while he was still running his school in Georgetown, in 1861.)

It was not enough for the Confederate commander to know that McClellan meant to advance. The rebel leaders also had to know what his exact strength would be; and Conrad went back to Washington to get that information "in the Spring of '62."

Captain Conrad secured his information with extraordinary ease, because one of his War Department spies had direct access to the original strength reports from McClellan's headquarters. The subagent in the War Department, however, was having problems of his own. He dared not be seen going through these secret papers extracting the needed figures. But he was able to report to Conrad that the War Department itself was making an official summarized strength report of McClellan's Army, "a tabulated statement, which could not help but prove an exceedingly interesting document." There was an anxious three-day wait. Then Conrad received word that a copy of the report would be lying on the subagent's desk in the War Department at a specified hour next day.

The two did not even need to meet. The War Department man made a copy, left it on his desk as agreed, and went to lunch. Captain Conrad, who knew exactly where to go, walked boldly through the Department's crowded corridors, winking at his friend who passed on his way to lunch, went to the man's desk, and found the paper. It was in Richmond two days later.

Apparently Conrad continued to get similar copies of other documents, for he says that, throughout the Peninsular Campaign, the rebel command "knew just what forces McClellan had, down to the exact number of pieces of artillery."

There was an immense irony in the situation. This was the time when Pinkerton was terrifying McClellan with his enormously exaggerated overestimates of Confederate strength, nearly double what the Southerners really had. As a result, McClellan (who, in fact, himself had greatly superior forces) was afraid to attack, believing himself hopelessly outnumbered. The rebel command, on the other hand, operated with exact knowledge of Union strength, plus knowledge of McClellan's psychology. Small wonder that both Johnston and Lee were able to hold off the superior Federal hosts. Lee, when he took command, knew well enough he was outnumbered, for he had been in Richmond advising President Davis, whose office was only a few doors from that of the intelligence officers. But he also knew that McClellan would not use the superior Federal numbers vigorously.

Eventually, Lee did just about what Johnston had done at Bull Run. He suddenly brought in his forces from the Shenandoah Valley, boldly concentrated on his left, and—fully aware that the Confederate Army, though much smaller, was "strong at the decisive point"—won the series of victories known as "the Seven Days."

Conrad says modestly that "the pirated tabular statement was a factor at least in the bloody contests, which ended with Gaines' Mill [June 27, 1862] and Malvern Hill [July 1, 1862]"—where Lee finally stopped, after forcing McClellan back to the James River.

Not till the Seven Days' fighting had actually begun did the Union command find out how much information the Confederates had. A certain "Colonel Washington," when captured, was found to have in his possession a complete and alarmingly accurate Order of Battle of the Army of the Potomac. This gave correct corps, division, and brigade organization and listed the correct regiments for each brigade. It also gave the names of division and brigade commanders and the approximate strength of each regiment.

The captured officer also had a map of the country around the Chickahominy, giving all Union divisional positions. These were so completely up-to-date that divisional positions changed only two days before were correctly shown.

"Colonel" Washington was quite obviously Lieutenant J. Barroll Washington, aide-de-camp to General Joseph E. Johnston, who was captured at Fair Oaks, May 31, 1862, and exchanged the following September. It was entirely natural for an ADC to be in charge of his general's papers, but he ought not to have carried them so near the front line.

Such details as this young officer carried could have come only from rebel spies with access to the files of higher Union headquarters. The data were almost certainly based on information Conrad had smuggled out of the War Department in Washington only a little while before. That august organization was beginning to be embarrassed as it discovered with what ease the enemy learned its plans. It was all the more embarrassed when news of the secrets captured with Lieutenant Washington—which should never have reached the public at all—appeared in the press.

IV

Before the Seven Days' fighting ended (July 1, 1862), McClellan's command was greatly reduced and General John Pope was given the new army of Virginia (June 26, 1862). About three weeks after Malvern Hill, on July 25, two spies whom Lee himself identifies only as "Texans" reached Confederate headquarters with full information of Pope's forces. These men located him, with 35,000 men, in and around Warrenton, Virginia. They also placed three regiments in the Fredericksburg-Falmouth area, with cavalry pushed across the Rappahannock River. The Texans also stated that seven heavy guns had been "sent to McClellan since he reached

James River"; but this was of no great importance, since it was clear that McClellan had been disposed of, for the time being.

These data did not wholly agree with a report from one J. Walker, in Hanover Junction, and Lee wanted more information. Two of Stuart's star secret agents were soon looking into the matter. Frank Stringfellow, of the 4th Virginia Cavalry, entered Warrenton itself. Conrad was called back to Richmond, to report to Secretary of War James A. Seddon. (He was also allowed to select a fresh horse.) Meantime, Robert E. Lee, basing his decision on all this reliable intelligence, moved his army up to the Rappahannock to confront Pope.

At a fairly early stage in his espionage, Conrad had begun to use the old Van Ness house as his secret headquarters. This was a mansion built by General John Peter Van Ness, a prominent politician, in the early 1800's, where the Pan-American Building now stands. At the time of the Civil War it was owned by an enthusiastic Confederate sympathizer named Thomas Green. Being isolated in spacious grounds, secure, in sympathetic hands, and only a few blocks from the White House and War Department, it was an ideal headquarters for Conrad's intelligence ring.

Three days after his conference with Secretary Seddon, Conrad was back in this lair, sending new instructions to his Washington staff. A double agent inside Lafayette Baker's secret service was instructed to warn him at once, if Baker seemed to have any idea that the spy was in the capital. His "trusty friends in the War Department" were ordered to meet him for conference on the steps of the Interior Department building that night. The underground line to Richmond was alerted to stand by for urgent dispatches at any moment.

Meantime, Stuart, with Stringfellow's help, had raided Catlett's Station (August 22–23, 1862), invading Pope's own tent, captured his dress uniform coat, and seized papers that made possible the victory of Second Manassas (August 29–31, 1862). As soon as the Confederate staff had had time to digest the contents of Pope's papers, Lee began the daring move that led to victory. Jackson's II Corps slipped away from the front August 25 and began its long swing through the Shenandoah and around Pope's right flank. On the twenty-sixth, Lee followed with Longstreet's I Corps. No one on either side knew quite what the situation was, except that it was changing swiftly. The Confederate generals needed a constant flow of intelligence and needed it in a hurry. Conrad in the Federal capital and Stringfellow in the field rose magnificently to the emergency.

Conrad started essential elements of information to Richmond at once: The Federals were rushing a skeleton army corps to the upper Potomac. Washington was empty, open, and helpless, anxiously waiting while McClellan reinforced Pope. The Federals were—for the first but not the last time—in terror lest Stuart's raiding cavalry gallop straight into Washington itself.

Conrad tried to ride out of the city, intercept Stuart, give him this information in person, "and urge him to dash into the city and capture Lincoln and his cabinet." But before he could do so, Pope's and McClellan's troops were moving north—while Captain Conrad reported their movements to Lee—"heading for the upper ford of the Potomac to protect Washington and Baltimore and prevent the invasion of Pennsylvania and the capture of northern cities."

All roads were closely guarded, and the usual routes into Virginia were hopelessly blocked by the mass of moving troops. Conrad hoped for a time, however, that he might be able to cross the Potomac farther downstream. He would then ride around the Union armies, turning west to Fredericksburg, then northwest to Upperville, Virginia, then west again to Ashby's Gap in the Blue Ridge. Somewhere along the way, he hoped to meet Stuart. If not, he still hoped to reach some telegraphic station far enough south to wire "any central point likely to reach the advancing troopers on their first invasion into Maryland."

But there was not time enough, and both plans failed. All Conrad could do was report to Richmond through the usual roundabout secret channels, hoping the Confederate Signal Service there could forward his intelligence to the Cavalry Corps. This was too slow. The vital intelligence did not reach Stuart till it was much too late. If it had been in time, Jeb could probably have led his horsemen into Washington itself, capturing Lincoln, wrecking the entire Union machinery of government—and perhaps ending the war with a Southern victory in 1862. As Conrad truly remarks, "at no time during the war had Washington been in such peril," though it was to be equally in peril a year later.

Conrad could still forward dispatches to Richmond, but Richmond could not reach Stuart. When he met the general some time later, after Antietam, Stuart assured him that if Conrad had been able to get word to him when his swift raiders were just outside the capital, "he would have dashed into Washington with his whole command and made the White House his headquarters!"

The disconsolate pair decided to attempt to seize the White House if such a chance ever came again. "I told him to look out for me on his next march of invasion," says Conrad, "for I would hold him to his promise." The same chance *did* come again, a year later!

Though there had been no way of informing Stuart in time, Conrad's other information went forward through the usual lines to Lee. It was supplemented and confirmed by other agents, including Stringfellow and Mosby.

Lee was also getting information at this time from an otherwise unknown spy named Charles T. Cockey, who operated an underground station for contraband and secret agents at Reisterstown, Maryland, northwest of Baltimore. This was part of a secret courier line from Washington. Cockey, who had begun operation early in the war, was not trapped until the spring of 1864, when he made the mistake of accepting a disguised Union counterintelligence man as a genuine Confederate. While Conrad was spying in Washington and while Stringfellow, Mosby, and their friends spied near the front line, Cockey was also supplying the Confederates with any information he could get.

All that is known of him is what the Union detective reported Cockey had told him: "When General McClellan was following Lee into Maryland [i.e., a few days after Second Manassas and just before Antietam, which was fought September 17, 1862] a man came to him from Washington and gave him the number of men McClellan had, and the direction McClellan had, and the direction he was going to take." This man was very probably one of Conrad's couriers from Washington.

Cockey went himself to Frederick, Maryland, and gave the information to Lee. This must have been between September 7 and September 11, 1862, the dates between which Lee's headquarters were there. At about this same time, McClellan was receiving Lee's famous "lost order," giving him the exact plans of the Confederate high command.

Both Cockey's communication line and his espionage probably received assistance from Dr. Adalbert J. Volck, a Baltimore dentist and a friend of Jefferson Davis, who was also a very good portrait painter, the creator of some distinguished work in metal relief, and a well-known caricaturist, whose work is still valued by collectors. (Dr. Volck's younger brother made the death mask of Stonewall Jackson.) To his other talents, the doctor added skill in smuggling medicine, artisans, mechanics, and recruits southward from Baltimore, where he operated a "safe house" for Confederate secret agents. Though the artistic dentist fell under suspicion and was sent to Fort McHenry several times, he came to no harm.

The alertness of their spies, which had served the rebel army so well before the Peninsular campaign and before Second Manassas, continued, perhaps even increased a little. So close was the Confederate watch on the Federal War Department that, when Burnside replaced McClellan on November 15, 1862, Lee had the news within twenty-four hours. When further information explaining Burnside's probable intentions was needed, Conrad put his War Department spies to work. Did Burnside intend to advance on Richmond? If so, would he come by way of Culpeper and Gordonsville or by way of Falmouth and Fredericksburg?

This time Conrad wasn't delayed. Within less than twenty-four hours he was able to report: "By way of Falmouth and Fredericksburg." His news was so important that Conrad himself took it personally to Lee's headquarters. As a result, Lee and the whole Army of Northern Virginia were entrenched at Fredericksburg on December 13, 1862, grimly waiting, when Burnside arrived—as predicted—on the other side of the Rappahannock.

Federal ineptitude in counterintelligence continued after Burnside arrived in front of Fredericksburg. Dr. William Passmore— English born but an enthusiastic rebel—was able to walk freely about the general's camp, posing as a mentally deficient peddler, selling market produce to the Union troops from an old cart. Burnside himself gave the spy a pass, authorizing him to enter the Union lines daily—as Passmore did for several weeks! Since the doctor was supposed to be a half-wit, people talked freely in his presence, with results said to have been very useful to Robert E. Lee. It is small wonder that Burnside was disastrously defeated at Fredericksburg.

Federal security was still so bad that some of this information may have come directly from the White House itself, through the gardener, John Watt. Conrad never admitted having an agent in the White House, and Watt never admitted selling intelligence to the enemy. But Conrad was at times very well informed as to Lincoln's movements, and Watt eventually had to admit that he had sold official secrets—though only to a newspaper. There is no doubt that the White House gardener could have been extremely useful to Conrad—and the Reverend Captain Conrad was not a man to miss chances. But Watt had been detected and dismissed months before Fredericksburg, and official secrets useful in that battle would have had to leak through such fellow traitors as he may possibly have left behind. None of this is nearly so incredible as it sounds. After all, a Negro girl spy, serving Jefferson Davis undetected in the Confederate presidential mansion, proved very useful to the Union.

When the Lincoln family entered the White House, Mrs. Lincoln had taken an immediate fancy to Watt, who had been a gardener there since 1852, and had taken him to New York to help buy plants for the White House grounds. Then, late in 1861, a news story by Henry Wikoff, *New York Herald* correspondent, revealed the contents of Lincoln's message to Congress before delivery, thus providing both the Confederate and the British governments with valuable advance information regarding the Mason-Slidell incident.

Wikoff was sent to the Old Capitol Prison and, when interrogated, did what no reputable newspaperman should ever do: He betrayed his source. A Congressional grilling forced Watt to admit what he had done, though he does not seem to have been placed on trial. He denied stealing a copy of the President's manuscript but admitted he had read the message surreptitiously and had then passed its contents on to Wikoff from memory.

Though this was some months before Fredericksburg and though there is no proof that Conrad ever used Watt as a source or that Watt left other spies behind him at the White House, the incident does reveal startling possibilities.

Two days after Lee had won his victory at Fredericksburg, Conrad was in Richmond, discussing with Jefferson Davis an espionage scheme so dangerous that Davis recoiled at the thought of letting him try it.

"I cannot bear," he said, "to think of our young men shot down or hanged as spies."

What the scheme was, Conrad never states explicitly. It seems to have been a plan for a larger network, continually at work in Washington instead of undertaking occasional special missions under Conrad's immediate direction. Davis told him to think his scheme over, whatever it was, and then, if he were still willing to accept the danger, he would be allowed to set up the new system.

Conrad was on his way to the Union capital next day, after selecting for himself "the finest horse to be had in the big depot" at the remount station outside Richmond. With the assistance of Secretary of War Seddon, he secured a boat with a four-man crew for crossing the Potomac, plus a body servant of his own, part Negro, part Indian, who served with him during all the rest of the war.

Lieutenant Charles Cawood, of the Confederate Signal Service, already had a permanent post on the lower Potomac, through which messages could pass at need. But Conrad now built a small shanty he called "Eagle's Nest" on a high cliff near Boyd's Hole, on the south bank of the Potomac, placing mines in the adjoining creeks and coves to prevent prying Yankee gunboats from interfering. Five men were stationed here. Conrad arranged for the already existing "Doctors' Line" to pick up messages in Washington and take them to a point on the Maryland side of the Potomac, opposite the shanty. "In less than twenty-four hours," says Conrad, "I could send a reliable dispatch from Washington to the Confederate capital." He himself was able to ride straight from the front door of the War Department in Washington to the front door of the War Department in Richmond. Messages passed back and forth without interruption until Appomattox.

None of these messengers was ever arrested. Only Dr. Wyvill

seems even to have been suspected. He was halted at the Navy Yard Bridge one night, on suspicion of smuggling "pills and quinine to the rebels." The Yankees rummaged through the hollow seat of the doctor's buggy but failed to notice the envelope tacked underneath.

Captain Conrad continued to journey back and forth between Richmond and Washington for a long time—probably till late 1863 or early 1864—without attracting the attention of the Federal authorities. But this happy state of affairs could not be expected to last forever. Lafayette C. Baker's detectives finally picked up his trail and even learned his name "about the middle of the war," probably some time in 1863. All this was promptly reported to Conrad by one of his own men, who had wormed his way into Baker's Federal counterespionage organization. Conrad gives this man's name as Edward Norton, a Confederate soldier who finally settled down in the U.S. secret service as a permanent Confederate spy in Washington.

VI

Realizing that, with Baker on his trail, he would not be able to accomplish anything in Washington, Conrad decided to vanish until the hunt cooled down. With characteristic audacity, however, he saw in his own danger a fine chance to convince Baker that the Confederate spy, Norton, was a true-blue Union man. He instructed Norton to make a full report to Baker, in which he was to show clearly that Conrad really was a rebel spy. This would clear Norton of any possible suspicion and would "give an appearance of loyalty to his work." It also gave Norton an excuse for meeting Conrad occasionally—ostensibly to spy on him—and this made it easier for Norton to pass on to the Confederates whatever information he had picked up while working as a Federal detective.

Late one evening, Norton met Conrad at a rendezvous outside the Patent Office with a last-minute warning. Baker was about to raid the Van Ness house. Conrad would have to leave Washington at once. At this critical moment the spy happened to be without funds.

Luckily, he was able to borrow $150 from a Confederate woman in Washington. With this he paid the captain of a river schooner for his passage, posed as the ship's cook when a Federal boarding officer appeared at Alexandria, and was able to report personally to Stuart that same morning. Norton had warned him just in time. Baker's men began ransacking the Van Ness house within an hour of his departure!

Some time after this, Conrad, in disguise, was caught by a Federal patrol and held to await investigation. As yet, no one had any idea he was a spy; he was being held merely on general suspicion. But his disguise would never stand investigation. To frighten off investigators, he promptly feigned the symptoms of smallpox. This got him out of one danger into another. He was placed in isolation among some genuine smallpox patients, from whom he was very likely to contract the disease.

Since, however, the guards themselves had no desire to be close to the smallpox camp, Conrad was soon able to slip away unobserved and begin the long walk to his secret station on the Potomac. Moving only at night, sleeping in thick woods by day, he evaded the patrols searching for him—who can hardly have yearned for close contact with a possible smallpox patient—and was soon safely back in his refuge at Eagle's Nest.

It is impossible to give exact dates for Conrad's doings, immediately after this. He appears to have stayed out of Washington for a time, leaving espionage there in Norton's hands, while he himself observed, scouted, received Norton's reports at Eagle's Nest, and sent them on. The official regimental records of the 3rd Virginia Cavalry (now in the National Archives) show Captain Conrad still listed as a chaplain, but "detailed on secret service for the C. S. Government," as late as May, 1864. On August 30, 1864, he was ordered to Richmond.

Making an entry about secret service in regimental records was, of course, in the last degree indiscreet, but it was only one more example of the carelessness about security that might easily have cost Conrad his life. He had begun to make a habit of calling on President and Mrs. Davis when he was in Richmond. On these occasions, Mrs. Davis delighted in introducing him as "a young man just back from Washington" who had been paying his "respects incognito to Mr. Lincoln and the family in the White House."

Jefferson Davis, professional soldier though he was, seems never to have realized the danger. Neither, for that matter, did Conrad! And, to do them both justice, nothing ever went wrong because of their indiscretion.

In June of 1863, Conrad ventured into Washington to get intelligence likely to assist Lee in the march to Gettysburg. Finding Washington almost stripped of defenses, he rode out to meet Stuart's raiders, whose swift march northward would soon bring them almost in sight of the capital. If he had not missed Stuart by an hour or two, the Confederates would have won Gettysburg and perhaps the war. It was his second misadventure of the sort.

In the spring of 1864, he again entered Washington in civilian clothes, visited Burnside's IX Corps at Annapolis, wearing a Federal chaplain's uniform, then returned to the capital once more to verify his information. This secret reconnoissance provided an important part of the intelligence that enabled Lee to anticipate Grant's advance into the Wilderness (May 5, 1864) with such astonishing accuracy.

At Charlotte Hall, Maryland, on the Potomac, Captain Conrad had the luck to meet a Union cavalry sergeant, commanding a small detachment at the spot where the captain hoped to have two of his assistants cross that very night. To make matters worse, they would be carrying a large and suspicious bundle consigned to General Robert E. Lee—and there were very good reasons why that bundle ought to go through safely.

Studying his man, Conrad decided the blue-clad noncom was open to a little bribery. He may also have guessed that the sergeant was not very bright. Taking a big risk, the Confederate spy explained that, though he was in a Federal chaplain's dress, he wasn't really an officer at all. He was just wearing a chaplain's uniform to get into Washington, because he had business there. The sergeant— who should have arrested the fraudulent chaplain on the spot— complacently accepted one of Conrad's ten-dollar gold pieces instead. (Scarce as gold was in the Confederacy, there was always enough for the spies.) In return, the disloyal noncom saw to it that the Potomac crossing was unguarded that night. The two secret agents found it easy to take across a large parcel that any rational patrol leader would have searched on sight.

A search, however careless, would have revealed something highly incriminating at first glance. For Captain Conrad's parcel contained a new and splendid Confederate uniform, specially made for General Robert E. Lee, the gift of a friend in Baltimore. This was, in fact, the superb dress uniform Lee wore at Appomattox— the one that caused Grant to apologize for his own shabbiness. What the victor would have said if he had known how his great opponent received that uniform, one trembles to imagine.

Conrad adds that with General Lee's new clothes went a magnificent pair of gold spurs for General J. E. B. Stuart. These now repose in the home of his grandson at Manhasset, Long Island, still in the silk-lined morocco case in which they were presented. They were a gift from an anonymous lady in Baltimore. From Conrad the spurs were sent to Dr. William H. Philpot, 4th Georgia Regiment, then stationed somewhere near Richmond. Why this was done and how Dr. Philpot sent them on to Stuart remains a mystery. Stuart wrote Mrs. Lillie Parran, widow of his friend W. F. Lee, who had been killed in action early in the war, "Did you know a lady in Balt[imore] (anonymous) had sent me a pair of elegant gold spurs?" He added, "They came while Flora [Mrs. Stuart] was here, and *she* buckled them on."

Ladies were always sending gifts to Stuart. Mrs. Parran brought him other spurs from St. Louis. Another unknown lady sent him a pair of gloves—"the best gloves of the kind I ever saw"—in 1863.

Conrad cannot, however, be correct in saying that he sent Stuart his gold spurs in the spring of 1864. Stuart himself says that he received them in 1862, and, in any case, he was mortally wounded May 11, 1864. Jeb did, as he lay dying, ask that *a* pair of spurs be sent to Mrs. Parran, but these would naturally be the spurs she had brought from St. Louis. The gold spurs from the lady in Baltimore have always been in the possession of the Stuart family, as they still are.

It is entirely plausible that Conrad sent Lee his uniform in 1864. If so, he had sent the spurs sometime earlier and in later years grew confused as to dates. It is also possible that he did send uniform and spurs together, as he says, but in that case he must have done so in 1862. His book, *Confederate Spy*, in which he tells the story, was written thirty years after the events it describes.

Confusion would be natural, for this package was probably only one of hundreds that Conrad's organization received from Baltimore. That city, besides being an espionage and recruiting center, was also a Confederate military supply base—secret, of course—from which were smuggled gold braid, officers' uniforms, presentation swords, and other military wares finer than the beleaguered Confederacy could supply.

Probably a good many local businessmen with strong Southern sympathies—or just with an eye on the dollar—were involved. One who can be identified was Christian Emmerich, a fashionable shoemaker. When the Federals finally caught up with him, they found he was running supply bases and recruiting stations both in his home and in his shop. A raid revealed a number of orders for Confederate uniforms, a stock of gold braid, a supply of Confederate uniform buttons, and Confederate letters, which he apparently meant to smuggle through the lines.

Emmerich's deliveries were assisted by a Baltimore and Ohio conductor and by a brakeman named Charles E. Langley, living only a few blocks away. The brakeman apparently continued espionage, for Federal counterintelligence files contain a report from Hagerstown, Maryland, dated February 2, 1863, on a certain Charles Langley, who is also called Jack, a short, thick man with heavy eyebrows. He had "black hair and wears it frizzled." He was said to have made three trips into the Federal lines, with papers better than any loyal citizen could get.

The splendid sword that Lee wore at Appomattox—and did *not* offer to Grant, despite a legend—may also have come from Baltimore. Another presentation sword, meant for Major Harry Gilmor, celebrated both as a cavalry officer and as a Confederate spy, never reached him. It was detected at a railroad station and the woman carrying it was arrested. After the war, Gilmor tried to buy it from the Union officer into whose possession it had fallen, but the new owner refused to sell.

6

J. E. B. STUART'S
SECRET AGENTS

PART 2.
Stringfellow and His Friends

Captain Conrad's endeavors were ably supplemented by a second group of scouts and spies in Stuart's intelligence service, of whom, after the war, Frank Stringfellow became the best known. Stringfellow was a suitable colleague in espionage for the Reverend Captain Conrad. Though not yet ordained, he became a clergyman of the Episcopal Church after the war; he possessed all Conrad's sincere religious zeal, plus all his boldness and skill in espionage.

Conrad's and Stringfellow's almost incredible adventures were really commonplaces in the lives of Stuart's spies. Such records as survive suggest that they were all equally bold and equally adventurous. But Conrad, who wrote two books, and Stringfellow, who frequently lectured to make money to support the church of which he was rector, are the only ones who became widely known. Captain (later Colonel) John Burke, the spy with the glass eye, talked sometimes of his adventures, and a few who listened thought to make notes—but far too few. Others in Stuart's group of spies, quite as venturesome and quite as valuable, seem never to have left any personal record of their exploits.

I

Two such unknowns were Captain John H. Boyle and Captain Charles Powell, who entered Dumfries, Virginia, a little while before Stuart raided the town in December, 1862. Dressed as civilians, they mingled with Union soldiers before the raid, then suddenly disappeared. When they returned to Dumfries with the raiders, Boyle was the staff officer who paroled Stuart's prisoners. This turned out to be a great mistake, for the prisoners remembered his face, later, after his capture. When the two again visited Dumfries as spies, in January, 1863, they were captured—Powell with the Union general Sigel's troops, Boyle at his parents' home in Upper Marlborough, Maryland.

When Boyle visited his home, curious neighbors learned that he was carrying more than a hundred letters to Jefferson Davis, Mrs. Davis, and other Southerners. A certain W. G. Hoben reported to the War Department, about January 20, that Boyle was again at his father's; that he had come there from Richmond the previous summer and then returned to Richmond; that he would leave again for Richmond some time during the week; and that he was invariably absent from home all day, returning very late at night.

That was enough for Federal counterintelligence. Boyle was soon in the Carroll Prison, which adjoined the Old Capitol, earnestly requesting Lafayette C. Baker to send him a pair of "dark blue pants" (his own property), as he was "very much in need of a pair of pants." Witnesses were being collected for his trial, to be held in the last few days of February, but in some way Boyle escaped hanging and rejoined the Confederates. A brigade commander's report praises him for his conduct at Gettysburg. There is no record of what happened to Powell.

Except for Stringfellow, Burke, and Conrad, there is no way of telling how many of Stuart's spies ventured into Washington. Stringfellow was often in the Union Army's lines and repeatedly in the Federal-held town of Alexandria, close to the capital; but he probably did not enter the city itself until late in the war. Stuart's other agents—or most of them—operated on the southern bank of the Potomac, much nearer to the Northern capital than any rebel had a right to be, but not within the District of Columbia itself, so far as is known.

The sources these secret agents used are, for the most part, unknown; but Stringfellow, like Captain Conrad and Mrs. Greenhow, had pipelines into Federal government departments; and John Burke also probably had a few of his own.

The rector spy's full name—by which no one ever called him—was Benjamin Franklin Stringfellow. When the war broke out, he was teaching Latin and Greek at a girls' school in Mississippi. With his gray-blue eyes, blond hair that curled a little, and slight stature—he weighed only ninety-four pounds—he was not an impressive military figure; but that turned out to be an advantage. With a little suitable padding in the right places, it enabled him to enter the Union lines disguised as a girl and return with his masquerade unquestioned. It also led numerous confiding Federals to underestimate him—until it was too late.

This deceptively fragile appearance for a time seemed likely to keep Stringfellow out of the war entirely, especially as he was afflicted with a persistent cough. So insignificant was his appearance that his first four efforts to enlist earned him four rejections. Eventually, Stringfellow contrived to join the Powhatan Troop, later Company E, 4th Virginia Cavalry, Captain John F. Lay commanding. There is a legend that Lay accepted the man nobody wanted only after this very eager volunteer had captured three of the captain's sentries and had marched them, at pistol point, before their astonished commander.

On May 23, 1861, a special election in Virginia resulted in a majority confirming the secession resolution of the legislature. On May 24, Federal troops crossed the Potomac and occupied Arlington. Seven days later, General Beauregard arrived to take command of Confederate troops at Manassas. Almost at once he found he needed to know whether Federal troops had occupied Alexandria (they had) and, if so, what they were doing there.

Company E, 4th Virginia Cavalry, was posted in advance of the regiment, close to the Potomac. Beauregard's orders soon reached Captain Lay: He must get a man into Alexandria, where there was an active organization of Confederate sympathizers, to learn as much as possible about Federal strength and probable movements.

Though there is no clear evidence, it is probable that Stringfellow was the man sent into Alexandria, where he was later to do a great deal of secret service; but, if so, he was back with the Confederates in time for the Battle of Bull Run.

In the following September, while Stuart was operating a cavalry screen around Dranesville, northwest of Washington, Stringfellow was permanently attached to the reconnoissance group of the Cavalry Corps. Two other men, Frank Deane and George Woodbridge, also of Company E, 4th Virginia Cavalry, were transferred at about the same time. The trio from Company E were joining a remarkable detachment, of whose exploits far too little can now be discovered. It included Captain Redmond Burke, Lieutenants Will Farley, B. S. White, T. S. Garnett, Jr., Charles Dabney, W. G. Hullihan, R. H. Goldsborough, Thomas Turner, H. Hagan, and John S. Mosby—the last soon to win fame as a guerrilla leader. Associated with them were Captain (later Colonel) John Burke, of Hood's Texan Brigade; Channing M. Smith, Company H, 4th Virginia Cavalry (Stringfellow's regiment); Manson Bradshaw, Company E, 4th Virginia (Stringfellow's own company); and perhaps a secret agent named Harwood, of Lee's Rangers. The Rangers were a mounted reconnoissance detail, operating under Fitzhugh Lee, nephew of the commanding general. Since Lee was one of Stuart's immediate subordinates, association between their intelligence men would be natural.

Channing M. Smith and Stringfellow must certainly have known each other, for Civil War cavalry regiments were small. Smith was a nephew of Robert E. Lee's chief of staff, Colonel R. H. Chilton, and at various times did secret intelligence work for General Wade Hampton, Mosby, and "Marse Robert" himself, besides his reconnoissance for Stuart. In a letter to Stuart on April 23, 1864, Lee mentions Smith and Stringfellow as particularly valuable in reconnoissance.

Will Farley, a low-voiced, mild-mannered South Carolinian of medium height and handsome features, was kept on Stuart's own staff "for such service as was needed," because he was regarded as "one of the most desperate fighters of Stuart's whole command."

Harwood is known only as the central figure in one quaint adventure. In 1862, when Stuart's headquarters were about seven miles from Harrison's Landing on the James River, the spy was ordered into McClellan's lines, disguised as a member of the 8th Illinois. On his way back from the river, he encountered a Confederate, whom he mistook for a picket strayed from his post. Forgetting that he was himself in Federal uniform, Harwood rebuked the man for leaving his post. He was not, however, addressing a derelict sentry but a Confederate cavalry officer, who was almost certainly Major Heros von Borcke, the Prussian professional soldier who had joined Stuart's staff. (The name is recorded as "Van Banch," but Harwood's knowledge of the Prussian Army was limited.)

Von Borcke—if this was he—promptly took Harwood prisoner, supposing him to be a Yankee from his uniform. When the astonished spy asked what command his captor belonged to, the stranger replied he was in Stuart's cavalry. In spite of that, Harwood decided to escape without revealing his true identity; but, while he was trying to think out a scheme, he and his captor met the 9th Virginia Cavalry, accompanied by "General Lee"—obviously Fitzhugh, not his uncle. Lee recognized and released Harwood at once. (That Von Borcke failed to recognize the spy is not surprising. Fitzhugh Lee would not reveal the identity of his agents, even to Stuart's staff, if he could possibly help it.)

Mosby had begun the war as a cavalry lieutenant, whose "energy and activity had been frequently exhibited," as a friend once remarked. But, as he was "never an easy or indulgent officer," he failed of re-election (in the days when Confederate soldiers elected their own company officers). The strict discipline that saves lives in action does not always make a competent officer popular. Lieutenant Mosby would have suffered the humiliation of being "busted back" to private if Stuart had not assigned him as a reconnoissance officer, after which he rose swiftly to success as a cavalry raider, employing some skillful spies himself—and, incidentally, winning the hearty admiration of his leading foeman, General Ulysses S. Grant.

II

Of equal value to Stuart and the Confederate cause were the two Burkes. Captain Redmond Burke may never, technically, have been a spy at all; for, though he engaged in all sorts of desperate reconnoissance missions, it is by no means certain that he ever wore disguise.

Redmond Burke was a large man, raw-boned, vigorous, and rough, with a special personal devotion to his general. Stuart once remarked in a letter home: "His child-like devotion to me is one of those curious romances of this war which I will cherish next to my heart while I live." He is said to have trained Stringfellow in scouting (not espionage) and on one occasion to have saved his life. He was killed in or near Shepherdstown, West Virginia, November 25, 1862, while attempting to escape capture.

The record of Captain John Burke, an out-and-out spy, exactly reverses that of Redmond. If John Burke ever did any ordinary field reconnoissance, it is not in the records. His reports are said to have aided Beauregard and Johnston at Manassas, and he seems to have been continually engaged in espionage until the middle of 1864, when he became adjutant to General Pendleton Murrah. Under the loose staff organization of the period, he may easily have retained intelligence duties, even as an adjutant.

Though a Texan devoted to the Southern cause, Burke had been born in Philadelphia and had lived in New York. He thus had a Northern accent, which long residence in Texas had never changed, so that he could pass as a Northerner at any time.

A third spy named Burke, whose first name is unknown, was a Federal agent. This man played the part of a Confederate sergeant so adroitly as to win golden opinions in the army on which he was spying. "If I had a thousand such men I could whip a brigade of Yankees," his admiring Confederate commander once remarked. A Confederate quartermaster, however, ordered to supply him with a horse and subsistence, strongly suspected he was supplying information to Admiral Farragut. This was certainly not John Burke, who is not known to have operated so far South or to have worked as a double agent.

In the spring of 1862, John Burke was with Jackson in the Shenandoah Valley; but his service with Stonewall must have been brief, for he was with Johnston during Magruder's retreat from Yorktown (May 13, 1862) and still with him when Johnston was wounded at Seven Pines (May 30, 1862).

He was with Stuart at a battle that one Confederate soldier, who

saw him there, calls "second Fredericksburg." This might refer to
the fight of Early's Confederates to pin down the Federals near
Fredericksburg (May 2, 1863), while Stonewall Jackson made his
famous flank march at Chancellorsville. More probably, however,
it refers to the Battle of Fredericksburg (December 13, 1862),
for the same soldier who mentions seeing Burke at Hamilton's
Crossing also mentions seeing Major John Pelham, whose guns
were stationed at Hamilton's (Railroad) Crossing during that action.

No matter which battle it was, a group of Confederate soldiers
were idly watching Stuart and Pelham ride past them near the
Crossing. As the soldiers watched, says one of them, "a tall, black-
haired man passed us on a horse, and went running the gauntlet
[sic] between our lines. I asked Major Pelham who he was, and he
said: 'One of the greatest scouts in the Confederacy. His name is
Burks' [sic], or I understood it as that."

John Burke was, in fact, tall and dark as here described. He was
also blind in one eye, a misfortune which he turned to good account: When in disguise he altered his appearance by either using
or removing his glass eye, as the situation might require, further
confusing Union counterintelligence by changing his hat and
"other apparel." Change of costume is, of course, an old device,
but there has never been another secret agent who could change
his eye!

Sometimes he entered the Union lines as a truck farmer. Sometimes he frequented Washington—at need even visiting government
offices—posing as a wealthy gentleman of leisure. When with the
Federal Army, he wore a Federal uniform, and carried a Union
major's commission. Toward the end of the war, he possessed three
different passes, one from Robert E. Lee, one from Meade, and one
from the Union cavalry leader, Pleasanton.

Burke completely astonished a Confederate reconnoissance
group sent to scout the road between Bristow Station and Catlett's
Station, which the Union Army was then using. As the rebels lay
watching, a column of Union soldiers marched down the road.
The hidden patrol stared in amazement at a Yankee major riding
with the column. One of the scouts turned to his noncom.

"Look, Sergeant, at that officer on the right at the head of the
column, don't you recognize him?" The sergeant did. In fact, the

whole Confederate detachment recognized their friend, John Burke.

This tale is much more plausible than it seems today. It was not unusual for mounted scouts on either side to fall in with an enemy column and jog cheerfully along, sometimes in their own proper uniforms, covered with the all-encompassing waterproofs, worn by both sides, from which only the enormous cavalry boots of the period protruded. Sheridan's Scouts did it repeatedly. The Confederate spy, Lamar Fontaine, claims to have managed the capture of an entire Federal wagon train with which he himself rode— in a Federal uniform coat, wearing a Federal cavalry hat, and riding a horse branded "USA." "I made a very fair Yankee," he remarks, complacently.

Not content with his visits to Washington, Burke at times extended his secret journeys to Philadelphia and New York. He visited the latter city once too often, was captured, and was started— under armed guard and in handcuffs—to Washington for court-martial. At a place called High Bridge, he leaped from the train into the stream below, and his guards, supposing their prisoner, with fettered wrists, would certainly drown, made no great effort to recapture him.

The Union guards did not, however, know that as a boy Burke had delighted in diving from high bridges, the higher the better. He reached the shore safely, manacles and all, and arrived in Richmond four days later. Presumably a Confederate sympathizer, somewhere along the way, helped him get rid of his irons.

Burke had various other narrow escapes. Once, betrayed by a servant girl in a private home, he was saved by the owner's daughter, who hid him under a mattress. On another occasion he hid under a lady's hoop skirt and on another occasion, more decorously, by lying on a beam while the Federals searched for him below. If this is true, he duplicated two of Stringfellow's exploits.

In one extraordinary adventure, while spying in rear of the Army of the Potomac, in or near Washington, Burke captured a Union captain. He had no wish to kill the man in cold blood. On the other hand, if released, the officer would immediately give the alarm. Burke finally told his prisoner that he had no choice but to kill him. The Federal exhibited a natural reluctance, there was some argument, and the captive won the debate. Burke spared his

life and contrived to get back to the Confederate lines all the
same, though there is no record how he did it.

A few weeks later, when Captain Burke, on another trip to Washington, put up at a hotel, the same Federal sent up his card.
Since there was nothing else to do, the Confederate received the
man who had so nearly been his victim. The Union captain had
come to warn Burke to be more careful. Union detectives were very
active. He himself had had no difficulty in recognizing and following the spy. What he had done, detectives might easily do. He then
invited his former captor down to the bar for a drink.

The story ends there. No one knows whether Burke accepted that
drink or not. But he did get safely back to his own lines. It was all
most irregular.

III

Some time in the latter part of 1861, Stringfellow was ordered to
meet E. Pliny Bryan, a telegrapher in the Confederate Signal
Service, at the Stone House Hotel in Manassas. The Confederate
Signal Service was also charged with espionage and secret communi-
cations, operating entirely under the central government in
Richmond.

Bryan had arrived in Washington in August, 1861, to arrange a
new line of secret communication, in entire independence of the
Greenhow and Conrad systems. Johnston's outposts had advanced
so far after Bull Run that they could look down into Washington;
and, to the surprise of residents, two powerful lights began to appear
on the far side of the Potomac, at five o'clock every morning. One
was on Munson's Hill, the other at "Taylor's Corner," on Upson's
Hill. People wondered what the rebels were doing, but no one
guessed the lights were guides for the new spy. Bryan was looking
for a Washington room with a view of the area between the two
lights. Confederates there would then be able to look down on his
window, through a powerful telescope that was being brought from
South Carolina. It would be easy to read Bryan's signals, since the
system was very simple: he merely had to move a coffeepot into
prearranged positions on the sill.

It is doubtful if this ingenious scheme ever worked or whether a similar scheme—by which an agent was to transmit messages by walking to right or left of a given point—was ever used. Just as everything was ready, General Johnston, deciding his troops were too far forward, pulled them so far back that the Confederates could no longer keep their observation posts, and Bryan, unable to use the new system, left Washington as secretly as he had entered it.

After the failure of this remarkable scheme, Bryan's espionage dealt mainly with the Northern press. The Confederates had, at first, attempted to discover the strength of the Union Army by having secret agents keep an eye on troops arriving in Washington; but they could not be sure how many troops were being passed around the capital instead of through it. They soon discovered they could learn a great deal more by reading the reckless revelation of Union troop movements appearing in the uncensored Northern newspapers. "From them," says a Confederate signal officer, "we learned not only of all arrivals, but also of assignments to brigades and divisions, and, by tabulating these, we always knew quite accurately the strength of the enemy's army."

Various Confederate sympathizers in the North collected the newspapers. At first these agents seem simply to have assembled the papers and then sent them on in bulky packages, as Confederate agents elsewhere continued to do throughout the war. There was a great deal of this kind of newspaper smuggling in the vicinity of Nashville, for example. But large packages of newspapers were not easily concealed, were hard to transport secretly, and were likely to arouse suspicion. What legitimate reason could a private citizen have for sending so many newspapers from so many Northern cities, especially if he were sending them South?

A secret courier line ran through Alexandria to Bryan's refuge, hidden farther down the Potomac—probably the same line, or one of the lines, used by Mrs. Greenhow, Conrad, Stringfellow, and others. To avoid burdening his couriers with bulky parcels, Bryan soon decided to have the newspapers searched for military information, within the Union lines. The resulting data on Federal strength and troop movements would require only a few sheets of paper, which the couriers could transmit swiftly and safely.

One of Bryan's resident agents is described as a dentist in Alexandria, whose name Stringfellow gives as Richard M. Sykes. This is certainly a pseudonym, for no such name appears in the Alexandria directory; and it is known that Stringfellow often carefully concealed the names of civilians who had helped him—even when the war was over.

Stringfellow was to live in this man's home, posing as a dental apprentice and assistant. The fact that he knew nothing whatever about dentistry was regrettable, but it couldn't be helped. Apprenticeship was still a usual way to study both medicine and dentistry, and the sudden appearance of an inexperienced learner in a doctor's office would be entirely natural. To give Stringfellow the utmost possible security, an elaborate cover story had been worked out for him. He was to assume the name of Edward Delcher —not an imaginary character but a real person of about Stringfellow's age, who had, until recently, been a dentist's assistant in Baltimore.

It was all planned with meticulous care. Any inquisitive Federal security man, snooping about in Baltimore, would discover that there was, or recently had been, a dental assistant whose name really was Edward Delcher. The detective would not, however, be able to find the real man. Bryan, who thought of everything, had considered that possibility, too. The real Edward Delcher could not possibly turn up at an embarrassing moment: he was on the banks of the Mississippi. There was no possible reason for the Federals—if they should become suspicious—to doubt that the young man in Dr. Sykes's office was exactly who and what he said he was.

Bryan, who was personally acquainted with the real Delcher family, provided a baptismal certificate made out in Edward Delcher's name. He also provided a medical certificate, showing that the supposed Edward Delcher was unfit for military service, though both the real and the pretended Edward Delchers were already soldiers in the Confederate Army. The certificate was meant to answer any possible questions why so young a man as Stringfellow was not in the army. If Stringfellow ever had to produce it, his deceptively frail appearance would confirm his story.

To make sure his disguise was even more perfect, Stringfellow wore a civilian suit, with the label of a Baltimore tailor, that had once belonged to the real man he was impersonating. Stringfellow was also given a vast amount of detail regarding the Delcher family, the kind of minute information a man would be likely to have about his own relatives and nobody else. All this Stringfellow memorized, so that he would be able, offhand, to answer any test questions.

A local resident, whose name Stringfellow later gave as Sam Whiteside (almost certainly another cover name, since no Whitesides can be discovered in the vicinity), guided him through the Federal outposts to his own home on the outskirts of Alexandria. As they approached the house, Whiteside went on alone, leaving Stringfellow a little distance behind him. Only when he had himself entered, to make sure no untrustworthy neighbors or Union soldiers had arrived in his absence, did Stringfellow's host allow him to enter, too.

The rebel spy spent the rest of the day hidden in the Whiteside house, still studying the small black notebook Bryan had given him, filled with intimate and minute details of his new "family." The father was supposedly a bootmaker living on St. Paul Place, Baltimore (though no bootmaker with such a name and address appears in Baltimore directories). There were two brothers, Harley Delcher, a Confederate soldier in Mississippi, like Edward Delcher himself; and John, a Union soldier, serving in West Virginia. (Since Maryland was a divided state which refused to secede despite much Southern feeling, such tragic family divisions were not unusual.)

When the Confederate spy took up his residence in Dr. Sykes's home, he found an old well under the floor of the dentist's office most convenient. By lifting a board, he could drop in huge quantities of newspapers, which—if they had been allowed to pile up with the trash of the Sykes household—would certainly have attracted embarrassing attention.

Each night Stringfellow placed his summary of the military intelligence, gleaned from the day's newspapers, in an envelope. He left this in a letter drop outside the eaves of the doctor's office. Each morning it was gone. That seems to have been all Stringfellow ever knew about it, and he seems never to have made any inquiries. The less he knew the better. So far as is now known, none of this material was either coded or ciphered; but as not one message was ever intercepted, that did not matter.

Probably the courier who took the messages was part of Mrs. Greenhow's network, for, on August 23, 1861, she was reporting to Richmond, "A line of daily communication is now open through Alexandria."

Stringfellow stayed with the dentist through the early part of 1862, without any real danger, though there were some nerve-wracking episodes. Once, in February, an emergency patient with a towel wrapped around his jaw suddenly appeared. A Federal major was at that moment in the waiting room, but the new arrival was in a great hurry for immediate treatment because of his "pain." There were sounds of agony from the dental chair, after which the patient left, still with the towel obscuring his face.

The man's suffering and his treatment were equally fraudulent. The patient was actually a Confederate agent bringing, not the usual newspapers, but a special report of such urgency that he had taken the risk of appearing at the office in broad daylight. It was alarming to find an enemy officer waiting there, however little the Yankee may have guessed what was actually happening.

The agent's report contained advance intelligence of Lincoln's personal order to McClellan to advance against Johnston's Confederates, who were still at Manassas, on or before February 22, 1862. It also reported McClellan's objections, his insistence that the roads were still impassable, and his preference for an attack route via Urbanna, Virginia, a town on the Rappahannock, almost due east of Richmond.

Important in itself, this report was specially valuable because it gave the Confederate staff at Manassas independent sources, each confirming the other. Mrs. Greenhow's reports of Lincoln's cabinet meetings, at which these same plans were discussed, must have come in at about the same time; and she herself adds that she was getting "minutes of M'Clellan's private consultations, and often extracts from his notes." (It is, of course, possible that the notes brought by the man with the imaginary toothache were Mrs. Greenhow's.)

McClellan's proposed line of attack would have brought the Federal Army into the rear of the Confederate position at Manassas. But Johnston now had ample warning. He upset the entire Federal scheme by simply withdrawing from Manassas to a safer line in the rear.

Complications of a highly personal nature, which might easily have revealed Stringfellow for what he was, now arose. He had been careful not to go near Emma Green, the Alexandria girl he meant to marry, and had not even allowed her to know he was in the town. Purely by chance, Emma brought her grandfather to the dentist, at a moment when Stringfellow happened to be in the outer office. In delighted amazement, Emma greeted him. To make matters worse, one of the patients in the waiting room at the moment was almost certainly a Pinkerton operative. The man was a genuine patient but, even off duty, it would be easy to make him suspicious.

There was only one thing to do, and Stringfellow did it, hoping that Emma would grasp the real situation. Coldly, he told the woman he loved that he didn't know her at all. There must be some mistake. He had never seen her before.

The quick-witted girl grasped the situation at once. She apologized prettily. Yes, indeed! A chance resemblance had misled her. She had mistaken Mr. Delcher for someone else. She was very sorry.

What all this meant Emma Green had not the least idea; but she trusted her Frank. When her grandfather's treatment was finished, she took the old gentleman quietly home, asking no questions.

There were still further complexities. Both Bryan and Stringfellow had always feared the dentist's wife, daughter of a Union officer. They had always thought that, if she came to suspect Stringfellow, she might report him to the provost marshal. In fact, Mrs. Sykes did soon guess the truth; and, though she did not report Stringfellow as a spy, she did something equally dangerous.

The scrupulous secret agent had, for some time, been uncomfortably aware that the lady seemed a great deal too friendly. The doctor had noticed it, too, and his manner toward his "apprentice" began to show a perceptible touch of frost. The dentist's wife had, in fact, no special interest in Stringfellow. But she had begun to feel her husband was growing indifferent, was now trying to make him jealous, and was succeeding only too well.

She appeared suddenly at Stringfellow's room one night with

alarming news. Dr. Sykes, taking an easy way to rid himself of his supposed rival, was at that very moment on his way to betray Stringfellow to the Union authorities! He would have to admit harboring a Confederate spy in his home for some months. But he could now say that he had himself been deceived, until that unfortunate recognition scene with Emma. Any charges Stringfellow might make, after his own arrest, would be discredited.

Stringfellow prepared to flee but, as he reached the door, heard cavalry moving in the street. Were they from the provost guard? Were they coming for him? Stringfellow did not wait to find out. The door led directly into the street along which the troopers were riding, so he climbed through a rear window and started for the Whiteside home at full speed.

When he came within sight of it, he took the precaution of watching from concealment on an adjoining hill. He did not have to watch very long. With their intended prey looking on from a safe distance, Union cavalry appeared, searched the Whiteside house and barn, then rode away baffled. Only when he was sure the very last Yank was gone, did the spy venture to enter. Whiteside, he learned had been killed, but his widow had kept Stringfellow's uniform ready for him.

Once again in gray, he was no longer a spy and could not legally be hanged; but he was still in danger. Striking out for the Confederate lines at Fredericksburg, he arrived safely, though only after a chase by a Union cavalry patrol.

Rejoining Stuart was difficult. There was no rail transportation. Johnston's retreating army was still using all the rolling stock there was. Eventually he found Jeb and his horsemen near Yorktown, Virginia, probably about mid-April, 1862.

During McClellan's advance on Richmond, Stringfellow, so far as is known, was sent on no more secret missions. This was the period in which Johnston, seriously wounded, had to be relieved of command and replaced by Lee (June 1, 1862). Stringfellow was, however, busy with ordinary cavalry scouting in proper uniform. With one or both of the Burkes, Will Farley, and John S. Mosby, he reconnoitered for Stuart in the famous ride around McClellan's army (June 12–14, 1862), after which Stuart mentioned him in dispatches as "particularly conspicuous for gallantry and efficiency."

IV

After McClellan's Peninsular campaign failed in the final crushing defeat at Malvern Hill, President Lincoln brought General Pope from the West to command a new army. Gradually more and more of McClellan's troops were moved north and handed over to Pope. On July 3, Burnside with his IX Corps was ordered back from North Carolina to Fortress Monroe. Which way would he go from there? Would he move up the James River and reinforce McClellan? Or would he move up the Rappahannock and reinforce Pope? What were the Yankees going to do? Would the beaten McClellan try again? Or would the next attack come from Pope's new army? The Confederate command had to know.

In the series of Confederate victories that now followed—Cedar Mountain, Groveton, Second Manassas—Stuart's scouts and spies played a very large part. Conrad, it is true, after securing information important in this crisis, failed to get it out of Washington; but Stringfellow and Mosby covered themselves with glory. They found the information that made the Confederate victories possible, and they brought it back to headquarters at the right moment.

Sometime in July, 1862, Mosby, Stringfellow, and one of the Burkes (probably Redmond) were detached as independent scouts and spies for Stuart. A little later, certainly before Second Manassas was fought (August 29–30, 1862), Farley and Lamar Fontaine reconnoitered together as far north as Fairfax Court House, where numerous rebel sympathizers were certain to have information for them.

No one knows what Farley and Fontaine accomplished. They, like Stringfellow and Burke, were probably in disguise, since they were in Yankee territory. Mosby remained in uniform—which saved his life when he was captured, July 20, on the platform of Beaver Dam station. Search of the prisoner revealed a note from Stuart to Stonewall Jackson, who had, by this time, brought his army eastward from the Shenandoah and was now operating with Lee around Richmond. In his message, Stuart told Stonewall that Mosby was "en route to scout beyond the enemy's lines," and any information he brought would be reliable. That naturally interested his captors.

It occurred to somebody that, if Mosby was as valuable as Stuart said, he was worth sending back to the Old Capitol Prison. But, since the guerrilla's reputation was not yet so widespread as it later became, none of the Federals realized what a remarkable prisoner they had. The Union authorities would have saved their army and themselves a vast deal of trouble if they had kept Mosby permanently in the Old Capitol, but instead they rashly exchanged him ten days later.

Mosby was sent from the prison to Old Point Comfort, there to board the "exchange boat," which, under a white flag, steamed back and forth on regular trips to Richmond, taking prisoners from each side back and forth. Since Old Point Comfort gives a superb view of Hampton Roads, the sharp-eyed guerrilla had a perfect chance to count the passing troopships, as Burnside moved his troops up the James River. Mosby could see instantly that IX Corps was on its way to support Pope, not McClellan. It was the first clear indication the Confederates had of this essential information.

None of the guards thought of keeping the Confederate prisoners where they would not be able to see what was going on, nor did anyone notice how alertly Mosby was observing everything. One Union soldier even remarked in his hearing that Burnside would soon join Pope at Culpeper. It was exactly the information needed, at that moment, to confirm other intelligence.

As soon as he reached Richmond, Mosby sped the news to Robert E. Lee. Lee flashed it by telegraph to Jackson, at Gordonsville, whence Jackson promptly advanced to smash Pope at Cedar Mountain (also called Slaughter's Mountain), August 9, 1862. This victory has sometimes been attributed entirely to Mosby's swift intelligence. It was certainly a great advantage to Jackson to know exactly where and when Pope's reinforcements were coming in, so that he could strike before their arrival; but other and equally important information was pouring in from Stringfellow and Burke, who were now practically living with the enemy.

Traveling at night and hiding in the daytime, Stringfellow and Burke penetrated far behind the Union lines without being discovered. Once Stringfellow—who really didn't like that sort of thing —had to knock a sleeping Federal picket unconscious. When he recovered his senses, the victim turned out to be a loquacious fellow, perfectly willing to tell all he knew, and able to reveal a great deal of useful military information. The man was actuated by no lofty patriotic fervor for the Union cause. He had joined the army, he said, mainly to get away from his wife! His most important news was that the Federals now meant to advance across the Rappahannock and attack Lee. Burke, having in the meantime received a bullet in the wrist, took the prisoner and the information back to headquarters, where he paused to have his wound treated.

The intelligence he and Stringfellow had gleaned from the talkative Federal confirmed the information Mosby had already supplied. Hence when, on August 6, 1862, Pope started his troops against Jackson, Stonewall knew all about his capabilities and intentions. Meantime, Stringfellow, whose home at Raccoon Ford, near Verdiersville, lay directly in front of the advancing Yankees, and who knew every inch of the ground, watched them from a safe distance, then rode back to the Confederate outposts, sent word to Jackson, and himself remained in observation. The Southern victory at Cedar Mountain, August 9, 1862, was almost inevitable after that, though Stringfellow continued to supply intelligence during the three days before the battle.

Close though he was to his home, Stringfellow took no heedless risks, even to see his mother. During the fighting at Cedar Mountain, he was ensconced in a thicket behind the Federal lines. As the rebels drove the Yankees back, the boys in blue came unpleasantly close to the spy's hiding place; but they did not catch him, and their near approach enabled him to observe them more accurately than ever.

By night, he saw fresh Union troops moving in from the direction of the Rappahannock. In the moonlight, he could not be quite sure of their numbers; but the long column looked like an army corps. If a whole corps really was coming in, he had important intelligence; but he needed to verify it. Prowling about in the dark, he caught a prisoner. Yes, the man told him, these were new Federal troops: Sigel's I Corps was arriving from Sperryville, to reinforce Pope.

A whole new corps! Stonewall must have this news at once.

Regretfully knocking yet another prisoner on the head—again, the only possible alternative to killing him outright—Stringfellow kept Sigel under observation for a short time, then started back for the Confederate headquarters with his news. On his way through the blue-clad army he was challenged only once.

"Pennsylvania Bucktails," he replied, mendaciously, knowing that famous regiment was in the area—and passed as a friend.

Stringfellow's intelligence was confirmed by a second report of Sigel's arrival, this time from Jackson's own cavalry. When the forces joined battle, Stonewall knew exactly what he was facing. Major John Esten Cooke, of Jackson's staff, wrote later, "It is probable the battle of Cedar Run, where General Pope was defeated, was fought in consequence of this information." In fact, Mosby, Redmond Burke, Stringfellow, and Stuart's cavalry reconnoissance share the credit. Thanks to Mosby, Stonewall was able to strike Pope before Burnside could arrive. Thanks to the other agents, he knew Pope's dispositions and all about Sigel's reinforcing corps.

Stringfellow still remained behind the Union lines when the battle was over; and on August 19, Redmond Burke, with his wounded wrist partly healed, brought him new orders from Stuart. The general wanted his star scout to observe the Warrenton area, to look for river passages near the town, and to locate the extreme right flank of Pope's army, which had been pulled back behind the Rappahannock.

That same night, Stringfellow entered the town, far behind the front line, wearing a Federal officer's blue uniform coat, though the rest of his uniform was Confederate. If in danger, he might be able to escape a spy's death by throwing off the coat and appearing in Confederate uniform, or so he hoped. In the darkness, the queer mixture of garments would not be noticeable—or so he also hoped. It is possible he was wearing the blue trousers that Confederate Army Regulations required, though few Confederates ever received them.

His espionage in Warrenton began at the Warren Green Hotel. This was a little risky, since he had put up there in earlier years and might easily be recognized, especially by Negro house servants, who were likely to be Union sympathizers. But, as it turned out, he had no difficulty of that sort—quite the reverse. The real trouble was that his disguise was a little too perfect. The first person he tried to question—a woman busy ironing clothes in one of the houses— would probably have been glad to give a Confederate soldier any information she had. But she made it abundantly plain that she didn't want to talk to any Yankee.

"Ask your own folks!" snapped the laundress, when he inquired about the location of "our" wagon train. But a Union soldier, who had overheard the conversation from an adjoining porch, was more helpful. When Stringfellow explained he had orders for the officer commanding the wagon train, the man told him the wagons were at Catlett's Station, a few miles southeast of Warrenton.

When it grew dark, Stringfellow risked visiting a local family named Brooks. These old friends told him that General Pope himself had ridden through Warrenton the day before, an interesting bit of information, for it is always useful to know where the enemy's commander is. Through the father of Colonel Charles Marshall, Lee's aide-de-camp, he also learned that Pope's headquarters, now at Catlett's Station, were protected only by a small guard. A large wagon train, the Marshall family said, had passed through Warrenton that morning, heading toward Catlett's Station. Presumably this was the train he had been asking about.

Always careful to confirm intelligence by personal reconnoissance, Stringfellow now rode toward Catlett's Station, approached the town as closely as he dared, made sure his facts were right, then rode all day and all night, reporting to Stuart about dawn. Jeb saw at once a superb chance for one of those swift and unexpected raids in which he delighted. He dashed off a report to Lee. The spy, he added, had promised to guide the rebel troopers "within twenty feet of Pope's Headquarters without detection." From Lee came one scribbled word: "Go!"

Stuart's raid on Catlett's Station, which followed, has been attributed entirely to Stringfellow, and this is doubtless true. It was a tremendous success. The raiders reached General Pope's own tent, capturing his dispatch book, filled with useful information, many other important military documents, one of his capes, and one of his uniform coats, with regulation gold lace, shoulder straps, and stars. The wagon train was exactly where Stringfellow said it would be.

But, though Stringfellow may have been able to take Stuart "within twenty feet" of headquarters, the guide who brought them to Pope's own tent was a Negro who had been captured en route.

He had lived in Berkeley County, Virginia, when Stuart had been on duty there in 1861. Recognizing the general, the slave explained that, though he was now servant to a Union officer, he was still devoted to his "own folks." He was perfectly willing to point out Pope's tent, adding that the staff tents adjoined it, and five officers' chargers were tethered there at the moment.

Jeb's cavalry always needed more horses. The 9th Virginia rode off to raid the staff tents and acquire some remounts.

One important part of Stuart's mission proved impossible. The timbers of the railroad bridge leading to Washington were wet with rain. They would not burn and the bridge could not be destroyed. The immense importance of the Union general's captured papers, however, compensated for this failure. Stringfellow says this was the intelligence "on the strength of which we could fight the second battle of Manassas [August 29–30, 1862]. Gaining the knowledge of the enemy's location, his force, the position of his reinforcements, and his *notions* of where *we* were and what we were trying to do, was of great value to us." Lee's military secretary, General A. L. Long, confirms this. Stringfellow thus compensated for Conrad's failure to get similar information through the lines to Stuart. It was a disappointment not to capture Pope himself, but that worthy had left his headquarters unexpectedly a little while before Stuart arrived, to supervise a fight along the Rappahannock.

The raiders did capture three hundred other prisoners; but it would have been better if they hadn't, for this small success very nearly cost Stringfellow his life a little while later. Among the prisoners was a captain who had had a clear look at Stringfellow's face. It seemed to make no difference at the moment—but that Yankee had a long memory.

As Stuart and his raiders withdrew, Stringfellow was detailed to stay behind in the rain and darkness to give warning of possible Federal pursuit. After it was clear there would be no pursuit, Stringfellow, who had had no sleep for two nights, sought the house of an "old citizen" to ask for a bed. Sometime later, he woke, at his host's shout of warning, to see Federal soldiers leading his horse out of the barn and the yard rapidly filling with blue uniforms.

Stringfellow fled on foot, out of the back door, over a fence, with bullets whizzing about him. Being now without a mount, he came suddenly upon a U.S. cavalry corral, crept along a ditch to the middle of the herd, cut out two horses, and reached his own army in time to serve as a courier during Second Manassas, the battle his espionage had produced.

V

In February, 1863, with prospects of a Confederate invasion of the North not many months ahead, General Stuart began to need "a regular and reliable communication with Washington City and its vicinity." Captain Conrad's organization was providing something of the sort, but Conrad was not in Washington all the time. Stuart decided to send Stringfellow to establish another and independent intelligence net, making certain "that no movement could either be made, or discussed freely, without my knowledge."

The communications seem to have been independent of the "Doctors' Line" and Conrad's secret station on the Potomac, about which even the trusted Stringfellow may not have been allowed to know. He remarked after the war that it was "necessary to have a reliable mail line between General Lee's camp and the Union capital city." This sounds as if he did not know that such a line already existed. To make his own communications satisfactory, he thought it "necessary to go over the line in person, to select our own agents, and to work the line thoroughly before returning to the army."

"I decided to go through the country myself," Stringfellow added, "and pick the agents."

To assist this communication system, he was given the right to use an entire cavalry company, commanded by a certain Captain John Farrow, of whom little else is known, but who was certainly a specially chosen man.

Stringfellow proposed to enter Washington through Alexandria. This would be dangerous if Dr. Sykes was still practicing dentistry in the town, but there would be compensation: Emma Green was still living in her old home.

As companions, the spy selected two young men who, since they lived in the area, would not have to explain their presence. One was Charles Arundel, whose home was somewhere in Fairfax

County, in which Alexandria is situated. The other is unknown. Finding all fords on Bull Run and Occoquan River guarded, the trio did not at first attempt to make any crossing anywhere. Instead, they watched the Federal picket line carefully, until they knew approximately where the sentries were posted and were sure the posts were about two hundred yards apart. They then crossed at points where there were no fords, knowing that these less likely crossings were less likely to be watched. Then they crept on hands and knees between two picket posts to the shelter of a woods near the Arundel home.

The Arundels gave them supper and provided blankets, with which the three secret agents retired to a neighboring pine woods, fearing a surprise search of the house. Next day they built small and inconspicuous defenses of earth and stone around their camp and settled down for a few days, while trying to find "the best man or woman for the work on hand."

The future clergyman now tried his hand at a little highway robbery. A Federal sutler, the Arundels told him, often paused at their house, being "fond of hot breakfast and a little chat before an old Virginia log fire." He would have a pass through the Federal lines— just what the Confederate spy needed. But the Arundel ladies made Stringfellow promise not to hurt the man. After all, they were Virginians, and the Yankee had been their guest.

Early in the morning, the spies, hidden in their pine wood, heard distant wagon wheels rattling over the frozen road. A moment later, "several of the girls" ran into the woods with news that the sutler was coming. The spies would have to capture his wagon by surprise, if they captured it at all. "There were men in it, though they did not know how many."

Young Arundel took a short cut across a bend in the road, hoping to go into ambush before the sutler passed. Too late! They arrived just in time for Stringfellow to seize the bridle of the lead horse. The driver at first showed fight but, with Stringfellow's pistol in his face, changed his mind. The other two, civilians on their way to visit "friends in the Army," were not inclined to heroism.

Taking from the sutler "a few things in the wagon useful to my friends in the country," plus a little United States currency, "by way of toll for using Virginia roads with a Yankee wagon," Stringfellow returned the horses and the wagon and released him. Though the man should at once have notified the provost marshal that his pass had been taken, he seems to have done nothing of the sort.

Stringfellow now started for Alexandria alone, having, as he admits, "a double reason." In other words, "I wished to get agents for my line; but I also wished to see the little girl who[m] two long years before I had 'left behind me.'" Apparently he had not seen Emma Green since that chance meeting in the dentist's office.

Fifteen miles from the town, he found shelter in the house of a Union sympathizer, a local woman with a son "in government employ" somewhere in the vicinity. This was bold to the point of rashness, for Stringfellow was still in Confederate uniform. But he talked of the girl in Alexandria and "the two long, trying years since I had seen my sweetheart." All the world loves a lover. Eventually the loyalist consented to help him, though she may not quite have realized that the young rebel had any purpose other than a visit to his Emma. She knew her own danger, however, and made him promise "not to mix her up" in the affair, if he were caught.

Stringfellow later remarked that, in all his adventures, he was "never afraid of a Virginia Union woman." He had no reason to fear this one, who gave him some of her son's civilian clothes, took charge of his Confederate uniform, and warned him of the place on the road where her son was working. It would be dangerous passing there, she said; he would certainly recognize his own coat. (That seems natural, for Stringfellow describes it as "tiger-colored.")

After a little inquiry, the disguised rebel found a practical way to enter Alexandria without arousing suspicion. A local woodcutter named Olander Devers made frequent trips into the town with loads of wood, then the most common household fuel. Visiting Devers would be difficult, as there was a Union cavalry picket a few hundred yards from his house.

Stringfellow avoided the door entirely, fearing a knock might start the dogs barking, and found an extraordinary entrance of his own. Near the chimney, two short logs had been loosened and a blanket had been hung inside to stop drafts. This must have been a specially devised entrance for secret service use, for Stringfellow seems to have known all about it. Silently moving the logs aside, he stepped in behind the blanket. Then, thrusting it aside, he stepped out before the startled Devers family.

This sudden entrance accounts for the story, sometimes told, that when Stringfellow entered, not through the wall but through the door, he was startled to find his host standing behind it with an ax. An ax there certainly was, in a woodcutter's household. And the sudden appearance of a total stranger, emerging from the wall in a tiger-colored coat, would be enough to make any woodcutter reach for it, but Stringfellow was never in any real danger. This was a staunchly Confederate family, with a son serving in "Mr. Lee's company"—which apparently meant Robert E. Lee's Army of Northern Virginia. The moment Stringfellow explained his mission and his needs, they were ready to aid him. Devers provided a horse, a cart, and a load of wood, which the secret agent drove openly into Alexandria next day. The sentry at Fort Lyon, outside the town, accepted his stolen pass; and all went well until Stringfellow reached the bridge leading into the town itself. At that moment, a U.S. Army wagon drove on the other end. Its driver gaped in amazement at the "tiger-colored" garment, which, it was clear, he recognized. But his effort to question its wearer failed. Stringfellow hurried past him, off the bridge, and away.

In Alexandria, he drove to a store kept by a man he knew he could trust (whose identity is still a secret). Devers, following at a discreet distance, picked up his horse and wagon and drove off. The kindly storekeeper went at once for Emma Green, brought her to the store, "not letting her know who was awaiting her," then tactfully vanished. It was the first of many meetings, with the shadow of stark tragedy overhanging the lovers' every tryst. Touchingly, Stringfellow adds, "Many happy days were spent in the city." He was now, he thought, "well fixed." His life was in danger every minute—but he could see Emma Green!

He took one necessary precaution. The provost marshal in Washington might at any moment cancel the pass taken from the sutler. It would certainly be canceled if the man ever admitted it had been taken from him in a holdup; and he would have to make an explanation of some kind the next time he wanted to go through the lines. Stringfellow, therefore, prudently became "R. M. Franklin, Store-helper," ostensibly a new employee in his friend's emporium.

He did, however, use the sutler's pass on two trips into Washington and was there able to enlist three or four more Southern sympathizers as additional agents. All these seem to have been in, or very close to, the office of Major General Henry Wager Halleck, "Old Brains," now general-in-chief of the Union Army. When these new secret agents began work, inside information flowed swiftly to the rebels, all of it apparently additional to what Captain Conrad was supplying. (Neither he nor Stringfellow ever refers to the other.)

Stringfellow was about ready to return and report on all this, when his career was nearly ended forever by pure bad luck. Rounding a corner hastily one evening, he encountered the same Federal captain he had helped capture at Catlett's Station the year before.

If they had passed casually in the street, Stringfellow's former prisoner—who had by this time either been exchanged or had escaped—might not have recognized his captor. But he could not help noticing a pedestrian who almost knocked him down. He had observed Stringfellow closely at Catlett's Station. It was still light. Recognition was immediate. It was also mutual.

Stringfellow fled, the officer shouted, pursuit began at once. Ahead, the fugitive saw the open door of a house, into which he dashed—probably already aware whose it was. He encountered an imperturbable old lady of rebel leanings, a friend of his mother's, who sat mending a tablecloth.

Mid-Victorian ladies are said to have been sticklers for the proprieties, but not this one. She lifted one edge of her enormous hoop skirt.

"Here, Frank," she said, and draped the tentlike garment around the crouching fugitive. (A girl in Fauquier County, Virginia, is known to have hidden her fiancé in exactly the same way.)

Breathless men in blue uniforms arrived at once. Stringfellow's rescuer, busy with her tablecloth and imperturbable still, was equal to the occasion. Yes, someone had dashed through the house and apparently out the back door. The baffled pursuers searched in vain and withdrew with apologies.

It was clearly time for Stringfellow to be getting out of Alexandria. "Patriotic Southern ladies," one of whom was almost certainly Emma Green, hired a hack and, with Stringfellow as driver, safely passed the outpost lines around Washington. It has been alleged that, to distract the sentries' attention, Emma flirted outrageously—as only a Southern girl can flirt—at every post they passed. However that may be, it is certain that no one paid any attention to the Confederate spy in plain sight on the driver's seat. It was an odd episode in the lives of a future rector and the rector's future wife. The two women had a new driver when they returned to Alexandria; but by that time the sentry had been relieved, and the change of drivers passed unnoticed.

On his return to the Arundel home, Stringfellow learned that his two companions had been killed and also found that the sutler he had held up was spending the night there. "I guess he didn't know me because trimming my hair, shaving, and putting on city clothes made a great difference in my appearance," said the spy in later years. The two shared a bedroom that night.

Stringfellow now met Captain Farrow, who greeted him as one raised from the tomb. "I thought you were dead. We heard you had been captured on the bridge going into Alexandria and hung."

With Farrow and some of his men, Stringfellow returned to raid the Federal outpost he had just passed. They brought off twenty-five prisoners and thirty-five horses, but Farrow was mortally wounded. Stringfellow, though nearly killed by one determined Yankee, who assailed him again and again, escaped with minor wounds, brought Farrow to safety, prayed with him, and rode off. "That was a sad and hurried parting." Ever the chivalrous warrior, Stringfellow was greatly disturbed because one Union soldier, "the poor fellow who had made so many efforts to kill me," had received some bad powder burns.

Back with the Confederate Army, he could reflect with satisfaction that his new network and its communication line from Washington was functioning perfectly. So was Captain Conrad's, though Stringfellow was probably not allowed to know very much about that.

Stringfellow was captured during the Gettysburg campaign, a few days before the battle itself. As when Mosby was captured, the Federals failed to realize how valuable their prisoner was and exchanged him almost at once, though not till the battle was over. Immediately after his own release, he led a raid to capture a Union general to exchange for General W. H. F. Lee, who had been captured a few days before Gettysburg (June 26, 1863). He failed to bag the general he wanted and brought back only a U.S. headquarters flag, an interesting trophy of no particular use. He was equally unsuccessful in one or two other kidnaping schemes.

Amid all this activity, he was able to spend a little while at his home near Verdiersville, in observation of Meade's army, though only as a uniformed scout, not as a secret agent.

VI

After Stringfellow's return to the Cavalry Corps, word came that his mother had been wounded in the foot by a stray shot fired in a skirmish near her house at Raccoon Ford, which had been taken over as a Union headquarters. Stuart sent him on a mission that would bring him into the vicinity, leaving the rest to Stringfellow. As a gift for the invalid, he took an autographed copy of the new biography of Stonewall Jackson, which the novelist, John Esten Cooke, had found time to write and publish, amid his duties as one of Stuart's staff.

Along the way, Stringfellow contrived to slip into a Federal camp and rifle the carelessly guarded tent of General Samuel Powhatan Carter. He was on the point of stealing the general's uniform when he discovered it was a bad fit. Rummaging further, he found a captain's uniform, obviously belonging to an aide, which fitted fairly well and would be a much more convincing disguise for a youthful spy than a major general's two stars. Then he heard—or thought he heard—someone approaching the tent and withdrew hastily, though not before scooping up all the papers on General Carter's work table.

Though he knew his mother was now in the hands of the Union Army, Stringfellow set off for the house anyway, hoping to slip in undiscovered. There was a skirmish—perhaps during his hasty exit from General Carter's camp—and he dropped the biography of

Jackson he was bringing as a present. Finding the book, the Federals were convinced they had killed him, though they found no body.

In this view they were entirely wrong. In fact, the body, very much alive, found them. Cautiously approaching his mother's refuge in the darkness, Stringfellow discovered it was full of Union soldiers.

Peering through a window, he saw a family slave approaching with a lamp. He scratched lightly at the window, hoping to get the woman's attention quietly, without attracting the soldiers' attention. The slave heard the scratch, lifted the lamp, peered out, recognized Stringfellow, thought she saw a ghost—report of Stringfellow's death had reached this headquarters, though no one had yet told his mother—and, in her terror, dropped the lamp and set the house on fire.

It was not a moment for a Confederate spy to linger, and the quick-thinking Stringfellow melted into the darkness, then emerged again, walked openly to a campfire, and lay calmly down, as if he belonged there.

The blaze inside the house was not very serious. When the excitement died down—the Negress's assertion she had seen a ghost did not alarm the Yankees—Stringfellow watched the back door till another family slave, "Uncle George," came out and headed toward the spring, carrying a pail. Taking care not to create another alarm, Stringfellow identified himself quietly, then sent Uncle George back to the house to get him some feminine garments. Thus arrayed, he stole up to his mother's room.

He was still there when an army doctor came to examine Mrs. Stringfellow's wound. Retiring to a closet, her son heard the medical man, as gently as he could, break to his mother the news of his own death. As proof, the doctor showed her the book Stringfellow had been bringing as a gift. The stricken parent was suitably sorrowful, though she did tell the sympathetic surgeon that, somehow, she could not quite believe her son was dead.

Inside the closet, meantime, Stringfellow, ignoring his own death, was hastily jotting down such other purely military information as the doctor let slip. Rarely can an agent make notes on the spot. These notes remained on the closet walls, undisturbed, for years after the war. Then a later householder whitewashed them over, happily so lightly that traces can still be seen.

Resurrecting her "dead" son by the simple expedient of letting him come out of the closet, Mrs. Stringfellow kept him in her room for several days. Here, he shared the invalid's diet, with an appetite so hearty that one Federal, seeing a generously loaded tray leaving the kitchen at each meal, wondered audibly how "one frail and wounded woman could eat so much."

Stringfellow was in no hurry to leave. It was pleasant to be with his mother; and, as he could get safely out of the house "on any night," he had a fine chance to observe the Yankees. Once assured of his mother's early recovery, however, he slipped away quietly after dark, carrying with him the papers stolen from General Carter. Delighted rebel intelligence officers, examining these documents, found they included the divisional payroll, which gave detailed and accurate information on strength, personnel, and organization. It was a treasure such as G–2's rarely find.

In late September, 1863—perhaps before, perhaps after, this visit to his mother, which cannot be exactly dated—Stringfellow was sent out with two or three men to get information of the Union forces near Culpeper Court House. On October 1, one of them contrived to pass the picket line and enter the Federal positions, posing as a teamster in the Federal II Corps, rejoining his comrades safely a few hours later.

Not satisfied with the information, the group remained in a secret camp they had made in a pine woods, within a few hundred yards of the Union position, concealed only by "little bushes" they had stuck in the ground by way of concealment.

The Confederates were still sleeping peacefully on the morning of October 2, 1863, when a few wandering Yankees, looking for persimmons, stumbled upon them and mistook them for their own men. A drummer boy lifted the corner of one man's blanket.

"Hallo, here!" he remarked. "We have better beds for you inside the lines."

As the blanket came off, someone cried, "They are rebels!"

Stringfellow woke to find himself covered by a Federal musket. Its owner greeted him sardonically. "Good morning, Johnny Reb! Wake up!"

But Stringfellow had a pistol under his blanket. He pretended to be only half awake, closed his eyes, and muttered, "Oh, go away and let me sleep, will you?"

The Federals laughed, but as they pulled off his blankets, too, the pistol blazed in their faces. One dead man fell upon him, masking the fire of the others. Stringfellow fired one or two more shots, probably killing two others, and fled. Some of the other Confederates probably also escaped.

During the early part of 1864, Stringfellow seems to have been mainly engaged in mounted reconnoissance with troops, rather than in espionage. On various occasions during these months, the frail fellow broke a Federal colonel's arm and captured his hat, overran an outpost, took an annoyed Federal lieutenant prisoner, stole forty-five horses with the U.S. brand, and ruined one of Mosby's night attacks by a premature and too impetuous assault—or so the disgusted Mosby declared.

VII

At about this time, the Confederates captured a young Yankee captain. When his papers were examined, they were found to contain a pass through the Federal lines for a girl named Sallie Marsten, living somewhere near Culpeper Court House. He had hoped, the captive explained disconsolately, to have the young lady as his partner at a regimental dance. As he was now on his way to prison, he would not be able to go dancing with Miss Marsten. Would Stringfellow take the letter to her?

Stringfellow knew the Marsten family well. One brother had been killed fighting for the Confederacy at Williamsburg. Another had been reported missing in action only a little while before. Sallie Marsten had crossed the lines trying to find some trace of him and had thus made the acquaintance of Stringfellow's prisoner, the captain. But there was no doubt the Marstens were staunch Confederates.

Stringfellow took the captain's letter to Sallie as he had promised and, before he left the Marsten home, arranged to borrow a ball gown and other feminine fripperies. He had to secure a Confederate pass that would allow "Sallie Marsten"—that is, himself—to pass the Confederate lines. He already had a Union pass, thanks to his prisoner.

Strange as this passage of dancing partners through the lines of an army in time of war may seem nowadays (and dangerous as any counterintelligence officer would think it), such episodes in the Civil War—at some times and on certain fronts—were not unusual. In 1863, General Grenville M. Dodge had to issue a definite order: "No ambulance officer to go outside the lines to bring in ladies to dances." Dodge was one of the three best intelligence officers in the Union Army. Yet even his officers had been incautious enough to give Confederate spies this dangerous opening!

Stringfellow retained his trousers, carefully rolled up under the voluminous hoop skirts, so that he could carry the deadly little pair of derringer pocket pistols he found useful in emergencies. There was no place to put them, in hoop skirts. At least, Stringfellow did not know of any. Perhaps he simply didn't know enough about hoop skirts, for a young lady in Tennessee, at about the same time, was packing her father's pistol beneath a similar garment with no apparent difficulty.

The Marsten ladies provided enough switches to make his hair look like a girl's. (This was less difficult for Stringfellow than it would be for a modern soldier. Civil War troops did not favor the "white sidewalls" cut of the modern service but wore their hair rather long. Generals Custer and Pickett let it flow to shoulder length.)

Not only did Sallie and her mother see that the spy was properly dressed for the ball; they rehearsed him in feminine behavior to such good effect that his masquerade was a complete success. His apparently frail physique helped. Daredevil though he was, Stringfellow had an appearance of artless innocence that was often very useful. A wartime comrade described him as "a beardless youth with a waist like a girl's" yet at the same time "in capacity and endurance far superior to any of his men." That same soldier, meeting Stringfellow's eighteen-year-old daughter long after the war, "could scarcely convince himself that his old captain was not before him."

The lieutenant at the Union outpost to whom Stringfellow presented his pass was skeptical. But the pass was perfectly genuine. It had been issued for the feminine guest of a genuine Union officer, known to be stationed in the vicinity. It came from proper and superior authority. The reluctant lieutenant had no choice but to honor it.

Though Stringfellow was well aware that there would be no eager young officer waiting to escort "Sallie Marsten" to the regimental dance, he knew soldiers well enough to feel sure there would be no lack of dancing partners, once he reached the local "Opera House," where the ball was being held.

As he entered, he heard one girl remark that she was seeing her partner for the first time in a year. His corps had just been brought back from the western front to Northern Virginia. The young lady's escort was probably in IX Corps, which, throughout the Civil War, moved about so much that it has been described as "a wandering corps, whose dead lie buried in seven states." These troops were brought east and then on to Annapolis, in April of 1864.

In a maidenly way, Stringfellow pricked up his ears: A corps movement would certainly interest the Confederate command. A few months later, as Grant's advance on Richmond began, Confederate intelligence would have a very special interest in IX Corps.

As the spy had expected, "Sallie Marsten" was not long without an escort. Stringfellow was soon joined by a far too loquacious major, who let slip the remark that Grant would be the new commander operating against Lee—the second vital bit of news Stringfellow collected at that dance. Appointment of a new enemy commander is military intelligence of the first importance. It means immediate changes in hostile tactics and strategy. Lincoln made Grant lieutenant general and commander-in-chief on March 9, 1864—whereupon Union tactics and strategy changed with dizzying speed. Within less than two months began the Federal offensive that ended at Appomattox.

Thus far, Stringfellow's audacious scheme had succeeded perfectly Then, suddenly, the suspicious lieutenant who had hesitated over Stringfellow's pass at the outpost line appeared, more suspicious than ever. Federal pickets had now reported seeing bushwhackers crossing the river with a Federal captain as prisoner. That led him to make a few inquiries. He discovered that Sallie's real escort was nowhere around. It was some time since anyone had seen him, on duty or off. There was something extremely odd about the whole business, and outpost officers are supposed to keep an eye open for oddities.

Without creating a disturbance, the young officer compelled the supposed young lady to leave the dance. Though convinced he had caught a spy, he never dreamed the slight and youthful figure before him was a well-armed and resolute rebel. They reached a secluded spot. Perhaps the scheming lieutenant had planned it that way. If so, it was a bad mistake. Stringfellow suddenly produced his two derringers, the wicked little guns having been designed for unexpected appearances.

After that, the hapless Yankee, with a pistol at his ribs, had to drive the spy's horse and buggy to the outposts, where, still with the pistol at his ribs, he passed his captor through and unwillingly accompanied him. At the riverbank he resisted at last and immediately became one more Federal whom Stringfellow had to knock unconscious.

The first Confederate sentry they met, a little farther on, was mildly surprised when, at his challenge, a young lady began to pull off her hair—and identified himself as Stringfellow, of the 4th Virginia, with a prisoner.

In his lectures after the war, Stringfellow often repeated these tales, but they were so badly reported that it is impossible now to tell what really happened. However, so careful an historian as the late Professor William E. Dodd, who in his youth heard some of Stringfellow's lectures, vouches for the fact that he did disguise himself successfully as a girl, several times.

So, for that matter, did Lieutenant Thomas Post, 1st Georgia, who entered a Union-held town and, like Stringfellow, attended a Yankee military ball in feminine garb. A Federal colonel invited him to dinner, and he was able to visit the entire encampment and note the condition of the troops. So also did Captain Frank Battle, who, visiting relatives in Nashville, completely deceived the occupying Yankee army by his feminine impersonation.

After Stuart was mortally wounded at Yellow Tavern, May 11, 1864, Stringfellow reported directly to Lee, also serving Wade Hampton and Fitzhugh Lee. He was one of the agents Robert E. Lee used in his very thorough reconnoissance before and during the

Wilderness Campaign. It was probably at this time that Stringfellow came close enough to Grant to hear him talking with his staff, though he could not bring himself to shoot an unsuspecting man in the back.

VIII

As Lincoln's first presidential term was ending, Jefferson Davis himself sent Stringfellow into Washington. The spy had hoped to get there in time to hear Lincoln deliver his Second Inaugural, March 4, 1865, and would doubtless have appreciated the famous words, "with malice toward none, with charity for all." But a heavy storm delayed him till the ceremonies were over. By an additional irony, he passed through Mrs. Surratt's Washington house, which had long been a way station for Confederate secret agents and became the base for the Lincoln assassins. (All sorts of Confederate agents, however, including spies and couriers, used the Surratt house. There is not the remotest suggestion that the scrupulous Stringfellow had any connection with the assassination of President Lincoln, though he did, at one time, toward the end of the war, work out an ingenious plot to kidnap him.)

Before entering Washington, Stringfellow had changed from Confederate to Federal uniform at the usual Potomac crossing at Allen's Fresh. Strolling down Pennsylvania Avenue from the Capitol, he met a soldier of the provost guard, looking for Union deserters or soldiers who had gone AWOL. But there was no trouble. Stringfellow had a perfect set of official papers. The provost's man, after examining them, cheerfully sent the Confederacy's most dangerous spy on his way.

On this mission, Stringfellow had again assumed the name of a real man, whom he believed to be at a safe distance. He gives the name as "Robert Hawkins." There *was* a Robert Hawkins in Company G, 2nd Maryland Infantry, who later transferred to Company K, 11th Maryland Volunteers. It is said Stringfellow believed that the real Hawkins was a prisoner of war in Confederate hands, who would not be released till his own espionage was finished. But some one seems to have made a terrible mistake. Hawkins had been in hospital for a long time and had then been on furlough.

But he had returned to duty February 15, 1865, and, as Stringfellow set out for Washington, was not a safely distant prisoner but on active duty somewhere near Baltimore! Worst of all, Hawkins was nearly due for discharge, and the place where he would be discharged would be Alexandria—the home of Emma Green, the town where Stringfellow himself did so much secret service!

If you searched all the muster rolls of the U.S. Army, it would be hard to find a worse name to use for Stringfellow's cover! But did all this appalling blundering make any trouble? None whatever! And Hawkins, the loyal Union man, lived on till 1890, wholly unaware of the nefarious use to which a rebel spy had put his name!

Stringfellow needed military identification papers only so long as he was in false uniform. He was soon back in civilian clothing, again posing as a dental student.

Putting up at the Willard, he slipped off to "a foreign embassy" to deliver a secret message from Jefferson Davis. (The "embassy" was certainly a legation; there were no embassies in Washington in the 1860's.) Either the paper was meant for secret delivery by diplomatic pouch to one of the numerous Confederate missions abroad, or else it was part of a last, desperate endeavor by the government in Richmond to stave off disaster by provoking foreign intervention. Whatever President Davis was trying to do, it was wasted effort. Lee would surrender to Grant the following month.

Stringfellow chose the Willard because Vice President Andrew Johnson was living there. Wherever the Vice President might be, there was certain to be much coming and going of important, or temporarily important, people, from whom a spy might glean a great deal. But he was well aware that a mere enlisted man, even if wounded, would become conspicuous if he stayed long at Major Willard's fashionable hostelry. Once suspicion was aroused, the provost guard might insist on medical examination of this wounded hero. That would never do. The wounded hero hadn't any wound. Hence, before question arose, he moved to the Arlington House, and thence to a series of boardinghouses.

Stringfellow's second duty in Washington was to approach an officer traitor in the Union Army. This man, whose identity still remains a mystery, was not a devoted rebel risking his life for the cause, like Mrs. Greenhow, Conrad, Stringfellow, and a hundred others. He was simply one of those scoundrels who occasionally appear in any army—very useful to their country's enemies—men who see in espionage an easy, if risky, chance to make some money and quite frequently do make it.

Since the Union officer had previously taken their payments, the Confederates hoped he would do so again. This time they wanted information on Union troop movements, on Union plans, and on possible contacts within the Union government. The blue-clad traitor met Stringfellow secretly in one of Washington's numerous parks, not far from the Capitol. At first the man hesitated when asked for more information, then seemed to respond to threats of possible exposure, but the two parted without any definite agreement.

At their second meeting, Stringfellow was surprised to find the rogue in company with other (and loyal) Union army officers. Though nothing special happened at this meeting, he came away with an uncomfortable feeling that he had in some way aroused suspicion. He therefore moved boldly into a boardinghouse much patronized by Federal detectives—the last place in Washington where an enemy agent would be expected.

Stringfellow's boldness was less successful than he had hoped. A woman detective, living in the boardinghouse, became especially suspicious and was clumsy enough to reveal her suspicion. In vain the Confederate spy tried to soothe her. He made friends, or tried to. Though he loathed checkers, he joined the wretched woman in one game after another. It was no use. Her distrust obviously remained. Eventually, as a test, she proposed, in the presence of all the boarders, a toast to Abraham Lincoln.

Any ordinary agent would have joined in the toast; hypocrisy is an essential of his trade. But the conscientious Stringfellow tried to save himself by explaining he never drank alcohol—and was challenged to drink the toast in water. It was too much. Foolish gesture though he knew it was, he raised his glass and defiantly toasted Jefferson Davis. Four men left the room at once, an obvious move, nearly as clumsy as Stringfellow's and the lady's.

With just time enough to vanish, Stringfellow sought other lodgings; and, in spite of his rashness, was able to graduate from his school of dentistry—not then a very scientific profession—a month after entering. There was only one consolation. Emma Green, aware of his danger, found lodgings with a family in the capital, so that she could at least be near him.

When, in early April, news came that the Confederates were evacuating Richmond, the spy decided that he had spent enough time in Washington. He was, as he soon found, too late in reaching that decision. He was actually in a livery stable, hiring a horse for his escape, when a detective approached him and began to ask questions.

Cool-headed and accustomed to danger, Stringfellow made a gallant bluff. He could show forged papers and a perfectly genuine new dentist's license. But the Federals had somehow received warning that the notorious spy Stringfellow was somewhere in Washington, perhaps because an indiscretion of Jeb Stuart's had allowed his name to appear in the press. They also knew—for it pays to know all about an enemy agent—that Stringfellow had once worked as a dental apprentice.

Luckily, however, the government's detectives did not seem to know what the much-wanted enemy agent looked like—no easy matter in that day, when photographs were far from common. Such descriptions of Stringfellow as they did possess seemed to this detective, however, to correspond with the appearance of the man standing before him in the livery stable. But the Federal agent evidently did not feel the resemblance was close enough to justify immediate arrest. All he did was ask questions. Taking advantage of the man's hesitation, Stringfellow abruptly referred him to the treacherous Union officer who had been selling him information. The Union traitor would have to vouch for the rebel spy. He could, to be sure, easily send the spy to the gallows. But if he did, Stringfellow could with equal ease send him there. What really happened, no one knows, except that Stringfellow was not arrested—for the moment. But his escape had been too narrow for comfort. It would not do to risk a second interrogation.

Stringfellow, like Conrad, knew where to find emergency help. It was now obviously dangerous to rely on livery stable nags. Stringfellow went to "a person whose name is linked in the history of those dark days" and received a carriage, horses, and a driver. The Confederate secret communications system was still working smoothly, while everything else was falling apart. Why had he not gone to his unknown friend in the beginning? Probably because he did not want to endanger this emergency exit unless he had to.

The spy and his equipage had traveled only a short distance when Federal cavalry appeared, asked for his papers, then said they would have to take him to higher authority. He managed to chew up and swallow almost all the incriminating documents in his pockets, stuffing them into his mouth whenever the narrowness of the road forced his guards to drop behind the carriage, where they could not see what he was doing. When his salivary glands failed, he chewed pine needles to stimulate their flow—a method that never fails. (I have experimented.) But he could not get rid of a report on the defenses of Washington, because it was too securely sewn into the lining of his coat—where it was found as soon as he was searched. A second lieutenant, on the outpost line, rather apologetically sent him under guard to Port Tobacco, Maryland.

When they paused at an inn during the journey, Stringfellow bought the sergeant guarding him a drink. The careless fellow was foolish enough to give the prisoner a chance to get his hands on an ax; but the tenderhearted spy could not quite bring himself to kill the man, in the very room where they had been drinking together. Besides, after listening to the noncom's rough talk, Stringfellow felt, on spiritual grounds, that the sergeant was not fit to die! He decided not to use the ax but to take chances on his own life at Port Tobacco.

The interrogating officer there indicated his willingness to accept a $500 bribe, but Stringfellow did not have the money. The good-natured Yankee sergeant, who had his own opinion of this officer, gave the prisoner a friendly warning: He must under no circumstances try to escape. Not having received a bribe, the corrupt fellow rather wanted a chance to shoot his prisoner "while attempting to escape"—after all, a very old game.

On the second night of his captivity, Stringfellow went to the water barrel for a drink and, with the guards watching him, opened the door far enough to throw out what was left of the water. When he closed the door, he carefully left it off the latch and just a little ajar—not enough to be noticeable but far enough so that it would open next time without a click. Later that night, he arranged blanket and pillow to look like a sleeping man and started for the door. He was almost out of the room when he accidentally jogged the elbow of a sleeping guard. The man woke at once, but accepted Stringfellow's explanation: The prisoner was only getting another drink of water.

Just before dawn, with the guards still sleeping, he tried again and this time succeeded.

Once free, he headed south for a mile. Before long he heard horses behind him. The pursuit had started. He took refuge in a woods, swung over a stream on a birch tree, hid behind an old log, covering himself with leaves. He could hear soldiers searching the woods for an hour. Then he heard them moving on, south. Presently another party combed the woods for him again. One man stepped over the log—but not on Stringfellow.

After twenty-one days of alternate concealment and travel, he reached Virginia. By this time he was suspected of being one of the Booth conspirators. There were no grounds for this; but, after all, he *had* been secretly in Washington while the murder gang was gathering there. He *had* lodged at the Surratt house. No place in Virginia was safe now. Soon, no place in the United States would be safe. He sought Canadian refuge.

Sometime in the summer of 1865, Stringfellow reached Hamilton, Ontario. How did he get there? It is not very hard to make a guess that, though unsupported by evidence, must come very near the truth. The elaborate system of Confederate secret courier lines and safe houses had never really been blown during the war. Through one of these lines, stretching across the United States to Canada, he passed safely.

Though the Confederate cause was now irretrievably lost, Stringfellow, a very young man, still had a future of his own. Something memorable and tender had happened during that last desperate mission in Washington. Emma Green may not have known all the desperate risks her Frank was running, but she could not fail to know he was a disguised Confederate soldier in the Federal capital or to realize the penalty of discovery.

Two sentences Frank Stringfellow wrote to "my own dear Emma" from his refuge in Canada tell the story—or rather, almost tell the story, then leave details that are a little tantalizing for the twentieth-century reader of a letter he was never supposed to read at all. The letter, dated April 2, 1868, begins: "Of course you remember the 2nd of April. Can you or I ever forget it?"

It suggests that, after being in love all through the Civil War, they became formally betrothed that day in April of '65—while Stringfellow was living in disguise, a spy in the enemy's capital, at every moment in danger of losing the life he so nearly did lose a few days later. How could Emma Green possibly have said no? She didn't, and their postwar lives together were long and happy.

7

SPIES IN THE SHENANDOAH

From the very beginning of the Civil War, the Shenandoah Valley had been a critical military area. Its extremely fertile farms did not, like plantations farther south, fill up the land with cotton or tobacco. They grew huge quantities of the foodstuffs Confederate soldiers needed; and, lying close to the main theater of operations, could supply the armies quickly and easily. In addition, the Valley was the natural invasion route for rebel armies marching north against Washington, Baltimore, Harrisburg, and Philadelphia.

Since the Valley was of such logistic and strategic importance, both sides stationed troops there from the very beginning of the war to the end; and where armies operate, intelligence services are busy. Rarely in military history have there been so many secret agents in so small and rural an area for so long. Espionage in the Shenandoah began long before Bull Run; and not until Sheridan at last crushed Early, by a masterpiece of espionage, did the sniffing and the snooping end at last.

In the beginning, these Shenandoah spies were in very little danger. There was at first no organized counterintelligence service to hunt them down. They were rarely caught and almost never exe-

cuted, though early in the war Stonewall Jackson hanged one
Union spy with exemplary speed. The numerous female secret
agents never very seriously risked their lives. No matter what the
Articles of War might say, neither side ever executed a woman
for espionage. After four years of war, a Confederate court-martial
at last summoned up enough courage to pass a death sentence on
the actress, Pauline Cushman, an unquestionably guilty Union spy
—who was rescued by Federal troops before execution. A regimental history comments drily that the ladies of Winchester, Virginia, "did a little spying in which they were almost always perfectly safe."

About as many natives of the Valley spied for the Union as for
the Confederacy, since political sympathies were almost equally
divided. At the northern end of the Valley, near Harpers Ferry,
Union sentiment was strong. Five Virginia counties there joined
counties farther west in seceding from the Old Dominion and setting up West Virginia as a new state.

But loyalties neither began nor ended with county lines. There
were enthusiastic rebel spies in the pro-Union counties that seceded from Virginia, just as there were devoted Union spies in the
staunchly Confederate counties farther south. Lieutenant David
Humphreys, 7th Virginia Cavalry, who collected information for
Jackson from Harpers Ferry, lived in Charlestown, in Jefferson
County. The Confederate girl spies, Belle Boyd and her mysterious
assistant, "Sophia B.," lived in Martinsburg, Jefferson County, also
the home of Mrs. Charles J. Faulkner, wife of a former American
diplomat who was now a Confederate officer. Mrs. Faulkner made
herself agreeable to Union officers and thus became "a medium for
communicating with the rebel authorities, communicating them
[sic] of all she learns." There were also Union spies in Martinsburg,
notably David Hunter Strother, a *Harper's* author and illustrator,
later a Yankee general, who had known Belle Boyd ever since she
was a little girl. Here, too, dwelt "Mrs. Hickey" and "Miss Frances,"
of whom there is no record save that they were detected in espionage for the Union in December, 1861.

Nancy Hardy, another Confederate girl spy, was probably also
a West Virginian. Captured in July, 1861, she is said to have killed
her Union guard, escaped, and then returned to the scene with a

force of Confederates. This is supposed to have taken place at "Summerville," which is probably identical with Summersville, West Virginia.

Just across the Berkeley County line from Martinsburg dwelt another Union girl spy. This was the Quaker schoolmistress, Friend Rebecca Wright, whose espionage for the Union, Sheridan declared, won the Battle of the Opequon for him. But in Winchester also lived the Yonley sisters, valued spies of the Confederacy. The Federal spy, Levi Strauss, whom Stonewall Jackson hanged for espionage, is said to have lived in Stonewall's own home town, Lexington, Virginia, deep in Southern territory. That Peter French and Harley Miller, of Hedgesville, in Berkeley County, were also Union spies is less surprising. Their homes were close to the Potomac, adjoining loyal Federal territory.

When, after winning at Bull Run the nickname he was to make famous, Stonewall Jackson returned to take command of the Confederate forces in the Shenandoah, he knew exactly the kind of military intelligence he needed and knew exactly how to get it. In early February, 1862, he had "my scouts constantly in the camp of the enemy" and by March 2 had surprisingly complete information. His instructions to agents were models of clarity.

"The kind of information I desire from behind the Union lines," he told his cavalry leader, Turner Ashby, "is the position of the enemy's forces, his numbers and movements, what generals are in command and their headquarters, especially the headquarters of the commanding general."

It is noteworthy that Jackson asked only for essential elements of information. He did not worry his intelligence service with impossible queries about enemy intentions—a bad habit common to many generals. It is also noteworthy that he was particularly careful to inquire who the Union generals were and where each one commanded. Identification of the enemy commander is always an advantage; but it was of more value than usual to Civil War generals, because so many of them had been cadets together at West Point and had later served together in the "Old Army." If you have known the enemy commander personally for years, it is much easier to know how to deal with him.

Partly by vigorous reconnoissance, partly by skillful secret service, the cavalry and the spies brought in the facts Stonewall wanted. Both Ashby in the Shenandoah and John Hunt Morgan in Middle Tennessee liked to forget about their rank, disguise themselves in one way or another, and boldly enter the Union lines. Morgan habitually posed as a farmer, drover, or even as a Federal officer; Ashby posed as a "horse doctor." Since farriers were few and veterinarians almost unknown, and since Ashby knew all about horses, he was warmly welcomed wherever he went, even in the North. Never detected—never, so far as is known, suspected—he visited the Federal troops as he pleased, observed at leisure, and returned, unmolested. Whatever damage Ashby may have done the Union Army, he did its horses a great deal of good.

On one occasion in early 1861, Ashby exchanged his usual thoroughbred for a hired plow horse, "rigged himself in a farmer's suit of homespun," and, posing as a "rustic horse-doctor," made his way north into Pennsylvania. Had he ridden his own fine charger, he would have roused suspicion; but, mounted on the borrowed nag, "with his saddle-bags full of some remedy for spavin or ringbone," he had no trouble visiting the Federal camp of General Patterson at Chambersburg. Thence, in due course, he returned by night "with an immense amount of information" for Jackson.

A secret report by Allan Pinkerton (still masquerading as Major E. J. Allen) to Secretary of War Stanton on June 25, 1862, lists a number of Confederate spies living in or near Winchester and Front Royal. One of these was a certain William Dana, whose house stood close to the Potomac, near Front Royal. After the battle there, Dana kept a sharp eye on everyone who crossed, noting who the Union sympathizers were and which local residents seemed to be helping them. Two suspected Union men were arrested and taken south—one, at least, on Dana's information. Suspicious local Unionists, not yet in trouble themselves, noted that the man went back and forth between Union and Confederate forces almost daily and were positive he was "acting as a spy on the movement of our troops."

The Federal counterintelligence man watching him plainly implies that Dana was reporting to Ashby's cavalry. Another informant states that Dana habitually reported to secessionists in Front Royal, whence communication with Ashby was quick and easy.

When, in March of 1862, Union forces were preparing to cross the Shenandoah, still another Federal informant eavesdropped long enough to hear the spy reporting their numbers and movement to Confederate soldiers, also in the town. (As the Union forces were still occupying it, these Confederates were presumably in disguise.) Dana's arrest was ordered July 18.

The Pinkerton report on Dana also mentions suspected Shenandoah spies named William Baltus, Charles Brown, Charles Cooper, Philip Williams, and a certain Kenly, of whom nothing else has ever been discovered. A great many more Confederate spies were probably never even suspected. Ashby's quiet reconnoissances in disguise among the Union forces remained a secret till long after Ashby had been killed in battle and the war was over. It is no wonder Jackson could write proudly in May of '62; "I have been relying on my spies for information of the enemy."

Jackson's success in preventing security leaks was due to extraordinary precautions. It is no exaggeration to say that Stonewall had, from the beginning of the war until his death, a better comprehension of security than any other leader on either side. Tradition credits him with the remark that, if he thought his coat knew his secrets, he would cast it off. That may have been a current maxim of the time—the same remark is attributed to Beauregard—but it expresses Stonewall's habitual practice exactly.

No military information leaked to the Federals from General Jackson's forces, because no one in General Jackson's forces had any information he could possibly let slip. General Jackson was usually the only man who had any idea what General Jackson was going to do next. What only General Jackson knew, General Jackson's opponents had no way of learning. As a result, the Federals were always being taken by surprise. His own much-irritated division commanders often had no inkling of their leader's intentions. They had their orders; and their orders, Stonewall thought, were all they needed to know.

This is hardly modern staff doctrine. But, though Confederate subordinates frequently did not know what their commander was doing, the Federals *never* knew—not until it was too late.

Such secrecy at times seemed absurd and was frequently exasperating—and not only to his command. At Fredericks Hall,

Louisa County, on Sunday evening, June 22, 1862, the General's hostess, a certain Mrs. Harris, inquired whether Stonewall would be there for breakfast. The general would like breakfast at the usual hour. But Mrs. Harris rose next morning to find she had no guest and no need to worry about his breakfast. At 1 A.M., Stonewall had set out on the long ride to Richmond, to attend a conference at which Lee, Longstreet, the two Generals Hill, and Jackson himself were to plan the Seven Days. The pass that Stonewall carried did not even name the bearer. It said simply: "One officer."

It was rather hard on Mrs. Harris's cook and even harder on Mrs. Harris. No one doubted the loyalty to the Confederacy of that excellent Virginia lady. But—one careless word? A casual, unintentionally indiscreet remark? An eavesdropping servant? One of the house slaves? (House slaves were likely to be pro-Union.) Lurking Federal spies? General Jackson didn't know. But of one thing General Jackson was sure: Information no one had would never reach the enemy.

On another occasion, one of Ashby's cavalry lieutenants asked a casual question or two. They were harmless enough, but Jackson turned swiftly to others standing near: "Arrest that man as a spy!"

Ashby, arriving at the right moment, saved the situation by tactfully explaining to Jackson that the lieutenant "had not much sense." Since Ashby knew more about espionage than anyone then in the Shenandoah, Stonewall was pacified. But one more indiscreet subaltern had grasped the principle of military secrecy.

Even Jackson's adored wife was chided when she asked her husband in a letter how he was getting on with the war. "What do you want with military news? Don't you know that it is unmilitary and unlike an officer to write news respecting one's post? You wouldn't wish your husband to do an unofficer-like thing."

Lee was nearly as careful of security as Jackson, though, as usual, he was tactful. Only his staff officers knew unit locations. Officers returning from leave had to go to headquarters to find out where their regiments were. Strangers looking for a given regiment had to pass through headquarters, whence they were sent on only if approved. Lee was also very cautious about revealing his plans. The sensational "lost order"—which did reveal all his plans before Antietam—was not lost by Lee himself or any of his staff, but by a careless corps commander.

I

It was natural that, with all this mystery in ordinary military routine, Jackson should envelop his secret agents in mystery deeper still. Only now and then does the record of an arrest, a surviving report like Pinkerton's, or a casual hint in the general's own papers show that Stonewall's spies were there, all the same—silent and deadly. By March 11, 1862, just before Stonewall's army drove northward to Kernstown, he knew not only that the Federals were also preparing to move, he even knew what they were going to eat. The boys in blue would carry three days' cooked rations. He was not sure, however, where they were going. Could it be Fredericksburg? What did the spies think? "Do any of your agents mention such a move?" he asked Ashby.

By March 19, the spies had reported on all bridges between Strasburg and Mount Jackson, and their list gave Stonewall a fine chance to hamper the enemy. Orders went out to Ashby: "Take plenty of time before the enemy comes up for burning bridges." Stonewall especially wanted "all the railroad bridges burnt at once." If the bridges were burned one by one, the Union engineers could swiftly rebuild them. But if all bridges were destroyed together, Union troop movement and supply would be badly handicapped. (It was the same method the Allies used before the Normandy landings in 1944.)

In these orders, Stonewall was very specific about other intelligence needs. He did not know the name of the present enemy commander. Would Ashby find out? It was reported that the Federals had offered $5,000 to anyone who would betray Ashby to them. Which Federal officer was making this offer?

Meantime, McClellan had been preparing for the Peninsular Campaign, in which he hoped to capture Richmond by advancing from Hampton Roads up the Peninsula between the York and James Rivers. To reinforce him, two divisions began to move out of the Shenandoah Valley. To keep these troops from strengthening the

Union attack against Richmond in the east, Stonewall marched
northward down the Valley to attack. New information came in at
once. When Ashby raided the outskirts of Winchester on March 22,
"some of the ladies" managed to get word to him that the Federals
were evacuating the town and a large column had already started
eastward to Berryville that very morning. The Federals now had
only four regiments in Winchester, plus a few field guns. Even
these would start for Berryville next morning, that is, Sunday,
March 23. (At this very moment, Captain Conrad's spy in the Federal War Department was supplying Richmond with an exact
strength report of McClellan's forces.)

Jackson knew that a Confederate movement northward, down
the Shenandoah Valley, would alarm the Federals. It always did.
As usual, Stonewall's estimate of the situation was correct. As soon
as he made this menacing march, Lincoln held back strong forces
in the Valley and used McDowell's I Corps to cover Washington,
in case Stonewall debouched from the Shenandoah. McClellan
protested angrily but uselessly.

After Jackson had actually commenced his march, he received
word secretly that Winchester was nearly defenseless. According
to one story, there were only four regiments. According to an unknown woman sympathizer, there were only two or three, guarding supplies. It was probably true—but not, unhappily for Stonewall, the whole truth. When the gray column's advance guard
reached Kernstown on the way to Winchester, about 10 A.M. on
March 23, 1862, the general expected no trouble and pushed on
vigorously. He had accurate information from Winchester, and he
thought he had accurate information from Kernstown, too.

For once, however, Ashby had not pushed reconnoissance far
enough, had not checked, rechecked, and completely evaluated
what the agents said and what his mounted patrols had seen. On
the afternoon of March 22, Ashby had driven in Federal pickets
and had actually entered the southern edge of Winchester. But he
did not find out that the Union general, James Shields, had deliberately marched his 2nd Division—as ostentatiously as possible—
through the town, dropping off only a provost guard and a few
pickets, then had quietly gone into bivouac farther north. That was
why Ashby had encountered only pickets.

Instead of feeble resistance by at most four Union regiments, Jackson ran into Shields's 8,000 men, who had dextrously been kept out of sight. As a result, Stonewall, with only 3,500 men, suffered the worst defeat of his career.

In neighboring Front Royal a young girl entered in her diary a note that Jackson had been deceived "by a miserable Yankee trick." She was sure he "had received forged despatches from Johnston ordering him into Winchester upon the plea that the enemy was evacuating that place to go for protection of Washington and Maryland." The youthful diarist was thinking of the fight at Kernstown as part of the advance on Winchester, as indeed it was.

II

To this period—either before or immediately after Kernstown—belong the adventures of Lieutenant David Humphreys, 17th Virginia Cavalry. The lieutenant was invited to resign his Confederate commission, to penetrate Federal territory and make a military survey of Harpers Ferry, in preparation for a raid by Jackson. Presumably Jackson would have marched on north to Harpers Ferry, if he had not been blocked at Kernstown.

It is regrettable that Humphreys does not give the exact date, but it can nevertheless be determined with fair accuracy. His description of snowy landscapes, combined with floods in the Shenandoah River, show clearly that he made his secret journey in early spring. This can only have been the spring of 1862, since Johnston, not Jackson, commanded in the Shenandoah in '61, and Jackson was with Lee in Virginia in the spring of '63. Furthermore, the description of the weather that Humphreys gives exactly fits old records of the weather in the Valley in early '62.

Confederate Army records show that Humphreys was an officer in Company B, 7th Virginia Cavalry, at Harrisonburg, Virginia, in 1862. It is reasonable to suppose that he set out, disguised as a civilian, some time before the battle of Kernstown, probably in very late February or early March. If the report he was expected to bring back from Harpers Ferry showed it was possible, Stonewall Jackson himself would assail this vital point, while Imboden and Mosby threatened Cumberland, Maryland, and Duffield threatened Martinsburg and New Creek, West Virginia, thus drawing Federal forces in several directions at once. All this was part of a Confederate effort to frighten the Federals into sending reinforcements to all these places, where the vital line of the Baltimore & Ohio Railroad might be cut. This was meant to weaken still further McClellan's forces operating against Richmond.

The whole scheme for Humphreys's mission was just a little naïve. The staff who planned it do not seem to have realized that a civilian caught spying would be hanged just as summarily as a disguised officer. They must have had certain misgivings on this point, however. Before Humphreys started, they had already picked out a luckless Federal officer, a relative of Secretary of State Seward, whom they proposed to hang in retaliation, if Humphreys should be executed.

Whatever the risks, the plan was carried out. Humphreys duly and ostentatiously resigned his commission. The resignation was duly and formally approved by Jackson, and—to make it as public as possible—the papers were read to the troops on parade. The amateur spy then rode to New Market in civilian clothes, went on foot to Massanutten, on to Strasburg, and so, via Castleman's Ferry, to his family's home near Charlestown.

Though he saw occasional Federal patrols, he was never discovered. At dusk, he followed in the rear of a Federal regiment till he reached the outskirts of the town, then hid in a haystack till midnight. Under cover of darkness, he made his way to his own house, where he found his wife absent and colored servants in charge.

A message brought to the house his brother-in-law, a physician who, being on friendly terms with the Chief Surgeon of the Union garrison at Harpers Ferry, though a devoted Confederate, held a pass from the Union authorities. Thus protected, Humphreys was able to travel the few miles to Harpers Ferry, enter the town, observe the Union garrison, secure the information Jackson wanted, and return with it the same night.

Suddenly, the Federals in Charlestown showed alarm. They had received warning that "rebel spies were in town." While this may have been a mere accident, not related to Humphreys's arrival, it did not make him feel comfortable; and, since he had all or most of the information he had come for, he decided to start back as soon as possible. Late on the night following his arrival, Humphreys made his way from his own house to his father's, carrying a new saddle on his back. Trusty Negroes had a horse ready. From somebody—probably one of the slaves—he learned that Federal patrols were on all roads; but this, to a man who had grown up in the area and knew all the byways, was no problem.

Humphreys rode twenty miles across country to the house of a trusted friend, formerly a laborer on his father's estate, now living near the river. The spy had to get across, but at first the man demurred, since the flood was both swift and high, filled with drift logs big enough to crush a horseman or sink a boat. Besides, the Union Army had tried to seize all boats. When Humphreys's friend at length consented to try, however, he brought out a small skiff, which he had hidden in a ditch in the woods. In this the two men fought their way across, while the boatman's wife watched anxiously and Humphreys's horse swam astern. The strength of the current forced them half a mile downstream before they reached the other bank. Then Humphreys from his side, and the nervous wife from the other, watched until the boatman landed at last.

At dawn, the lieutenant reached "General Jones" and reported. (Presumably, this was John R. Jones, who was named brigadier about this time, though never confirmed in that rank.) The spy's report was telegraphed to Jackson, and it is probable that this intelligence was one of the essential elements of information that led Jackson to advance down the Valley. If he had reached Harpers Ferry he would probably have taken it, and the resultant terror in Washington might have led Lincoln to countermand McClellan's Peninsular Campaign altogether. In the end, all Humphreys's perils, courage, and success led to nothing—a common tragedy of the intelligence service.

But though the fight at Kernstown was a tactical defeat, neither the spies who brought Jackson the intelligence he needed (most of which was accurate save for the error as to Federal strength) nor the Confederate troops who were forced to withdraw had wasted their time. The spies had supplied Jackson with enough information to accomplish his main strategic mission: The Union forces that had been moving east, out of the Shenandoah, to support McClellan, had to be recalled. This delayed McClellan's concentration against Richmond and gave more time to prepare for the defense of the capital—which was a complete success.

8

BELLE BOYD

PART 1.
The Charming Rebel and the Artist Spy

Most romantic of the numerous young ladies who spied for the South was the fascinating Belle Boyd, daughter of a storekeeper in Martinsburg, who, when she began her career as a secret agent, was just seventeen. Though the town is today in West Virginia, it was still in the Old Dominion when the Civil War began—and the sympathies of the Boyd family were ardently Virginian.

Though this agreeable young thing's ability to make almost any male in either army do exactly what she wanted has created a legend of devastating beauty, Miss Belle wasn't really an especially pretty girl. Surviving portraits show that she looked rather like one of those horses she rode so perfectly—a long face, a very long nose, and prominent teeth. She had, however, a fine figure, or so it is reported—though how anyone could guess that, considering the yards and yards of drapery covering maidens of the Civil War period, even on horseback, it is hard to understand. The fact is, Belle Boyd was one of those girls who don't have to be pretty. She had a way with men, especially young men, even more especially with young men in uniform, who became her willing slaves at a glance or, at most, after a very few glances—a situation most convenient for a lady spy.

"A splendid specimen of feminine health and vigor," remarked one of her jailers, after holding her in custody for some months —but he remained conspicuously silent about her looks.

To learn how feminine health and vigor, plus immense personal charm and a magnificent figure, can help a girl, do but consider Belle's matrimonial record, in addition to her record of wheedling useful military information out of susceptible Yankees. The first time she was sent to prison, she emerged engaged to marry a fellow prisoner (though the marriage never took place), and her admiring jailer is said to have provided a trousseau. When the U.S. Navy caught her aboard a blockade runner, she promptly became engaged to the Yankee naval lieutenant placed in charge. Then she persuaded him to abandon the Union cause, give up his commission, and wed her.

It was Belle's charm, plus her dashing horsemanship, plus her facile conquest of anyone in a blue uniform who seemed likely to possess useful military information, that led to various spiteful tales about her. For none of these does the least foundation appear to exist. She was called a camp follower—and she did, indeed, visit her soldier father in camp, accompanied by her mother! The Associated Press sent out to newspapers of May 31, 1862, an extremely inaccurate story referring to poor Belle as "an accomplished prostitute who has figured largely in the rebel cause." This was pure libel. All it meant was that the Federals were smarting over the stinging defeat Stonewall Jackson had inflicted on them at Front Royal a few days earlier, an affair in which Belle had, indeed, "figured largely."

She was, in fact, a perfectly respectable girl. The worst that can be said about her comes from Miss Lucy R. Buck, a young lady of about Belle's age, who lived at "Bel Air" plantation, not far from Front Royal. Miss Lucy did not in the least like Miss Belle. She thought her a forward, nasty creature and said so in a very private and very outspoken diary, which still survives.

The two girls met for the first time on New Year's Day, 1862, while Belle, already deep in secret service, was visiting in Front Royal. To Lucy Buck she "seemed all surface, vain & hollow," one of those girls Lucy "felt to be false and heartless." Three months later, Miss Buck was still "not at all favorably impressed."

There was some justification for Miss Lucy's unfavorable opinion. You can't exactly, by any standard, describe Belle Boyd as diffident, retiring, or discreet; and she *was* a forward creature, when there was a chance to collect information or otherwise aid the Confederate cause by a little expert flirtation.

I

It was natural that Belle should take to espionage, which was more or less a family specialty. Her cousin, Captain William Boyd Compton, 31st Virginia Militia, was in and out of the Federal lines during most of the war, was eventually caught, was sentenced to death, and made a sensational escape. Lieutenant Colonel William R. Denny, possibly a relative, serving in the same regiment as her kinsman, was an active secret agent, to whom Belle regularly reported. Her maternal uncle, Captain James W. Glenn, took a hand in guerrilla units, probably spied himself, and had certainly been associated with Andrew Laypole—hanged for his activity behind the Union lines—and with Major Harry Gilmor, a friend of Belle's though no relative, who added Confederate espionage to ordinary mounted reconnoissance. Another relative, Colonel John E. Boyd, was sentenced to death for spying, though, like Compton, he escaped the gallows.

Belle began her services to the Confederacy as a (highly unofficial) military courier and as a nurse, but this was a mere incident of the first Shenandoah campaign. Her father, Benjamin R. Boyd, had enlisted in the 2nd Virginia, one of Stonewall Jackson's regiments. In early July, 1861, when Jackson, defeated at Falling Water (now West Virginia), fell back through Martinsburg, two soldiers were so ill with fever they had to be left there. Belle, with her personal maid, Eliza, was helping care for these invalids when a Federal captain with two of his men entered. Belle says the officer had an American flag in his hands. It seems a little odd—officers usually leave the flag with the color sergeant; but the captain may have been requisitioning billets and placing flags above each house he took over.

According to Belle, he waved the Stars and Stripes over the sick men, calling them "—— rebels." Rebels they certainly were, but Belle resented that officer, the flag he brought with him, and the naughty word he used.

"Sir," said she, haughtily, "these men are as helpless as infants and have, as you may see, no power to reply to your insults."

"And pray," inquired the astonished Yankee, "who may you be, Miss?"

Belle was too furious for speech. The Negro maid answered for her.

"A rebel lady."

"A —— independent one, at all events," replied the discomfited warrior, with a regrettable repetition of the naughty word, but he withdrew, flag and all. In a book she published four years later, Belle apologizes for quoting "his exact words," even with suitable dashes.

When Martinsburg ladies tried to move the sick men to another house, Federal soldiers interfered again, and again Belle rose to the emergency. Seeing a pair of shoulder straps passing in the street, she appealed for help. A little commissioned authority reduced the obstreperous boys in blue to order, and the volunteer nurses took their patients on to their new quarters. Belle marched beside the stretcher of one wounded rebel with a pistol—which, fortunately, she did not use—while two Boyd family slaves carried him through the streets.

But the safe arrival of the patients did not end the impetuous young lady's troubles. The Union troops had both a victory and the Fourth of July to celebrate at the same time and—being half-trained, half-disciplined recruits, for whom war was still more or less a lark—grew tumultuous once more. Some of them, hearing that Belle's room was decorated with rebel flags—as, indeed, it was —raided the Boyd house to tear them down. Though Belle herself had no chance to get rid of these incriminating banners, her quick-witted slave, Eliza, ran up to the bedroom in time to snatch them all down and burn them.

Having failed to seize the Confederate flags, the Yankees proposed to display their own above the offending house. Then Belle's mother was heard from:

"Men, every member of my household will die before that flag shall be raised over us."

The boys in blue went right ahead with their flag-raising, one soldier making himself particularly obnoxious. Belle was furious. "My indignation was aroused beyond control, my blood was literally boiling in my veins."

The village maiden drew a pistol and fired. The offending Yankee fell, badly wounded. The others decided they did not really want to raise a Union flag over the Boyd household and, strange to say, attempted no immediate retaliation but picked up their comrade and carried him away.

The Boyd household hoped they were rid of them, but there was an uneasy impression that this time, perhaps, Miss Belle had gone a little too far.

She had.

A slave rushed in. The soldiers had come back. They were piling combustibles against the house and getting ready to burn it. A messenger dashed off to headquarters. Before the fire could be lighted, a guard detail arrived to discourage the would-be incendiaries.

There may be confirmation of Belle's story in the local graveyard. Private Frederick Martin, Company K, 7th Pennsylvania Volunteers, was buried in Martinsburg, July 7, 1861. There is no record of the cause of death—but there was no fighting in that area at that time. It is queer, however, that a certain Private "Fritz" Martin, also of Company K, 7th Pennsylvania, was mustered out of service, alive and well, July 29, 1861, as shown by U.S. and by Pennsylvania military records! Apparently some clerk in the adjutant's office made a mistake and failed to check a muster roll carefully. There doesn't seem to be much doubt that Private Martin was really dead.

II

Extraordinary as the story of this shooting sounds, it is probably true. Belle Boyd herself tells it, and other equally extraordinary tales in the book of adventures she later published can be verified by unimpeachable contemporary statements. Nor was the incident of the slain soldier so unusual as it now seems. Belle Boyd was not the only impetuous Southern maiden who could shoot straight and fast. Virginia Moon, later spy and courier for the Confederacy, demonstrated her rebel sympathies at the Female College in Oxford, Ohio, by shooting all the stars out of the flag above the college building. Where, in a young ladies' college, Virginia found her pistol remains a mystery today, as it was to the college then. But find it she did. After which, Virginia (and, let us hope, her pistol) left the Oxford Female College with the utmost speed.

Southern girls of the period do not seem to have been in the least gun-shy. Cordelia Lewis Scales, aged nineteen, living near Holly Springs, Mississippi, writes to a girl friend in 1863: "I never ride or walk now without my pistol." When Union troops invaded her father's house and tried to search her trunk, Cordelia faced them with her "very fine six shooter" and drove them off.

"She's a trump!" exclaimed an admiring Yankee, and the colonel of the 26th Illinois sent his band to play "Dixie" for her.

Alice Ready, a young Tennessee girl, sister-in-law of General John Hunt Morgan, prepared to shoot any Federal who dared enter her room. On at least one occasion Alice carried her father's pistol strapped under her hoop skirt, though she never had to fire it. How the young lady expected a "quick draw" from beneath a hoop skirt is hard to understand. But the feat was not impossible. After all, Frank Stringfellow did manage to get two derringers swiftly from the trousers he wore underneath his hoop skirt and capture a Federal officer.

Southern damsels were sometimes unexpectedly adept with other weapons. In Warrensburg, Missouri, a dauntless damsel named Mary Bedichek went to the rescue of her father, when he was attacked by Union militia. After Mary had wielded a knife effectively on two of them, the overenthusiastic militiamen gave up. Exactly as in Belle Boyd's case, the Federal officer who investigated the episode not only gave Mary complete official clearances; he also gave her a pistol for use in future emergencies.

Miss Marina Gunter (later Mrs. Joseph Harris) of Putnam County, Tennessee, could not prevent Union bushwhackers from threatening her father; but when they began to beat him outside the house, and "when she heard the licks and her old father's groans," Marina—like Belle, a seventeen-year-old—rushed upon his assailants with an ax, killed two, and wounded a third so badly that he died. Once again, the Federal command approved, and its Nashville headquarters provided protection against future assault.

III

On July 9, two days after Private Martin's burial, a local artist presented himself at the headquarters of Major General Robert Patterson, commanding the Union Army in the Shenandoah. The artist, who brought with him vital and absolutely accurate information, was David Hunter Strother, still a civilian in 1861, though eventually to become a Union general. Strother was no mere amateur. For some years, as "Porte-Crayon," he had been making a reputation as illustrator and author for the House of Harper, and he had illustrated *Harper's Weekly's* reports of the John Brown raid and trial. Like Belle Boyd, whom he had known ever since she was a little girl, he was a native of Martinsburg, familiar with the area.

Strother had been observing Johnston's army for some time. In view of his artistic reputation, the Confederates had innocently let him wander about camps and bivouacs very much as he pleased, so that he soon knew all there was to know about their forces. Hence when, on July 18, 1861, Johnston began his carefully screened withdrawal from the Valley, the Union's volunteer spy understood exactly what was happening and kept a close eye on the moving columns. One of Strother's informants continued watching until the troops began crossing the Shenandoah River. That left no doubt they were on their way to Bull Run.

Strother was thus able to report everything to the besotted Patterson almost as soon as it happened—and was not believed by anyone except a certain staff colonel named George H. Thomas, soon to be famous as "the Rock of Chickamauga." The information was confirmed by two other northern agents, working south from the Union lines, but Patterson's headquarters paid no attention to their information either. If the hesitant general had accepted the intelligence brought him, he could have attacked Johnston's rear and stopped his march, even if he did not defeat him. The Con-

federates at Manassas would then have had no last-minute reinforcements. This, as already pointed out, would have meant a
Union victory.

When the 2nd Virginia Infantry (part of what would soon be
known as the Stonewall Brigade) moved back from the Potomac
on its way to Bull Run, Strother, the Union spy, stood in the streets
of Martinsburg, watching the men march by. No one can doubt
Belle Boyd was watching, too, for her father was in the ranks of the
passing regiment. There is an odd irony in the thought of the two
spies, who knew each other well, standing in the same little town,
at the same moment, Belle spying eagerly for the Confederacy,
Strother for the Union.

When Union forces entered Martinsburg, the delightful Miss
Boyd began to gather a fair amount of information from young
officers, who always find it hard to keep from talking too freely to
smiling young sirens. And, according to Belle herself, "whatever I
heard I regularly and carefully committed to paper."

This, of course, was all wrong. An agent within the enemy's
lines—even an as yet unsuspected agent like Belle—ought not keep
any notes at all. The agent is then able to face sudden searches
with equanimity. (There are few pleasures greater than watching
the other side's counterintelligence diligently searching for documents that do not exist.)

Though she had a cipher, Miss Belle not only took the wholly unnecessary risk of writing out everything in clear and in her own
handwriting; she did worse: She kept it lying about, where accident or sudden search might reveal it. Any curious sentry, any
suspicious patrol into whose hands a packet might fall, could read
the contents, and a little investigation would identify the handwriting. Fortunately, Union counterespionage methods were
equally clumsy. Belle's methods, however amateurish, at first
worked well enough to fool the Federals.

As a useful sideline to espionage, she soon added a little gun-
running. Knowing that the Southern forces were always short of
arms, she began to steal Union officers' swords and pistols, and she
probably also stole any other munitions of war she could lay her
pretty little hands on.

Such thefts were really easier than they sound. Sabers were, in those days, no mere ceremonial ornaments. They could be really useful in self-defense, and most officers carried them. But a heavy, clanking scabbard is a nuisance off duty. Hence the temptation, in leisure moments, to take off belt, saber, pistols, and all, and hang them up with hat and coat. Belle Boyd and various other light-fingered maidens found this most convenient. A girl could hide a fair-sized arsenal under her hoop skirt and slip the weapons away to some convenient hiding place, thence, in due course, to be secretly delivered to the Confederate Army.

The 28th Pennsylvania was somewhat perturbed when, in October, 1861, it found—buried in the ground or cached in barns and outhouses in Maryland—200 sabers, 400 pistols, 1,400 muskets, and equipment for 200 cavalrymen. Not even Belle Boyd could steal all that without assistance.

This kind of theft went on in various Virginia towns. In Winchester, for example, where Belle Boyd sometimes operated, one family, as late as 1863, was keeping a regular supply of Federal swords and pistols in the attic, "to hand over to the Confederates when they came." Under the Presbyterian Church was a choice assortment of sabers, some of which had been smuggled through the streets, "each wrapped by itself in an old bag to keep from clashing."

In addition to the information she herself collected, Belle at times carried information that others had brought her. Once at least (and probably a good deal oftener) she had the help of a local girl, whom she identifies only as Sophia B., who is known to have walked seven miles, carrying reports to Stonewall Jackson's headquarters, and seven miles back.

Two devoted Negroes also served at times as couriers. Like many slaves, these were wholly trustworthy, happy in bondage, willing to serve the Confederacy, even though it was fighting to keep them in slavery, because they were devoted to Miss Belle. One was her personal maid, Eliza, who throughout her life, even as an old woman in her days of freedom, still sent letters to her adored mistress, recalling their adventurous days together—dictated letters, because Eliza was wholly illiterate. The other was an old Negro man, proud possessor of an old watch, inside which he carried Belle's reports—carefully folded small enough to slip inside. Exactly who he was, few people were allowed to know then, and nobody knows now.

Almost certainly, Belle also had the assistance of her relative, Stephen D. Boyd. He sent a long report from Charlottesville on July 28, 1862, dealing at length with the strength of Pope's army, which the Confederates would hopelessly defeat only a month later, perhaps using some of this very information. Probably he had been working with Belle from the very beginning, though this is guesswork.

Belle's line of communication could not possibly remain secret very long, when she herself operated with so little caution. Before long—probably rather late in 1861—one of her reports was intercepted. It was unsigned, but there were plenty of eager Unionists in and around Martinsburg who could identify her handwriting and were glad to do so.

A Federal captain appeared at once. Miss Belle must come with him to headquarters. There an indignant colonel and a group of Union officers confronted her. They read her a suitable extract from the Articles of War, which, of course, included the death penalty for espionage. They also scolded her severely. Communicating secret intelligence to the enemy. A very naughty girl, indeed! That seemed to be about as far as the irate officers cared to go, since they were clearly not a formally convened court-martial.

Serenely aware that, if it had not already hanged her for shooting a Union soldier, the Union Army certainly wouldn't hang her for a trifle like espionage, Belle listened, more or less patiently, to the scolding. Then, apparently, she decided it was time to go home— and went. Bowing politely, with a murmur of "Thank you, gentlemen of the jury" (there was no court and, of course, no jury!), she swept haughtily out of headquarters. These very soft-boiled army officers sat there and let her go! Apparently they had decided that homicide and espionage were nothing more serious than girlish whims.

In October, 1861, Belle visited her father in the Confederate camp at Manassas Junction and, while at the camp, rode as a courier for Generals Beauregard and Jackson. After that she spent the winter of 1861–1862 quietly at home in Martinsburg. The Federals had withdrawn; even Jackson was inactive; there was little for a lady spy to do, and it must have seemed rather dull. But it was not dull very long.

The Federals had not withdrawn very far, and susceptible young men with shoulder straps on their blue uniforms were not far away. Miss Belle rode out from Martinsburg one evening with two young gentlemen in gray. For once, Belle's horsemanship failed her. Her mount bolted toward the Union lines. Her escorts, knowing the Federals would shoot them but would not injure Belle, very sensibly took cover in an adjoining woods. Here they watched helplessly while their army's leading female secret agent was carried into the enemy's outpost line.

Outpost officers, however, are likely to be subalterns. Subalterns are likely to be young. The Union pickets were very gallant when the runaway came pounding into their lines. Someone caught the frightened horse, and Belle, not at all disturbed, was at once a center of attraction. It was a familiar role; and Belle Boyd, being Belle Boyd, enjoyed herself.

She was so sweetly helpless that two cavaliers offered to escort her beyond the lines. If they had been more experienced, they would have taken an escort, but few junior officers on either side were very experienced as yet. Besides, young men somehow rarely wanted to take a squad along when they went riding with Belle Boyd.

As the three moved out beyond the outposts, one of these hapless youths unfortunately made a casual remark, sadly lacking in tact, about "cowardly rebels." It didn't mean anything. It was the kind of thing very young officers are likely to say at the beginning of any war.

The youthful warrior who said it had no idea of the identity of the delightful young creature he was escorting, or he might have been more careful, for that regrettable phrase sealed his doom. Inwardly seething with fury, Belle guided these blithe youths, who were expecting nothing more exciting than a short gallop with an agreeable girl, straight into a trap.

She knew exactly where her two Confederate escorts were lurking, and thither she led the Yankees. Able, without being seen themselves, to watch the little cavalcade approaching, the hidden rebels rode out at the last moment. Belle's Union escorts were

taken completely by surprise. Everyone was just a little embarrassed—except Belle.

"Here are two prisoners that I have brought you," she told her
Confederate escorts. Turning to the dismayed Federals, she added,
maliciously, "Here are two of the 'cowardly rebels.'"

There was an awkward pause. Then:

"And who, pray, is the lady?" inquired one of the men in blue.

"Belle Boyd, at your service," replied that young lady.

"Good God! The rebel spy."

There was nothing to do but take Belle's Union cavaliers back
as prisoners; but someone at Confederate headquarters seems to
have felt compunction. The Union officers had merely been trying
to help a Southern girl who was having trouble with her horse,
and that is not a military operation. They were sent back to their
own lines within an hour—though what the officer of the guard
had to say when they arrived, one trembles to imagine.

IV

In the early spring of 1862, while Belle's father was on furlough
at home in Martinsburg, the Federal army again began moving
southward along the Shenandoah Valley. Martinsburg would soon
be no place for a Confederate soldier, and Private Boyd thought it
would be no place for his daughter, either. Belle went farther south,
to Front Royal, but she had scarcely arrived when Stonewall Jackson, defeated at Kernstown (March 23, 1862), was driven back,
far beyond Front Royal. When the Federals marched into that
town, too, Belle decided she might as well go home to Martinsburg.

Her second arrest followed before she could get there—iron-
ically enough, on one of the rare occasions when she was doing no
spying at all. She had just boarded the Martinsburg train when a
Union officer entered her coach.

"Is this Miss Belle Boyd?"

"Yes."

The officer had an order for her arrest, but Belle had a pass from
General James Shields, the local Union commander. Since each
paper more or less canceled the other, Belle's puzzled captor did
not know quite what to do. But, as he already had a detail of

prisoners for Baltimore, he took her with him and turned her over to General John Dix, the commander there, the same officer who had presided over the inquiry into Mrs. Greenhow's doings. On the way, Belle—out of pure deviltry—managed to procure a small Confederate flag, which she waved defiantly en route. The Union guards, who had a sense of humor, were undisturbed. They decided it was "an excellent joke that a convoy of Confederate prisoners should be brought in under a Confederate flag, and that flag raised by a lady."

As usual, Belle soon managed to get her own way. General Dix, who didn't in the least want his new prisoner, "confined" her in the Eutaw Hotel, one of the best hostelries in the city, for about a week. Then he sent her home to Martinsburg.

By the time Belle returned from her luxurious "imprisonment" in Baltimore, the Federal command—though it had no idea how much espionage she had been doing, or how long—was well aware that Belle needed watching. Belle herself says she was "placed under a strict surveillance, and forbidden to leave the town." Then Mrs. and Miss Boyd asked the provost marshal for a pass to go south to Winchester, thence to Front Royal, and so on to Richmond.

Delighted with the prospect of getting completely rid of Belle Boyd forever, the provost marshal in April or early May, 1862, provided a pass which allowed her to leave Martinsburg. Rarely have so many people been so glad to see so charming a girl go so far away—the farther and sooner, the better! At Winchester, Lieutenant Colonel James S. Fillebrown, of the 10th Maine, after some hesitation, gave the Boyds a new pass to Front Royal—and thereby made one of the worst blunders any soldier ever made.

Perhaps because she expected to be in Richmond soon, Belle about this time threw caution to the winds and did what no secret agent in history ever did before or has ever done since: She gave an interview about her espionage to the press—partly in reply to the attack on her character.

It was a correspondent of the *New York Tribune*, then in Strasburg, who led her into this blazing indiscretion. Getting Belle to talk was easy. The Associated Press had questioned her virtue, and she was naturally furious.

"She pleads guilty to nearly all the charges made against her," wrote the *Tribune* man, "as far as they refer to conveying information to the enemy, carrying letters and parcels from rebels within our lines to those without, and performing acts of heroic daring worthy of the days of the Revolution; but when they assail her virtue, and class her with camp cyprians, she denies them in the strongest terms possible."

The Northern press had indeed printed some appalling tales about her, and it was perhaps the prospect of refuting these that led her to talk to the correspondent at all. "To be called 'an accomplished prostitute,'" said she, is something she "did not expect from Yankee gentlemen."

Here followed some personal description by the interviewer, which, though perfectly true and not wholly unflattering, was scarcely the kind of thing likely to please an impulsive girl. Said the correspondent: "Without being beautiful, she is very attractive. Is quite tall, has a superb figure, an intellectual face, and dressed with much taste."

"Very attractive . . . superb figure . . . much taste." Compliments all very well in their way. But does any woman forgive the man who says she has "an intellectual face"—and this "without being beautiful"?

The *Tribune* man also added a protest: "Why she should be allowed to go at will through our camps, flirt with our officers, and display their notes and cards to her visitors, I am at a loss to know." Then the wretched fellow became wickedly derisive. Because Belle especially admired South Carolina, he said, she wore "a gold palmetto tree beneath her beautiful chin, a rebel soldier's belt around her waist, and a velvet band across her forehead, with the seven stars of the Confederacy shedding their pale light therefrom. It seemed to me, while listening to her narrative, that the only additional ornament she required to render herself perfectly beautiful was a Yankee halter encircling her neck."

During their stay in Front Royal, the Boyds lived with Belle's aunt and uncle, who kept a small hotel, which was also their home. When the Union general, James Shields, and his staff took over the hotel, the owners moved into a neighboring cottage.

It was the best spot in Front Royal for a Confederate agent. From her new home Belle could see officers passing to and fro—and the officers could see Belle. As usual, the results were disastrous. There was on the general's staff a susceptible "Captain K." There is not much doubt that this was Captain Daniel J. Keily, aide-de-camp. He fits perfectly Belle's description of "Captain K.," and there is one further bit of evidence: The real Captain Keily was wounded in the face at Port Republic, and immediately after that battle, Belle Boyd went to call on a wounded Federal officer, a friend of hers, near Port Republic.

The story of Belle's call is told by Thomas Ashby, a sixteen-year-old relative of the Confederate cavalry leader. Ashby notes that after Port Republic, two wounded officers were taken to his father's house. One was a German, the other a member of Shields's staff. As Captain Keily was the only member of Shields's staff wounded at Port Republic, he was that other officer. Young Ashby, who approved of Belle Boyd no more than Lucy Buck did, is extremely scathing about this incident: "When she came to see the wounded German officer she was playing the game of flirt and lowering the dignity of her sex." But Belle was not calling on the German at all. She had come to see the wounded aide with another purpose in mind. As aide to General Shields, Keily always knew a good many things the Confederates would be glad to learn.

The captain became a devoted suitor. He wrote verses to Belle. He sent flowers. He probably flirted with her—and it is more than probable that Belle encouraged him. In the course of all this, young Keily inevitably let slip some secrets of the staff. Belle herself says maliciously that she was indebted to her devotee "for some very remarkable effusions, some withered flowers, and last, not least, for a great deal of very important information."

One gets an idea of this delightful young creature's *modus operandi* from her former opponent in espionage, David Hunter Strother, who had, by this time, become a colonel on the staff of Major General N. P. Banks. Strother arrived at Front Royal "in the cars," for a day of official business with General Shields. He found Belle Boyd, whom he already knew, "looking well and deporting herself in a very ladylike manner." Belle was quite unaware that Strother, too, had been spying. She had no hesitation, therefore, in showing him evidence of her prowess among officers of his own army—innumerable brass buttons from Union uniforms. She even "sported a bunch of buttons despoiled from General Shields and our officers." The guileful minx must have asked Colonel Strother for one from his own uniform to expand the collection, for he adds, noncommittally, "She seemed ready to increase her trophies."

A day or two before or after this, Belle achieved one of her most famous feats. The date was probably May 14 or 15, 1862, certainly some days before Shields marched out of Front Royal to join McDowell at Frederick on May 22.

In the east, around Richmond, the Confederacy was now hard pressed. McClellan would at last be crossing the Chickahominy, uncomfortably close to the city, on May 25. In the Shenandoah Valley, Jackson at the moment seemed to be in great danger. Banks's army, of which Shields's division was now a part, would soon move against him from the north. Frémont's army was to move in upon him from the west. It was to be a perfect "squeeze play," in which the Yankees would have overwhelming numerical superiority.

During all this time, the enterprising Miss Boyd had been getting a continuous flow of military information from General Shields's enamored aide-de-camp. It was probably from him she learned that, before his division marched, Shields would hold a final "council with his officers" in "what had formerly been my aunt's drawing room." Being familiar with the house, Belle knew that a hole in the floor of the closet of a bedroom above opened through the ceiling of the drawing room below. Though this has often been described as a knothole, Belle herself says it was "a hole that had been bored, whether with a view to espionage or not I have never been able to ascertain." It is hard to think of any other reason for a hole just there.

Either there was no guard or not a very vigilant one. As soon as the blue-uniformed officers had assembled, the girl slipped quietly upstairs, lay down with her ear to the hole, and listened. The council lasted till one o'clock in the morning, and Belle heard every word. When the sabers had clanked away into the night and it was safe to cross the courtyard, she went back to her own room and enciphered a report of what she had heard. Then, afraid to trust even her family's slaves, she saddled her own horse quietly and started "in the direction of the mountains."

Only a little while before, General Shields had refused to give her a pass to Richmond, explaining that Jackson would soon be completely defeated—after which she could go anywhere. But the Union Army had issued passes to "Confederate soldiers returning south"—that is, paroled prisoners of war. How did an enemy agent, instead of a paroled prisoner, happen to have a parolee's pass? All the lady herself says is that some of these useful papers, through "various circumstances, had never been put in requisition."

It is not hard to guess the "various circumstances." Some paroled rebel had turned his pass over to Belle, being perfectly sure he knew the country well enough to evade Federal pickets and patrols and get home without it. Either Union staff officers worded their passes rather vaguely or the Union sentries were extremely lax. The papers were made out to male soldiers. Yet the sentries, without question or suspicion, accepted one presented by a young girl riding alone toward the enemy in the middle of the night. (Perhaps they were simply made out to "bearer." If such a pass came from divisional headquarters or higher, a sentry would assume the solitary woman rider was a Federal agent.)

Once through the Union outposts, Belle knew exactly where to go. Fifteen miles ahead was the house of "Mr. M." There she would find either Turner Ashby or someone who could take a message to him.

She banged vigorously on the door and finally got a response from upstairs:

"Who is there?"

"It is I."

"But who are you? What is your name?"

"Belle Boyd. I have important intelligence to communicate to Colonel Ashby: is he here?"

"No; but wait a minute: I will come down."

The mistress of the household, when she appeared, was cautious. Where was Ashby? The mistress of the household was suitably vague. Even when told the girl had to see him "without the loss of a minute," she declined definite information. She would say only that Ashby's troops were in bivouac, "a quarter of a mile farther up the wood."

Ashby, however, was not nearly so absent as his cautious hostess had been pretending. As Belle was remounting, another door opened, and the missing colonel emerged. He had evidently been listening till he recognized the voice of his midnight visitor.

"Good God! Miss Belle, is this you?"

She handed him the cipher report, but as deciphering would take time, she also gave him an immediate and rapid oral summary of what she had overheard. Two hours later, having ridden past a sleeping Union sentry, Belle Boyd was safely in bed at her aunt's house, though, by the time she had unsaddled, day was breaking.

One can't help wondering what Belle's mother thought of all these goings-on by a daughter still in her teens. Apparently in Mrs. Boyd's eyes, as in her daughter's, military necessity overrode considerations of Victorian propriety.

When, in March of '62, the Federals had first tried to withdraw troops from the Shenandoah to aid McClellan, Stonewall had frightened them into keeping the troops where they were, even though Kernstown had been a Confederate defeat because of false intelligence. Again in May of '62, the Federals saw a chance to move forces eastward to support McClellan, whose prospects of taking Richmond seemed better than before.

This time, Jackson had better intelligence, for the plans Belle had heard General Shields and his staff making were for their own eastward march to support McClellan. Shields meant to take most of his troops. He left behind in Front Royal only the 1st (Federal) Maryland Infantry, supported by one squadron of cavalry and one battery of field artillery. Belle Boyd, in her eavesdropping, could hardly have failed to hear most of these details; and, as soon as a horseman could ride south from Ashby's bivouac, carrying the news Belle had brought, Stonewall knew as much about the proposed march as General Shields himself.

9

BELLE BOYD

PART 2.
AN END TO ADVENTURE

Now followed the three most adventurous days in Belle Boyd's habitually venturesome life. On May 21, 1862, she bluffed her way
through the Union picket lines and into Winchester, without a pass.
On May 22, she made contact with a Confederate secret agent
there and received from him two packages of documents and a
small but highly secret note. A little later that morning, she was
arrested with the documents in her possession—a perilous situation,
out of which she managed to wheedle her way, as usual. A few
hours later, she was safely back in Front Royal. There, next day,
May 23, immediately after luncheon, she would hear the crack of
Southern rifles and, in the most famous of her exploits, would dash
out across the battlefield, with vital and accurate last-minute intelligence for Stonewall Jackson.

I

Belle had good reason for her Winchester journey. There dwelt in
Winchester, at this time, a Confederate spy whom Belle describes
only as "a gentleman of high social position"—probably the same

man Jackson's staff officer, Major Henry Kyd Douglas, saw bringing intelligence to the rebel camp, a short time after Belle's visit
to him. Douglas never knew who he was and knew better than to
ask questions of General Jackson; but there is not much doubt that
the gentleman was Lieutenant Colonel William R. Denny, who
lived in Winchester and devoted himself to espionage. Since Union
forces in Winchester occupied "Angerona," his residence there, he
and Belle usually met quietly in the garden.

Probably Belle knew in advance that the agent would have intelligence for her when she prepared, on May 20, 1862, to visit
Winchester next day. For that she needed a pass, and Belle submitted her request to Major Tyndale, of Philadelphia, provost
marshal in Front Royal. At first Major Tyndale refused to grant
it. Then he relented and agreed to issue it next day, probably
only to get rid of Belle Boyd; for, when she returned next morning
(May 21), the major had "gone on a scout," without leaving the
pass.

Though he thus escaped from Belle, Major Tyndale's reconnoissance was one of the least successful in military history. May 20,
1862, was the day when Stonewall Jackson's ragged column was
turning out of the Shenandoah into the Luray Valley, on the east
side of Massanutten. Quite undiscovered, it was advancing secretly
northward, toward Front Royal at the Luray Valley's end. That
night the rebels were in bivouac at Luray, well to the south of the
town, but drawing dangerously near the unsuspecting Federals
there.

When Major Tyndale came back from his scouting, Jackson
was a day's march nearer Front Royal. But neither the major nor
anyone else in the Union Army had any idea of his approach.
With his rebels almost ready to pounce, all the Yankees still imagined that "Old Jack" was still at Harrisonburg, far to the south. On
the morning of May 21, 1862, about the time Belle Boyd heard the
disappointing news that she would get no pass, the boys in gray
were breaking camp at Luray or had already begun their march to
Front Royal.

Failing to get intelligence of the enemy was only one of Major
Tyndale's mistakes that day. He had also been quite wrong in
imagining he could stop Belle Boyd by withholding a scrap of

paper. Not in vain had that entrancing maiden been assiduously cultivating the acquaintance of young Federal officers in Front Royal. Among them was another youth—quite as susceptible as Captain K.—whose name Belle gives only as "Lieutenant H." As a Federal officer, the lieutenant could travel to Winchester at any time. Better yet, he was an officer of the cavalry squadron that provided the pickets guarding Front Royal. His troopers would never dream of halting their own officer. Nor would they halt any lady he was escorting.

Dear little Belle was sweetly appealing.

"You profess to be a great friend of mine," she told Lieutenant H. "Prove it by assisting me out of this dilemma, and pass us through the pickets."

The wretched youth hesitated only a few moments before agreeing. Mounting the box of her carriage and taking the reins, he prepared to drive Belle and a girl cousin to Winchester. Jackson's veterans were, by this time, well on their way northward in the Luray Valley.

At "Bel Air," the Buck family house near Front Royal, Miss Lucy had risen early that morning to write a letter Belle was to carry to Winchester for her. Miss Lucy walked over to the Strickler House with this. But there she saw "a carriage at the door in which was seated the young lady with a Yankee officer." She withdrew in horror. Miss Lucy would not entrust her letter "with one who appeared upon such familiar terms with those whom we most dreaded." Keeping her letter, she "went on up to see Cousin Mary." Once more, Miss Buck objected to Miss Boyd's conduct; and that was really most unfair. Belle couldn't possibly spy on the Federal army without associating with Federal officers.

In Winchester, next morning, the "gentleman of high social position" called on Belle to hand her two packets of papers. One of these, he said, was "of great importance." The other was "trifling in comparison." It contained one of those Northern newspapers which Confederate staffs read eagerly, because they were filled with military intelligence that should never have been printed. The spy also gave Belle what appeared to be "a little note," which he described as "a very important paper."

Belle was to send these three papers—the "little note" especially—along her own courier line "to Jackson or some other responsible Confederate officer." Neither of the two spies had the least idea how close Jackson was by this time, nor does Belle ever say when or how these messages reached him.

The immediate problem was to get the papers safely out of Winchester. The more important packet she gave to her Negro maid, as less likely to be suspected than herself. The other less important packet, and the little note, she kept. The lieutenant soon took over the packet Belle had given to her slave girl, perhaps because he had noticed that Belle had written on both packets, "Kindness of Lieutenant H." A Union officer was less likely to be suspected than a personal maid. Though Belle says she wrote on the packets "unguardedly," she was certainly hoping the inscription would help get them past any merely casual inspection.

At just about this hour, on this very day, Stonewall Jackson, still undiscovered, was moving up the Luray Valley, east of Massanutten.

When Belle was ready to start back from Winchester to Front Royal with all this secret intelligence, she sent Colonel Fillebrown her request for a pass, together with a bouquet. The flowers did the trick—or so Belle was allowed to think. Her pass came back at once, with a polite note, thanking her "for so sweet a compliment."

But Fillebrown was no susceptible lieutenant. He was in his middle thirties, he was a good deal brighter than he let himself seem, and his eyes were wide open. Neither Belle herself nor the gentleman of high social position who gave her the incriminating documents had noticed a Negro quietly watching the papers change hands. The slave informed Union headquarters in Winchester. Someone there must have wondered how, if Belle needed a pass now, she had ever reached Winchester without one. It was a provost marshal's business to wonder about these little matters.

Someone, probably Fillebrown himself, telegraphed a query to Front Royal. It reached Major Tyndale, the same officer who had refused to issue a pass for Belle's trip to Winchester in the first place. The major, annoyed by Belle's trickery, sent back an indignant reply. Fillebrown took suitable measures.

As Lieutenant H. and his feminine passengers reached the picket line, two mounted men closed in upon their carriage, one on each side. Miss Boyd did not like their appearance— "two repulsive-looking fellows, who proved to be detectives." But, under the circumstances, she may have been prejudiced.

"We have orders to arrest you."

"For what?" asked Belle, who knew very well.

"Upon suspicion of having letters."

Back the party went—Belle, her cousin, who "trembled like a poor bird caught in a snare," and the lieutenant.

The detectives took them to headquarters of the 10th Maine Infantry, where Colonel George L. Beale asked if the lady had any letters. Indeed she had, replied the artful minx, with an air of girlish innocence, well knowing she would be searched if she denied it. As calmly as she could, she drew the least important packet out of her basket and handed it over. All might have been well, if she had not already scribbled on it that unfortunate line, "Kindness of Lieutenant H."

This at once involved the young officer, who seems to have been stupid enough never to have suspected what Belle was really doing. There was nothing for the girl to do but brazen it out. "This scribbling on the letter," she assured the colonel, meant nothing at all. "It was a thoughtless act of mine."

The lieutenant, whose eyes were slowly opening, now produced the package Belle had asked him to carry. This, too, was marked "Kindness of Lieutenant H." Things began to look bad for the lieutenant. When the package was found to contain a copy of the vitriolically anti-Federal *Maryland News-sheet*, things looked worse than ever: "The Colonel entertained no further doubt of Lieutenant H.'s complicity." But Colonel Beale was not too furious to notice that the girl was holding a scrap of paper.

"What is that you have in your hand?"

It was, of course, the note which, she had been told, was the most important of the three documents. Belle's native boldness saved her.

"What—this little scrap of paper?" she inquired. "You can have it if you wish: it is nothing." And she approached the colonel as if to hand it over willingly. She was prepared to emulate Harvey Birch, the hero of Cooper's novel, *The Spy* (which she had read), and swallow the paper if her interrogator reached out to take it. But Colonel Beale was now so angry with the lieutenant that he ignored the lady's offer and did not take the paper.

The pair drove back to Front Royal and were, for the moment, let go—but not because the U.S. Army trusted either of them. Secret orders went out to keep Miss Boyd under surveillance; the indiscreet lieutenant was soon facing the court-martial that ended his military career.

II

Surveillance over Belle did the Federals very little good, for by the time she reached Front Royal on May 22, Stonewall Jackson, his presence still unknown to the Federals, was almost ready to pounce. Colonel Beale had failed to seize the little note which the gentleman in Winchester thought the most important part of his information. Belle either sent it on through channels or handed it over personally, when she met Jackson next day.

When the girl and her mother—and Miss Lucy R. Buck—went to bed in Front Royal that night (May 22), Stonewall Jackson and his Confederates lay wrapped in their blankets, undiscovered, only ten miles away. The Union scouts had still not pushed reconnoissance far enough to the front and had failed to find them. Colonel John R. Kenly, commanding the 1st Maryland (Union) Infantry in Front Royal, had not been wholly idle. He had pushed one patrol a little way down the Luray Valley, where it had captured a lone Confederate. Under interrogation, this man admitted that a rebel column was on its way up the valley; but both Kenly and his superior, General Banks, assumed this was some small force on a minor mission.

Everything was quiet all the next morning. The noon hour passed. Then, suddenly, there was a rattle of musketry, and Kenly's outposts, a mile and a half south of the village, came scurrying in. A total of 17,000 men—Early's troops reinforcing Jackson's—bore down on his single weak regiment, which had an infantry reinforcement of two companies and an artillery support of two guns!

That indefatigable diarist, Miss Lucy R. Buck, was out calling when the attack began. She says she heard "the quick, sharp report of a rifle and another in rapid succession," then "saw the Yankees scampering over the meadow below our house"—the outposts falling back.

There was a great deal of excitement among the blue uniforms, but none of the ladies chatting with Miss Buck knew why. There had thus far been very little firing. Then another girl "rushed in with purple face and dishevelled hair crying, 'Oh, my God! The Hill above town is black with our boys.' . . . Ma and I did not wait . . . but started for home in double quick time, all the [while] hearing the firing exchanged more and more rapidly. Nellie, spy-glass in hand, clapping her hands exclaiming, 'Oh, there they are. I see our dear brave fellows just in the edge of the woods on the hill over the town! There they are, bless them.' "

Some of Ashby's cavalry emerged from woods near the court house. The excited women saw "a grey figure upon horseback seemingly in command"—probably Turner Ashby himself. Someone called, "Only see! The Yankees run." Everyone leaned out a back window and saw, with delight, "contrabands [i.e., fugitive slaves] and Yankees together, tearing wildly by." A slave rushed in, shrieking that the rebels were coming and the Yankees were making an "orful fuss in de street."

Belle Boyd, who had been dutifully reading aloud to her grandmother and a cousin, saw her chance. She ran to the door. Confused Union troops were everywhere. A not very bright Federal officer gave Jackson's spy precisely the information Jackson needed (rarely has so dangerously loquacious a blockhead held a commission in any army): Yes, the rebels had already driven in the outposts, and "now we are endeavouring to get the ordnance and the quartermaster's stores out of their reach."

"But what will you do with the stores in the large dépôt?"

"Burn them, of course."

"But suppose the rebels come upon you too quickly?"

"Then we will fight as long as we can by any possibility show a front, and in the event of defeat make good our retreat upon Winchester, burning the bridges as soon as we cross them, and finally effect a junction with General Banks's force."

Belle already knew that Banks, at Strasburg, had only 4,000 men. She knew the force at Winchester, north of Strasburg and Front

Royal, was also small. It could be reinforced from Harpers Ferry. She also knew that Generals Shields and Geary, though now on the march, could be recalled—though it would take time. She even knew where Frémont's army was—far enough away to present no immediate danger. A good many careless Yankee officers must have chattered to the Charming Rebel in the last few days.

She could now give Jackson full information on enemy capabilities, even the enemy's exact intentions, the valuable supplies in Front Royal, the location of all supporting troops. The information was absolutely fresh and must reach Jackson at once.

Belle prepared to make sure it did.

But, before she left the house, the prankish creature paused an instant to play a rather painful practical joke on an unsuspecting Yankee. A. W. Clark, war correspondent for the *New York Herald*, had a room in the house. Belle didn't like Clark, who is said to have tried to force attentions on her.

Hearing the firing, the newspaperman dashed from his room, meeting Belle on the stairs and nearly knocking her down.

"Great heavens! What is the matter?" exclaimed the agitated journalist.

Belle was tart. "Nothing to speak of, only the rebels are coming, and you had best prepare yourself for a visit to Libby Prison."

Clark rushed back to his room to gather up his papers. The door stood open, with the key on the outside. Quietly closing the door, Belle turned the key and was off. Clark soon managed to climb out through a second story window, but Belle's little trick delayed him long enough to let the Confederates catch him.

Through field glasses, from a balcony, Belle spotted the Confederate advance guard, only three-quarters of a mile away and moving rapidly on the town. If she could only get word to them of Front Royal's defenseless situation, these troops would pass it back to Stonewall, who would certainly have a command post well to the front. She rushed downstairs, looking for a messenger.

Several men "who had always professed strong attachment to the cause of the South" were standing about. Would any of them carry intelligence to General Jackson? The group were something less than heroes.

"No, no," they said, "you go."

Putting on a white sunbonnet, Belle set off. (Mid-nineteenth-century ladies never went outdoors bareheaded. Tanned skins were not fashionable, and even in the midst of battle there was room for thought of Belle's complexion, which was probably noteworthy.) Through agitated Yankees in the street she made her way out of the little town and into the green fields beyond. Federal artillery was firing at rebels in the road. Federal infantry was firing from windows of the local hospital, and Confederate artillery was pounding the hospital from which the fire was coming.

Though she tried to escape observation, Belle was directly in the cross fire of both armies, and her costume was conspicuous. The white sunbonnet made a fine target. So did the contrasting colors of her blue dress, "with a little fancy white apron over it." She herself was always sure the Federals tried to shoot her. If they did, they were doing the right thing in trying to stop a dangerous spy; but a great deal of lead was flying through the Virginia atmosphere that morning. Once a shell landed near her—Belle thought within twenty yards. But there were no contact fuses in those days. The girl had time to throw herself flat before it burst.

She approached the 1st (Confederate) Maryland Infantry and Hay's Louisiana Brigade—advance troops—which were "naturally surprised to see a woman on the battlefield." She waved her sunbonnet toward the town. The troops cheered her and rushed on. She could see no other Confederates. She knelt to pray. The direct answer to the maiden's prayer was Major Henry Kyd Douglas, of Stonewall Jackson's personal staff, who rode up at this moment. An instant later, she saw the Confederate main body, moving up.

Both Belle and Douglas later wrote down their recollections of the incident. The staff officer says that, while the general paused to estimate the situation, he himself had a moment to look around. He saw "the figure of a woman in white glide swiftly out of the town." (Belle's white apron and bonnet were more conspicuous at a distance than her blue dress.) The distant figure made a circuit, then ran up a ravine toward the Confederates. "She seemed, when I saw her, to heed neither weeds nor fences, but waved a bonnet as she came on, trying, it was evident, to keep the hill between ourselves and the village." He pointed her out to Jackson "just as a dip in the land hid her."

General Richard S. Ewell suggested that Major Douglas ride to meet her. Stonewall gave the order and Douglas dashed away. It took him only a few minutes to regain sight of "the romantic maiden whose tall, supple, and graceful figure struck me as soon as I came in sight of her." (Belle's features may have been irregular, but even on a battlefield men noticed her figure.)

A moment later, the running girl saw Douglas. She called his name. The major, who had known her for years, was startled as he recognized the breathless figure.

"Good God, Belle," he exclaimed, taking her hand. "You here! What is it?"

"Oh, Harry, give me time to recover my breath."

She handed over a "little note"—probably the one she had brought from Winchester—and added orally that the Federals meant to burn the bridges. The gray cavalry must seize them before that happened.

Colonel Richard Taylor (later Lieutenant General) also remembered the scene. Though naturally he and the others, after a lapse of years, differed as to the exact information Belle brought, they all agreed it was important. Taylor evidently saw her as Douglas was escorting her to the general:

> Past mid-day we reached a wood extending from the mountain to the river, when a mounted officer from the rear [obviously Douglas] called Jackson's attention, who rode back with him. A moment later, there rushed out of the wood to meet us a young, rather well-looking woman, afterward widely known as Belle Boyd. Breathless with speed and agitation, some time elapsed before she found her voice. Then, with much volubility, she said we were near Front Royal, beyond the wood; that the town was filled with Federals, whose camp was on the west side of the river, where they had guns in position to cover the waggon-bridge, but none bearing on the railway bridge below the former; that they believed Jackson to be west of Massanutten, near Harrisonburg [as he had been, but that was some time before]; that General Banks, the Federal commander, was at Winchester, twenty miles north-west of Front Royal, where he was slowly concentrating his widely scattered

forces to meet Jackson's advance, which was expected some days later. All this she told with the precision of a staff officer making a report and it was true to the letter.

Belle's information was indeed "true to the letter," though General Taylor, remembering the episode fifteen years later, wasn't quite so accurate as Belle. The town was not full of Federals. "The Yankee force is very small," is what Belle herself says she told Jackson.

Major Douglas says that when he met her, she stood with her hand against her heart and gasped out, "I knew it must be Stonewall when I heard the first gun. Go back quick and tell him that the Yankee force is very small—one regiment of Maryland artillery and several companies of cavalry. Tell him I know for I went through the camps and got it out of an officer. Tell him to charge right down and he will catch them all. I must hurry back. Good-by. My love to all the dear boys—and remember if you meet me in town you haven't seen me today." Apparently Taylor heard part of a similar conversation, though he may be reporting only what someone told him.

Douglas raised his cap. Belle kissed her hand to him. Jackson, it turned out, had never heard of her—which probably means all her intelligence had passed through Turner Ashby, who, as a proper matter of intelligence routine, would have given as few agents' names as possible. Jackson, riding forward, asked Belle if she wanted an escort and a horse for her return. Belle thanked Stonewall but declined. The sooner she got back to Front Royal, and the less conspicuously, the better.

A few minutes later, Douglas saw a distant flash of white at the edge of the village. Belle was waving her sunbonnet. She disappeared among the houses of Front Royal.

Jackson's problem had been solved. Knowing the enemy's strength, he pressed the attack. The Confederate troops rushed the town. The Union commander was killed. The hopelessly outnumbered blue uniforms fled.

After the town had been taken, Douglas found Belle on the pavement in front of the little hotel, chatting with some Federal officers (all prisoners now) and some of the arriving Confederates. Belle knew them all. She had made it her business to know the Federals. And the Confederates included old acquaintances. Her cheeks were still flushed with excitement "and recent exercise." She greeted her old friend, Major Douglas, "with much surprised cordiality." Douglas bent from his saddle. Belle pinned a red rose on his uniform. It was "blood-red," said Belle—and her "colors." Douglas must remember.

Major Douglas rode back to Stonewall. Anyone in Front Royal could see how surprised Belle had been to encounter her old friend; but Belle's exploit had been a little too public to be long a secret. Most of Front Royal had been watching that battle. The entry for that same day in Miss Lucy R. Buck's diary says, "Speaking of boldness reminds me of an exploit attributed to Miss Belle Boyd Wednesday. Tis said that she wished some information conveyed to the army about the time of keenest firing and not being able to get any one to go for her, she went herself to a most exposed point, where the bullets fell like hail stones about her riddling her dress. I know not what truth there is in this rumor." Belle Boyd told the story herself—but only when she was safe in London, in 1865.

Presently a dismal little column of prisoners passed, under guard, the disconsolate Clark among them. He glared at the triumphant girl. "I'll make you rue this. It's your doing I am a prisoner here." You can hardly blame the correspondent for being irritated, but his plight was not really very serious. Jackson released him on June 5.

III

Belle's last attempt at espionage before the Federals finally placed her where she could do no more harm can probably be dated in June, 1863, during the Confederate advance to Gettysburg. Her old friend, Major Harry Gilmor, had orders to enter the Union positions near Winchester, headquarters of Major General Robert H. Milroy. General Micah Jenkins, under whose orders Gilmor was serving, had set up headquarters at Fisher's Hill, near Strasburg. While he was getting ready to start from Woodstock, south of Strasburg, he met Belle Boyd. The two were old acquaintances, having met in the first autumn of the war. In no time at all, Belle knew he was on a secret mission and was begging to be taken along.

Any other girl in the entire Confederacy would have met with a flat "No." But poor Gilmor, who didn't in the least want her along, tried to get rid of her by explaining she would have to get permission from General Jenkins. That seemed to settle it. Everyone went to bed; and Gilmor, up with the dawn, was ready to slip away, when he discovered that Belle had quietly made off with his saber and pistols. Before he knew quite what to do, down the stairway came Belle Boyd, in a neat riding habit, "with a pretty little belt around her waist, from which the butts of two small pistols were peeping, cased in patent leather holsters." She had guessed Gilmor would try to evade her and had stolen his arms to forestall him.

Seeing there was no way of escaping her, the major took her to headquarters, where Belle tried to wheedle Jenkins into letting her go, while Gilmor, standing behind her, made frantic gestures of dissent. The general—who could take a hint—refused permission. Belle was furious.

The episode at Front Royal probably became rather widely known, but a few weeks later another escapade of Belle's came to the attention of the Federals. On July 2, 1862, a suspicious medical officer of the 2nd Division, I Army Corps, reported directly to Secretary Stanton that yet another Federal officer was entrapped by her wiles: "The celebrated Belle Boyd the 'Rebel Spy' now in Front Royal has apparently fallen in love or is anxious to make a victim of the Medical Director of the 1st Army Corps (Dr. Rose)."

A Federal posing as a Southerner made friends with Belle, and the incautious girl rashly asked him to carry a message to Jackson. Pinkerton himself visited Front Royal to look into her doings. Belle was soon on her way to the Old Capitol Prison. Though detained there for some time, she was not brought to trial but was eventually released and sent south. From Richmond she set out for Europe aboard a blockade runner, was captured, contrived to become engaged to the Union naval officer commanding the prize crew before he could make port, was briefly confined in Boston, where she greatly disconcerted the United States marshal in charge of her, and was thence sent on to Canada and Europe, where she married her Yankee sailor, now dishonorably discharged from the U.S. Navy. When her husband, returning to the United States, again fell foul of the government, she wrote a flaming letter to Abraham Lincoln, threatening to tell all she knew. Lincoln was probably not very much worried, but—Belle's husband was released!

There has been much dispute as to the real value of her services. She was too much of an exhibitionist to be a really good secret agent. "Some of her methods as a spy subjected her to harsh and hostile criticism," wrote a Georgia soldier. The youthful Thomas Ashby sneered at her: "Just a kind of circus rider." One of her Federal jailers thought her "undeniably good-looking, fine figure, and merry disposition," but was not inclined to take her secret service very seriously. It wasn't secret enough, for one thing. He had the impression of "a woman governed more by romance and love of notoriety than actual regard for the Southern cause." Still, he was willing to admit, "she could have been dangerous had she possessed equal good sense and sound judgment."

But that wasn't what Turner Ashby thought, or what Stonewall Jackson said, in a letter of thanks after Front Royal—a letter that unhappily disappeared in the Chicago fire. As for the Federal government, it took her seriously enough to arrest her three times and finally to pack her off, first to Richmond, then to Canada, to make sure she should never again come near the U.S. Army—and especially its younger officers!

10

LAST SPIES
IN THE SHENANDOAH

After a year or two of experience, Federal spycatchers began to
improve in their work along the Potomac and in the Shenandoah,
and Federal courts-martial began to lose their earlier hesitation
about passing death sentences. Bold exploits like those of Belle
Boyd and Colonel Strother became more difficult, but they did not
cease. When in early November, 1863, General John D. Imboden
established headquarters at Kratzer's Springs, north of Harrisonburg, he was still receiving abundant intelligence from many civilians in the "lower valley"—that is, the northern end of the
Shenandoah. These active spies were people "living at home who
performed most useful outpost duty," observing and reporting
constantly.

"Many ladies were, in this regard, very useful to us," the general
adds. "I often received information from them sooner than my
scouts could report it, as they frequently have to hide in the day
time and only travel at night, while a lady or male citizen would go
about as they pleased."

Early one morning in December, Imboden received a note from
Moorfield, in the northern part of the Valley. A recently wounded

Confederate soldier, with one arm still in a sling, had ridden all night to bring it to him. The note consisted of a few lines only, but "its contents made me spring from my seat and order the whole command to move in thirty minutes." Though the note was unsigned, Imboden knew perfectly well where it came from. It was "in a dainty, but familiar female hand." It came from "a beautiful accomplished girl, whose brother was an officer in my command." While visiting a friend, she had seen Averell's cavalry moving south, had hidden in an upper room to count them, and had reported 3,000 cavalry, 3,000 infantry, some artillery, and 200 loaded wagons. As soon as the troops passed, she had ridden home and tried to find a Confederate scout. Since there was none in the vicinity, she sent the wounded man. Scouts who had seen Averell confirmed the report half a day later.

Fitzhugh Lee's cavalry turned out with Imboden, hoping to cut off the Yankees, who were obviously heading for Staunton, to destroy the railroad and stores there and to raid Lexington, Lynchburg, and Salem. They hoped to catch Averell at Covington but failed. Early, commanding in the Shenandoah, managed to cut him off from Staunton, and the Federals succeeded only in burning Salem.

The Shenandoah spies continued to keep an eye on Averell's cavalry. In the following April, a Confederate general was able to follow his movements, thanks to "information obtained direct from one of Averill's colonels." This does not imply treason—only that the colonel talked carelessly where a spy could hear him. The general himself says that he had the news from "one of my scouts and spies, perfectly reliable," but—probably for good reasons—he does not go into details.

Four disguised Confederates were captured in the Shenandoah Valley, or near it, during 1863—Andrew Laypole, alias Isidore Leopold, Captain William F. Gordon, Captain William Boyd Compton, and Colonel John E. Boyd. All four were sentenced to death, though only Laypole was executed.

At the outbreak of the war, "Leopold," as Laypole called himself when in disguise, had enlisted in the 1st Virginia Cavalry, the regiment that had been J. E. B. Stuart's first Confederate command. After serving for some time on "special duty" for Stuart, in 1862 he was first captured by soldiers of the 2nd Massachusetts, who were making a raid to suppress guerrillas. As Stuart's star scout, Redmond Burke, was killed in this raid, it is fairly clear Laypole was already engaged in secret reconnoissance, as well as in guerrilla warfare. The official congratulations sent to the successful Federal commander specifically mention "Leopold" as a guerrilla. There was no accusation of espionage, however; and, perhaps for this reason, Laypole was soon free again. It is not clear whether he escaped or was exchanged.

He now joined Company D, 12th Virginia Cavalry, and was soon deep in secret service of some kind, which probably included ordinary espionage. On April 12, 1863, soldiers of the 1st New York Cavalry and the 12th West Virginia Cavalry captured him again, near Shepherdstown, West Virginia—in disguise and obviously a spy.

The local Union commander, General Robert H. Milroy, who didn't like the prospect of hanging a prisoner and was very eager to get rid of him somehow, wrote to General Robert C. Schenck, three days after the capture, "I think it would be best to turn Leopold over to the civil authorities of Maryland. Shall I do this?" The civil authorities, of course, would not execute the man—at least, not for espionage; but General Schenck evidently disagreed, for the prisoner was sent before a court-martial.

Though Leopold obviously was a spy, the judge advocate decided he could not prove it and withdrew this specification while the court-martial was actually sitting. Leopold was nevertheless convicted of a murder committed during guerrilla operations. He had been within the U.S. lines from about November 1, 1862, to about April 20, 1863, during which time, the prosecution said, he had been "robbing, plundering, maltreating, wounding and killing" civilians.

The most interesting thing about the court-martial is evidence given by General Milroy, whose troops had made the capture. The general testified that when he interrogated Laypole, the prisoner had offered to change sides and serve the Union—presumably as a spy. When Milroy's intelligence interrogated the man, Laypole supplied a good deal of information about the Confederate intelligence service and the Confederate forces in general. Then he asked to talk with Milroy in person.

Brought before the general, Laypole offered to give more information of the same sort and wrote out "a list of Scouts and Spies for each rebel Genl." He described the various individual agents, revealed the area where each was operating, "and offered to help checkmate them." None of these offers to turn his coat saved Laypole. He was hanged on the gallows erected for Captain Compton, who had escaped a few days before.

Captain William F. Gordon had entered service as a first sergeant in the 31st West Virginia Volunteers, in May, 1861. In June, 1862, his name begins to appear on the rolls as "absent without leave"— which is sometimes a convenient way to cover up an assignment to secret service. The records show that, although his company commander soon had a shrewd suspicion whither his missing first sergeant had vanished, he did nothing whatever to bring him back. The notation on one monthly return of Gordon's company says: "Some accounts represent him as being a compositor in 'Richmond Enquirer' office and others as being with General Jenkins cavalry." Gordon had been an editor printer of the sort common in rural journalism before the war. He may have left his company to become a compositor again. Presumably this was cover for whatever he was really doing. Technically he was a deserter; but, instead of being punished as such, he was eventually promoted to captain and assigned to Jenkins's Cavalry Brigade.

A jump from sergeant to captain was certainly not meant as a reward for desertion. It all looks as if Gordon had been "pulled out" for secret service, the facts being concealed by falsifying the records. The company clerk had to put something in to cover up the first sergeant's secret mission, and the AWOL entry was the best fiction he could think up.

By the spring of 1863, Gordon, now a captain, was surreptitiously busy on Confederate affairs of some kind in and around his former home at Sycamore, a village near Clarksburg—not, perhaps, in disguise but certainly wearing that universal favorite of the Confederate Army, a U.S. Army overcoat. He entered Harrison

County, of which Clarksburg is the county seat, on April 15. He had been spying elsewhere during the first half of April, and probably a good deal earlier.

He had escaped arrest once by dressing as a girl and on another occasion by hiding in a loft. Probably his main concern was secret recruiting for the Confederate Army, but he was certainly within the Union lines in disguise.

The Federals had for some time suspected that Gordon was lurking about near Clarksburg; but not until April 15 did they search the home of his father-in-law, Stephen Bassett, at Sycamore. The search at first revealed nothing. Then the commanding officer thought he detected "a strange feel in respect of some floor boards" in Mrs. Bassett's room. Pulling up the carpet, the Yankees found a small trap door. Pulling that up, they found Captain Gordon, lying on a quilt. The Federals, who knew all about Southern hospitality, didn't believe a Southern family would lodge a guest—much less a son-in-law—permanently under the flooring. They believed it still less when search revealed a ciphered document.

Gordon had been reporting to another Confederate agent, a certain Major Armsey; and the Federals, when they secured Armsey's cipher key, could tell just about what the two had been doing. They had to admit, however, that when Gordon was captured his clothes "were of the character of a Confederate uniform"—except for the inevitable Federal blue overcoat. There was dispute whether the overcoat had been so completely dyed that it could no longer be regarded as Federal uniform.

After the Union squad had arrested the captain, they also arrested his mother-in-law and other members of the Bassett family. The others were set across the Confederate lines, but Gordon himself went before a court-martial, which sentenced him to death.

Orders reached Fort McHenry on November 19, 1863, directing that he "be shot to death with musketry on the parade ground of the fort between noon and 3 P.M. of November 20." When November 20 came, Lieutenant H. B. Smith, of the Union Army, was dolefully contemplating the order. He knew he would have to command the firing squad, and he didn't like the idea. Then, only a little while before the hour set for the execution, came a telegram from Washington. The sentence was commuted to imprisonment at hard labor—from which, of course, Gordon would be released after the war.

It was just as well that the Union authorities took this humane course. Judge Robert Ould, the head of the Confederate Commission for the Exchange of Prisoners, had selected a Union officer to be hanged as a hostage, if Gordon were executed. But, as Gordon's sentence was commuted, both officers lived, and Gordon flourished for many years, when the war was over.

Belle Boyd's cousin, Captain William Boyd Compton, was another West Virginian in Confederate service who, about this time, barely escaped execution as a spy. He had served in the 31st Virginia with Lieutenant Colonel William R. Denny, for whom Belle acted as a courier. After being imprisoned in the Old Capitol twice and in Fortress Monroe once, the colonel was rather reticent as to his secret service. But he did once remark to his daughter that he had been "liable to sudden death for his activity after he got out of prison" and would, on one occasion, certainly have been hanged if the Yankees had searched him. The colonel must have been an active secret agent, but his tale is lost now.

Compton is known to have returned at least twice (and probably a good deal oftener) to his home in Fairmont, West Virginia, near the Pennsylvania line, while it was in Federal hands. He had two good reasons: He had been ordered back to recruit for the Confederate Army. But, as his defense counsel said, pleading for his life at his court-martial, "Love too beckoned him forward." In other words, the second reason was Miss Kate Kerr, described at the court-martial as "a particular lady friend." Miss Kerr was, in fact, Captain Compton's very particular friend, indeed. He was engaged to marry her, and he eventually did.

Compton was captured twice, each time by the same Union officer, Captain John H. Showalter, a West Virginian in the Union service. Compton was caught the first time visiting Miss Kate, at the Kerr house, in 1861; but there seems to have been no charge of espionage, and he was eventually exchanged as an ordinary prisoner of war.

Late in the following year, Compton received authority from the Confederate War Department to enter West Virginia and recruit a battery of horse artillery. Nothing seems to have come of this; but in March, 1863, he was sent back to raise a company of irregular infantry for bushwhacking behind the Union lines. Though Compton, when captured, denied that he had as yet enlisted any recruits, he was not in Confederate uniform, and the papers he was carrying were enough to hang anybody. They included a list of equipment for the forces he was to raise, which showed that the Confederates meant these troops to operate in at least partial disguise. The table of equipment assigned each man one overcoat, and an added note specified, "Yankee overcoat if possible."

One night in March, 1863, Captain Showalter was riding in a dimly lit passenger car, when the train reached Valley River Falls and Compton boarded it. He was wearing a slouch hat, gray trousers, a gray coat with brass buttons, the whole covered by a dark overcoat. Showalter did not at first realize who he was. When the Union officer finally recognized him, there was nothing to do but arrest him and seize his papers.

As Compton was out of uniform and within the Union lines, he was sent to Baltimore for court-martial, was there convicted, and was sent to Fort McHenry for execution. Here he was confined in a double-security "room within a room," with various other prisoners. After Compton's arrival, another Confederate officer was brought in, charged with violation of a flag of truce. When this accusation was shown to be baseless, the man had to be released; but a careless jailer had failed to note that he had been carrying a razor and pocket knife—which useful articles he left behind for his fellow prisoners.

Jefferson Davis threatened to hang five Union officers in retaliation, if Compton died; and by June, 1863, the execution had been "suspended." The next year, however, the Union authorities decided to get on with their hanging.

The pocket knife offered Compton his last hope, and he seized it promptly. Climbing on a box that had been left in the room, he stuck his knife in the ceiling and announced to his fellow prisoners, "Boys, I am going out right through here." Prisoners stood guard at all windows and the door, while Compton and others hacked a hole through the ceiling and the timbers of the roof.

By nine o'clock that night (May 15–16, 1864), they had cut

through everything but the tin of the roof. To prevent accidental discovery, this covering was left intact until the last moment, when a certain Captain Gubbins cut a man-size hole—or what he meant for a man-size hole. After the moon went down, about 1 A.M., Compton and four companions climbed through. At the crucial moment it became apparent that Captain Gubbins had slightly miscalculated the required dimensions, and the hole was a little narrow. One man, stouter than the others, almost lost his trousers while his companions were trying to drag him through the jagged cut in the tin, but he got through at last, with his trousers more or less intact.

Once out of the prison building, they crossed the wall by throwing stones at a timid sentry and then dashing at him, out of the darkness, with a shout of "Charge!" It was all very startling, coming out of the silent night; and the sentry, who had no heroic inclinations, flung down his musket and fled, quitting his post just long enough to enable the escaping prisoners to scramble over the wall. They all reached the South in safety, though one man insisted on pausing in Baltimore long enough to call upon a young lady.

Colonel John E. Boyd, like Compton a relative of Belle Boyd's, was a veteran of Early's reconnoissance group. There is no record of what kind of intelligence work he engaged in. Some of it may have been overt reconnoissance in the field, in proper Confederate uniform, but there is no doubt that he engaged in espionage in disguise when necessary. It is practically certain that he operated against the brilliant group of Union scouts and secret agents commanded by Major H. H. Young and operating for Sheridan in the Shenandoah. He had been so active and so effective that the infuriated Sheridan, who knew very well what Boyd was doing, threatened to "hang him higher than Haman" if he ever caught him.

When Boyd finally *was* caught, in January, 1865, hiding in his father's house, he was out of uniform and had important military papers in his possession. There was a hasty scramble to hang him, he was taken at once to Winchester, and sentenced to death within two days.

Sheridan's interrogators tried to make their prisoner talk, in fear of death; that was, and is, standard operating procedure with prisoners accused of espionage who seem likely to possess useful information. Boyd was offered a reprieve, if he would disclose the route by which Confederate secret agents had been entering Sheridan's lines. But, as this would have meant capture and death for five other spies who had come in along the same route Boyd had been using, he refused and went to Fort McHenry for execution.

From his window, one day, Boyd observed Union soldiers digging a grave and getting a coffin ready. Without any idea that his own death was imminent, he asked a sentry for whom they were meant and was told, "Some d——d rebel spy." The grave was, in fact, his own—or intended to be his—though neither Boyd nor the sentry realized it at the moment. Barely in time, Colonel Ward Hill Lamon, of the Union Army, interceded with President Lincoln, and the sentence was commuted to solitary confinement.

Colonel Boyd lived to a ripe old age as a successful lawyer in Harrisonburg, Virginia, invariably a leader in Confederate veterans' parades and said to be one of the two finest figures on horseback, in a town filled with fine horsemen.

Captain Compton, too, had remained in prison long enough to see the gallows erected for his execution, but had escaped in time. A few days after Compton vanished through the prison roof, the gallows meant for him were used to hang Laypole, in sight of fellow Confederate prisoners, watching gloomily from the cells.

11

SECRETS IN TENNESSEE

The Confederates needed no spies in Tennessee so long as their own army controlled the state. But when, after Grant's victories at Forts Henry and Donelson in February, 1862, they had to evacuate Nashville, Southern espionage began at once; and when the rebels were driven south from Shiloh in early April, still further espionage became necessary. They were then driven out of Corinth, Mississippi, in May and, at New Year's, 1863, out of Murfreesboro, Tennessee, to Tullahoma, far south of Nashville, not far north of the Alabama boundary.

Here, for a time, General Braxton Bragg made a stand, with two of the Confederacy's boldest cavalry leaders protecting his flanks. Nathan Bedford Forrest was on his left (western) flank, at Columbia, Tennessee; John Hunt Morgan on his right (eastern) flank at Liberty. Tennessee, where the two armies faced each other, was a nominally Confederate state, though in fact Northern and Southern sympathies were about equally divided. There had been enough votes to take Tennessee out of the Union. But many a Tennessee boy joined the Union Army; and many a pro-Union civilian was ready to assist the Federals by spying, scouting, guiding refugees, identifying rebel spies, and supplying information.

I

Almost as soon as they had evacuated Nashville, February 25, 1862, the Confederates realized that they needed a better local intelligence organization. There would have been no difficulty in setting one up in Nashville and leaving it behind when they departed—an old, old method which has often produced results. It would have been very easy, before the evacuation, to choose, as resident agents within the town, loyal Confederates who were residents already. These people would have had no need for cover. Their presence was completely accounted for; they had always lived in Nashville. All they had to do was keep quiet—and use their eyes and ears—after the Federals marched in.

Nothing of the sort was done, and the Confederates had scarcely left the city when they found they had left important documents behind. Governor Harris remembered he had thrown into a waste basket in his own office some documents that might compromise five or six men. He contrived to communicate secretly with ex-Governor Neil S. Brown, who laid hands upon the papers. Probably Harris's messenger was M. A. M'Laugherty, who, because of a permanently injured right hand, could not serve in the field and became a permanent secret courier and smuggler of military goods. (On one occasion, he delivered papers from Harris to Brown in the Public Square in Nashville, the two "barely recognizing each other" as they passed.)

An agitated supply officer discovered, at about the same time, that he had left all his vouchers behind. There was nothing for it but to send in another spy, and a military clerk named W. H. Holman volunteered. The Federals quickly caught and jailed him, but he does not seem to have been tried for espionage.

Not long afterward, probably in March, 1862, a Union soldier from Tennessee, Private George H. Morgan, Company A, Hamilton's Brigade, volunteered for this job. Private Morgan went first to a cousin at Sparta, southeast of Nashville, thence to his father's house in Jackson County, a little farther north, then to the home of a minister in Lebanon, directly east of Nashville, and thence into the city itself.

After all these mysterious prowlings, he still found it impossible to get his hands on the vouchers, and it began to seem dangerous to stay much longer in Nashville. But Private Morgan was a persevering individual. He moved across to Edgefield, on the opposite bank of the Cumberland River. There he settled down to wait, while a woman agent, in Nashville, began looking for the missing papers. When she eventually found them, she passed them to Private Morgan, who was able to make his return journey without any trouble at all. It seems to have been the first of many similar exploits.

At about the same time, not more than a week after evacuating Nashville, the Confederate command began to worry about what the Federals might be doing there. General Hardee issued orders to another Morgan—the celebrated cavalry raider, General John Hunt Morgan—to "send a spy into Nashville to see what the enemy is about & especially to bring me some later northern newspapers." Nothing further is known about this, but John Hunt Morgan usually provided exactly the intelligence he was supposed to get.

Three days later, with a small force and a steely glitter in his eye, General Morgan set out in person (March 7, 1862) on a more difficult mission. He proposed to capture a Union general. Any general would do. Morgan wanted his prospective prisoner merely as an exchange for General Simon Bolivar Buckner, whom the Federals had captured when he surrendered Fort Donelson. But no general officer of the Union Army was at the moment near enough the front line to be captured.

Unable to secure the prisoner he wanted, Morgan decided to use a disguise and see if he could get prisoners that way. He and his men put on blue Federal overcoats over their gray Confederate uniforms. These were a sufficient disguise. Little of the trousers was visible—and Confederate uniform regulations called for light blue trousers, anyway.

Morgan found a Federal outpost with a detail of ten men, commanded by a not very bright sergeant. Keeping his pose as a Federal officer, Morgan rebuked the innocent noncom severely for failing to prevent Confederate raids. He then placed the entire detachment under arrest, ordered them to stack arms (an officer or soldier under arrest is at once disarmed), and announced he would report the whole matter to General Ormsby Mitchell, the local Union commander. The disconsolate Federals, though somewhat surprised, nevertheless obeyed orders. By the time they understood what was really happening, they were on their way to Murfreesboro as prisoners.

Though passing himself off as a Federal was a favorite trick of Morgan's, it was not always successful. During a spring raid in 1862, he appeared late one night at Palmetto, a town in southern Middle Tennessee, posing as "Colonel Johnson, U.S.A." Being in blue uniform himself, he apparently hoped no one would examine his men's uniforms—usually nondescript, at best. He might have succeeded, had not a sharp-eyed young girl noticed that neither uniforms nor equipment completely corresponded with the Union Army's or with Morgan's own. Though discomfited, he was able to lead his men to safety.

After he had been promoted to colonel, in early 1863, the raider seems to have given up pranks of this sort, though he still delighted in other trickery, especially fraudulent telegrams.

II

It was not difficult for either side to find scouts who knew the country well and could reconnoiter in comparative safety, even in uniform; but most of these men donned either civilian clothes or the other side's uniforms, when they thought it would help—and thus became spies. The division of sympathies in Tennessee created a special danger. Every one in a given area knew almost everybody else. A local man spying for the Confederacy would be recognized by local Unionists; a spy for the Union might be recognized by Confederates; and a stranger was suspect, *ipso facto*.

All this was still further complicated by a great deal of family, social, amatory, and even gastronomic visiting across the lines. As one of Morgan's troopers remarked, "when the boys learned that there were pretty girls & something good to eat all around them they would take the chance of a fight or a horse race any time to see the one & enjoy the other."

Unromantic counterintelligence men in the Union Army made it their business to learn which girls were receiving visits of this sort —and then watched their houses. So did inquisitive pro-Union neighbors. They also watched homes suspected of harboring Confederate spies, whether sons of the family or mere visitors. But no risks deterred the ardent young soldiers.

The most famous of Confederate spies in Tennessee, Sam Davis, gladly rode an extra secret fifty miles, whenever his intelligence duties brought him within that distance of his home in Smyrna. During these visits, Sam's parents took every precaution to conceal his presence. The boy habitually tethered his horse, War Bonnet, some distance from the house, concealed by a huge boulder (which now bears a bronze tablet). When Sam's signal—a tap on the windowpane—sounded unexpectedly in the night, the Davis family at once put out all lights. Only then did Sam come indoors.

After he had feasted on home cooking, all traces that an extra meal had been served were concealed. Slaves, though usually loyal, might talk. The younger children always stayed in bed, at least pretending to be asleep, till their mother was sure it was safe to call them to see their brother; and they were warned never to mention Sam's visits to anyone, even after he had gone. The parents always feared that Federal counterintelligence might place their home under perpetual surveillance and so, sooner or later, trap their son. But this never happened. It is doubtful if the Federals knew anything at all about him, until at last they captured him by pure luck.

This kind of thing went on all along the line. The famous Maryland secret agent, Walter Bowie, often penetrated the Federal lines for intelligence, recruits, and supplies—but also to call upon his fiancée. A young trooper of the 1st Maryland Cavalry was caught returning to the Confederate Army after a visit to his home in Delaware, a slave state that had not joined the Confederacy. A court-martial sentenced him to death, but his sentence was commuted and he was held as an ordinary prisoner of war. Three soldiers of the same regiment, also condemned, were spared by the merciful Lincoln, though not till they were literally at the foot of the gallows. In another of these cases, Lincoln commuted a death sentence because, as he himself remarked, he "was satisfied from the evidence there was a woman in the case and the conduct of the young man was pardonable."

Romance and gastronomy combined in a nearly fatal adventure near Jackson, Mississippi, when two Confederates visiting behind the lines there left a safe island refuge in Pearl River Bottom, near Jackson, because one of them wanted to see his sweetheart and both of them wanted some of her mother's cooking. They were caught; but one persuaded the Federals he was too frail to be a soldier and the other posed as too stupid to be dangerous—which was not at all the truth.

Sergeant George D. Shadburne, star spy for Hampton's Cavalry, managed to spend an entire two weeks' furlough near Skinker's Ford on the Rappahannock, not far from Fredericksburg, at the home of a widow blessed with two daughters—"beautiful, refined and charming and of a most lovely character." Shadburne had no trouble from the Union soldiers who swarmed around him during his vacation in their midst; and it is not surprising that, as one of his officers remarks, during this two weeks' interlude in wartime, Shadburne's "cup of roseate bliss was nearly full."

When he left, however, Shadburne almost paid with his life for this agreeable fortnight. Everyone in the vicinity asked him to carry letters south. In addition to these mildly incriminating documents, he carried his own diary.

With one companion, he was caught as he passed the lines and taken to a town that seems to have been Fredericksburg. He managed to "faint," near the edge of a sidewalk, and dropped the diary into a gutter, unnoticed. He also got the letters, which his companion was now carrying, and pushed some of them into an adjoining yard, until a dog began to bark. He then hid what he had left under a brick.

He had not, however, been able to get rid of a promissory note, made out to himself, which identified him. Sent to a prison barge in the James River, in manacles—described as "a desperado whose capture had long been desired"—he was able to offer the three Yankee soldiers guarding him $3,000 apiece to release him. Pri-

vates Vandervoort, Holmes, and Glutz manfully resisted temptation, but their incorruptible virtue did very little good. Shadburne
escaped anyhow, without assistance, and saved the money. He
had been able to pick the locks of his own fetters as well as
those of a fellow prisoner, after which he swam ashore, stole a
small boat, and returned to the Blackwater Swamp near Petersburg.

Romantic or homesick youngsters were willing to take desperate
chances. To a soldier in time of war, when each meeting might
be the last, a visit home or to an attractive girl was worth any risk.

Usually, at least. There were occasional disappointments. John
N. Opie, one of Stuart's cavalrymen, rode in broad daylight past a
line of Federal troopers, all blazing away at him on his way to
visit a girl with whom he thought, at the moment, he was in love.
He escaped unharmed; but, to his intense disgust, the lady took
a casual view of her suitor's perils. She spent most of their time
together, which he had very nearly bought with his life, writing
letters for him to take back to others. Opie paid several subsequent calls, almost equally dangerous. But when the same thing
happened each time, Opie looked around for another girl.

Equally reckless was the visit Francis Hawks Govan, one of
Forrest's troopers, paid to his parents at Holly Springs, Mississippi,
in 1862 or 1863. Though Holly Springs was an important Federal
supply base, Govan was not on an intelligence mission. Nevertheless, he found the situation a little awkward when he reached
his father's house, for by this time the Govan family had other
guests. One of them was Ulysses S. Grant, and he had brought
Mrs. Grant with him, to say nothing of a large number of men in
blue uniforms.

Private Govan—a bold youth, or he would not have been riding
with Forrest—knew perfectly well General Grant was living in
the Govan home. He thought, however, that he could get into the
house undetected, even in Confederate uniform, by climbing a
fence or slipping through a back gate after dark. This time, fortune did not favor the brave. A former Govan slave, recognizing
him on the back porch, notified the Federals. The young rebel was
upstairs, chatting with his mother, when a staff officer suddenly
appeared and marched him downstairs to General Grant. The

conversation that followed was written down by a son-in-law, who was sure that it ran just as he heard it from Govan.

"Young man," remonstrated Grant, "what are you doing here within my lines and in the very home I use as my headquarters?"

Perfectly aware that he might be a prisoner of war but that he couldn't possibly be considered a spy, young Govan replied boldly.

"I came, sir, in uniform, merely to see and visit my mother."

"How did you get into my lines?"

"I was reared here and know every path and every street."

"Do you know that it is wrong for you to do this?" (It wasn't wrong, as a matter of fact, but it *was* risky.)

"Yes, sir, but I felt that I must see my mother, and I came in full uniform as a soldier of the South."

Grant turned to his officer: "Take this young soldier back upstairs, and you, young man, remain there with your mother until further orders."

Being a prisoner of war can, of course, be acutely uncomfortable, but not in your mother's custody. Later, the young rebel is said to have dined at the same table with General Grant. Within twenty-four hours, he was given an escort beyond the lines and there set free.

Occasionally, these bold young men added to the risks they ran, out of sheer bravado. Captain Frank Battle, of "Fighting Joe" Wheeler's command, traveled from Tullahoma to his home on Mill Creek, near Nashville, to see his mother, sister, and sweetheart. It was a very satisfactory home leave until he made up his mind to enter Nashville with the sweetheart, to "see what the Yankees were doing"—a visit that might easily have gotten him hanged. (That it might have gotten the girl hanged, too, seems to have occurred to neither.)

Being slender, young Captain Battle could wear his mother's and sister's dresses easily, and he was also able to keep his voice high enough to avoid suspicion. Carrying passes issued to his aunt and mother, only two weeks before, authorizing them to enter Nashville, the Confederate officer and the lady reached the Federal picket line, only to find that the Federals were no longer honoring any passes at all. The girl, however, was carrying several bottles of wine for a sick aunt in the city. One of these she sacrificed to make glad the heart of the officer of the guard, who gratefully let the pair through the picket line, regardless of orders.

After that, all went well, until a Union Army wagoner accidentally backed against their buggy. Forgetting to behave like a lady, Captain Battle blasted the man with some strong language, which should have roused suspicion but did not. (It is perhaps true, as has occasionally been hinted, that some Southern belles had vocabularies rather more robust than the moonlight-and-roses tradition suggests.)

Having visited their Nashville relatives, the apparently feminine pair drove peacefully home, carrying a bundle of newspapers—which the Confederate command later found most interesting.

One of the most unpleasant experiences any young rebel had, during one of these innocent calls upon girls within the enemy lines, fell to Samuel Burke, 20th Tennessee. While spending a furlough surreptitiously at home within the Union lines, Burke went to see a Miss Cherry, whose home was a few miles from Triune. Pro-Union neighbors passed word to the Federal command at Franklin. Yankee cavalry appeared, forced one "Cupe" Burke—certainly not in the role of Cupid—to guide them to the Cherry home.

Samuel Burke, knowing the girl was in no danger, withdrew to the second floor and fired at the first head that came up the stair—which belonged to the unfortunate "Cupe," who had a Federal pistol at his back. Realizing by this time that his date was not going to be a conspicuous success, Sam Burke prudently slid down a rope, reached the ground, and vanished. Love will find a way, however. Sam persevered in his rudely interrupted courtship and eventually wed the lady.

Young men willing to accept such risks without orders were, of course, unusually bold and occasionally got into trouble through sheer deviltry. In early 1864, a group of four Confederates slipped through the lines, not far from Smyrna, Tennessee, "to see the homefolks." Everything went well until, on their way back to their own army, the quartet, chancing to see some seventy-five Union soldiers on the Smyrna road, decided to attack them! Their hope was to deceive the Federals into thinking they were part of a larger force and thus frighten them long enough to seize their teams and wagons. The result was about what one might expect at odds of seventy-five to four. The gay young rebels barely escaped with their lives.

Not all Federal troops were so lacking in cordiality to visiting Confederates. A detachment of about forty Union Home Guards met a Confederate group in broad daylight on the road near Triune, Tennessee. At two hundred yards, their commander, going forward under a flag of truce, ascertained that the enemy were merely on a visit home to get new socks, underwear, breeches, and something to eat. The two detachments made a strictly unofficial private armistice of their own, for two weeks!

Occasionally, spies ran extra risks out of pure good nature, carrying personal letters or gifts, though every document and every article added to their peril. One of General Bragg's girl spies, operating out of Kentucky into Tennessee, carried the sword and spurs of Major Frank M. Gailor, killed at Perryville, October 8, 1862, to his widow in Memphis. The spurs were no problem, but the sword was an awkward object for a lady to conceal on her person and would be very hard to explain if discovered. It was easier, however, for a lady in a hoop skirt than it would be for a damsel in modern dress. (It has been alleged, by people who had every chance to know, that a Southern girl who was really in earnest about what she was doing could conceal an entire uniform— boots included!—under her hoop skirt, without rousing Yankee suspicion.) General Bragg's intrepid young female spy, whose name is unknown, tied the sword "around her waist under her hoop" and clanked through the Federal lines undetected.

When Federal occupation authorities later found the weapon in the widow's possession, they confiscated it. Mrs. Gailor went to the local Union commander, General Charles C. Washburn.

"If you were to be killed tomorrow you would like your wife to have your sword."

"Of course you can have that sword," said the gallant general.

This same Confederate lady later smuggled intelligence to Forrest in preparation for his raid on Memphis, in which the chivalrous General Washburn barely escaped capture.

III

Perhaps the first espionage mission into Nashville by a young girl was undertaken to oblige one of Morgan's lieutenants, whom she had probably known while the Confederates occupied the city. The two famous daredevils, Morgan and Forrest, planned a sudden joint attack on the city. Morgan was to move in from the rebels' extreme right (eastern) flank, Forrest from the extreme left (western) flank. If rebel cavalry, coming from east and west at the same time, suddenly attacked Nashville, anything might happen. But no one knew exactly what the Federals were doing. (They were, in fact, planning to attack Morgan that day or the next.) Neither did anyone know how strong the Federals were.

Someone would have to enter the captured city and find out. Morgan sent Lieutenant George C. Ridley. His orders were to ride, with ten picked men, on the route Liberty–Alexandria–Lebanon–Goodlettsville, getting as near Edgefield (just across the river from Nashville) as he could, without causing alarm. At that point he was to halt and send in a spy.

General Morgan probably meant the lieutenant to disguise one of his own men and send him into the city, but Lieutenant Ridley knew a trick worth two of that. Also—like any normal lieutenant—he knew a girl.

Taking his command quietly across the Cumberland River at Payne's Ferry, the scheming lieutenant soon found a "trusty young lady." This plucky female rebel set out valiantly for Nashville, while the soldiers "scattered in the vicinity"—probably to their own homes. Within twelve hours, the "trusty young lady" returned with complete plans of the field fortifications around Nashville, plus an exact strength report, and the precise location of every Union regiment or battery. Since no one ever gathered military intelligence on that scale in twelve hours, it is plain that rebel spies in Nashville had already been at work for some time and had prepared reports in advance.

Once he had secured the intelligence he had come for, Ridley and his exultant cavalry struck out for the town of Liberty, where they had left Morgan. But they suddenly encountered a much larger force of Federal cavalry, also on their way to Liberty. The Federals, too, were looking for Morgan.

Lieutenant Ridley's secret orders covered just such a contingency. If cut off from his own lines, he was to return southwest instead of southeast and report to Forrest instead of Morgan. Approaching Columbia, he came to a Williamson County village then known as Snatch, now called Peytonville.

Not quite sure where he was, but certain he was near the enemy, Lieutenant Ridley sent his orderly-sergeant to the nearest house to ask for a guide. The woman who came to the door regarded him askance. There was no man there to guide him.

She was lying and the sergeant knew it. As he had approached, he had seen a man about the place. He and his men were, he assured her, "Rebel scouts" trying to reach Columbia. The woman persisted in her tale. When the lieutenant himself appeared, she repeated it. The lieutenant was firm. He had to have a guide and he, too, had seen a man at the house. The door slammed in his face. From within, he heard the defiant lady call:

"Ring the bell and blow the horn!"

Instantly the big farm dinner bell sounded, while from the second-floor porch a girl began blowing a horn "like an old-time chicken peddler." In the stillness of the darkening countryside, the noise could be heard for miles; but Lieutenant Ridley, a determined, though still courteous, young man, shouted through the door:

"Madam, we are not to be frightened in this way; the guide must come."

The clangor of the bell, the blasts from the horn, continued. The invisible ladies within the house remained adamant. The scouts were still arguing, when down the road came the drumming of many hoofs. Then shots. Horsemen charged down on the surprised and alarmed Confederates. A whole company seemed to be attacking. However that may have been—it is easy to exaggerate numbers in a night attack—their assailants sounded, acted, and shot like a force much too large for Ridley's. The lieutenant and his men rode for their lives, while the air around them buzzed venomously with bullets.

For the next two hours, there was a running fire fight, in which no one seems to have been seriously hurt. (Shooting at half-visible men in the dark, when both marksmen and targets are going full speed on galloping horses, is not at all like target practice.) In the end, Ridley escaped into a woods and let the pursuit gallop past.

The Confederates were now without guide, without food, without shelter, and still completely lost, with no idea where Columbia and Forrest's headquarters might be. A dim light showed in a farm-house. They knocked. From within, another feminine voice:

"Who's that?"

"Madam, we are Rebel soldiers trying to get to Columbia; we are lost and want a guide."

"No guide here! Poke your head in that door, and I'll blow your brains out!" replied this inhospitable Southern matron.

"Madam, we must have a guide, and if you don't open the door, we will have to break it down."

"Marth' Ann," cried the irate woman behind the door, "ring that bell."

Martha Ann—whoever she was—obeyed.

Again a brazen clangor burst upon the Tennessee night. Again hoofbeats sounded on the road. Again there was a burst of shots. Again the Confederates rode for their lives, their lieutenant pain-fully aware that Generals Morgan and Forrest were both in dire need of the information he was carrying, and that the prospect of their ever getting it seemed increasingly remote. Again Lieutenant Ridley and his men shook off their pursuers—after about two hours.

When morning came, they met, at last, a friend of the lieutenant's, who was trying to get back to Union-held territory secretly, after visiting a son in the Confederate Army. This man told them that they were on the right road to Columbia. Then a scout asked "what they meant down there at 'Snatch' by ringing bells and blowing horns," and the truth came out: It was not always easy to tell the armies apart. Federal uniforms by this time were likely to be faded, worn, and stained. Confederates habitually wore Federal overcoats whenever they could get them, and their own uniforms were fre-quently nondescript. Ordinary bushwhackers might be on either side or might be mere ruffians intent wholly on plunder. They might be wearing Confederate uniform, Federal uniform, or almost anything else. In emergencies, all neighbors turned out shooting, whenever they heard the bell and horn signals. They did not inquire which side they were shooting at; they simply commenced shooting.

Ridley's hapless Confederates had been chased by Confederate sympathizers all night long.

Ridley found Forrest at last, turned in his documents, and started to rejoin Morgan, who was now at McMinnville, some distance southeast of Liberty. He had probably been forced back by the same Federal troops Ridley's little command had stumbled upon the day before.

Still the adventures of the lieutenant and his horsemen were not quite over. The scouts scattered, about sundown, to look for food, as they expected to be riding the rest of the night. The lieutenant and Sergeant Seth Corley, waiting on the road between Eagleville and Shelbyville, saw a horseman in civilian clothes riding down a lane.

They stopped him. Where was he going? "About ten miles above there to see some of his people." His speech didn't seem quite right. The drawl of rural Tennessee is unmistakable, and this fellow's accent was "not that of a Southern man." Sergeant Corley noted also that the stranger was riding a horse branded "U.S." with a U.S. Cavalry saddle. That was not in itself suspicious. So did many a Confederate soldier. But why was a civilian riding one?

By this time the others, well fed, were returning from the neighboring farms. Lieutenant Ridley, with his men again assembled, decided to search the stranger's saddlebags.

The clothing there was not quite what normal civilians carry. In one saddlebag was a Confederate captain's uniform; in the other, a Federal major's. It did begin to seem a little doubtful which side the man was on. Nor was it easy to believe he was merely paying a visit to friends. He was within the Confederate lines, or dangerously near them, and he didn't seem quite sure which of his two uniforms he ought to be wearing. Nor could he explain why he wasn't wearing either.

Lieutenant Ridley and his men took him along as a prisoner, first seizing the two revolvers he was carrying—rather heavy armament for a peaceful civilian. But Ridley was not acquainted with the ancient trick of wearing large, visible, and impressive pistols where they can be seen, meantime depending, in real emergencies, on a small one concealed in a pocket or elsewhere, to be unexpectedly produced. This man had three pistols, not two, as Ridley thought.

After the prisoner and his guards had ridden a few miles, they reached a dark woodland. Here the mysterious stranger suddenly drew a derringer and fired—almost in Ridley's face. Though the bullet pierced his hat and not his head, the lieutenant was irritated. He brought down the Union spy with a single shot, while the Confederate troopers fired from the rear.

When one of the rebel scouts pulled off the stranger's boots—the Confederate Army, always badly shod, was always looking for footgear—he found more evidence against the dead man. Between the lining and the outer leather were orders from Federal headquarters in Nashville. He was a spy, on his way to Shelbyville and Tullahoma (Bragg's headquarters) to examine roads and find out Confederate strength.

IV

Though the name of the young lady who went into Nashville as Lieutenant Ridley's courier has never been revealed, she may have been any one of a number of girl spies, living on farms not far outside the city. Few of these girls were ever caught by the Federals, whom they happily "dated" and gaily deceived for years.

Thanks to this feminine assistance, General Morgan's intelligence operations usually worked more smoothly than Lieutenant Ridley's calamitous (though ultimately successful) reconnoissance. Morgan's successful raid of December 7, 1862, which completely surprised the hapless Federals at Hartsville, Tennessee, was made possible by a chain of civilian volunteer couriers, whose success was determined, at the most critical moment, by a young girl in a sunbonnet.

A Federal brigade, commanded by a certain Colonel C. B. Moore, who was not nearly careful enough about reconnoissance, occupied the town of Hartsville, which lies northeast of Nashville. A civilian named John Hinton had for some time, with the assistance of friends, been watching Moore's troops, knowing (or guessing) that Morgan might intend to raid them. By pooling their observations, Hinton and the others were able to work out an adequate report on the strength and disposition of the Federals, after which the next problem was to get the information safely to Morgan.

Hinton took it through the Union picket lines, but, fearing that he might be seized with the documents on his person, hesitated to make the entire journey to Morgan's camp. Stopping at the home of a widow named Kirby, about four miles from Hartsville, he explained his problem. Mrs. Kirby's daughter, sixteen or eighteen years old, sewed the papers in her sunbonnet and rode off to see an uncle, two miles farther on, along the Cumberland River. Thence her cousin, a boy of ten or twelve, took the papers the rest of the way.

Twenty-four hours later, fully informed, knowing exactly where to attack and how many Union soldiers he would find, Morgan swept down upon the hapless Colonel Moore, captured the entire brigade, including the colonel himself, and was safely off before the startled Federals in Nashville could send relief.

It was a perfect example of how dangerous a very small group of spies can be, to even a very large force. Proper counterintelligence measures, or even adequate use of patrols, by Colonel Moore would have saved the entire brigade and might even have made it possible to trap the raiders.

Many Tennessee girls gave assistance of this sort. In Savannah, well to the south of Nashville, dwelt a family named Irwin, which included three sons (at least two of whom were in the Confederate Army) and five daughters, between the ages of fourteen and twenty-three, reported as "very beautiful." Though all maidens were described as lovely in that genteel era, these girls certainly had all the charm that espionage requires. Before long, they had so bewitched an unidentified newspaper correspondent that he was furnishing "full information of General Halleck's movements, to be given to Beauregard."

It was easy to pass on information wheedled out of the lovelorn journalist, since Savannah was close to the route used by Confederate secret couriers. General Halleck, furious when he learned what was happening, expelled all correspondents from camp.

One of the most daring of these Tennessee girls was Mary Overall, living with her sister, Sophia Overall, her mother and her stepfather, John A. Jordan, at Triune. Mary was about nineteen and—according to her future husband, the extraordinary spy and saboteur, Captain John W. Headley—"an enthusiastic Southern girl." Headley was one of the Confederates who had managed to escape from Fort Donelson before Grant forced its surrender in 1862. On the way south he had spent a little time in a house where Mary Overall and her mother were also guests. The pair may have been previously acquainted. They were certainly very much in love before very long and were married soon after the war.

Sometime in 1863, probably rather early in the year, Morgan sent Headley to collect military intelligence, preparatory to an attack on Nashville. Headley was instructed to begin by paying a secret visit to Ned Jordan, who lived near the village of Triune, close enough to the city to be well informed. Jordan was the son of Dr. Clem Jordan and brother of Mary Overall's stepfather. The whole family were living in the doctor's house.

Though Mary Overall may not yet have become an outright spy, she knew all the right people and just where to go for accurate military information.

As secret missions go, this one of Headley's was rather easy, since the nearest Federal garrisons were at Murfreesboro and Franklin, fairly close to Mary's house. Headley simply rode down the "pike," reached Dr. Jordan's at one o'clock in the morning, and began to discuss with Ned Jordan the best way of getting secretly into Nashville.

Mysterious callers arriving in the middle of the night were no novelty in wartime Tennessee, but Headley had made noise enough to wake the household. He heard women talking upstairs, then the words: "That is Headley's voice." Presently Mary Overall and her mother joined the conference.

Let Headley go into Nashville himself? Definitely dangerous. The two women had a much better plan. Mary, her sister, and a friend named Lucy King would enter the town, where they were well known. Their friend, "Dr. Hunter, in a drug store," would soon collect all the information Headley needed.

Meantime, they turned Headley out of the house. Southern hospitality was all very well, but no private home in Tennessee was safe for a man on such an errand as his. Headley bivouacked in a convenient brierpatch on a ridge about a mile from the pike, keeping a lookout from a wooded hill. Here the younger Jordan visited him from time to time—probably as little as possible for safety's sake. Headley took meals at two adjoining houses, one of them the Cherry farm where "Cupe" Burke was killed.

DeWitt ("Dee") Jobe, another Confederate spy, whose home was in Middle Tennessee and who also was staying away from his friends' houses by night, joined him in the hide-out there. Next day, Jobe was off on his intelligence assignment again, but Headley had to lurk in his brierpatch nearly a week before Mary Overall had completed arrangements for her Nashville visit. The time and care she took in planning helps explain why the numerous girl spies in Tennessee were so rarely caught. Cover was well prepared before they went out on a mission.

Whatever Mary's arrangements may have been, they made entry into occupied Nashville very simple. The Overall sisters and Lucy King went to visit a certain Mrs. Angie Claude at Flat Rock, three miles from Nashville. The other two girls probably knew exactly what Mary was doing; and Mrs. Claude's son-in-law, one Henry Tanksley, who drove their carriage, was an old hand at military intelligence.

The Federals saw nothing suspicious in such a visit. It was natural for the girls to visit relatives. It was equally natural for Tanksley to drive a carriage for his mother-in-law's guests. It was probably no accident that, when Mary Overall reached Nashville, two of Tanksley's nieces had been invited to Fort Negley by Federal officers. Would the visitors like to join the party? They would—for this was an important part of the Federal defenses.

While the girl spies were observing Fort Negley, Tanksley was moving quietly about Nashville, securing information, most of which seems to have dealt with Federal strong points. The group brought Headley so much information that he felt prepared to "guide Morgan into the city on one hand and out on the other." To supplement this, Mary brought additional "information in detail." Headley lingered to verify his facts—perhaps also to spend a little time with Mary; but he sent on a report, unsigned because he knew his handwriting was identification enough. He could justify lingering in pleasant society, for it brought him "additional information, all of which corresponded with that furnished by Miss Overall and Mr. Tanksley."

Eventually the counterintelligence of the Union Army caught up with Mary, who, however keen an observer she may have been, was untrained, impulsive—and nineteen. Her troubles started when a rebel courier named Trammel, on his way south with espionage reports, was killed by Union cavalry at War Trace, south of Murfreesboro. Papers found on his body were sent to General Robert H. Milroy, then commanding defenses of the Nashville & Chattanooga Railroad. This was in late 1864 or early 1865. Among the papers, Milroy found a spy's report signed "Mollie." At this moment Mrs. Dollie Battle, whose husband had been killed at Shiloh, and her daughter Sallie, arrived on horseback, either to ask for Trammel's body or to make sure it received proper burial.

"Dollie" sounded a good deal like "Mollie." Milroy at once accused the Battle ladies of having written the "Mollie" letter and also of having supplied a horse to a spy named Houton, or Van Houton, of whom nothing else is known. Both were arrested and repeatedly interrogated.

Finally, when Mary Overall learned what was happening, she wrote to the Union command in Nashville that she was the much-sought Mollie. But her courage—though it got Mary herself into trouble immediately—did the Battle women no good at all; General Milroy simply put Mary in prison too. By this time, however, it was May of 1865. Lee had surrendered at Appomattox. The Confederacy was dead. Mary Overall took the oath of allegiance and got out of jail. Mrs. and Miss Battle were held in prison two weeks longer, then simply released. They even got their horses back!

Three other maidens, dwelling a few miles from Nashville, were equally useful in Confederate espionage. One was Miss Robbie Woodruff, a Mississippi girl whose mother had settled on a farm about ten miles outside the city, who used to go peacefully into town, collect rebel secret dispatches, and, in equal peace, depart with them. Her success was not hampered by the fact that she was extremely attractive.

Following an age-old secret service method, Robbie Woodruff dropped her documents in a duly designated hollow tree, stump, or log—the letter drop apparently changed from time to time—and then went quietly home. The regular Confederate couriers, who always knew where to look, picked up the dispatches at their leisure; and neither Miss Woodruff nor any courier so far as is known was ever caught or even suspected.

Hand in glove with Robbie Woodruff were the Misses Ann and Kate Patterson, the daughters of two physicians, who dwelt a few hundred yards apart on the Nashville Turnpike. Dr. Everand Mead Patterson had helped plan Confederate espionage; and his wife and daughter Ann were extremely active in assisting rebel scouts and spies, whenever opportunity offered. Kate Patterson was the daughter of Dr. Hugh Patterson, whose share in secret service can now only be guessed at, though he certainly had the Confederate sympathies of the rest of the family. His prominence as a Mason was of great help to his daughter in extracting small but important favors from guileless Yankees. As she had been at school in Nashville when the war began, Miss Kate had many useful acquaintances there, who could help gather information. She was further assisted in smuggling supplies by a false bottom, permanently installed in her buggy. Her sister and Robbie Woodruff were also active spies, and Mrs. Everand Patterson lent a vigorous hand upon occasion.

Mrs. Patterson, Kate Patterson, and Robbie Woodruff, together, on December 24, 1862, decoyed a Federal spy into the Patterson house, while Private Richard H. Adams, Jr., 51st Alabama Cavalry, and one Jake McCain, a Texas soldier, lurked in hiding, and a third Confederate kept their horses ready (and invisible) at a safe distance.

The ladies had had plentiful experience in this kind of thing. They had long made a practice of signaling messages from a designated window to watching Confederate agents. In the daytime, if Federal agents were in the vicinity, they drew the blind. At night, they opened the blind and put a light in the same window, to convey the same warning. Cautious rebels, watching from afar, could govern themselves accordingly.

The alert girls were quick to spot "a certain individual" who claimed to be a cattle buyer. He appeared in the countryside around Nashville far more frequently than was natural, if livestock purchases were his only aim. Besides, he was never accompanied by any cows! At best, he seemed "rather mysterious," and the Pattersons thought it odd that he always appeared just before, or during, Federal troop movements. His pose as a cattle buyer made a good excuse for prowling about farmhouses and examining the terrain between them.

Besides, the fellow asked too many questions. Not, it may be said, that asking did him much good. The girls, by this time thoroughly suspicious, always answered him obligingly; but their answers were regrettably lacking in candor. Said that admiring Confederate, Private Richard H. Adams, "the best strategists could hardly have shaped answers more calculated to mislead."

While supplying false information to the Union Army, the two Confederate sirens kept Adams and the other Confederate spies and spy-catchers fully informed of the comings and goings of the mysterious cattle buyer. But all this plotting did very little good. Again and again the Confederates tried to trap him; always the elusive Yankee evaded their snares.

Finally, on December 24, 1862 (a date that suggests the Federal spy was part of the network that General Grenville M. Dodge was then slowly extending through the whole Confederacy), at about four o'clock "in the evening" (the usual Southern word for afternoon), Privates Adams and McCain approached the Patterson farm. "The signal being all right," they went cautiously up to the house itself, where they found Mrs. Patterson and at least two of the girls —possibly all three, though Adams does not mention Kate.

Adams took the further precaution of entering by the less conspicuous back door and leaving McCain outside on guard. "The young ladies" met him with the news that the suspected Federal had been "out the evening before and that morning." They also reported "what they had seen and heard"—probably the movements of other Yankee scouts and patrols or possibly larger troop movements.

At that moment, McCain, on watch outside, reported that a man was coming across a field "to the right and somewhat to the rear of the house." While the Confederate soldiers kept under cover, the girls peeked out.

They identified the approaching stranger at once. This was the "very man." He was sure to stop at the Patterson house again, "as he pretended to be anxious to buy a fat cow from Mrs. P." As he came closer, Adams and McCain climbed into the loft of a log kitchen adjoining the Patterson dining room. The third Confederate, with the horses, was under cover already, so that he roused no suspicion.

The stranger appeared at the door, asking for food—a natural enough request in that hospitable land. The delighted Adams and McCain listened with interest as he explained that he was exhausted after watching Confederate movements all day. This seems to have been his first admission of what he was really doing.

"From his conversation," said the listening Adams, "he seemed to drop the occupation of cattle buyer—as the army was advancing and he had frequently outwitted us."

Mrs. Patterson helpfully remarked that she had seen Adams (whose name she gave) and four other Confederates "out that morning." To dispel the luckless Federal's possible doubts completely, the guileful matron added that she thought Adams "came from the direction of Nashville and seemed well informed." Adams and his party had been "going in the direction of Lavergne," a town about halfway between Nashville and Murfreesboro, in which Kate Patterson would eventually live as Mrs. Kyle.

Having kept the Federal busy listening to her chat while she cooked, Mrs. Patterson now placed before him a "nice meal" which was quite enough to occupy a hungry man for some time.

While the ladies thus kept the Yankee's attention, the two Confederates climbed down from the loft. Adams moved silently, but McCain made a little noise. No matter. One of the girls promptly smashed a large dish, while Mrs. Patterson loudly complained that now her "last dish was done," meantime overturning a chair to make a little more noise. Given this opportunity, the two Confederates slipped into the dining room with their pistols drawn and still unobserved by the hungry Yankee, who at the moment was mainly interested in Southern home cooking—all the more so because he had had nothing to eat since the night before.

Suddenly, the poor wretch found two steel muzzles at his head. A stern voice told him to unbuckle his belt and let his own arms fall. Even though seated with his legs under the table, quite unable to resist, the man delayed, explaining coolly "that he was a farmer and did not wish to be disturbed at his meal." Tapping him on the head with cold metal, Adams told him again to drop the belt. This time he complied. While Adams kept him covered, McCain pulled it away along the floor, noting, with glee, holsters containing "two beautiful Colt Army pistols."

Search of the prisoner's person revealed suspicious papers. Meanwhile the women, "as a blind," were loudly complaining at such treatment of their guest. But, in spite of their (quite insincere) protests, the victim was tied up and hustled away.

The Confederate intelligence officers who received the prisoner pronounced him a valuable find. The papers he was carrying were in a clever code, which made them seem like the ordinary notations any cattle buyer would make. More closely examined, they revealed the positions and strength of Confederate troops.

The spy was hurried off to higher headquarters, probably Bragg's; and, though there is no record of his fate, there is not much doubt what it was, for General Bragg was a harsh soldier, the only Confederate officer ever known to have sentenced a woman spy to death. He was not likely to show any special mercy to a male Yankee spy, caught *flagrante delicto.*

12

TRAGEDY IN TENNESSEE:
COLEMAN'S SCOUTS

When General Braxton Bragg took command of the Army of Tennessee in 1862, his intelligence service was at first under command of Colonel J. Stoddard Johnson, a Virginian, who at once began organizing espionage networks, mostly amateur but very active, in various parts of the theater of operations. Before long, however, he handed the whole problem over to General Benjamin F. Cheatham, a Tennessean widely acquainted with the people and the country around Nashville.

I

Ordered to set up an intelligence system, Cheatham turned to local people whom he knew he could trust. One of the first men he consulted was a certain Alfred H. Douglas, about whom not much is known, and John G. Davis, elder half-brother of the future spy, Sam Davis—at that time still unknown—and of Oscar Davis, still a mere boy, who from time to time undertook secret missions that an adult could scarcely have accomplished. Cheatham also consulted Dr. Everand Mead Patterson, a local physician who had joined the

Confederate cavalry while his wife, son, and daughter took an active hand in secret service. The Davis and Patterson families were connected by more than espionage: John G. Davis became the husband of Kate Patterson, daughter of Dr. Hugh Patterson, whose house stood near that of his brother, the other Dr. Patterson.

Very late in 1862 or 1863, Douglas and John G. Davis were sent to report on Union forces in Nashville, which Bragg's volunteer agents had not fully studied.

In view of their practical experience, Cheatham consulted both men, before appointing Captain Henry B. Shaw to command the proposed new intelligence unit, after which the three together selected other personnel. The captain was a former steamboat owner, approximately forty years of age. Since his home was in Nashville, he had "superior advantages for obtaining information & Northern Papers." Of these advantages he had already been making full use for some time. He had begun by supplying information to General Earl Van Dorn in Mississippi, had later been an intelligence agent for Generals Forrest and Wheeler, in and about La Vergne, Tennessee, southeast of Nashville, and was closely associated with the Davis family. Both Sam and Oscar Davis were his trusted agents, while John G. Davis became his business partner as soon as the war ended. (The two were killed together by the exploding boiler of a steamboat, which they jointly owned.)

Shaw reports that, on April 2, 1863, some time before Bragg actually assumed command in Tennessee, he was told to organize "a company of scouts composed of men from various commands who were familiar with the country & well acquainted with the people." A fellow spy says that Sam Davis was detached from the 1st Tennessee Infantry to Shaw's group "about the middle of April."

Because he died on the gallows, refusing to save his life by betraying his fellow soldiers, Davis has become the best known of the group—better known, indeed, than Shaw himself. But the brave youngster was one of at least forty-five scouts and secret agents in Shaw's band, all specially chosen, all brave, and all devoted to their cause.

This figure is probably too small, since many of these men must have vanished without a trace, as spies do. It is true that four veterans of the band, engaged in reminiscences after the war was over, set the probable total as low as thirty and thought that Captain Shaw, in an emergency, "could gather about fifteen good men." But this very low figure does not allow for couriers en route to Bragg and others resting in the safety of the Confederate lines, after the exhaustion of a secret mission. Shaw himself seems to have avoided keeping records—as is wise, in a service such as his. It is also possible that the whole forty-five were never in service at the same time. Some may have been added to the roster later, replacing men who had been captured, killed in skirmishes, or executed.

It is possible, too, that some of the Confederate spies cooperating with Shaw's group really belonged to other intelligence organizations. Thomas F. Martin, Company I, 11th Tennessee Cavalry, who had been detached by General Joseph Wheeler as an "independent" scout, appears to have been one such man. Martin worked in cordial cooperation with Sam Davis and Polk English, whose uncle's farm provided one of the secret bases for Shaw's men. When these three were out on a mission together, one of them usually carried back their reports—probably no farther than the base where Captain Shaw happened to be—while the other two remained in observation.

Though Shaw, Douglas, and John Davis were careful to select as their secret agents, whenever possible, young men whose homes were in Middle Tennessee, Shaw himself brought in a few with special qualifications, from outside the state. One of these was Sergeant Richard B. Anderson, from a Texas regiment.

Texan or not, the sergeant soon knew Middle Tennessee and Mississippi as well as any native. During the cavalry fighting along the Mississippi, General Van Dorn had begun using him as a "private scout" (plainly a euphemism for the espionage in which Anderson was actually engaged). As Shaw had also been spying for Van Dorn during this period, it is clear enough why Sergeant Anderson was drawn into his group. Shaw undoubtedly knew exactly what Anderson had been doing, before he brought him to Tennessee.

There is not much doubt that Anderson was the unnamed agent whom Van Dorn sent into Holly Springs, Mississippi, before his raid of December 20, 1862, because the man knew the town "like the back of his hand." Van Dorn had learned—and this information can have come only from spies—that Grant was collecting enormous quantities of supplies there; and he proposed to block his advance against Vicksburg by destroying those supplies. But first he had to have reliable information from inside Holly Springs.

That Van Dorn selected Sergeant Anderson for a secret mission of such importance indicates that the sergeant was already an experienced agent. He was to examine the Federal base, ascertaining troop strength and dispositions. After accomplishing this successfully and prowling about among the Federal troops for some hours, Anderson, on his way back, met Van Dorn's advancing column and gave him the welcome news that the Federals had no suspicions and all was quiet in Holly Springs. Some spy, probably Anderson himself, even reported that they "were preparing a grand ball."

At five o'clock on the morning of December 20, Van Dorn thundered into town at the head of 5,000 cavalry, capturing huge quantities of supplies and ammunition together with hundreds of Union soldiers—not to mention Mrs. Ulysses S. Grant, to protect whom the gallant Confederates immediately posted a special guard. (The incident is not so unusual as it seems. Both Mrs. Lee and Mrs. Beauregard were, at one time or another, in Federal hands and were treated with the same courtesy.)

Van Dorn died in May, 1863, shot, not by a Union soldier but by a jealous Southern husband. Apparently Anderson joined Captain Shaw and his merry men in Middle Tennessee immediately after Van Dorn's death.

Most clandestine organizations of this sort took their names from their leaders, but this group was never—or almost never—called Shaw's Scouts. Because Captain Shaw's *nom de guerre* was "Colman," or "Coleman," his devoted band were always known as Coleman's Scouts.

II

When the organization of Coleman's Scouts was completed, Shaw had under his command a group of fearless youngsters, who, in view of the nature of their services, must all have been volunteers. They almost had to be volunteers. No matter what advantages their local associations and their intimate knowledge of the country gave them, theirs was always desperate and dangerous work, as was that of their Federal opponents. (Stringfellow once told a friend that he had never expected to come back alive from *any* of his missions.) One of Shaw's agents remarked that he would rather go into ten battles than on even one intelligence mission. "The secret service men were braver than the average soldier," said Union General Dodge; and, in view of his known admiration for Sam Davis, there is no doubt he meant the agents of both armies.

At least eleven of Shaw's group were captured, including Shaw himself. Sam Davis was executed. Richard Dillard and DeWitt ("Dee") Jobe were killed as helpless prisoners for refusing to give information. After Jobe's death, "Dee" (presumably also DeWitt) Smith, a kinsman, swore never to take another Federal prisoner and himself slaughtered about fifty Federal soldiers in revenge. Badly wounded and captured at last, he was condemned to hang, but died of his wounds before the date set for his execution. Everand Patterson was court-martialed and sentenced to death, but escaped. Samuel Patterson received a death sentence, but he, too, escaped—in company with a Union soldier, who was also under death sentence and didn't like the idea. Joshua Luck, sent before a court-martial, was acquitted. Thomas M. Joplin, after capture, was "stolen from Nashville" by Ann Patterson—a tale that would be worth the telling, if the facts could be recovered.

The perils of the scouts were fully justified by the immense importance of the information they brought. When Bragg fought at Chickamauga, he had full information on Union strength and even knew where the Federals would cross the river. On the morning of September 21, 1863, the day after the battle, Sam Davis and another scout named Will Hughes came into Shaw's command post near Nashville, after penetrating into the city itself. News had been received there that the Union troops in Chickamauga itself were demoralized and that General Rosecrans, in local Federal command, had admitted he was at the mercy of the rebels. The usual courier line through Decatur, Alabama, having been cut, Anderson and one companion, who had come in early the night before, were ordered to carry this information to Bragg as best they could. They reached his headquarters after riding 120 miles in thirty-six hours, without changing horses.

After this, Bragg, for some reason, ordered Shaw to move his intelligence men back to the main army. It immediately became apparent that this was a blunder, and they soon returned to the vicinity of Nashville.

Sergeant Anderson probably does not exaggerate when he says that "Bragg knew every move his opponent made. He knew who commanded every brigade in the enemy's army; he knew how much artillery and its calibre. After the battle of Stones River [Murfreesboro] he knew what loss the enemy sustained and was advised to push his victory, which, however, he failed to do."

The disgusted sergeant was probably also right in feeling that Bragg habitually failed to make proper use of the abundant military intelligence the spies provided. After Chickamauga, said he, "the great wonder to us was that he did not capture all of the Federal forces there. He waited on Missionary Ridge and waited until Sherman marched through from Memphis with a big army and left General Dodge in Pulaski with ten thousand men to prevent Bragg's scouts from keeping tab on all he was doing."

Though the main reason for the success of Coleman's Scouts was their own courage and determination and the skill of their leader, there were other reasons for their success. Their greatest advantage was that they were operating in country with which they were entirely familiar. "Dee" Jobe was said to know "every private road through all the hills between the pikes from Triune and Murfreesboro." The same thing could have been said of most men in this special group. Coleman's Scouts were frequently in dire need of "private" roads, their business usually being of a very private nature, for which ordinary roads were dangerous, even by night.

Operating mainly in their native state, near their own or friends' homes, Shaw's men were always sure of food, shelter, and—if they needed it—concealment. They also knew where to find more or less informally organized local networks of men and women, especially young girls, ever alert for military intelligence and always willing to enter Federal camps, forts, or garrisons, posing as harmless local residents and already on friendly terms with the Yankees.

In spite of these advantages, Confederate soldiers assigned to secret intelligence were in constant danger of exposure. Pro-Union neighbors did a good deal of amateur counterespionage, watching the houses of known Southern sympathizers on whose farms there were any signs of unusual activity. The spies had to be specially careful not to bring the people who were helping them under suspicion. They visited farmhouses for food but did not linger, usually retiring to the woods or to convenient cornfields and brier-patches for the night. If the danger was great, they did not risk visits to the farmhouses even for food. Women and young boys brought it to their hiding places. They left their horses hidden at a safe distance in the woods, lest hostile neighbors notify the Yankees or overcurious Yankee patrols find strange mounts in a farmer's stable.

At various points near Nashville, Franklin, and Columbia were secret letter drops, some in hollow trees, some under rocks, some in various other places, where Shaw's men could pick up papers secreted by local spies. One letter drop was at a street corner in Nashville itself.

"We communicated with men inside who furnished information, but we never knew who they were. Henry Shaw [i.e., "Coleman"] knew, and I suppose he was the only one," says Sergeant Anderson. This was not always the case, however. That lovely and devoted little daredevil, Kate Patterson, often dropped her messages in a hollow tree, but she and many other girls of the neighborhood were well acquainted with the secret messengers, who paused at the local farmhouses on their desperate errands.

Anderson also says the couriers who carried the information never "knew its nature," because it was "all in cipher," so that, if General Grenville M. Dodge, head of Federal espionage in this theater, "had procured it he would have been none the wiser." This doubtless was the usual rule and certainly a wise one. But ciphering and deciphering require a vast deal of time, which a secret mission's chief does not always have. The messages Sam Davis was carrying on his last mission were entirely in clear, and they told General Dodge and his court-martial enough to hang that gallant lad. Other agents in Shaw's band at times memorized the dispatches they were carrying—an old device—in case their papers had to be destroyed to protect their own safety.

Shaw's men had two secret rendezvous, where they could report, rest, and find food and the luxury of indoor lodging, in perfect security. Approaches were continually guarded, so that, when the Yankees did at last discover one of them, the spies had all vanished. Both these lairs were near Campbellsville, in Giles County, Tennessee, some distance south of Nashville and not far from the Alabama line, one at the farm of Squire Schuler and the other at Big Creek, on the farm of Thomas English.

III

In setting up his group of spies, Shaw was more or less following the pattern of many other similar organizations on both sides. In the Union Army, such groups included the Jessie Scouts, organized early in the war by Frémont and named in honor of his wife (not in honor of a wholly mythical Colonel Jessie, as is sometimes said); Sheridan's Scouts in the Shenandoah Valley and at Appomattox; and Blazer's Scouts, organized to operate against Mosby. For the Confederates, there were Henderson's Scouts, operating along the Mississippi, Carter's Scouts, also operating in Tennessee; and the Iron Scouts, in the Blackwater Swamp, of whom George Shadburne was one. Almost all such organizations, except perhaps Captain Richard Blazer's Federals, habitually combined legitimate scouting in uniform with out-and-out espionage in disguise. Usually these were small units, rarely if ever more than a hundred men.

Unhappily, the stories of most of these intelligence units can never be told for lack of records, though a very little is known of Henderson's Scouts. The visiting British Guards officer, Colonel Fremantle, met their commander, Captain Samuel Henderson, at Johnston's camp, within sound of the guns at Vicksburg, in May, 1863. Fremantle learned there were about fifty, whom he describes as "a fine-looking lot of men, wild, and very picturesque in appearance." He was allowed to know that they were "employed on the hazardous duty of hanging about the enemy's camps, collecting information, and communicating with Pemberton in Vicksburg."

Henderson and his men begin to appear in military records in 1863, and their reports continue until the end of the war. While Grant and Sherman were struggling down the Yazoo toward Vicksburg in 1863, they were constantly under the eyes of these alert Confederate agents, whose information flowed promptly back to Pemberton's headquarters. How much of this was due to uniformed reconnoissance and how much of it was espionage by disguised agents, the scattered records rarely show. In February, 1863, General Pemberton informed General Loring that Henderson's Scouts reported the Federals "through main obstructions in [Yazoo] Pass." At that time at least one man was "scouting in civilian's dress through the country." Another of Henderson's men, a certain F. F. Voorheis, stated a little later that because of high water he was "compelled to go to the Pass in a skiff." This sounds as if the agent were right in among the Federals, in which case he was certainly in disguise. Though various dispatches show that Henderson was not made prisoner when Vicksburg surrendered and that he continued intelligence operations whenever needed, there are no details except the flow of his reports.

The achievements of Coleman's Scouts are more fully reported than those of other groups because local historical enthusiasts in Tennessee began collecting material a few years after the Civil War and have continued their work ever since.

IV

Shaw and his men were operating against two large and efficient intelligence agencies. One was the Union Army's local group of spy catchers, directed from Nashville by William Truesdail, whose official title was Chief of Police in the Army of the Cumberland, a civilian, though sometimes called Colonel. The other was the central intelligence organization which Grant had set up for the Union's western army, directed by General Grenville M. Dodge, an excellent combat officer, who had shown a special talent for military intelligence during the early fighting in Arkansas and Missouri.

Truesdail had been a banker and real estate speculator in Erie, Pennsylvania, where his experience as deputy sheriff and police justice had earned him a reputation as an investigator of fraud and other crimes. (It was a deserved reputation. In one instance he recovered $30,000 of embezzled cash.)

Both Truesdail's and Dodge's counterintelligence men circulated in Nashville and in the country round about, posing as good Confederates, to ferret out spies and also the smugglers who ran contraband goods and Negroes south.

Since many of these spy catchers, though loyal Union men, were genuine Southerners with appropriate accents, it was often fairly easy for them to gain the confidence of suspects. One of Truesdail's men, posing as a Confederate sympathizer from Iuka, Mississippi, wormed his way into the confidence of a rather clumsy Confederate agent named Ogilvie Byron Young, who, after escaping conviction as a spy in Cincinnati in 1861, was operating in Nashville in the autumn of 1862. As a result, the spy catchers were able to seize a hollow-heeled boot stuffed with maps of the Nashville forts and with full details on Union strength and dispositions, plus confidential Confederate dispatches brought back from Europe by a Mrs. Ranney, supposedly the wife of a major in the 6th Texas. With the boot, they also seized C. J. Zeulzschel (a shoemaker of Union Street, Nashville, who had prepared the hollow heels) and Young himself. Both men went to the Federal prison in Alton, Illinois.

It was another of Truesdail's men who trapped an agreeable lady, known only as Mrs. Ford, who was engaged in smuggling quinine across the lines. Other Truesdail men caught Dr. J. R. Hudson, a Nashville physician, with a large quantity of morphine plus an alarming array of revolvers, shotguns, and ammunition.

One of the Northern counterespionage agents, whose name is given as "Blythe," posing as a paroled prisoner with a pass from Bragg to enter Nashville, overtook a certain Mrs. Clara Judd, walking along the road. ("Blythe" was almost certainly Captain Delos Thurman Bligh, a friend of Pinkerton, then or later chief of detectives in Louisville, and the same man who had arrested Ella M. Poole.) He offered Mrs. Judd a buggy ride into the city; but when, on the way, they encountered Federal and Confederate officers conferring under a flag of truce, he became suspicious. He had heard one of the Confederates mutter to her, a little too loudly, "If they won't let you in you can go across the country—about four miles—to my father's, and there they will run you through the lines anyhow."

Blythe, or Bligh, concealed his suspicion, and, since he had a Confederate pass, the lady trusted him enough to confide that she was on her way to Louisville to buy quinine and other medicines for Confederate military hospitals. She also meant to study the troops along the tracks of the Louisville & Nashville, in preparation for a raid by John Hunt Morgan, who habitually sent a spy ahead of his cavalry.

Truesdail, after hearing Blythe's report, told him to go to Louisville with her and keep her under observation. Since the Federals thus knew everything Mrs. Judd was doing, they soon had ample grounds for arresting her. Both she and Blythe were seized near Mitchellsville, just south of the Kentucky border, on the way back; and Blythe, to maintain his cover, was roughly handled, "according to previous arrangement."

Mrs. Judd went to the military prison at Louisville and then to the one in Alton, Illinois. She turned out to be a native of Minnesota, widow of an Episcopal clergyman in Winchester, Tennessee. She admitted carrying letters from Bragg to "persons north," she had been caught smuggling, and the provost judge thought she was "probably a spy." Still, she did give the Federals information on Morgan's coming raid on Gallatin, Tennessee, which turned out to be correct (though nobody thought to warn Gallatin); and there was the usual hesitation about hanging a woman. The authorities at Alton paroled her and sent her to her original home in Minnesota, "to remain there during the war."

General Dodge's organization, with about a hundred agents, operating from Tennessee to Richmond and to the Gulf of Mexico, was a more formidable opponent than Truesdail's relatively small and local force of military police. Dodge's network was designed primarily as a positive intelligence service, collecting information on the Confederate armed forces; but it could (and, upon frequent occasions, it did) detect and capture Confederate spies. The Chief of Scouts was the redoubtable L. A. Naron, a native of Alabama, but devoted to the Federal cause. Since his home was in Chickasaw County, Alabama, General Sherman dubbed him "Chickasaw," and the nickname stuck. Naron was universally known as "Captain Chickasaw" until he wearied of espionage and retired, in the midst of hostilities, to live with his family in Illinois.

Dodge's resident agents and some, at least, of his couriers were Southerners like Naron, indistinguishable in manner, appearance, and accent from Confederates. Like some of Truesdail's men, these Union agents could live and travel among Southerners without being suspected. It was Dodge's agents, not Truesdail's, who became aware of the secret activity of Coleman's men, apparently captured numerous messages, realized how dangerous their espionage was, and began a diligent effort to uproot the whole system. Truesdail should have been alerted to this new danger, but there is no evidence of cooperation between the two counterespionage systems.

13

THREE WHO CHOSE DEATH

PART 1.
THE SAM DAVIS TRAGEDY

By coincidence of a strange and tragic sort, within a period of
about six months in 1863–1864, three young Confederate secret
agents—two of them from Coleman's Scouts—were forced to
choose between ignominious death and betrayal of their comrades.
All three chose death.

The first of these courageous youngsters was Sam Davis, barely
twenty-one years old, of Smyrna, Tennessee, who, at the very foot
of the gallows, refused a final chance to save his life—the last of
several such offers—and died at the rope's end three minutes later.
The second was an Arkansas boy, David O. Dodd—somewhere in
his early teens, too young to join the Confederate Army, but nevertheless a volunteer secret agent. Captured and condemned at
Little Rock, he, too, received the same offer of a chance for life
and, in the same way, refused it. The third man, Dee Jobe, who
had grown up at Triune, not far from Sam Davis's home in Smyrna,
was neither tried nor formally executed. He was simply tortured
to death by the Union soldiers who captured him. He managed
to destroy the secret message he was carrying, refused to talk, resisted torture, and died—silent to the end.

To make coincidence stranger still, a second Samuel Davis, a Virginian, was condemned to hang as a spy about a year after the execution of Sam Davis of Tennessee. Both were probably related to Jefferson Davis, however distantly. To add a final touch, on the very day when David O. Dodd was hanged in Little Rock, another Confederate boy, also named Dodd, was hanged for espionage in Knoxville.

<h1 style="text-align:center">I</h1>

Though he was operating alone when the Federals captured him, Sam Davis was not always a solitary adventurer. In his earliest recorded exploit, he was one of a trio cooperating with a larger group of agents, on various missions. After his victory at Chickamauga, General Bragg knew that Union reinforcements would certainly be sent against him from Middle Tennessee, Alabama, and perhaps Kentucky, where Grant had his most easily available troops. How many would there be? When and where would they move? Which divisions would Grant choose?

Sam Davis was one of several agents sent in to find out. Another was P. N. Matlock, of Carter's Scouts, later a successful physician, practicing medicine in the very terrain where he had once prowled on secret service. Another was James Castleman, also a resident of the locality, like Matlock probably a soldier in Carter's Scouts. Matlock wrote out an account of their adventures, the manuscript of which has fortunately been preserved.

Chickamauga was fought September 19–20, 1863. On the twenty-fourth (Matlock says, "on Thursday after the great battle of Chickamauga"), Bragg sent for Matlock and Castleman and himself personally gave them their orders. They were "to go on scout [i.e., spy] service on the Louisville and Nashville railroad and ascertain the numbers of troops from Bowling Green, Ky., to Nashville."

At the same time, unknown to them for the moment, Sam Davis was being sent into nearly the same area. He had orders to ascertain the strength of Federal units between Nashville and Decatur, Alabama; and he was carrying money for the illicit purchase of U.S. Army pistols. If these three agents succeeded, Bragg would have full information on all Union troops along a line deep into Kentucky on the north, straight across Middle Tennessee, and south into Alabama—and his soldiers would have a few extra pistols.

When Matlock and Castleman returned to quarters from their talk with Bragg to get ready for their trip, they found they were going to have company. Another secret party—whose names Matlock gives as Mose Clift, Tom Brown, Elihu Scott, and James Freeman—were also going into the Union lines. Brown was part of Shaw's intelligence group. The others may have come from Carter's Scouts. With the possible exception of Brown, they were not primarily concerned with military intelligence. Their main duty was to bring back recruits for the Confederate Army. Sam Davis was not in the party at all—not yet.

The group proceeded to the home of one Meredith Saunders, near Sugg's Creek Camp Ground, within, or nearly within, the Union lines. Here Matlock and Castleman left the recruiting party and went on a special mission of their own. When they returned, they found the others had secured fifteen recruits and had been joined by two Confederate officers. (Who these officers were and where they came from remains a mystery.)

Since the recruiting party was waiting for more men to come in, Matlock and Castleman took advantage of the delay to visit their families. They went first to the Castleman house, on the east side of Stone River, about sixteen miles southeast of Nashville and not very far from Smyrna, the home of Sam Davis. At sundown, they went on to visit Matlock's family, who lived seven miles closer to Nashville. First hiding their horses in a wood, they approached the turnpike about half a mile from the Matlock house—the spies' usual routine. Going ahead on foot, they suddenly saw someone run across the pike, about fifty yards from them. They hailed the mysterious stranger, who turned out to be Sam Davis. As he also had orders taking him to Nashville or its vicinity, Davis proposed they all go together. This would make it easier for the other two to enter the city, since he already knew exactly where the Union pickets were posted.

About nine-thirty that night, they reached the Matlock home, where they found Mrs. Matlock's brother, Dr. A. P. Grinistead, just back from Nashville—doubtless with a great deal of useful information. After copious consumption of Southern home cooking and an hour or two of casual chat, the spies withdrew, to sleep in a cedar thicket, south of the house.

Next morning, with six-shooters safely buckled out of sight under civilian clothing, the three musketeers set out for Nashville, meeting, en route, a Negro with a two-horse wagon, in which they rode the rest of the way. They knew the Union pickets paid little attention to travelers entering Nashville. Getting out again would be the real problem.

Taking a room openly at the St. Cloud Hotel, the trio agreed to stay together at all times and fight to the death, if detected. After dining at the hotel, they stumbled upon a man named Watson, who at once recognized Castleman. Recognition might have been disastrous; but Watson, with sons in the Confederate Army, had no thought of betraying them and was eager to help in any way he could. He agreed to buy pistols from Yankee soldiers, some of whom were willing to turn a dishonest penny by trading with the enemy—and the spies were liberally supplied with dishonest pennies for just such purposes.

Watson proposed storing these illegal purchases in an outhouse near his home in South Nashville, where they would be safe until the spies picked them up on their way back to Bragg's army. If, in the meantime, the men were arrested, there would be nothing to identify them as gunrunners. All this was dangerous for Watson, since Nashville civilians had been ordered to hand over all arms in their possession or "concealed with their knowledge," but he ran fewer risks with the pistols stored outside his home.

While waiting for Watson to make his illicit purchases, Davis and his friends, strolling about the city, soon noticed that many Federal officers tethered their horses outside the courthouse, carelessly leaving their pistols strapped to their saddles—a bit of information which they noted for future use. It would be convenient to have horses for the return journey. Besides, no matter how many pistols their friend Watson might buy, the Confederate Army could always use a few more—not to mention spare horses and saddles.

Next day they had a friendly dinner with three Union generals, two of them wounded, and listened with edification to an instructive tactical discussion of the recent battle at Chickamauga "and how the d——n Rebels fought."

During their stay in Nashville, the three had seen, from a distance, a good many people they knew. So far, except for Watson, they had seen them in time and had managed to avoid them, but such luck could not last forever. It was time for them to leave.

They made some final purchases—new hats, boots (articles that most Confederate soldiers badly needed), and ten pairs of spurs. At dusk they strolled hopefully to the courthouse. Waiting till several officers had tied their horses in the vicinity, they selected the three best Federal mounts, making sure each saddle had two revolvers strapped on, and headed quietly for Watson's house in South Nashville. Here they picked up two sacks filled with Yankee pistols and rode on to safety. After a midnight supper at the Matlock house, they retired to the cedar thicket to take stock of their loot, finding themselves the richer by three additional horses, new hats, new boots, new spurs, and fifty-three pistols—forty-seven from Watson and two from each of the stolen chargers.

Taking one horse, four pairs of spurs, and eight pistols, Sam Davis rode away. His two companions never saw him again. Young Davis knew that still other Confederate agents—who, even now, cannot be positively identified—were also in the vicinity of Nashville; for Bragg, eager to secure complete intelligence, had honeycombed the area with them. Matlock and Castleman knew only that Davis was going to Triune, southeast of Nashville, to meet two of these spies—who must certainly also have belonged to Shaw's "Coleman" group. Matlock thought the men Davis was meeting were Thomas Joplin and Dee Jobe, but he was never certain.

Davis's late companions went on to their rendezvous with the recruiting party, armed the recruits with their stolen weapons, and went back to report to General Bragg.

"He thanked us for what we had done," says Matlock, simply. Well he might!

II

For a short time after this episode, Sam Davis disappears from all records—as spies frequently do. He reached Bragg's camp safely—perhaps during the last week of September, 1863, since he was sent out again in late October or early November, probably not until November 10, 1863.

Bragg soon found that he needed further information. He had to know what new Union divisions were coming in, when they would arrive, what routes they would follow. Shaw was ordered to find out. It was an urgent mission, as Bragg's whole tactical plan would depend on what Coleman's Scouts could learn. They were to send or carry this information southwest, from the vicinity of Nashville, to Decatur, Alabama, whence a secret courier line would carry it to Bragg's headquarters on Missionary Ridge, outside Chattanooga.

The mission was so important that Captain Shaw went in himself, taking a small group, including Sam Davis, from near Chattanooga and perhaps gathering up others en route. When he began observation behind the Union lines, Shaw had with him Alexander Gregg, Samuel Roberts, Billy Moore, Polk English, J. Tom Brown, Joshua Brown, and Thomas Martin.

Two more of Shaw's men, Dee Jobe and Tom Joplin, who were operating around Triune, College Grove, and Nolensville that summer, may have accompanied the group. Jobe made a practice of entering Nashville in disguise, to drink with Union officers for the sake of such bits of intelligence as he could pick up. On one such occasion, by leaving the saloon a little before his boon companions, he was able to ride off with the three best horses in sight, running them safely off to his hide-out in the hills south of Nolensville. Sam Davis had done the same thing, but he had Matlock and Castleman to help him.

Shaw's experienced men slipped in through the Federal outposts without adventure. Probably Shaw was wise enough not to let the whole group travel together; and he certainly made them scatter once they were inside the Union lines, since they had been assigned to observe different Federal units at separate posts. Davis, and probably the others, remained in more or less continuous touch with Shaw.

By November 9, 1863, Shaw and his spies had gathered enough information to necessitate another report to Bragg. With the report went the usual bundle of Northern newspapers, in which careless reporting still allowed much valuable military information to appear. All this reached Decatur, Alabama, at nine o'clock on the evening of November 10, so that Bragg certainly had the information by November 12, at latest.

About this time, certainly in the late autumn of 1863, A. L. Sharp, who had at one time had Sam Davis as a pupil, chanced to meet him. The young soldier incautiously remarked that he had been detailed as a scout for Bragg's headquarters. Though that was a technical breach of security, there was no great harm in it, since Sam had said nothing about espionage. But it was really dangerous for him to add that he was operating in Middle Tennessee. That was equivalent to admitting that he was a Confederate secret agent, since the whole area was held by Union troops. To make matters worse, Sam observed, "We have orders to go in again next week," adding that, if he came within fifty miles of his home in Smyrna, he would "make a dash to get there."

The schoolmaster pricked up his ears. His wife was living in or near Smyrna, and he gave his former pupil a letter for her, which Davis *père* could forward.

Davis left Bragg's camp on his last mission, November 10, 1863; and at the same time a large group of other agents, from another reconnoissance group, set out on the very special intelligence mission Bragg had ordered.

Before very long, Shaw began to suspect that unidentified Federal troops were moving into Lynnville, a small town north of Dodge's headquarters in Pulaski, and sent one of his agents, Billy Moore, over to find out. Moore was captured because he approached a Confederate household, where he was well known, and gave his usual signal, running his hand lightly over the blinds. When men emerged, he did not at first realize they were Yankees, and was easily captured. The Union men who had seized him were good-humored and, when their new prisoner complained of the cold, took him inside and seated him by the fire, into which he was able to drop some of his secret papers, surreptitiously. When given corn pone and bacon, he added his identification papers to his diet and washed them down with buttermilk. After a few days, he was able to leap from a second-story window and escape. A new spy replaced him, entered Lynnville, and returned safely—though without identifying the new Union troops there.

A further indiscretion by Sam Davis added to the risks. As he approached his target area, he encountered a roving band from the 4th Alabama Cavalry, sent to reconnoiter terrain near the towns of Winchester and Fayetteville, Tennessee, and Athens, Alabama. The local guide promised them had failed to appear, because of illness in his family. Local Confederate sympathizers, however, sent word that "a Confederate scout who came in here this evening" would replace him. The new guide turned out to be Sam Davis, just arrived from Decatur, the town that served as advanced base for Confederate agents entering Tennessee.

Davis rode north with the Alabama horsemen all night, reaching Fayetteville, Tennessee, in time to breakfast openly at the local hotel. There the group separated: Lieutenant Cal J. Hyatt took a detail eastward toward Winchester, while Davis and others moved toward Tullahoma, a little farther north, pausing to dine with a Confederate farmer—another of Davis's locally useful acquaintances. After rejoining Hyatt, they paused again to shoot up some incautious Yankee cavalry. Lieutenant Hyatt and his men then started south, toward Huntsville, Alabama, to rejoin their regiment.

Davis, invited to return to safety with them, replied he had still to complete his mission for General Bragg. It was bad enough to admit he was on a special mission, which he should have discussed with no one, but Sam rashly volunteered the information that he was trying to locate Federal troops in Middle Tennessee, learn their strength, and collect data on fortifications. Captain Shaw's other secret agents, he added, were already at work near Columbia and Pulaski. No doubt he knew he was talking to trustworthy Confederates; but it was, nevertheless, the kind of remark a man on a highly secret mission ought never make. Had any of these men been captured, or talked accidentally to the wrong person, or had any not actually been the genuine Confederate soldiers they seemed to be, Union intelligence officers might have learned everything. A few days later, this same guileless willingness to trust any man in a gray uniform led Sam Davis to his death.

After leaving the cavalry, Sam appeared in the night, about November 13–15, 1863, at the house of Dr. Everand Patterson, where he gave his usual signal, a pebble flung against a window. By this time, it was more dangerous than ever for an agent to spend a day in a private home, and Sam told Kate Patterson that he would go on to the "Rains Thicket," also called "Rains's Woods," for the day. This was a wild, densely wooded area of some three hundred acres, half a mile north of Dr. Patterson's house, along the Nolensville Pike. Here stood three houses, belonging to various members of the Rains family, whence the name. The area is still overgrown, and it is clear Davis chose it as a hide-out for that reason. When spies were concealed there, local sympathizers signaled their approach by a "bob white" signal.

Sam's lair was not very far from Dr. Patterson's, for when Kate Patterson rode out with breakfast for Sam and feed for his horse, she expected his coffee to keep warm in an earthenware jug. Telling the story thirty-three years afterward, remembering it all, the lovely Kate, now a middle-aged woman in her second marriage, added, ". . . and, oh, he did enjoy his good warm breakfast." Later, Robbie Woodruff, like Kate Patterson a local girl spy, went out to join them. Later still, two "little Patterson boys" brought dinner. Sam Davis spent one of the last few days of life that remained to him picnicking cheerfully in the company of two extremely pretty girls.

Davis gave Kate Patterson a list of things to get in Nashville, including the latest newspapers, while he remained hidden in the Rains Thicket. His younger brother, Oscar, who for some reason was not at the Davis home in Smyrna, took him some "nice things to eat" during the day. He found Sam sleeping but so alert that he was up, pistol in hand, before his brother could reach him. Kate Patterson returned about sundown, and "that night Sam started for the South." He did not go directly, since he did not leave Shaw's secret headquarters with dispatches for Bragg until the nineteenth. Between the Rains Thicket and his rendezvous with

Shaw, he seems to have had no difficulty eluding Union troops. No one knows what he was doing in the next day or two—probably resting at one of the two secret rendezvous of Coleman's Scouts.

Kate Patterson was sure that when he left the Rains Thicket Sam Davis was carrying nothing incriminating. He was on his way back from Bragg's headquarters and could easily carry the general's instructions, if there were any, in his head. Newspapers, if Kate gave him any, were not incriminating. In general, Shaw's men never carried suspicious documents if they could help it. Joshua Brown and Captain Shaw himself, captured about the same time as Sam Davis, a few days later, were not even suspected of espionage and were treated as ordinary prisoners of war. General Dodge did not learn their real identity until Brown himself—no longer a rebel spy but a respectable New York broker—told him the facts.

About November 18, Captain Shaw decided that a new report, together with another bundle of newspapers, must reach Bragg at once. There was important intelligence: General Grant had gone to Chattanooga to take personal command against Bragg. General Sherman's troops were moving in the same direction. General Dodge had moved his troops from Corinth, Mississippi, to Pulaski, Tennessee. Did that mean he would soon march his wing of XVI Corps after Sherman? Certainly there was soon going to be another Union attack on Bragg. Joshua Brown, who had seen and counted all the artillery and almost every regiment in XVI Corps, believed it was moving gradually toward Chattanooga.

Davis met Shaw somewhere near Pulaski on Thursday, November 19, 1863. Shaw provided him with a fresh horse and handed over the report, together with other incriminating papers. A memorandum book taken from Davis's person at his capture tells the story. It contains the entry: "Met Coleman in the road. One package tied up; letter sealed; twelve miles from Mt. Pleasant." Court-martial witnesses said only that Sam had a "package of papers, one of them sealed up in a yellow envelope the ballance [sic] of the package except letters, seemed to be newspapers."

Shaw had given Davis Louisville and Cincinnati papers, three "washballs" of soap, three tooth brushes, and three blank books for General Bragg, which Kate Patterson had smuggled out of Nashville a few days before. After these reached Union headquarters, General Dodge himself, in need of such rare articles, took them over for personal use.

Though he had a cipher, Shaw sent his highly incriminating dispatches in clear. Probably he dared not take time to encipher them, since the information was urgent and few of his couriers had been intercepted. But it was needless to mention the names of Bragg and his staff officer, Colonel McKinstry, when code names would have done quite as well.

Still more rashly, Shaw reported to Bragg that Billy Moore had just been captured. This piece of carelessness was enough to identify the prisoner as a spy and lead to his execution if the dispatch fell into the hands of an alert Union counterintelligence man. It did fall into Union hands, but—fortunately for Moore—into the hands of Yankee officers too slow-witted to take advantage of the blunder and search guardhouses and jails for a prisoner named William Moore. The other data in the message—Union artillery, reserves, railroads, a wagon train, troop movements, even the movements of Confederate spies—could also have been veiled in innocent-appearing code, even if there was no time to cipher.

Sam Davis spent either the night before he met Shaw (November 18, 1863) or the night after meeting him (November 19) at Big Creek, the home of Polk English. Davis had probably come directly there from the Rains Thicket.

Big Creek had been a spy rendezvous so long that even the Negroes knew what was going on, but all these slaves were loyal to their masters. The farm was situated near Lynnville and Campbellsville, Tennessee, just north of Pulaski, where General Dodge had now placed the headquarters of the left wing of XVI Corps. The location was a great help to rebel intelligence, since Shaw's men could live in safety near the enemy's headquarters, while trusty slaves went down into Pulaski, where the agents themselves were too well known to be comfortable. Houston and Martin, the devoted slaves who usually made these trips, never roused Federal suspicion. It was easy enough for them, since few Northerners had any idea of the devotion of some Southern Negroes to their masters, Yankees being likely to assume that all slaves fa-

vored the Yankee cause. Until about the time Sam Davis was captured, Dodge's counterintelligence agents had never located Shaw's
two espionage bases. Two or three Union spies who approached
too near had been seized, severely interrogated, forced to admit
who they were—and then bluffed into believing they had been
captured by ordinary guerrillas.

Either on the eighteenth or the nineteenth of November, Davis
took time to observe "the line"—a term that probably refers to the
railroad rather than to the picket line. Meanwhile, Polk English
and the slave, Martin, went to Pulaski. Boldly approaching Union
headquarters, they had the luck to overhear two careless officers
discussing Confederate espionage. This naturally interested the
eavesdroppers, especially as the Yankees seemed to have Sam
Davis's exploits in mind, though they probably did not mention
(or even know) his name.

About this time, General Dodge's usual monthly report was due,
and his military secretary—probably one of the two chatty officers
—had left a penciled draft on the office table before the final,
approved copy was made in ink. In some way, this reached Captain Shaw. One story is that the office porter, having been given
some papers to burn, saw the importance of this one and turned
it over to the spies. More probably the thief was Houston. Shaw
himself said, after the war, that the papers were stolen from
Dodge's table "by a negro boy that once belonged to Mr. Bob
English, near Lynnville." It is entirely possible the rough pencil
copy was stolen after the official copy had been made. In that
case, Dodge's staff probably assumed the rough staff work had
been burned and never guessed the truth.

At any rate, Houston got hold of the papers in some way and
turned them in at Thomas English's farm on Big Creek with the remark that they might do "Marse Sam" some good. Houston was
right. They were very valuable indeed, for they described the
Union forces at Murfreesboro, Shelbyville, and Pulaski. When the
spies Robert Owens and Alfred H. Douglas came in that night,
Sam Davis already had the papers. Probably he took them without
notifying Shaw, from whom he may already have received his instructions.

Sam Davis was also carrying detailed drawings of the fortifications at Nashville and other towns in Tennessee, probably including Pulaski. These plans may have come into the spy's hands through several channels that did not involve treachery within the Union Army. They may have been among the papers stolen from Dodge's headquarters. They may have come from a local civil engineer in Nashville. They may have been made by a Nashville druggist with a talent for drawing, who sometimes served as a Confederate spy. They may also have come from some unknown girl agent in Triune or through Robbie Woodruff or Kate Patterson, both of whom were encouraging Yankee admirers in the hope of getting information.

A local legend in Franklin avers that the papers really came through a certain Mrs. Sally Carter, a resident there. No one knows where or how Mrs. Carter got them—if she did get them. She is said to have passed them on to a Nashville leather dealer, George Lumsden, who was stopped by Union cavalry, but not before he had hastily dropped the papers over a fence, out of sight. When the Yankees released him, Lumsden gathered up the documents and passed them on.

That Mrs. Carter was involved is extremely probable. She is credited with having already sent Bragg advance intelligence that may have brought on the Battle of Murfreesboro. She is said to have learned Federal plans while visiting Nashville, then to have slipped through the lines to her home in Franklin, where she turned the information over to an officer who passed it on to Bragg.

When Davis commenced his ride to Bragg's headquarters on November 19, Tom Joplin commenced the journey with him, but they soon separated, probably for greater safety. That evening, not long after their paths divided, Joplin ran into Federals, but though shot and badly wounded, struggled on to Bragg's army.

III

Young Davis had done his best to secrete the incriminating documents he carried. He had sewn some of his papers into his saddle. Others he put in the enormous cavalry boots of the period, which were so big that some troopers carried an extra pistol there. He was more ingenious in devising hiding places elsewhere about his person or in his light baggage. He carried a hank of yarn over his shoulder—probably with papers tied into it; for he threw it off, as soon as possible, when he realized he was a prisoner. Inside his haversack was a ball of yarn, an easy hiding place for secret papers, such as American spies, the "Green Boys," had used outside Philadelphia during the Revolution. A single quick toss, and the spy was rid of dangerous documents.

Lurking somewhere about was a supposed Confederate officer, aided and protected by intensely pro-Confederate local people, who probably never realized the man was not what he seemed. Worse still, General Dodge had recently sent a number of his best operatives into the field, looking for the rebel spies they knew were there.

Before he started, Sam Davis had been told that a Confederate captain was somewhere in the vicinity, trying to get back to his own lines. Unless two Confederate captains—one genuine, one a spy—were wandering about at the same moment, the "Confederate" was really General Dodge's Chief of Scouts, "Chickasaw." The local people who told Davis about him did so in good faith, and their mistake was natural enough. A genuine Confederate reconnoissance officer might easily have ventured too far forward and then found himself cut off. In such a predicament, he would naturally conceal himself and appeal to local sympathizers for help. Captain Chickasaw, who knew this, acted accordingly. He had been fooling his Southern compatriots for years.

There is a story, plausible enough in itself, that Davis was himself trying to find Chickasaw, as a companion for his return journey. A strange situation: The hunted Confederate spy seeking the Union spy—who was hunting him! This may explain why Davis had no suspicion of the two imitation "Confederate" soldiers who soon met him, questioned him, and turned him over to Chickasaw—who rode up in a Confederate captain's uniform. Sam Davis had no reason to fear Confederates. He carried hidden on his person a pass authorizing him to move as he pleased about the Confederate lines; it was one of the papers that hanged him a few days later.

Chickasaw, star of the Dodge organization, had been living

during the early part of 1863 "on the run," in Alabama and Mississippi. Having finished that secret mission, whatever it was, he had returned to Dodge's headquarters and was now directing the recently enlarged Union counterintelligence group who were looking for Coleman's spies. Assisting Chickasaw in this assignment was the only slightly less formidable Sergeant James Hensal (or Hensel), of the 7th Kansas Cavalry, the "Jayhawkers." Hensal's skill in military intelligence was second only to that of Chickasaw, whom he was soon to succeed as Dodge's Chief of Scouts.

Chickasaw's agents had for some time been capturing alarmingly accurate reports, one of which was signed "E. Colman" (though the pseudonym is usually given as "Coleman"). No one had any idea who Colman, or Coleman, might be, except that he was head of a dangerous enemy spy ring. Dodge himself was much disquieted.

To make matters still worse for Shaw and his men, a Confederate prisoner had escaped. He must have been an important prisoner, since Chickasaw himself joined in the hunt, and other agents poured into the area in unusual strength. Chickasaw had also sent a special patrol of three other disguised Union soldiers on a thorough reconnoissance along the Tennessee River. Cavalry of XVI Corps swarmed on the roads, for Dodge was moving troops and needed a strong cavalry screen on his right (southern) flank. The uniformed patrols were not specially looking for spies; but they were certain to halt and interrogate any unexplained individuals they found wandering about.

With the years, various legends have grown up around Sam Davis's capture. The facts, however, are clear enough in the sworn record of the court-martial, which has long lain forgotten among General Dodge's papers in Iowa. In these papers, the story is told by the four men who knew it at first hand, testifying under oath, only a few days after the events; and it is here published for the first time. Two Union soldiers, both spies for General Dodge operating under Captain Chickasaw, and Chickasaw himself were the witnesses. Sam Davis gave his own version, which was essentially the same.

Chickasaw's men, Privates Joseph E. Farrar and R. S. King, met Davis on the road about fifteen miles south of Pulaski and stopped him. All three were in Confederate uniform (except for Davis's dyed Federal overcoat, such as many Confederate soldiers wore). The real Confederate was not in the least suspicious, supposing he had met two fellow soldiers who were merely a little overzealous about conscription.

Farrar and King were clever enough not to arrest him. They continued to insist on "conscripting" him. Apparently the dyed Federal overcoat made it possible for them to pretend not to notice the genuine Confederate uniform underneath. This threat of conscription tricked Sam Davis neatly into admitting what he really was. The two men seemed genuine. It was natural for Confederate scouts to be reconnoitering in front of Bragg's army. They would, he felt sure, let him pass the moment he proved he was a secret agent carrying intelligence for the high command. He tried to explain matters.

There was no sense in conscripting him for the Confederate Army. He was already in it. He *had* been in it for the last three years and he was "a true Southern man."

To prove it, Sam Davis then did the worst thing he could possibly have done. He displayed his pass, signed "Capt. E. Colman Cmdg Co. of Scouts." Shaw had given him this to get him past Confederate patrols and pickets, and he would have been quite right in showing it—if Farrar and King had really been in the army whose uniform they wore. Davis even went a step further: When Farrar refused to honor the pass, he offered to show him "something else," doubtless meaning the dispatches for Bragg.

The two Union soldiers, having by this time seen enough to feel sure of the truth, wasted no more breath in interrogation. They refused to examine further papers, announced they were going to "conscript him by Authority of Col. Cooper for the Confederate Service" (Colonel Samuel C. Cooper was Adjutant General in Richmond, in charge of conscription and recruiting), and took their prisoner at once to Captain Chickasaw, whom they had no difficulty in finding.

Neither they nor Chickasaw had as yet revealed their true identity. As it seemed natural for Confederate soldiers to take him to a Confederate officer, Davis responded frankly to Chickasaw's questions. When asked "how he became arrested, He said the boys played Sharps on him." Davis had still not realized his danger.

Hence, when Chickasaw asked "what he was going to do with them dispatches," he repeated the truthful story he had already told Farrar:

"He said that he was bearing a dispatch, and if I was a true Southern man I ought to recognize his pass and let him go on. He stated that he was right from Bragg's Army. He left there on the 10th of the month and was then on his return."

This is the authentic story of the capture, as told to the officers of the court-martial just after the event and under oath. When, a year or two later, Captain Chickasaw retold the story in print, he did not change it; but he did add details that the court had not needed to convict the prisoner. "I sent out two of my scouts, dressed in Confederate uniform. While on their return to camp they met a young man dressed in rebel uniform, whom they conscripted for the rebel army."

The young spy pretended, at first, to be very indignant and

told them they were doing wrong, that he was on special business from General Bragg, all of which was of no avail, my scouts persisted in taking him before their Captain, who could act at his pleasure. They then demanded his arms which he hesitated for some time before delivering up, and said he did not believe they were Confederate soldiers, he would never give them up, that the whole Federal Army could not take them from him alive. They had now approached to within about two miles of our camp, when this young man discovered that he was a prisoner in the hand[s] of Federal scouts. He attempted to escape by putting spurs to his horse, but the scouts were on the watch, and the moment he made an effort one of the men caught his horse by the bridle rein. He was taken to headquarters, and upon examining his person was found a water-proof haversack filled with letters and papers for General Bragg. Among them was a despatch from General Bragg's chief of scouts in Middle Tennessee [i.e., Shaw, alias Coleman], giving the exact number of men in General Dodge's command, together with all his late orders and a late paper from Nashville. Other papers were found proving this young man to be a spy.

After the war, Dodge retained among his personal papers the record of the Davis court-martial, including the original copies of "Coleman's" letter to Bragg's provost marshal and the pass Sam Davis was carrying. The text of the letter shows clearly enough why Davis was convicted—legally or not: It contains information on troop dispositions: "The Yankees are still camped on the line of the L & ARR. Genl Dodges Hd Qrs are at Pulaski. His main force is camped from that place to Lynnville. Some at Elk river & 2 Regts at Athens." There are details on the Nashville defenses and the movements of the Confederate spies; also, an amusing personal message for Bragg: "I also send for Genl Bragg three washballs of soap, 3 more toothbrushes & two Blank books. I could not get a larger size Diary for him I will send a pr Shoes & Slippers some more Soap Gloves & Socks Soon—"

Realizing that this unusual prisoner had better be taken back to the main body of the Union Army with as little fuss as possible, Chickasaw and at least one of his men set out with Davis, who still may not have realized where they were taking him.

At least two of the numerous Federal reconnoissance parties that had gone out scouting that morning—in their own proper blue uniforms—were in the area toward which Chickasaw was riding, and these were soon joined by a third. Chickasaw's assistant, Sergeant James Hensal, was in the field, and so was a detachment of the 7th Kansas Cavalry, the "Jayhawkers." The troopers may have been under Sergeant Hensal's command, for, though he was now on detached service, he belonged to this regiment.

At about the same time, a squad which included a soldier named John S. Randall, 66th Illinois Infantry, was coming down the road on a special mission. What that mission was, Randall, who later told the story, does not say. Probably he did not know and had been ordered simply to accompany the squad; but, as he was attached to Dodge's own guard, the mission, whatever it was, may easily have had something to do with the secret service system Dodge had long been operating.

When this detachment reached a crossroads, or road junction, which Randall does not identify, the men concealed themselves in the bushes. It is clear they were somewhere near the Jayhawkers. No account of the affair explains why so many soldiers had to be in hiding at that particular place on that particular day.

Captor and captive rode into the Federal ambush—which Chickasaw may or may not have known was there—and both were arrested. Farrar and King seem simply to have disappeared, still in rebel uniform. Hensal says he saw only two men riding down the road. Chickasaw says he had three men with him—that is, Farrar, King, and Davis—but he does not say he had them with him all the time. He does not say how he identified himself. Hensal, of course, knew him well.

When the Jayhawkers and the infantry swarmed out of ambush, Davis may still not have realized the situation. Chickasaw may have allowed himself to be treated as a genuine prisoner. If Farrar and King fled, they were doing only what real Confederates would certainly do.

Sam Davis must soon have begun to realize, however, that there was something very odd indeed about the men who had arrested him, for it was not long—though perhaps only after the Jayhawkers appeared—before he began to get rid of incriminating papers, as well as he could. He managed to throw away a skein of yarn he had been carrying on his shoulder and the ball of yarn in his haversack. In the general excitement of the capture, no one troubled to pick up the yarn.

Search at once showed that Davis was an enemy agent. The papers in his haversack and the incriminating documents in his boots and saddle were speedily discovered. Not until then, however, did someone remember seeing the prisoner throw away yarn. Union soldiers went back and found it, with the papers hidden in its meshes.

The prisoner could not get rid of the bulky package of newspapers, but they were not really very incriminating. What sealed his doom was his Confederate pass, signed by Shaw as "E. Colman," and the letters to Bragg's provost marshal. The fatal bit of paper still looks exactly as it must have looked when taken from Sam Davis. Folded down almost to the size of a postage stamp, it is exactly like any paper that a soldier has carried for any length of time, on active duty in the field—worn, crumpled, stained with perspiration and the dye the perspiration dissolved from the uniform.

Even a hasty examination of the documents showed at once that the locally operating group of rebel spies was alarmingly well informed. That was, from General Dodge's point of view, bad enough; but far more serious was the plain evidence they con-

tained that the "Colman" group was getting extremely confidential
data from someone high in Dodge's own command. An engineer
himself, the Union commander felt sure the drawings taken from
his prisoner were the work of a military engineer.

Dodge was almost equally eager to identify the mysterious "E.
Colman," who was obviously spymaster for Bragg in Middle
Tennessee.

When Sam Davis was brought to headquarters, Dodge wanted
to know where "Colman's" spies were getting so much and such
dangerously accurate intelligence. He also wanted to know the
routes they were using to penetrate the Federal lines, the names
of the other spies, and "Colman's" true identity. If Davis would
give this information, Dodge would spare his life. If not, Sam
would hang. The general made this offer several times, at different
interviews. Each time, Sam Davis refused; and Dodge, though
secretly admiring his courage, could only send him back to prison.

Though he didn't know it, General Dodge at that very moment
had the mysterious "Colman" and one of his best agents, Joshua
Brown, among his prisoners at Pulaski, confined in the same prison
as Sam Davis. While Chickasaw had been prowling about the
countryside, other Federal soldiers had been sent out to find the
hidden headquarters of the rebel spies. They did find the Schuler
house and there, or near it, captured "an old, seedy, awkward-
looking man in citizen's clothes," who described himself as "Dr.
Shaw," formerly a Confederate Army surgeon. They took him
back to Pulaski and locked him up, having no idea they had captured the much-wanted head of the whole intelligence ring.

Joshua Brown, when captured, had a great deal of dangerous
information, but he had memorized it all and, if he had ever had
any papers, had gotten safely rid of them. He was therefore regarded as an ordinary prisoner of war. The other Brown in the
spy ring, J. Tom Brown, was also captured near Nashville, about
this time; but he, too, remained unsuspected. Shaw, Davis, and
Joshua Brown, captured within a few days of each other and all
sent to the Pulaski jail, recognized each other instantly, of course,
but were careful to give no sign of recognition. Brown soon escaped. Shaw was never suspected till he was in prison at Johnson's

Island, near the Canadian border. When a Federal stool pigeon, posing as a former Confederate spy, was put in the same cell, Shaw guessed the truth at once and was careful to say nothing incriminating.

Davis's tragedy moved swiftly to the hanging on November 27. Knowing they were safe themselves, while still unidentified, and painfully aware that nothing they could do would save Sam Davis, Captain Shaw and Joshua Brown waited anxiously in the Pulaski jail to see whether Federal pressure could, in the end, persuade him to betray them. Both knew that, after one word from him, they were both dead men; and Shaw, though he professed complete confidence in Davis, became nervous each time he saw him taken away for interrogation. This happened several times, for, besides General Dodge himself, the local provost marshal, the chaplain who attended Davis, and Captain Chickasaw all tried to persuade him to save himself by revealing the secrets of the spy ring; but the gallant youngster steadfastly refused.

John S. Randall, of the 66th Illinois, one of the soldiers who had been in the ambush near the scene of the capture, was now sent into the jail, disguised as another prisoner. (Apparently he had not been near enough Sam Davis at the time of the capture to be recognized.) Randall may not have been the only Union stool pigeon playing this ancient game. He himself always believed that other ostensible prisoners associating with Davis were really Federal detectives on an errand like his own.

IV

Once it was clear that Sam Davis could not yet be frightened into talking, the Federals wasted no time. Orders convening a "military commission"—that is, a court-martial—had gone out the day he was captured, and the court convened November 22. It was one way to force on the prisoner a realization of the peril in which he stood. He might still weaken when he faced the court—or the gallows.

At the court-martial, there were two charges, each with one specification:

Charge 1: "Being a Spy." Specification: that he had come "secretly" within the Union lines to gather intelligence But it was never specified that he was in false uniform.

Charge 2: "Being a carrier of mails communications and information from within the lines of the U.S. Army to persons in arms against the Government." The specification to this charge simply said that he had been arrested carrying mail to the rebel army.

The witnesses were Captain Chickasaw first, then Privates Farrar and King, the two men who had made the capture.

All three testified to the facts already stated. The crucial point was—or would have been, if the court-martial had known any military law—whether Sam Davis was in proper Confederate uniform. Chickasaw did not testify on this point, probably because he had not been present at the actual capture.

Farrar was asked to "state what was the dress of the prisoner when taken."

Answer: "He seemed to have been dressed in his own uniform except one of our [i.e., Federal] overcoats dyed black or of a dark cast which he wore."

(It was, in fact, an overcoat which his brother Oscar had gotten from a Federal deserter; there is no doubt it had been dyed.)

King was asked the same question: "State what kind of dress the Prisoner wore when arrested."

Answer: "He had on something like a gray suit, dressed in Southern clothes."

Question by the judge advocate: "Did he wear the uniform of the Confederate army?"

Answer: "Yes Sir he did."

At that point, Davis could (and should) have been acquitted and sent back to the Pulaski jail as an ordinary prisoner of war. He was in his own uniform—and the men who captured him said so. Therefore he was not a spy. He had indeed carried dispatches. But what of it? That was an ordinary military duty. He had carried dispatches within the Federal lines? Why not? That, too, was an ordinary military duty.

This was a very queer court-martial. To begin with, the defendant had no defense counsel. It is true he had been offered counsel and had declined. But this was a capital case. Ought any prisoner go on trial for his life without counsel, especially a young and inexperienced boy? The first charge was destroyed by the prosecution's own witnesses. The second charge was not an offense at all. No sensible judge advocate would ever have gone to trial with it. In other words, the court-martial was a series of farcical blunders by volunteer officers very imperfectly acquainted with the rules of land warfare. But it was tragedy, not farce, for Sam Davis.

The court adjourned the same day to consider its verdict. Next day it found the prisoner guilty on both charges and sentenced him to be hanged on November 27—which, by another irony, was the day after Thanksgiving.

Everyone concerned was much distressed. The boy's captors, after three years of war, knew how to appreciate devotion to a cause. General Dodge was particularly impressed by his prisoner, dark-haired, standing six feet, "a fine soldierly-looking young fellow, not over twenty." Sam was again offered not only life but freedom—if he would give information. Dodge was tactful enough to take the boy to his private office before making the last offer he himself would make personally.

When Sam still refused, the Union Army regretfully prepared to hang him. Various Pulaski ladies were allowed to visit him. So were the local Methodist minister and Chaplain James Young, 88th Ohio. To the latter the boy, at the last moment, gave his dyed Federal overcoat. The chaplain kept it for several years after the war, then sent it back to Tennessee. It is still cherished in the War Memorial Building in Nashville.

Toward the end, the prisoner was kept handcuffed. Joshua Brown remembered how young Davis was brought into a room where other prisoners were eating. Without a sign of recognition, Brown handed him a piece of meat. Unable to handle knife and fork, Davis picked it up with both hands.

Although citizens begged to have the execution take place farther from the town, the officer in charge insisted on erecting his gallows on East Hill, immediately northeast of Pulaski. He meant the ghastly spectacle to be a deterrent to other rebel spies he felt sure were somewhere about.

They took Sam Davis from the jail with arms pinioned, placed him in a cart, and seated him on his coffin. From the jail window,

Shaw and Brown watched the dismal little procession. Davis's arms may have been freed or somewhat loosened after he had mounted the death cart, for Brown says the boy saw his two friends and saluted as he passed. To the customary mournful drumbeat, the guard carried him out of the town. The doors and windows of Pulaski houses were closed. One woman lay on her bed with a pillow over her head to shut out the dreadful sound. She would never know how much that Union drummer boy—to the end of his long life—admired and respected the young spy he was escorting to the gallows.

Having reached the scaffold, Davis asked the Union officer in charge how long he had to wait.

"Just fifteen minutes," said the Federal. "I am sorry to be compelled to perform this painful duty."

"It does not hurt me; I am innocent; I am prepared to die and do not think hard of you."

He was interested in the latest news from Bragg's army and remarked, "The boys will have to fight the rest of the battles without me."

He had to endure a final, dreadful—and obviously deliberately planned—test of his endurance. A soldier heard an officer at the gallows say, "Mr. Davis, you have but five minutes to live unless you give up your secret." The victim refused three times. At the last moment, just before or just after this incident, Captain Chickasaw galloped on the scene. It might have been a reprieve—but it wasn't, not quite. Chickasaw merely brought a last chance to accept Dodge's offer. The boy could still save his life; he knew how. A Union soldier, six feet away, heard the conversation.

"Do you suppose I would betray a friend?" asked Sam Davis. "No, sir; I will die a thousand times first. I will not betray the confidence of my informer."

Chickasaw gives very nearly the same account of this episode at the gallows' foot. He says he told Davis he was not the man who ought to be hanged—"and if you would yet tell me who General Bragg's chief of scouts was, so I might capture him, your life would yet be spared." Sam Davis, who knew very well the man Chickasaw wanted was at that moment a prisoner in the Pulaski jail, still unrecognized, looked his tempter in the eye: "Do you suppose were I your friend that I would betray you?"

Life, Chickasaw reminded him, "was sweet to all men."

He was not that kind of man, returned Davis. "You may hang me a thousand times and I would not betray my friends."

There was nothing more to say and only one thing to do. They adjusted the noose. Someone noticed that, at the last moment, Davis stood very straight and "put his hair back," apparently doing the best he could, with hands that were either bound or manacled. Someone thought to note the grisly fact that the victim fell three feet and thirty inches. There was apparently no pain and no struggle. Davis swung motionless.

He seems, mercifully, to have died at once. Less than two minutes had passed since he had refused Captain Chickasaw's last offer of his life.

"I wish that man could have gotten away," said a Union soldier as he marched from the scene. A good many others felt (and said) the same thing. They knew the chance for life Davis had been offered—and the price. As soldiers, they respected courage.

The drummer boy in blue who beat the dead march for the execution was a mere lad named L. W. Forgrave. All his life after, in St. Joseph, Missouri, he remembered the horror of the execution and Sam Davis's supreme courage. He used to tell his sons about it, drumming the march on the arm of his chair as he talked.

Chickasaw felt about the same way: "Thus ended the life of Samuel Davis, one of General Bragg's scouts, a noble, brave young man, who possessed principle. I have often regretted the fate of this young man, who could brave such a death when his life rested in his own hands. His mind was one of principle, though engaged in a wrong cause."

An Indiana girl named Mary McEwen received letters from two soldiers who saw the tragedy. It was hardly the thing a boy describes for a girl, but these young soldiers did. "He displayed a great amount of courage and died bravely," wrote one; "he stood it like a man," wrote another. "He could of saved his life by telling who his captain was that was inside of our lines, and some men in our army that helped him." A third Union soldier made two entries in his diary: ". . . he stood it like a man . . . he never paled a bit but stood it like a hero."

Still a fourth Union soldier, Thomas Edward Swarts, 66th Illinois, wrote his brother on the very day of the execution, a letter filled with admiration and regret:

> I was to see the Spy who was hung today he was caught last week it is said a sargt of the 7th Ills Inf and chicasaw (a scout) they wer out on a scout and came across him and said they wanted him as a conscript in the rebil army he then told them who he was they brought him to this place and he was hung today 20 m after 10 the drop fell he was game to the last never flinched he had the No of Canon in our Division and the No of the Regts there stringth &c he was about 21 very good looking and smart. . . . this piece of roap is what I got to remember him by I cut if off my self dont let anyone have any of it or unrap it. . . . I heard the fellows name who was hung today was Sam Davis.

Sometime later, a fellow prisoner in the Union prison camp at Johnson's Island found Captain Shaw in tears. Shaw handed him the copy of the *Pulaski Citizen* he had been reading. It contained the story of Sam Davis's execution.

14

THREE WHO CHOSE DEATH

PART 2.
Dee Jobe, the Other Sam Davis, and the Dodds

DeWitt Smith Jobe, known among his army friends as "Dee," was the second member of Coleman's Scouts who preferred to die rather than betray secret information. Sometime in the late summer of 1864, he entered the Federal lines with Tom Joplin and a few others. Their orders were to examine the little towns of College Grove, Triune, and Nolensville, along the Nolensville Pike, which led north to Nashville. Jobe was on completely familiar terrain, since his home was in Triune. (His elder brother, Benjamin A. Jobe, had also served as a spy, though nothing is known of his exploits.) Joplin certainly, and the others probably, had also grown up in this general area.

I

The group had agreed among themselves that, in case of imminent danger, they would scatter and continue operations separately, working as far apart as possible. Each man would thus have a better chance of getting back with the intelligence Bragg needed. Danger of some sort must have arisen on August 29, 1864, for Jobe rode alone all that night to reach the home of one William Moss, set back from the turnpike about two hundred yards, between Nolensville and Triune.

Moss, who had two sons in the army, gave him breakfast. Afterward, Jobe hid on a neighboring farm, pausing at the farmhouse to see a girl from Triune named Betty Haynes. It has always been a legend in the vicinity that Jobe secured a good deal of information from a local girl, and Betty Haynes may have been his source. A nephew says that Jobe also got information from "his true & tried friend, Miss Bettie Puckett."

Whether by treachery or accident, the Federals learned a Confederate agent was about. Fifteen mounted infantry from the 115th Ohio, commanded by Sergeant Taylor E. Temple, arrived from Murfreesboro and, when they found no one, began to search. According to one account, they examined the entire countryside with a large telescope and, through it, saw a horseman riding past a cornfield on a neighboring hill. His presence seemed worth investigating. Bettie Puckett, who knew exactly where Jobe was, "endeavored to decoy them in a different direction," but it was no use.

Following the hoof marks, Temple's patrol soon caught up with Dee Jobe, who had just time to chew up the papers he was carrying before the Federals seized him. He was then about six miles from his home.

Whether the horseman the Federals had seen was Jobe himself or someone trying to communicate with him is doubtful. Another account by a veteran Confederate officer who knew the country and its history well says Jobe was found sleeping in a thicket. Both stories may be true. The fugitive may have been seen moving from his first refuge and may have been discovered after he had gone to sleep in the second.

Then followed one of the most horrifying episodes of the Civil War. It was plain Jobe had military information. When he refused to reveal it, the Union troops tried torture. Like Sam Davis, Dee Jobe stood firm.

But not for Dee Jobe was the relatively easy death of the gallows. His captors began by demanding what had been in the papers he had destroyed. Jobe refused to say. They threatened to kill him. He still refused. Instead of slaughtering him on the spot (you can't get information from a dead man), they beat him over the head, knocked out his front teeth—and still learned nothing. They then put a leather strap around his neck and dragged him over the ground until they either strangled him or broke his neck. (By a curious irony, Sergeant Temple also died of a broken neck—but that was not until 1919.) The yells of the torturers could be heard a mile away.

After this act of savagery, the Union soldiers began to develop compunctions, or at least admiration of Jobe's courage. He was, some of them said, the bravest man they had ever seen. The Union men left the body lying by the road, where a young woman, a friend of the Jobe family, happening to pass with an escort, found it. Dismounting, she spread a handkerchief over the face, and it was probably she who notified the family. "Old Frank," a slave who had nursed the young soldier in childhood, brought the body home and dug a grave in the family "burying ground," which, as usual in the South, was not far from the home.

The dead man's cousin, DeWitt Smith, of the 45th Tennessee, left his regiment at Chattanooga and returned home to avenge Jobe's death. He began near Tullahoma. Here he entered a camp of sleeping Union cavalry, stole a butcher knife, and went from one tent to the next—each tent containing eight men—killing every one. As Smith was cutting the fifteenth throat, the last man stirred in his sleep and sat up. Smith fled.

So, at least, declares Tennessee tradition. It is obviously doubtful that so much slaughter was possible in complete silence, though similar feats were managed in the Indian wars. Smith could always rely on cooperation from Rutherford County people, furious over the torture of Jobe. He once forced two Yankee prisoners to accompany him to a farmhouse, where he calmly molded bullets while the housewife cooked a meal for him, then marched his captives about half a mile, shot them both, dropped their bodies in a sinkhole, and affixed labels: "Part of the debt for my murdered friend, Dee Jobe." At times Smith carried six pistols at once, plus a musket—or so tradition avers. He had hoped to kill General Rosecrans himself and once shouted at a dying Negro corporal, whom he had just shot, "By God, you saved Rosecrans' life."

II

By a curious coincidence, there was a second Confederate spy also named Samuel Davis, also captured, and also sentenced to death. The two were almost certainly—though distantly—related.

Lieutenant Davis, an infantry officer, badly wounded in Pickett's charge at Gettysburg, had been captured, and, after some time as a Federal prisoner, had escaped. Probably because of his wound, the Confederate Army sent him to Andersonville as an officer of the prison guard. Scarcely had he reached there when the commandant's serious illness made Davis acting commandant; and he thus became a familiar figure to many Union prisoners. That made all the trouble.

Davis might have ended his services to the Confederacy without further adventure had he not chanced to pay a midwinter visit to Richmond. As Christmas, 1864, fell on Sunday, many festivities were postponed to Monday, December 26. In a joyous throng in the Spottswood Hotel, the lieutenant came upon one Harry Brogden, a Marylander in the Confederate Signal Corps, which included the espionage service. Brogden had orders to proceed to Canada with dispatches, a mission for which he felt no enthusiasm whatever. Davis, eager for a change, offered to go in his place.

"That remark," he observed afterward, "nearly cost me my life."

Brogden's orders were officially transferred; and within twenty-four hours Lieutenant Davis, carrying a British passport, with his hair dyed, and in civilian clothes, was on his way north. As his home was in Delaware, there was no danger that he would betray himself by a Southern accent. He traveled under the cover names of Willoughby Cummings and H. B. Stephenson, and at his capture gave his name as Stewart.

The papers Lieutenant Davis was carrying dealt with the trial of John Yates Beall, a Confederate naval officer who held the now-forgotten rank of Acting Master. Beall had captured two steamboats on the Great Lakes and had tried to seize a Federal naval vessel. After this, he had tried to capture a military train on the railroad between Buffalo and Dunkirk, New York, and had, instead, been captured himself. As a naval officer in disguise, he was found guilty of espionage. Though sentenced to death in September, 1864, he had not as yet been executed, and the Confederate government was making every effort to save him. Officials in Richmond wanted to supply Confederate representatives in Canada with evidence that Beall was a legitimately commissioned officer of the Confederate Navy. How this could save him, when he had been captured in disguise on Northern soil, no one ever explained. Probably the Confederates hoped to encourage Canadian diplomatic protests.

At that time, two Confederate officials—Jacob Thompson, a Tennessean who had been Secretary of the Interior under Buchanan, and Clement Claiborne Clay, who had been U.S. Senator from Alabama until 1861—were busy in Canada with all sorts of Confederate plots. They had plans to seize Great Lakes shipping; plans to burn Buffalo, Detroit, and other border cities; plans for raids into northern territory, like that on St. Albans, Vermont. Beall's attempts had been part of these schemes; and it is possible some of the papers Davis carried may have had to do with these other plots as well as with the effort to save Beall.

Davis passed secretly across the Potomac at Pope's Creek, Maryland, a route regularly used by Confederate couriers and agents, entered Washington easily, and went on to Toledo. Dropping into a hotel lobby there, while his train was delayed, he listened to an officer of the U.S. Navy reading aloud from a newspaper account of how the Federal authorities were looking for a Confederate secret agent, carrying exactly the papers Davis was carrying.

"Ah," said the officer, "how I would like to catch the damn rascal who carries those papers; it would be the making of me or any one else that caught him."

Davis politely assented, but "you bet I did not tell him I was the damn rascal."

He reached Detroit, via Columbus, Ohio, crossed to Windsor, Ontario, and got in touch with Thompson. After some weeks in Canada, he began the return journey with a great many secret messages. Though he memorized the most important of these, he also had his "coat sleeves full of closely written white silk." The advantage of writing military secrets on silk was that it did not rustle or crackle under searching fingers, as paper was certain to

do. Confederate couriers going to and from Canada habitually
did hide documents in their sleeves.

The lieutenant had been discreet, had committed no blunders,
and would have completed the return journey successfully, save
for one handicap which he and the Richmond central office
should have thought of before he started. Nobody remembered
that Davis's face was well known to numerous Union prisoners at
Andersonville, some of whom had been exchanged within the last
few weeks. If he met any of these men, they would recognize him
at once; and they would have a lively and un-Christian interest in
seeing their former jailer given a taste of prison life himself.

On the second day of the return journey, the inevitable happened. Somewhere near Newark, Ohio, Davis boarded a train carrying several exchanged Union soldiers, one of whom had been in
Andersonville only about three weeks before. Frank Beverstock,
3rd West Virginia Cavalry, and Archibald Parker, Company M,
16th Illinois Infantry, both former prisoners at Andersonville, consulted together. Parker remembered Davis as a Confederate officer
in "a Lieutenant's style or rig." He was now wearing a plug hat,
and his hair had been dyed, but they were sure it was the same
man. They approached him.

"Is not your name Davis?"

"No," said the lieutenant, "my name is Cummings." He showed
a British passport. Unconvinced, they persuaded the conductor to
telegraph ahead to the provost marshal at Newark. Beverstock
posted himself at one door of the car, Parker at the other, to
prevent escape. Eventually Davis yielded:

"Well, boys, you have got me."

The provost marshal was on the platform when the train pulled
in, and they marched Lieutenant Davis from the car. A guard
appeared. When Davis admitted carrying dispatches, Beverstock
asked what had been in them. But the lieutenant was not to be
trapped. "He run out his tongue and said, aha!"

The ex-jailer of Andersonville was promptly stowed in the
Newark jail, not without a certain enthusiasm among his former
captives.

Now, however, a rather badly trained provost marshal bungled
everything. Though there was no doubt that Davis was a spy, he

was searched so carelessly that only his money, watch, and chain were found. No one suspected the messages hidden in his coat sleeves. Everything worked out as the Confederates in Canada had hoped when they wrote those messages on silk. The Union searcher did not hear the revealing crackle of paper and looked no further.

Worst of all, when the search was over, Davis was not held incommunicado but was turned loose in a large room, occupied by numerous other prisoners. It had a large stove—exactly what Lieutenant Davis needed. As soon as his guards disappeared, he ripped the linings out of his sleeves and dropped the silk, with its incriminating messages, into the fire.

Quick destruction of the dangerous lining of the lieutenant's sleeves did not save him from a death sentence, nor did it preserve the secret of this favorite Confederate trick. By January of 1865, while Davis was still on his mission, a U.S. consular agent in Toronto reported to the Secretary of State that Confederate spies were sending messages in coat linings, though he does not mention the use of silk. He also added that they were making highly reduced photographic reproductions of other messages and concealing them in coat buttons—a very modern touch in that day, when photography was in its infancy.

With the gallows looming in front of him, Davis remembered the papers he had carried from Richmond to Canada in the effort to save Beall. He knew that already the Confederate authorities had sent other papers to prove that Beall's second in command, who had been captured earlier than his chief, was also a properly commissioned Confederate officer. Perhaps the army officer who had tried to save the two naval officers might save himself by proving that he, too, held a Confederate commission and was acting under orders. (It is hard to see why anyone entertained such hopes, since all three had been caught out of uniform.)

Davis therefore offered to secure for the court-martial the testimony of the Confederate President, supported by that of Judah P. Benjamin, Secretary of State and former Secretary of War, that he was only a bearer of dispatches, not a spy.

The court-martial had no interest in testimony from enemy officials. No matter how exalted, they could not possibly appear as witnesses; and their depositions would be suspect. Whether Lieutenant Davis had done any actual collection of military intelligence or was merely carrying secret messages did not matter. He was a disguised enemy officer, secretly in Union territory. Disguise was enough to make him a spy, no matter what he had been doing. He received a prompt death sentence and was sent for execution to the prison at Johnson's Island in Lake Erie, near Sandusky, Ohio.

After the trial, all members of the court-martial that had sentenced him shook hands with him, each "expressing his personal regret at my unfortunate position." But that did very little to console the condemned man, sitting in a solitary cell with ball and chain, while he waited for the rope.

On February 1, 1865, the prisoner was allowed to see a newspaper clipping, announcing his execution for February 17, and that night he was given a copy of the official record. A few days earlier, a friend of prewar days had appeared in his cell and had promised to notify Davis's friends of his danger. He was humanely treated by the Federal captain in charge, who even mailed letters for him, and news soon arrived that "your Baltimore friends are fully apprised of your situation, and will spare no effort."

"Fighting Joe" Hooker, the local Federal commander, who had been sent west after his defeat at Chancellorsville two years earlier, was heard to remark, "He's no spy"—but he approved the sentence of the court-martial. Lieutenant Lewis A. Bond, the judge advocate who had prosecuted Davis, wrote to express regret and to compliment his victim on his "manly conduct and heroic bearing." He also granted Davis's rather odd request that one or two members of the court might be present to see him hanged!

Then, on February 9, the prisoner received private assurance that he was not going to be hanged, after all. This was confirmed on the eleventh, but only unofficially. And no amount of unofficial assurance could possibly save his life. Though execution was scheduled for the seventeenth, no official message had reached the prison by the sixteenth.

President Lincoln had, in fact, telegraphed on February 13. Meant to save Davis's life, this telegram nearly got him hanged—first because it was delayed, then because it was so ambiguously worded it seemed to authorize the hanging. For once the author of the Gettysburg address had been careless with his literary style. President Lincoln had telegraphed Hooker, "Is it not Lieut. S. B. Davis, convicted as a rebel spy, whose sentence has been commuted; if not, let it not be done." Which, if it meant anything, meant "Commutation denied. Hang the man."

Some staff officer, knowing Lincoln's eagerness to mitigate the harshness of court-martial sentences when he could, translated this into a reprieve, but headquarters were unpardonably slow in relieving the condemned man's anxiety. On February 15, Davis saw the gallows being erected. At ten o'clock on the night of the sixteenth, fully expecting to die next day, he sent a message to the prison commandant, asking to be allowed to walk to the gallows: "I could and would walk and would give him no unnecessary trouble." Then he lay down and went to sleep.

Up by five, he dressed, breakfasted, and sat down to wait. But, however courageous the lieutenant may have been, he did not find it a very cheerful morning. He could see the morbid crowds which, by seven o'clock, were arriving to see him die. He could see the rope being tested and stretched and could hear the band practicing the Dead March. When Union officers came in to ask for autographs, he scribbled "a few verses."

At this gloomy moment, the commanding officer walked into the cell, ordering sentries and everyone else out.

"I have a commutation for you; your sentence is commuted."

"I am glad to hear of it, sir," said Davis—which was an understatement.

"It was hours before I realized my life was saved," he wrote later. Beall, whom he had come to save, was hanged February 24, 1865.

Lieutenant Davis went to Fort Delaware in irons. Here he rather tactlessly remarked that he had handled more prisoners than the fort commander "had ever seen in one body, and I had never ironed a man." This earned him a beating, after which he went for six weeks to a cell in Albany and finally, after citizens there protested his treatment, to prison hospital. Even then he had to give a promise not to escape—which made very little sense, as Lee had already surrendered. Later he went to Fort Warren, Boston.

For months after Appomattox, the Federal authorities tried to show that Davis had been sentenced to life imprisonment and could never be released. But the men he had himself held prisoners at Andersonville protested, and he was released December 4, 1865. The implacable Stanton was still growling that the man should have been hanged.

Long afterward, Lieutenant Davis remarked: "I don't want to feel as I did from the 1st to 17th of February, 1865."

When Appomattox was twenty years in the past, Brevet Major Lewis E. Bond, U.S.V., the judge advocate at Davis's court-martial, was sitting one day in his Cincinnati office. A stranger entered.

"I presume you do not remember me," said he. "My name is Samuel B. Davis." He stretched out his hand and they had a friendly chat. As Davis rose to go, Bond asked a question:

"Lieutenant Davis, will you not tell me before you go why you came to this state in 1864?"

But Lieutenant Davis stuck to the secret service tradition. Twenty years had passed, but he still wouldn't talk.

"That," said he, "is a secret that will die with me."

So Lieutenant Samuel Boyer Davis *was* more than a mere secret courier!

III

Save for the name, the identity of their intelligence work, the family relationship, and the courage with which each faced death, there is not really much similarity in the stories of the two Samuel Davises. But the tragedy of Sam Davis in Tennessee had an almost exact parallel in the fate of the equally brave David O. Dodd in Arkansas. Both were captured with incriminating data on Union forces in Union terrain; both were carrying papers that indicated expert connivance somewhere; both were mere boys; both were asked for the names of those working with them; both refused; both were offered their lives for betrayal; both refused that, too—and both were hanged. Two Union officers later contributed to a monument for Davis; at least one Union officer to a monument for Dodd. Even the names of the places where they were executed were the same: Davis was executed at Pulaski, Tennessee; Dodd in Pulaski County, Arkansas.

There were, however, differences in the two cases. Davis was a soldier, Dodd a civilian; Davis was an experienced secret agent, Dodd an amateur on his first mission; Davis, being in uniform, ought never to have been regarded as a spy; Dodd, being in civilian clothes, certainly was a spy.

Young Dodd came of a Texan family that had moved to Benton, Saline County, Arkansas, near Little Rock, which is in Pulaski County, where the father had established business interests while his son was still a child. The boy had been a student at St. John's Masonic College, in Little Rock; but about the time the war began, he became ill and left to study telegraphy. He was soon employed in the Little Rock telegraph office and, later, after the Union Army entered the city, began clerking in Union sutlers' stores. When the family went south, he entered the telegraph office in Monroe, Louisiana.

The elder Dodd soon decided someone ought to return to Little Rock to look after the family property and, thinking that the boy's youth would enable him to get into the city without difficulty, sent David. This purely business trip would have presented no problems if young Dodd had not been induced—by someone who has never been identified—to collect military information. He needed a pass to travel through the area the Confederates still held. General James A. Fagan, local commander, also a resident of Saline County, provided one. Dodd himself said, not long before his execution, that the general refused to issue it, except in return for espionage. Someone unquestionably did encourage the boy to bring back information on Federal positions, strength, and "plans" (which may mean either war plans or maps). When arrested, he was carrying full details on Union artillery and brigade organization, which could have been of interest only to Confederates. Since no officer would expect a youngster without training to collect this kind of intelligence unassisted, it is clear that David Dodd had been told to make contact with one or more agents in Little Rock. Whoever these people were, they were protected by a cover so good that it has never been penetrated.

Young Dodd rode into Little Rock with another Confederate spy, just before Christmas, 1863, probably on Christmas Eve, about a month after Sam Davis had been hanged. The second agent was Frank Tomlinson, nearly the same age as his companion, from the town of Pine Bluff, about whom little is known. Whether their meeting was deliberate or accidental, whether either confided to the other what he was doing, are questions that have never been answered. The two had no difficulty passing Federal guards on their way in, but they separated when they reached the city—as any sensible spies would do, if they possibly could.

Tomlinson—whose mission was to collect intelligence either by his own efforts or with the aid of resident agents—got his information quickly but, in some way, roused suspicion. With Federal troops in pursuit, he escaped across the river, into what is now North Little Rock. Here he found refuge in the house of a farmer, who dressed him in girls' clothes, including a sunbonnet to hide his face, and set him to work. His pursuers searched the house but paid no attention to the young lady, busily occupied with what seemed to be ordinary household routine. When they were gone, Tomlinson set out to submit his report.

David Dodd at first aroused no suspicion in Little Rock, where for some time he moved about with entire freedom. He was an agreeable youth—"an unusually handsome and manly, though extremely modest little fellow," said a girl who knew him. He found lodgings at the home of his aunt, as if on an ordinary family and business visit. He relied on a paper dated December 2, 1863, from the Federal post at Princeton, Arkansas, directing scouts and pickets to let him pass. He also carried a certificate from his father, dated December, stating his age and further stating that he had "no connection with the Army." (This was not quite true, but the father may not have known of his secret mission.) The boy had taken the further precaution of appearing before the provost marshal in Little Rock on New Year's Day, 1864, and taking the prescribed oath to the Union, under Lincoln's amnesty proclamation of December 8, 1863.

Spy or not, during the Christmas holidays he lived the normal life of a mid-nineteenth-century teen-ager, dancing and seeing a good deal of three girls: Mary Dodge, supposed to have given him information; Mary Swindle, who went to a dance with him; and Minerva Cogburn, to whom he brought letters from his sister. Some Little Rock girls "were in the habit of receiving information from Federal army officers," and these three may have been gathering information for Dodd.

Mary Dodge (later Mrs. William George Whipple) is said to have been "the one who gave David the information that he had written in code in his book." Whatever Mary may really have been doing, her father, Dr. R. L. Dodge, had very little doubt she had been dabbling in espionage and feared the Federals would find out. When Dodd was arrested, the doctor packed his daughter off to relatives in Vermont as fast as he possibly could. Mary herself was not allowed to know of the arrest and did not learn of the execution till a long time afterward.

David Dodd was in Little Rock only a few days, arriving at Christmas, or just before, and starting back December 29. With him he carried a memorandum book containing notes on the "composition" of the Union forces (this must mean the strength and disposition reports the Confederates had asked him to get). This incriminating data the inexperienced boy had naïvely written out in Morse—certain to attract attention and perfectly easy for any telegrapher to read. The notebook is now filed with the court-martial documents in the National Archives, together with two carefully braided locks of girls' hair, which Dodd was carrying with him, probably keepsakes from Mary Dodge and Mary Swindle. He had also been foolish enough to keep his pass from Colonel W. C. Crawford, commanding the Confederate outposts; Federal and Confederate money; and "two letters from Rebels of this city [Little Rock] to parties outside our lines." But he had been careful to leave a loaded derringer pocket pistol at the home of his uncle, Washington Dodd, on the Upper Hot Springs road, some miles from Little Rock.

The returning spy rode a mule out of the city, passing one sentry without question; but he was halted by a Federal picket about eight miles on the road toward Hot Springs, southwest of Little Rock. Here, Dodd told Daniel Olderbury, Company E, 1st Missouri Cavalry, that he was going fifteen miles into the country to see friends. That seemed reasonable, as did his reply to a further question that he meant to travel on the Hot Springs road. Olderbury told him to proceed, adding that, as Dodd would not need the pass any more, he would keep it. Olderbury did keep the pass until he was relieved. Then, as a matter of routine, he tore it up.

"I did not know he was arrested when I tore it up," he told the court-martial later, with a faint note of apprehension.

Dodd was now beyond the Federal lines and apparently safe. He jogged along on his mule till he reached the house of his uncle, Washington Dodd, on the Upper Hot Springs road, about eighteen miles from Little Rock. Here he recovered his Derringer and in the afternoon started back toward Little Rock but turned off on a southerly crossroad, which would take him to the Benton road. He was now only a mile or two from the picket post at which he had given up his pass.

At the point where the crossroad joined the Benton road, he ran into another picket, commanded by Sergeant Frederick Micher, Company B, 1st Missouri Cavalry. Sergeant Micher, looking up, saw his "inside Vidette" (cavalry sentry) halt a civilian who was "coming into the main road." When the Federals asked for a pass, Dodd explained that the picket on the Hot Springs road had already taken it. Why he did not present his pass from the Federal post at Princeton, which was addressed to all pickets and scouts, is not clear. He still had it, for it was among the documents presented at his trial.

Asked where he lived, Dodd said Little Rock, which was more or less true. Where was he going? "To a man's by the name of Davis." Where was he going from there? "Down on some creek to get him a horse."

The sergeant did the only thing he could do: He sent the mysterious traveler to regimental headquarters, where First Lieutenant C. F. Stopral demanded either a pass or some other identification. Again the puzzle arises: Why didn't Dodd hand over his Federal pass? Instead, he handed over the memorandum book, in which he had made notes in Morse. Alas for him! The lieutenant knew enough telegraphy to spell out some of the Morse alphabet. He gazed upon the dots and dashes with suspicious eye. What he read was rather more than suspicious:

"The 3rd Ohio battery has four guns. Braes 11th Ohio Battery has six guns." He had trouble with another passage, but it seemed to be about 18-pounders—anyhow, not quite the sort of thing an innocent young civilian ought to be carrying around, especially in Morse code. The lieutenant himself took the prisoner to Captain George W. Hanna, 1st Missouri Cavalry, who also had a post on the Benton road and was at the moment, in spite of his rank, commanding the regiment. When Stopral displayed the Morse code in the memorandum book, Hanna commented, "That looks suspicious."

When Dodd explained that his pass had been taken from him at the picket line on the way out, the captain asked if he could recognize the man who took it. When Dodd said he could, the captain sent him out to the picket line under guard. The guard had, however, been changed by this time. It would have been easy enough to examine the guard roster and find the right man, but no one seems to have bothered. The prisoner went to the guardhouse.

When he was searched there, he was found to have Confederate States currency, local bank notes, Confederate postage stamps, the loaded derringer pistol, and letters concealed "between his shirts." One letter was Minerva Cogburn's reply to the letter he had brought from his sister—ordinary friendly correspondence between young girls. There was no military intelligence in any of the letters.

The prisoner was sent back to the provost marshal, and Captain Robert C. Clowry, Assistant Superintendent of the U.S. Military Telegraph, later President of Western Union, was called in. Under his expert scrutiny, the Morse notes in the memorandum book turned out to be even more incriminating than had at first been suspected. In addition to the notes on Federal artillery that Lieutenant Stopral had been able to read, other notes in the memorandum book read: "Three brigades of Cavalry in a Division, 3 regt. in a brigade, brigade commanded by Davidson. Infantry 1st Brigade has 3 regt. 2nd Brigade has 3 regts. one on detached service. 1 Battery 4 pieces Parrots Guns, Brig Gen'l Solomon commands a Division. Two brigades in the Division. 3 rgts. in one brigade and 2 in the other. 2 Batteries in the Division."

Clearly, this was espionage.

Rather naïvely, Dodd tried to persuade the officers of the court-martial that "the information entered in my memorandum book was regarded by me simply as a piece of polite information. It was intended only for reference, at any time in conversation with my associates—all I expected to gain by it was character for attention and observation of passing events." There was, he added, no special motive for writing it in Morse—just practice.

It was not really a very good story, but it was the best the terrified lad could extemporize. Dodd submitted these statements—and others equally unconvincing—in a statement obviously written by his two lawyers. No court could be expected to believe them; and the war-hardened officers of the court-martial brushed them aside, found the prisoner guilty, and sentenced him to hang.

Well-meant civilian efforts to save him failed. General Frederick Steele, in local command, is said to have been sure the boy had accomplices because of the excellence of certain maps found on him; but no maps were put in evidence at the court-martial. The tale is probably due to confusing Dodd with Sam Davis. Maps or no maps, however, Steele could hardly have failed to realize that so much accurate and detailed intelligence must have been supplied by observers in Little Rock itself. It was vitally important to find these intelligence sources and cut them off. That was exactly what General Dodge had felt when Sam Davis was captured.

Just as Dodge had done, Steele offered Dodd his life if he would reveal the identity of his informants. At the very least, this would have involved Mary Dodge and probably several other people. A Union veteran says that Dodd replied, "General, I can die, but I cannot betray confidence. I am alone responsible for these papers." That certainly wasn't true, but it was a gallant lie.

They hanged him January 8, 1864, on the campus of St. John's Masonic College, where he had once studied. Mary Swindle, who had been at a dance with him the night before his capture, saw her dancing partner taken past her father's house on his way to the gallows. Apparently Dodd, like Davis, was given one last chance on the scaffold to save himself by betrayal, for his last words are said to have been: "I have no disclosures to make; hurry up your execution."

An inexperienced hangman bungled matters badly. There was no cloth with which to bandage the boy's eyes, but he told his executioner calmly, "You will find a handkerchief in my coat." The hangman's rope was too long, so that Dodd fell with his feet touching the ground, and soldiers had to haul up the rope hastily. In spite of this, however, a Union soldier who describes the execution says he died instantly and painlessly.

There was a black-bordered advertisement in the local paper next day: "The friends and acquaintances of David O. Dodd, are invited to attend his funeral this Evening at 3 o'clock, from the residence of Mr. Barney Knightin." His grave in the Mount Holly Cemetery, Little Rock, is still an Arkansas shrine—and part of the inscription is in Morse code.

His fellow spy, Frank Tomlinson, reaching his home in Pine Bluff safely, received an honor accorded no other spy in history—a parade in celebration of his return!

The ghastly series of coincidences was not yet quite played out. There had been a second Davis; so there was a second Dodd. On the very day when the Union Army hanged David O. Dodd in Little Rock, it also hanged E. S. Dodd, private in Terry's Texas Rangers, also on charges of espionage, at or near Knoxville, Tennessee. Perhaps this verdict could have been justified on technical legal grounds. Like many another Confederate soldier, Dodd *was* wearing some captured "blue clothing," which he had neglected to dye Confederate butternut or gray. But he was not seeking military intelligence; he was merely trying to rejoin his command.

Dodd's horse had been killed in a skirmish during a raid into territory held by the Federal Army. In such predicaments, Texas Rangers usually got their unhorsed men away by riding double; but, where this was impossible, the dismounted men tried to follow the mounted Rangers back to their base, secretly and on foot. Dodd admitted to the court-martial that he had been wearing a mixed uniform, which did include articles of clothing captured from the Union Army—something the Confederate Army frequently did when the alternative was to have no clothes at all. Some of Dodd's clothing was blue. He insisted he had always worn his own uniform hat, with the star of the Texas Rangers on it. Just how a man plainly displaying his proper unit insignia can be charged with espionage has never been clear to anybody but those particular court-martial officers.

Unfortunately, he had kept a diary, in which he noted at least one occasion when he had posed as a Federal soldier. Dodd insisted that he had done this only to secure food and directions. Union courts-martial were, however, feeling vindictive because some of their own men had recently been hanged by the rebels. Dodd's partially false uniform was regarded by this court as enough to make him technically a spy, even if he had done no espionage; and the court was merciless.

The execution was even more bungled than the one in Little Rock. The rope broke, precipitating the victim, half dead, to the ground. He revived sufficiently to gasp, "Release me, please," after which they hanged him all over again—this time more adequately.

Even more pathetic than the Davis and Dodd tragedies, because one of the victims was so much younger, was the hanging of two boys of fourteen and sixteen by the Confederates, not long after the Davis execution. They, too, were charged with espionage. Details are—perhaps fortunately—lost. The lads were brought, handcuffed, to the gallows, where the younger, in terror, began to "beg and cry and plead most piteously." The older boy kicked him and bade him "show the rebels how a Union man could die." Nothing else is known of the story. Even their names are lost. Some martinet had been foolishly insistent on the letter of the law.

15

THE GAY DECEIVERS:
MORGAN, BEAUREGARD,
AND ELLSWORTH

The star wire tapper of the whole Civil War was a gay and guileful rebel named George A. Ellsworth, a telegrapher of Canadian birth, who accompanied General John Hunt Morgan on his raids into Kentucky. General Beauregard—a rather gay deceiver himself, who often managed to stuff Union generals with spectacularly false information and who appreciated a talent for mendacity in others—is sometimes credited with being the first to recognize Ellsworth's peculiar abilities and commend them to Morgan. Ellsworth himself says that he personally sought out Morgan. But it is certainly true that Ellsworth met Morgan in Mobile, Alabama, and joined his cavalry there, only three days after Morgan returned from a conference with Beauregard in Corinth.

I

Beauregard had long since proved his own ability to fool Union generals. It was he who—knowing that General Halleck, besieging Corinth in the spring of 1862, was ready to attack with greatly superior Union forces—scared him off by pure deception. The wily rebel ordered a great many trains to pull into Corinth with as much whistling and general noise as possible. Each train, empty or not, was greeted with resounding Confederate cheers.

Hearing this perpetual uproar, the Federals attributed it to incoming reinforcements for Beauregard. But it really indicated the gradual withdrawal of Beauregard's army. Departing trains, heavily loaded with troops, slipped out of Corinth in silence. It was these same trains, returning empty to carry away more troops, that received all the cheers.

Beauregard's bluff, however, failed to deceive railroad men serving in the Union Army, who convinced Major General Grant that the Confederates were secretly evacuating. They could, the railroaders assured him, tell, by putting their ears to the rails, "not only which way the trains were moving, but which trains were loaded and which were empty." Loaded trains, they said, had been going out for several days and empty ones coming in, cheers or no cheers. But Grant could not convince Halleck, whose subordinate he then was.

About the middle of May, 1862, General John A. Logan also told Grant that the Confederates had been evacuating Corinth for several days. The Federals could, said Logan, take the town with a single brigade. But Halleck refused to permit the attempt—and Halleck was in command.

Even after Beauregard had gotten all his Confederates safely away, the clever Creole was still not done with his tricks. He left behind, in the empty town, an imposing array of dummy artillery and similar devices. These continued to delude Halleck, even though this impressive array of guns never seemed to do any firing.

The extent of Halleck's gullibility is incredible. On May 21, 1862, nine days before Beauregard withdrew his troops, a New York correspondent reported that the Federal commander had "an exact and comprehensive plan of the enemy's fortifications at Corinth." The plan was supposed to show "the position of every gun in the works." Halleck, the news story added, had "great confidence in this intelligence." The *Cincinnati Gazette* unconsciously helped along Beauregard's bluff by a dispatch explaining "that Beauregard has been receiving exceedingly heavy reinforcements is very probable. The prisoners and deserters all say so; spies bring in the same story."

Beauregard must have chuckled. By that time a large number of the guns were wooden dummies, or soon would be. In any case, even if the *Gazette*'s information was correct, it was insane for Halleck to let a correspondent get it. The newspaper story let the Confederates know what information the Federals had. Since the information was wrong, the situation was even worse, for now Beauregard knew his little joke was succeeding perfectly.

General John Pope, at the head of one of Halleck's besieging armies, was just as blind as his commander. At 1:20 A.M., May 30, 1862, when little or nothing but a covering detachment of Confederate cavalry was left in Corinth, Pope was reporting: "The enemy are re-enforcing heavily in my front and left. The cars are running constantly and the cheering is immense every time they unload in front of me. I have no doubt, from all appearances, that I shall be attacked in heavy force by daylight."

To maintain these Federal delusions as long as possible, Beauregard left enough buglers in Corinth to sound the usual calls long after there was no Confederate army there to hear them.

When daylight came on May 30, there was no sign of the Confederates. At 7 A.M., Union patrols, snooping about the outskirts, met with no resistance. Pushing on a little, they discovered there were no rebels anywhere in town.

Beauregard's devious ways had by no means ended when the Union troops marched in. The Confederates had left behind the girl spy, Aurelia Burton, and perhaps other girl spies who were never discovered. How long Miss Burton had been spying, no one knows. It was September, 1862, before one of her letters was intercepted, describing the northwestern part of the town as the Federal weak point and "giving with remarkable precision all the information necessary for attacking it." Having scanned this remarkable document, the Federals resealed it and sent it on; but Aurelia was carefully watched and eventually arrested, while the weak points she had indicated were promptly strengthened.

How Beauregard became acquainted with Ellsworth—if he was acquainted with him—and why he sent the telegrapher to Morgan —if he did send him—remain mysterious questions. But there is no doubt that a senior commander who could play tricks like Beauregard's would fully appreciate Ellsworth's value to that other military jester, John Hunt Morgan.

Ellsworth's early career is obscure. During the first year or two of the war, he was Assistant Superintendent of the Texas Telegraph Company. He enlisted June 1, 1862, in Company A, 2nd Kentucky Cavalry (Duke's), in Chattanooga. This may have been a second enlistment, as Ellsworth says he "enlisted again" when he joined this unit. On July 1, he was detached as a telegraph operator and promoted captain.

II

A few days after he and Morgan met in Mobile, after Morgan's return from visiting Beauregard in Corinth, Ellsworth was with the raiding column that Morgan led out of Knoxville into Kentucky in early July, 1862. The troops moved: Knoxville–Sparta (Tennessee)–Celina (Cumberland River)–Tompkinsville (Kentucky)–Burkesville–Glasgow–Versailles–Lebanon–Cave City (Horse Cave)–Rolling Fork River–Springfield–Harrodsburg–Lawrenceburg–Midway–Georgetown. Though he had everything his own way as far as Georgetown, Morgan did not press his luck too far, prudently turning back in time by way of Paris, Richmond, Crab Orchard, and Somerset, and reaching Monticello, Kentucky, on July 22. He was safely back in Tennessee on August 1. He had led his men 1,000 miles in less than a month, capturing and paroling 1,200 prisoners and losing only 100 of his own 800 troopers.

A large part of this success was due to Ellsworth's shameless telegraphic fabrications, sent to various Union stations. Befuddled by these adroit fictions, the Federals rarely knew where Morgan was and never knew what he was going to do next. Ellsworth's own description of these pranks he played, during this and other raids, shows he and his commander shared the same impish delight in tricking the Federals. But, though Ellsworth was, indeed, a kind of military Puck, he was a great deal more than that. His waggish wires served two vital military purposes. The messages he sent caused alarm, confusion, or delay among the Yankees. The messages he picked up by wire tapping warned Morgan well in advance of what the enemy was doing or was going to do.

Some of Ellsworth's telegrams, to be sure, served no military purpose whatever. They were sent for pure amusement, when the raiding cavalry was ready to move out, and secrecy no longer mattered. Morgan found it just as diverting as Ellsworth did to send jocular or sarcastic telegrams to leaders on the other side.

When the column reached Cave City, Kentucky, about dusk, Morgan himself led a detail of ten or fifteen men, including Ellsworth, toward the Louisville & Nashville Railroad, a vital Union supply line. Being largely limestone country, Kentucky is full of caves, and one well-known cavern, Horse Cave, stood near the railroad. About half a mile away from this landmark, with a heavy thunderstorm approaching, Morgan halted his little band, while Ellsworth cut into the Louisville-Bowling Green telegraph line—so carefully that the Louisville operator, who at that moment happened to be sending, noticed nothing.

The first word Ellsworth heard was "Morgan." After listening a moment, he realized that General Jeremiah T. Boyle, Union commander at Louisville, was telegraphing orders to Colonel Sanders D. Bruce, at Bowling Green, for the pursuit and capture of Kentucky's rebel invaders. Bruce was to support a certain Colonel Houghton. The general was indiscreet enough to add that Houghton's force was too small to venture as far as Glasgow (which Morgan had already passed). He wanted Bruce and Houghton to combine forces and move along the line of the Louisville & Nashville, intercepting Morgan there if he tried to move farther north to wreck the railroad.

Unhappily for General Boyle's tactical plans, Colonel Bruce never received the message. Nor did any other Federal operators south of Horse Cave receive the further messages that followed, including a great many messages for Federal troops in Nashville. With Morgan's personal assistance, Ellsworth concocted replies to delude the Federals in Louisville into believing that Bruce, Houghton, and the Nashville operators were receiving all messages as usual.

During this adventure, Ellsworth acquired the nickname "Lightning," which clung to him for the rest of the war. A thunderstorm broke not long after he had tapped the wire, and he sat at his instrument in the darkness with electricity playing around him. A scout named Ben Drake exclaimed, "Old Lightning himself!" John Allen Wyeth, also on this raid, adds to the tale. A suspicious Federal operator, who found Ellsworth's touch unfamiliar, queried, "Who are you? And what's the matter with your office?" To which Ellsworth nonchalantly replied, "O.K., lightning." Both tales may be true, and both probably helped create the nickname. Ellsworth himself says he was always known thereafter as "Captain Lightning" or "Morgan's Lightning."

Sitting through two hours or more of a rainy night, with water up to his knees, Ellsworth listened to messages from Louisville, Nashville, and other towns—none of which went beyond the point where he had cut the wire. Many of these were commercial telegrams, countermanding shipments of money and valuables, lest Morgan lay hands upon them.

Morgan seized the opportunity to perpetrate a characteristic practical joke. He had Ellsworth send a message, signed John H. Cogel, to a man named Hunter, in Lexington, instructing Hunter to send two barrels of whiskey to Cogel in Nashville. Some weeks later, Ellsworth had a chance to read copies of the resulting interchange of telegrams. Hunter had duly forwarded the barrels of whiskey to Nashville. No one there had ordered them, and Cogel—whoever he may have been—had no intention of paying transportation charges. Both barrels had to be sent back to Lexington at the expense of the much irritated Hunter.

Such pranks, like the undelivered civilian telegrams—which had never gone beyond Ellsworth's cut in the wire—were of no immediate military importance. But later, when Union operators and businessmen found what had happened, everything had to be done over again. This overburdened the wires, caused general confusion, and added to the Federals' troubles.

Of much greater importance was a message which Morgan intended to be false but which, by pure accident, turned out to be true—thereby adding credibility to his next fabrications. The raider forged a dispatch, supposedly from Union headquarters in Nashville, to Union headquarters in Louisville. This mendaciously reported he was somewhere near Gallatin, Tennessee, when he was actually near Cave City, Kentucky, fifty or sixty miles away. Then he added that Forrest's cavalry had attacked Murfreesboro and was now advancing on Nashville.

Morgan had certainly not intended to let any truth at all slip into these imaginative flights. He was just happily telling lies to the enemy. He had no idea what Forrest's intentions were. His report of the raid on Murfreesboro was pure invention. He simply hoped the news would worry the Yankees. When, by pure coincidence, Forrest really did attack Murfreesboro a few days later (July 13), that bit of accidental truth made all the other fabrications seem authentic!

Having thus collected a great deal of genuine information and having spread a great deal of false information, the cavalry jogged on.

When the column was within three or four miles of Lebanon, about dusk on July 11, it was fired on by Home Guards, who put up a resistance so spirited that Morgan could not enter the town itself until two or three the next morning. Then, with his commander, Ellsworth went to the telegraph office. "A light was burning and the Office Had the appearance of having been very lately deserted—all was quiet usual Click was not to be Heard although everything was in readiness to receive or send a message."

The silence was brief. Within a few minutes, some office signing Z began to call B. Ellsworth did not know where either office was, but he gave the usual answer indicating an operator was ready to receive: "I.I." Immediately Z asked, "What of the marauders now?" Lebanon was the office that would naturally receive such a question and Ellsworth assumed (correctly) that B was Lebanon. He replied briefly that "we were still holding them at bay," whereupon Z volunteered the information, "There are 800 troops here Coming to Your aid."

This was of great interest to Morgan, who might have to fight them. But where were the eight hundred? In other words, what station was Z? The Federal day operator at Lebanon, D. E. Martyn, who might have supplied the information, was now crouching along a small stream, practically a sewer, whose current, as Martyn said later, "odoriferously effervesced noisome effluvia."

But, as Martyn also remarked, "It was an awfully good place to hide in." He was never captured.

Few Union messages were going through at that hour in the morning, and the key was silent. Ellsworth improved the time by reading the office file of dispatches of the day before. Among them, he soon found a message to General Boyle, in Louisville, reporting that four hundred "marauders" were approaching Lebanon. This was good news for the Confederates. General Boyle and his Federals would be badly puzzled. They would now have two locations for Morgan and his men—Gallatin, Tennessee, and Lebanon, Kentucky, many miles apart. They would also have an exaggerated strength estimate.

Ellsworth now picked up the further news that the 60th Indiana was on its way to Lebanon. Presumably, this was the reinforcement promised. A special detachment went out to destroy the only bridge over which they could pass.

Eventually, Z, who turned out to be W. H. Drake, night operator at Lebanon Junction, sent another query: "What news? Any more skirmishes after your last message?"

"We drove what little cavalry there was away," replied Ellsworth.

Z now inquired whether "the train" had yet arrived. Ellsworth said no, it hadn't; and, by the way, how many troops aboard it? Five hundred, said Z, 60th Indiana, Colonel Owens commanding. This was also useful information for Morgan, but it grew increasingly important to know where station Z was. Morgan wanted to ask the question outright, but Ellsworth pointed out that any real Union operator at Lebanon would certainly have known that. Such a question would give the whole Confederate game away.

Finally, Ellsworth invented an imaginary "gentleman here in the office," who "bets me the cigars" that Z could not spell the name of the town where his station was located. Z, or Drake, rose to the bait at once.

"L-e-b-a-n-o-n J-u-n-c-t-i-o-n," he clicked. ". . . how did you think I would spell it?"

"He thought you would put two b's in Lebanon."

"Ha! ha! ha! He's a green one."

"Yes, that's so," agreed Ellsworth, who, having now learned Z's location, could afford to be agreeable.

When William R. Plum, day operator at Lebanon Junction, took over, Ellsworth for the first time aroused suspicion. Martyn had escaped so swiftly that the Confederate had had no chance to study his style of sending. Consequently, the very first fraudulent message stirred Plum's suspicions. Coming on duty, the Union day operator had sent a casual message. Ellsworth had replied, "O.K." It seemed queer to Plum. There had been rumors of rebels about. Who *was* on the other end of that wire? "O.K." didn't sound like Martyn, who never used that signal.

Drake, who had not yet left the Lebanon Junction office, ridiculed Plum's fears. He was sure the man on the other end of the wire was Martyn, for during the night he had been "talking with him by the hour." Plum allowed his fears to be allayed, and his suspicions were not again aroused when the supposed B—that is, in fact, Ellsworth—tapped a message that his key would be silent for a little while. He was going to take a nap. The truth was that Morgan had, at that moment, entered the office and told Ellsworth to close it down. The ruse worked perfectly. Plum, in reply, merely warned B not to oversleep. It was a long time before any Federal operator began to wonder about Lebanon's silence.

That nap explained everything perfectly, while Morgan, his telegrapher, and his troops rode on to Versailles. After dark, Ellsworth with a squad went off toward Frankfort to tap the wires. The Federals seemed to be taking a defensive attitude; but there was little other information, and it was nearly dawn before the squad reached camp again.

Three miles from Midway, on July 15, 1862, Morgan sent Ellsworth into the town ahead of the column to capture the telegraph operator there, before he could announce the Confederates' arrival. Taking Private Cabel Maddox with him, Ellsworth walked in on the unsuspecting local operator, one J. W. Woolums. "There was not much uniformity in our Uniform," Ellsworth wrote later. "We were in Citizens dress—our arms Consisted of a pair of Navy sixes"—which ordinary civilians, in those days, had every reason for wearing.

Ellsworth noticed at once that the telegraph poles outside the building carried two wires, only one of which entered the station. When Woolums explained that the upper wire, not connected with his instruments, was the military wire, Ellsworth sent Maddox up a ladder to cut it. When Woolums, still not realizing he was a prisoner, protested, he learned the worst. The two Confederates then forced the luckless man to send an innocent telegram to Lexington. This merely asked for the correct time, but it gave Ellsworth a chance to get some idea of the other operator's style.

By the time Morgan and his troopers rode into Midway, Ellsworth was in control of the wire, and the Federals had no chance of telegraphic warning. Imitating Woolums's style as best he could, Ellsworth soon found that all military messages were passing over a through wire running directly from Lexington to Frankfort. Having discovered this, he cut Frankfort off entirely and began talking to Lexington, posing as the Frankfort operator. Soon after he began this, a telegram arrived from a conductor in Lexington, asking whether it was safe for his train to enter Midway. Seeing a chance to bring a whole train into Morgan's grasp, Ellsworth at once replied, "All right; come on. No signs of rebels here."

This kind of thing could not go on forever without being detected. By July 13, General Boyle, the Union commander in Louisville, who had been growing suspicious, wired the War Department: "The rebels undoubtedly have control of telegraph all around us"—a message he probably sent north to Ohio and over an eastward line there, to keep it out of Confederate hands. It did, however, reach Midway, where Ellsworth heard it, doubtless with a chuckle.

Despite their fear of wire tapping, the Federals had to risk some use of the southward telegraph line. On that same July 15, Ellsworth picked up a message from General William T. Ward, in Lexington, ordering the Federal commander in Frankfort to start troops to Midway, while Ward moved his own soldiers into neighboring Georgetown, north of Lexington. Morgan, said this telegram, had left Versailles at 0900 and was moving along the Midway road to Georgetown.

As a matter of fact that was not what Morgan had done—yet. But it was exactly what he meant to do; and, if Ward were allowed to make this move, Morgan would have to fight him. It was, therefore, desirable to decoy the Federal troops in another direction, out of the path of the raiding rebels. Ellsworth promptly concocted another of his deceptive dispatches. Morgan, this fallacious document reported, had already passed Midway and was on his way to Frankfort. Ellsworth signed the name of Woolums, the genuine Midway operator, who, as a prisoner, had no chance of reporting the truth. Needless to say, Morgan had no intention of going anywhere near Frankfort.

In about ten minutes, Ellsworth, to his delight, intercepted another telegram from General Ward to Frankfort, hastily ordering its Union garrison back to town. Ward also sent warning that Morgan, with 1,000 men, was advancing on them. "This dispatch received from Midway, and is reliable," cackled General Ward. All this was good news for the advancing Confederates, since it removed a fairly large hostile force from their intended route.

Flushed with this success, Ellsworth drew further on his imagination. Ward's estimate of Morgan's strength was very nearly accurate. Such a figure was not nearly terrifying enough to keep the Federals worried. Ellsworth therefore wired Louisville as if he were really wiring from Frankfort: "Tell General Ward our pickets are just driven in. Great excitement. Pickets say the enemy must be two thousand." After that, ominous silence from Frankfort.

In fact, a state of beatific peace reigned in Frankfort. But, with the wire secretly cut, Ward had no chance of learning that. And the Frankfort operator, on the other side of Ellsworth and receiving immediate replies from him, supposed the usual military telegraph circuit remained wholly undisturbed.

All Ellsworth had to do to produce an alarming effect was to stop sending messages date-lined Frankfort. The imagination of the badly worried General Ward in Louisville would suggest a terrible picture of outnumbered Union troops, battling valiantly against overwhelming Confederate hosts. All this kept his forces far away from Georgetown—and therefore nothing disturbed Morgan's peaceful march thither.

At some point during these interchanges, Plum, the Lebanon Junction day operator, whose suspicions had already been aroused once, and then quieted, arrived in Frankfort. Plum says that, by this time, even the local operator there was beginning to have doubts, for Ellsworth was not imitating Woolums's style well enough to deceive other Union operators very long.

Federals in Frankfort began to take precautions. The train the Confederate operator had tried to lure into Midway was called back to Lexington. Military dispatches for Lexington were now enciphered and routed through Cincinnati, on wires the rebels could not reach. In this way, General Ward must ultimately have learned the truth—but it was too late then.

Before abandoning the Midway office, Ellsworth grounded the circuit there and left it open on the Lexington end, "to leave the impression that the Frankfort operator was skedaddling, or that Morgan's men had destroyed the telegraph."

When the raiders reached Georgetown, about ten o'clock that night, the local Union telegraph operator assured Ellsworth that the line had been out of order for some time. Suspecting that the Union man was lying, Ellsworth used a method traditional among old-time telegraphers: he touched the wire to his tongue. Currents in those days were weak, and the faint electric impulses were most readily received on moist and sensitive tissues. As Ellsworth had expected, there was still current, but the Union operators were silent, now well aware that the enemy was probably listening. Ellsworth wished to keep silent, too, but on Morgan's orders he finally called Lexington and, with his commander's permission, told as much truth as possible, even reporting Morgan's presence in Georgetown. He added one ingenious lie to account for anything unusual in his "fist."

"Keep mum; I am in the office, reading by the sound of my magnet in the dark. I crawled in when no one saw me. Morgan's men are here, camped on Dr. Gano's place."

Naming Dr. Gano was a delicate local touch, meant to give verisimilitude. Dr. Steven F. Gano and Dr. Andrew Gano were both practicing in Georgetown, and both had houses not very far from the town. The other operator was at first deceived, or pretended to be deceived.

"Keep cool," advised Lexington. "Don't be discovered. About how many rebels are there?"

Ellsworth replied he didn't know. Presently Cincinnati, too, was asking for information. But Cincinnati was already suspicious: "How can you be in the office, and not be arrested?"

"Oh," tapped Ellsworth, "I am in the dark and am reading by magnet." It was a plausible story, but not quite plausible enough to satisfy Cincinnati. Someone there immediately set a trap.

"Where is your assistant?"

"I don't know."

"Have you seen him today?"

"No."

Ellsworth was again telling the truth, but this time the truth was fatal. He certainly had not seen an assistant. For—as Cincinnati knew very well and Ellsworth did not—the Georgetown operator had no assistant. Ellsworth's first messages to Cincinnati had not sounded quite right. His reply to the last question proved there was a rebel on the Georgetown end of the line. Cincinnati must have spread the word at once.

Though Ellsworth's luck was slowly running out, by this time it didn't matter very much. Morgan was ready to turn back, and the Union leaders were in a state of confusion that would last till he was safe in Tennessee. The Federal telegraph operators, however, were now being cautious. At Cynthiana, Ellsworth found the line out of commission. At Paris, the local man had fled with all the instruments. Ellsworth apparently made no effort to use his own.

When he cut in at Crab Orchard, however, he heard orders from General Boyle, locating Morgan (accurately this time) and starting Union troops after him:

"Pursue Morgan. He is at Crab Orchard, going to Somerset."

Then Ellsworth's game was again exposed. He heard Lebanon (whence he had himself sent so many fabrications) warning Lebanon Junction (which he had so elaborately hoaxed), "George Ellsworth, the rebel operator, may be on the line between here and Cumberland Gap."

Ellsworth also heard some Union "precautionary suggestions" at or near Crab Orchard, and it was useful to know what the enemy was doing. But he totally failed when he called "MC," that is, operator James Jones, at Mt. Vernon, Kentucky. Guessing at once, "from the style of the operating," that this was Ellsworth, whose mischief-making was known by this time, Jones replied, "Our troops are here preparing to cut Morgan off in the direction of Somerset. I think we will bag the rascal."

This was pure bluff. The Federal troops at Somerset consisted of Jones himself, a convalescent soldier, and forty home guards—but the Confederates didn't know that! A proud telegrapher later asserted that "Morgan was fairly driven by telegraph." Whether that was true or not, Morgan certainly did move on Somerset immediately.

About nine o'clock on the night of July 21, as the Confederates approached the town, word came down the column, "Lightning to the front!" There was no response till Ellsworth was discovered, fast asleep on his horse. Morgan sent him ahead with two men to capture the Somerset telegraph office, before the operator there could send out a telegraphic warning. An hour later, seeing only one light in the quiet country town, Ellsworth judged it must be the telegraph office, approached quietly on foot, and entered just as Ellison, the Somerset operator, dropped out of a back window and fled.

Ellsworth had barely taken over the key of the departed Ellison when a message came through from James Meagher, Union operator at Stanford, Kentucky. Meagher had been out repairing the line near Crab Orchard which Morgan's men had just finished cutting. He was now, unknowingly, reporting to the man responsible for the break.

By this time well aware of Ellsworth's tricks, Meagher suggested that he and the Somerset operator ought to have a private recognition sign, so as to be sure they were talking to each other. The Confederate operator solemnly agreed to the Union operator's suggestion: "Before signing we will make the figure 7." (This is the exact device used for identification by the Germans, when communicating with their armistice delegation within the French lines, in November, 1918. The German delegates were to regard as genuine any radio dispatch that included the number "3048.")

Meagher seems to have had no idea how badly he had been fooled till some of Morgan's horsemen—probably flankers—clattered into Stanford. He ran for it then, was wounded climbing a fence, but escaped. As a friend remarked afterward, Meagher had already been a prisoner of the Confederates once, and after that "there was no catching Jimmy."

The puzzled Federals in Louisville were presently asking for information of Morgan, adding that Federal intelligence knew he had left Crab Orchard for Somerset at 1 P.M. on July 21. Ellsworth replied that he had no information of Morgan, which was more or less true, as Ellsworth and his companions had ridden far ahead of the column and Morgan himself had not yet reached Somerset. About noon of the twenty-second, Ellsworth asked Louisville for permission to have a nap, which Louisville strenuously forbade, on the ground that Union troops were planning to capture Morgan and might need information from Somerset at any moment. At 2 A.M., he was given permission to get some sleep, but with strict orders to be on duty at 6 A.M. He slept till eight, was vigorously rebuked by Louisville, and pacified the command there by reporting there was still no news of Morgan. This kept the Federals quiet until the Confederates were ready to leave Somerset.

Since the raiding column had now nearly completed its circle and was again approaching the Tennessee border and safety, Morgan seized the opportunity to indulge his sense of humor. He gave Ellsworth a derisive telegram to his ancient journalistic foe, George D. Prentice, a Louisville editor, ending with the news that he had "destroyed $1,000,000 worth of Government Stores" and was "now off for Dixie." The million-dollar estimate was probably no idle boast. Somerset was a supply base for medical, quartermaster, and ordnance stores, with several thousand stand of arms and a vast deal of ammunition.

At the words "Government Stores," the Louisville operator broke in to ask what he meant. Ellsworth told him to wait for the end of the message. When that came, the signature of John H. Morgan explained everything. The Union man asked who Ellsworth was and received his real name. He wanted to know when Morgan really did get to Somerset. Eleven last night, said Ellsworth, adding "that the next time we Came I wanted him to let me off earlier and not Keep me up until two oclock looking for Morgan."

"I think He saw the Joke," says Ellsworth, "for His Ha Ha came over the line."

Morgan also sent a telegram to General Boyle, beginning "Good morning, Jerry," explaining that the Confederates now had "all your dispatches since the 10th of July on file," and inquiring politely, "Do you wish copies?" There was also a mocking message for George W. Dunlap, U.S. Congressman from Kentucky.

There was one oddly chivalrous interchange. From Barboursville came a plaintive message signed by W. G. Fuller, superintendent of Union telegraphs, reminding Morgan that he had captured Fuller's field glasses and pistols, in a raid on a Union construction camp in the preceding January (1861): "Please take good care of them." Back flashed Morgan's reply: "Yes; I have your field glasses and pistols. They are good ones, and I am taking good care of them. If we both live till the war is over, I will send them to you, sure." But Morgan did not live.

Ever the humorist, Ellsworth, as he closed down till the next raid, sent one last message promoting himself to a very high but entirely imaginary office, in a telegraphic order of his own:

> Such instances of carelessness as were exhibited on the part of the operators at Lebanon, Midway, and Georgetown, will be severely dealt with. By order of
>
> G. A. Ellsworth,
> Gen'l Military Sup. C. S. Teleg. Dep'mt.

III

Ellsworth's successful chicanery, especially when followed by the sarcastic telegrams, ought to have made the Federal telegraph operators suitably skeptical. But when Morgan made his swift dash from Sparta, Tennessee, to Gallatin, north of Nashville, in August, 1862, Ellsworth was again able to play all his usual tricks. His success was probably due to the brevity of the raid. It was all over and Morgan was riding south, with the whole Federal garrison as prisoners, in two or three days. The Federal operators hardly had time to realize that Ellsworth was back and engaged in his usual mischief on the wires, before his derisive farewell messages began to come in. By that time, the raiders had vanished.

Gallatin was then occupied by the 28th Kentucky, a Union regiment raised in that divided state, which contributed soldiers to both sides. Preliminary secret reconnoissance was entrusted to one of Morgan's innumerable spies. This man—an apparently agitated civilian—rushed frantically into the town a few days before the raid, explaining he had barely escaped being drafted into the Confederate Army and begging for refuge until the Confederate recruiting officers left the district in which he lived.

Sympathetic Federals cared for the "fugitive," thus giving him a fine chance to study the area and ascertain, among other interesting facts, that Colonel William P. Boone, regimental commander, had his quarters in the local hotel, some distance from his troops. It was probably this spy who located the telegraph office and the camp of the 28th Kentucky. The man was playing what the Federals learned to call a "Morganish trick." Whenever possible, Morgan sent an agent ahead into any town he meant to raid.

Thanks to this clever fellow and to Morgan himself, the Confederates knew exactly where to go when they entered Gallatin. Morgan, posing as a Union officer, had personally visited Gallatin and examined the telegraph office in the preceding March, 1862. The new report from his secret agent merely brought the intelligence file on Gallatin up to date.

The raiders set out on August 10, 1862, and on August 10 Morgan detached a certain Captain Joseph de Shea (or Desha) to enter the town and quietly capture Colonel Boone. With the kidnapers went the redoubtable Ellsworth. Leaving their horses a mile outside the town, the Confederates made their way in on foot, hidden by the surrounding cornfields, arriving at dawn. They found the colonel in his hotel room, dressing, made him prisoner, assured his agitated wife that he would not be injured, and withdrew, carrying Boone with them.

Ellsworth also knew exactly where to go. With one companion he set off for the railroad station, where, on the second floor, J. N. Brooks, local ticket seller, expressman, and telegrapher, had his bedroom.

"Surrender!" bellowed Ellsworth, thundering on the door. "I demand it in the name of General Morgan."

Brooks opened up, sleepily, to find himself "looking down the barrels of four Navy pistols." His situation was hopeless, and he knew it.

Though triumphant thus far, Ellsworth was uncomfortably aware that he and his companion were all alone with their prisoner, only a few hundred yards from the Union camp. Presently, however, they heard the hoofs of Morgan's incoming cavalry. They were safe. As it was too early to use the telegraph, Ellsworth accepted his philosophical captive's invitation to breakfast.

With the regimental commander in his hands, Morgan closed in at once on the sleeping 28th Kentucky. He was in a position to destroy the whole regiment before any sentry discovered him. Knowing they had no chance to resist, the Kentuckians surrendered —on the orders of Colonel Boone himself, according to some accounts. Since Brooks, the operator, had also been caught sleeping, not a word of warning reached the wires.

Breakfast over, Ellsworth compelled his prisoner to send a message asking about trains. Having no choice, Brooks complied, but he used his key as awkwardly as he dared, in a style quite unlike his own, hoping to rouse suspicion at the other end. Either this clumsy sending or the unusual hour did strike Jimmy Morris, the operator at Northeast Nashville, as queer. The Gallatin office usually opened at half past seven. There was nothing urgent about this inquiry. Why was Brooks getting up at half past four in the morning to send it?

Just what Morris did is not clear. He certainly did something— subsequent events show that. But he could not tick off a warning to other operators without warning the intruder in the Gallatin station. Apparently he sent a messenger to the nearest headquarters, with word that there was something wrong at Gallatin.

Other Nashville stations seem to have been slow in getting the warning, for at 7:10 A.M. an operator at Franklin and another operator somewhere in Nashville (who was certainly not sending from Morris's key at Nashville Northeast) flashed word that No. 6, northbound for Louisville, was on time.

About eight o'clock, however, Ellsworth heard a certain Conductor Murphy asking Nashville for orders to bring his train from Franklin, Kentucky, to Gallatin, about twenty-five miles to the south, across the Tennessee line. Nashville promptly refused, but Ellsworth pricked up his ears. Making sure Nashville could not hear him, he called Murphy, at Franklin, cancelling the previous order and instructing him to bring his train on to Gallatin.

A Confederate reception committee was waiting when Murphy's train steamed in, and Morgan's men rejoiced over twenty freight cars, loaded with Federal supplies and fifty fresh horses for the Army of the Cumberland. "Mr. Murphy took the joke very well and said He would run again on the Same orders," Ellsworth reports.

When No. 6 rolled into Gallatin, Morgan's men were at the station. No Northern operator as yet knew what had happened to Conductor Murphy and his freight. Nashville supposed Murphy was still obeying orders to lay over at Franklin. But No. 6 was another matter: It was running on schedule, and stations beyond Gallatin would soon begin to wonder why the train did not appear. Ellsworth decided to convince Union operators that, whatever might have happened to No. 6, it had not happened at Gallatin. Pretending that he himself was anxious about the train, he therefore began asking Nashville why No. 6 had not appeared.

The Nashville operator, as a joke, not realizing how truly he spoke, replied, "Guess Morgan's got her; she left on time with twenty-four cars, six loaded." Soon after 9 A.M., the Federal operator at Bowling Green also began asking what had happened to No. 6.

"Not yet arrived," replied Ellsworth, laconically and untruthfully.

The anxious Bowling Green operator now called Nashville to ask about rumors of Confederates between there and Gallatin.

"Nary rumor," replied Nashville.

Soon after this, Ellsworth heard Nashville announcing that another passenger train was just pulling out. About 10:45, however, Nashville suddenly became suspicious and began asking Ellsworth a series of seemingly casual questions, the real purpose of which Ellsworth recognized at once. He suspected that someone on the passenger train—which had failed to reach Gallatin as announced —had seen Confederates; that the train had been run back to Nashville; and that the Federals there had thus been warned. It is more likely, however, that Jimmy Morris, at Nashville Northeast, had at last succeeded in getting a special courier through, with news of the exceedingly odd telegraphic style that Brooks, at Gallatin, had suddenly and inexplicably adopted.

Ellsworth sent for that unhappy man, still a prisoner, and ordered him to take the key again and give correct answers to Nashville's queries. Probably poor Brooks continued to send in a style as unlike his own as possible, but he did not dare send the wrong answers. If he did, Nashville would show increasing suspicion. Then Ellsworth would take him as a prisoner to Dixie. If he cooperated, he would probably be released.

"Who is at the key?" inquired Nashville.

"B," replied either Ellsworth or Brooks, at Gallatin.

"Who is B?"

"Brooks."

"What Brooks give your full name," insisted Nashville.

The full name was supplied, but still Nashville's skepticism remained.

"Who was that young lady that went with You and I to Major Fosters the other Night?"

"Don't know you—never went with any young lady—Don't Know Major Foster," clicked the key in Gallatin.

Nashville now reported that, as Ellsworth had suspected, the passenger train to Gallatin really had been turned back. A Negro had met it, four miles from Gallatin, "saying John Morgan Has the town."

With grim humor Ellsworth telegraphed orders for the unfortunate Negro, who had patriotically reported the exact truth, to be arrested and jailed.

"Everything is quiet Here."

"I am satisfied but the Superintendent is not," said Nashville. "He wants to know What that was He sent you by express yesterday."

It was a question that would have baffled Ellsworth completely, but Brooks supplied the answer:

"A jug of Nitric Acid."

"Correct the train will start again the negro has been arrested."

There was one other question, perhaps a little earlier in this entertaining dialogue:

"Mr. Marshall, the Superintendent of the Railroads, is not yet satisfied that you are not Morgan's operator, and he wishes you to tell him who you wished to take your place while you were gone on leave of absence; how long you wished to be gone, and when did you wish to go?"

Again Brooks—under pressure—obliged.

"Tell Mr. Marshall I wished Mr. Clayton to take my place while I got a week's leave to go to Cincinnati."

Marshall, at last convinced that all was well, gave orders for the next north- and southbound trains to proceed as usual, his orders of course being audible to all stations along the way, including Gallatin. The Nashville train left at 11:15.

After that, routine messages followed until 4 P.M., when Nashville, greatly excited, called to say both trains had "returned the second time." Confederates certainly were in Gallatin, whether the telegraph operator there knew it or not. What had become of the Nashville train that was already missing?

Ellsworth was gently evasive until about four o'clock. Then, while Morgan himself was in the office, Nashville called, asking who was now at the Gallatin key. Ellsworth asked what to say.

"Tell him anything you please," said Morgan. "We will leave Here at 5 Oclock." The Confederates had abandoned all hope of getting another train. The Union men by this time knew all too well who Ellsworth was.

"I am Ellsworth," confessed that worthy.

"You d——m wild Canadian what are you doing there?" replied Nashville Northeast.

An admiring audience of young ladies, clustered in the telegraph office, had joined in hearty rebel laughter as they heard one telegram after another read out. Now one of them wrote out a dispatch to George D. Prentice, the Louisville editor: "Wash" Morgan, cousin of the raiders' commander, was coming to Louisville to take Prentice's scalp, it said.

Laden with booty, Morgan's cavaliers withdrew to Hartsville, Tennessee, with a sense of duty done. Before leaving Gallatin, Ellsworth took Brooks's pocketbook, which had $40 in it, as legitimate spoils of war. He also seized $50 or $60 that he found in the telegraph office. The aggrieved Brooks protested to Morgan, who

forced Ellsworth to return the pocketbook and its contents, plus a
new coat and shirt.

IV

The Federals were now on their guard against Ellsworth. He accompanied Morgan on another raid through Kentucky that ended
only after the battle of Perryville (October 8, 1862). But, though
he tapped wires to good effect, he himself mentions no more of
his deceptive messages.

Ellsworth was not with Morgan on his raid along Rosecrans's
lines of communication reaching into Tennessee, December 22,
1862–January 1, 1863. But Morgan did have another telegrapher,
named Aud, of whom nothing else is known. This man had worked
in the telegraph office at Louisville not long before the raid and
knew a good deal about the Union forces there. Morgan had him
cut in on the Federal line at Munfordville, Kentucky, with a dispatch to General Boyle at Louisville, supposedly from the Union
general commanding at Bowling Green. This asked for immediate reinforcement, alleging that Morgan—who actually was nowhere
near—was about to attack Bowling Green. Boyle, replying that he
had no troops to spare, foolishly gave the disposition of his forces.
That was exactly the information Morgan wanted.

Again Morgan's sense of humor led him to reveal his own trick.
He sent another of his derisive telegrams to General Boyle, "calling
him 'a bright young man and smart boy,' ending with characteristic
vulgarity"—or so said an indignant Federal. He followed this
with a message for a girl he knew in Lexington, Kentucky, asking
the Louisville operator to forward it!

Sometime later, probably in January, 1863, Ellsworth ventured
into Kentucky in disguise, tapped the Federal wire at Cave City
again, and spent two weeks listening to official Federal messages.
He lived and worked in a thicket two hundred yards from the
track, where he had set up his instrument, and sometimes amused
himself sitting by the railroad and watching the trains pass. On his
way back, with three or four hundred copies of official Union telegrams—enough to hang anyone—he was discovered and chased by

Federal cavalry, eluded them, and returned to Morgan's camp. The telegrams went on to Bragg.

In March, 1863, he was tapping Federal wires near Gallatin, "near the Tunnel on the Louisville and Nashville RR." In his first twenty-four hours, he took down a message describing an impending movement of Union troops that needed an immediate checkmate. Starting at five in the afternoon to warn Morgan, he rode all night. About dawn he met a Union cavalryman. There was a pistol fight, and Ellsworth was hit four inches above the ankle. He rode twenty miles with only one foot in a stirrup till he could get a conveyance to McMinnville, where he could find medical aid.

Morgan let him recuperate till June, then ordered him back to duty for a raid into Ohio. On his way across Kentucky, somewhere near Burkesville, Morgan detached Captain Ralph Sheldon and Ellsworth, with a small force, to pass around Columbia, Kentucky, and destroy bridges and culverts on the Louisville & Nashville Railroad. Sheldon also hoped to capture a train or two.

As the little force approached Lebanon about 4 A.M. on July 4, 1863, they paused to tear up track, went on about five miles to Lebanon Junction, tore up more track, and settled down to wait for the next train. When it did not arrive, Ellsworth cut into the line, as he had the year before, and began calling Z (Lebanon Junction), signing B, as he had in 1862. With incredible carelessness, the Federals had not troubled to change the call letters.

Ellsworth nearly ruined his chances for future mischief then and there, because he did not know what messages the real Lebanon Junction operator, E. H. Atwater, had been receiving. He asked why the train was delayed.

"Why," protested Atwater, "you sent a message around by Danville, Lexington, and Louisville this morning, saying a party of Rebels came to within three miles of Lebanon and destroyed the railroad and telegraph and not to let trains come. And now you ask where they are!"

Only quick and expert lying saved the situation. Ellsworth replied glibly, "Well, that was the report brought in by some drunken section men, who were probably on a Fourth-of-July spree; and, failing to get your office, a message was sent round by Lexington."

After hearing that—perhaps remembering what had happened the year before—Atwater demanded a confirmatory statement from "Mr. Knox," the ticket agent at Lexington. Reflecting that he "Could sign Mr Knox's name as well as I Could any other," Ellsworth concocted a suitable message and supplied the signature:

"My telegram of this morning was based on reports brought in by some drunken men and is without foundation. Let the train proceed."

Ellsworth then added a glowing account of the prospective Fourth of July celebration at Lebanon and invited Atwater to come as his guest, receiving a tentative acceptance. The 8:30 P.M. train from Louisville had puffed into Lebanon Junction about this time, and the worried conductor, who had heard guerrillas were about, asked Atwater for news. The operator reassured him, flashed to Ellsworth the welcome news, "the Train is off I must go—" and swung aboard.

Sheldon hastily got his men into position opposite a break in the line and waited.

The train chugged along undisturbed, pausing a few miles outside the town to take on a guard of Union soldiers. Before it had quite reached the first break in the line, the Confederates flagged it to a halt, "as we did not wish to Hurt any one on it." The engineer began to slow down too late, struck the break, and derailed at least part of his train. The train guard opened fire at once, after which the Confederates also began firing. There was a lively little fracas for about twenty minutes, during which Atwater set out down the track to get aid from Lebanon. Almost at once he ran into his prospective host, Ellsworth, and two or three other Confederates, who made him prisoner. The two men had, of course, never seen each other.

Ellsworth asked the captive's name.

"Atwater."

"You are the operator at Z," said Ellsworth, "and I was talking with you over the line this morning, having cut the wire and connected this instrument. I found out what I wished and am the one who invited you to Lebanon. I am Ellsworth, George Ellsworth, Morgan's operator."

Atwater, not unreasonably, suggested that Ellsworth, having

invited him to Lebanon as a guest and then trapped him, at least owed him a drink; but before that problem could be settled, Federal cavalry appeared in the distance. Ellsworth and his companions rode for their lives.

Atwater was free. He now had the satisfaction of tapping the line himself and sending General Boyle, in Louisville, news that Morgan was somewhere near Lebanon.

This seems to have been Ellsworth's last major deception, though he presently had the satisfaction of capturing three Union telegraphers. He himself was captured, however, as were most of Morgan's men, in the advance through Indiana and Ohio. After his release, he took charge of all Beauregard's telegraphy. By poetic justice, he found Union operators, on two or three occasions, tapping his own wires.

16

FALSE ORDERS, WIRE TAPS,
FRAUD, AND DECEIT

Though no other general succeeded in deluding his foes with the unscrupulous guile and cheerful abandon of the intensely godly Stonewall Jackson, military hoaxes were numerous on both sides. All of them were bold, most of them ingenious, a surprising number successful, and a few extremely funny.

This contest in deceit included false orders delivered at critical moments by spies in false uniforms, forged telegrams, false flag signals, deceptive movements of railroad trains, and wooden cannon, like Beauregard's—sometimes called "Quaker guns" because they shed no blood.

I

Occasionally, false orders were given to Union troops by Confederate officers actually wearing Confederate uniform, who were not recognized for what they were, either because of darkness or the excitement of battle. Though the thing seems incredible, there are three well-authenticated instances of this; and if all the facts had been recorded a good many more could certainly be found.

Such military pranks were all the easier because both sides spoke the same language. Few commanders, in the urgency of combat, thought to question an unknown "staff officer" or "courier" who, with an appropriate air of confident authority, delivered an order from "the general." Fewer still paused to consider the authenticity of his accent.

Such spies, of course, had to make sure they had the name of the right general, and their dialects could not be very noticeably from the wrong side of the Mason and Dixon line. Some were selected for their speech, others were given speech training. Sheridan's fraudulent Confederates, who swarmed among the genuine rebels in Ewell's Confederate II Corps, in the Shenandoah, and later among Lee's forces at Petersburg and Richmond, were carefully taught as much as possible about the Confederate Army, its units, and the names and exact commands of even junior officers. Southern spies like Stringfellow and Gilmor were careful to have the same information about the Yankees.

The only spy on either side known to have been caught because he made a mistake about an enemy officer's name was one of Sheridan's men. Disguised as a Confederate officer, this agent had the misfortune, not long before Appomattox, to deliver a false order—supposedly from one of Lee's generals—to the indignant Confederate general whose name had been forged! The luckless agent would certainly have been hanged, but for Lee's surrender, after which all Union prisoners, including spies, were released.

A few weeks after the Seven Days battle, one luckless Yankee perished because he underestimated the care with which Longstreet observed details. Dressed as a Confederate courier, the Yankee approached the general on August 21, 1862, with a forged message, purporting to come from Stonewall Jackson and intended to move I Corps in the wrong direction. But Longstreet, personally acquainted with all Jackson's couriers, realized at once that the message was a fraud and ordered the man hanged on the spot. The poor fellow was hardly dead before his boots were being pulled off by an ill-shod rebel.

Sometimes darkness or the confusion of battle enabled an officer, even though properly clad in his own uniform, to give orders to the enemy—misleading orders, needless to say—and then ride placidly away, without discovery. Even if detected, these men could not be accused of espionage, since they were not disguised. Most officers who played this trick had wandered accidentally into the enemy's lines and were simply brazening it out. Naturally, they gave the worst orders they could think of.

Protagonist in the most spectacular incident of this sort was the Confederate general, Leonidas Polk. As the battle of Perryville was closing in the dusk of October 8, 1862, Polk saw troops firing on the Confederate brigade of General St. John Liddell. Peering through the gathering darkness, he could see the blazing muskets of troops who seemed to be Confederates, too. As he had no aide or staff officer with him at the moment, the general rode up to the firing line himself and ordered the nearest officer to cease fire. Couldn't he see he was shooting his own men?

"I don't think there can be any mistake about it; I am sure they are the enemy," replied the officer.

"Enemy!" cried Polk. "Why, I have only just left them myself. Cease firing, sir; what is your name, sir?"

"My name is Colonel Tanner, of the 22nd Indiana; and pray, sir, who are you?"

Only then did General Polk realize he had ridden into a Yankee regiment. He also realized there was nothing to do but keep up his pose as an indignant and very senior Union officer.

"I'll soon show you who I am, sir," he snarled, shaking his fist. "Cease firing, sir, at once."

Turning his horse, the general departed with impressive dignity, cantering along the rear of the Federal firing line and, as he went, ordering the men to cease fire. Polk confessed later, "I experienced a disagreeable sensation, like screwing up my back, and calculating how many bullets would be between my shoulders every moment." None of the Union soldiers fired at him, and Polk, reaching cover behind a small cluster of trees, galloped hastily for his own lines. Once in safety, the general was unkind enough to concentrate the fire of 3,000 Confederate muskets on the soldiers of the 22nd Indiana, whom he had just ordered to cease fire.

In the dusk of that same evening, Major Charles S. Cotter, then chief of artillery for the Federal general, McCook, repeated General Polk's blunder but was identified before he had any chance to give false orders. The major had been out selecting artillery emplacements and had finished moving an Indiana battery into position on the extreme right of Rousseau's Federal Division. He was riding toward a neighboring woods to select two more gun positions when he saw a group of soldiers in the twilight. He rode over to ask why they were not advancing. Too late, Cotter found that he had ridden into General Polk's staff, probably not long after the general himself had escaped from the 22nd Indiana. Less fortunate than Polk, Major Cotter was immediately taken prisoner by the Confederates.

One of Major Harry Gilmor's cavalry officers played the same trick Polk had played—but deliberately and even more brazenly. Gilmor's horsemen had been sent forward to drive off troopers of the 6th U.S. Cavalry who had been raiding Confederate pickets near Smithfield, Virginia. Gilmor had been told that there were only 200 Union raiders. His information was correct when he received it. But he had not been told that several thousand of Sheridan's troopers would soon move in behind them.

Gilmor's men had overwhelmed the 200 Union cavalrymen and were joyfully "running" them when they suddenly beheld much larger forces on their front and flanks. Captain Gus Dorsey saved this critical situation by riding up to one of the Federal columns and—"in a loud stern voice"—bellowing the command: "By fours, right about wheel. March!"

The Federal commanding officer should have looked more closely at Dorsey's uniform. But the rebel's parade-ground voice and the habit of obedience were too much for him. He dutifully repeated Dorsey's command, and, to Gilmor's delight, the Union column rode off to its own rear, giving Gilmor just time to escape.

While Grant was attacking at Belmont, Missouri (November 7, 1861), Confederate Major General Benjamin F. Cheatham had an adventure much like Polk's and turned it to advantage in much the same way. Cheatham rode unexpectedly into a cavalry squadron. Assuming it was Confederate, he asked what unit it belonged to.

"Illinois cavalry, sir."

Cheatham saw that the speaker had recognized him for a senior officer, without noticing his uniform. This was entirely possible in 1861, even in daylight, for during the first months of the war neither side had a single recognizable uniform. Militia units were still wearing special "regimentals"—gray for the Yankees of the 7th New York and the 28th, 66th, and 71st Pennsylvania, blue for the rebels of the Richmond Blues.

Cheatham recognized his danger but kept his head.

"Oh! Illinois cavalry," he said calmly. "All right; just stand where you are." The Union officer dutifully obeyed orders; and Cheatham, having thus, singlehanded, immobilized an enemy unit with one bold bluff, rode peacefully away—only to stumble into still another group of Federals. Seeing a mounted officer approaching from another Union regiment, they also supposed he must be a Union officer. The Confederate general escaped to his own command with no further difficulty.

Exploits like Polk's or Cheatham's were, of course, only lucky accidents, of which they were quick-witted enough to take advantage. But spies sometimes deliberately disguised themselves as enemy staff officers or couriers, so that they could carry false orders to enemy commanders, after which they faded hastily and discreetly into the landscape, before anyone thought to demand identification. One of the boldest and most successful of these was Halifax Richards Wood, attached to the divisional staff of the Confederate major general, R. F. Hoke.

In May, 1864, Union General Benjamin F. Butler landed at Bermuda Hundred with two Federal corps and began an advance up the James River, toward Drewry's Bluff. Butler extended his left until he had nearly enveloped the Confederate right. Hoke saw at once that, if Butler managed to get completely around the rebel right, he would soon be in control of the road to Richmond. Without troops enough for a fight, Hoke had to find some way to hold the Federals back until Confederate reinforcements could arrive.

Wood saved the day. Donning a blue uniform, he rode in a wide arc around Butler's flank until he was far behind the Union forces, then rode boldly forward, as if coming up from the Federal rear. When he reached Butler's headquarters, he reported, in feigned excitement, that large (and entirely imaginary) Confederate forces were landing from the James, in Butler's right and rear. Wood then rode off quickly, as if in haste to return to Federal headquarters, thus avoiding questions.

Before he could get back to the rebel lines, General Hoke's anxious Confederate staff saw that the Federal flanking movement had suddenly ceased and that Butler was already making hasty changes in his dispositions. Then Wood rode in with his story. He had gained enough delay to stave off defeat. During the night Confederate reinforcements came in to support Hoke. Butler was soon bottled up in Bermuda Hundred, and, for the time being, Richmond was saved.

After the war, this tale was confirmed by Colonel Peter S. Michie, of Butler's own staff. Michie had suspected Wood was a rebel spy —but not in time to stop him—and there had been a delay in checking the information that he brought.

The Union forces also used this same trick at times. Grant's victory at Chattanooga in November, 1863, was assisted by a false order which was delivered by a Northern agent disguised as a Confederate. This added considerably to the confusion of the Confederate retreat.

Before Sherman attacked the Confederate Northern flank on Missionary Ridge, Bragg had placed his wagon train at Chickamauga Station, immediately east of the north end of the Ridge. The train was to be held here, with teams harnessed and hitched to their wagons, so that it could move out instantly, if, as Bragg correctly feared, he was forced to fall back.

Somehow, Union intelligence knew all about that wagon train and its orders—probably through General Dodge's spy system. Presently, a man in Confederate uniform rode in among the wagons with orders to unhitch, unharness, and feed the horses. Naturally, the teamsters obeyed. The horses would be fresher when needed.

Eventually, Bragg did have to withdraw. Late that afternoon, the sullenly retreating rebel line came over the hills and looked down in amazement on the wagon train that was supposed to be ready to withdraw instantly: "Such a sight as met our gaze beggars description. All our supplies down in that field, teams unhitched, teamsters cooking supper and everything as calm as if there was not a Yankee in twenty miles, and all the time Sherman was coiling his line around us. There was nothing to do but fight out of it."

The teamsters hitched up as fast as they could and pulled out at full speed. The hard-pressed Confederate line, on the hilltop, held off the Federals long enough to cover their retreat.

Realizing too late that the supposed wagon master who had delivered the order was a spy, Confederate cavalry set out in pursuit. They "got pretty close to him and chased him into Sherman's lines," but they couldn't catch him.

(Sheridan's brilliant intelligence officer, Major H. H. Young, once rode up to a Confederate battery so placed as to be very dangerous to advancing Union troops and ordered it to a new position where it was harmless. Young, who spent half his time in a Confederate uniform, had no trouble getting his orders obeyed.)

Such deception was especially easy because both sides wore oilskin capes in wet weather, and the Confederates also wore a great many Union overcoats. This, says John Esten Cooke, of J. E. B. Stuart's staff, was not "formal assumption of any disguise." Though not all Federal commanders accepted this easy-going attitude, Stuart himself did. Late in 1863, Stuart was with troops who charged a Union roadblock north of the Rapidan. When the Confederates paused, the staff noticed a mounted man in an oilskin, riding a little forward, apparently to get a better view of the retreating Yankees.

"Who is that?" asked Jeb.

"One of the escort," replied an officer.

"No! You are mistaken. Halt him."

The man was brought back and confronted by Stuart.

"What do you belong to?"

It was hopeless to bluff any longer. "The First Maine," said the man in the oilskin, sheepishly. Stuart burst into roars of laughter and sent him to the rear as a prisoner. Then Cooke, who had been "certain he was a good Southerner," remembered that the prisoner *had* seemed to be listening to Stuart's remarks with special attention. But there were no charges of espionage.

Mosby, who refused to wear a false uniform, found it easy to enter Union lines in an oilskin cape and converse with the enemy "as one of them."

II

Sometimes the Confederates managed to deceive the Yankees without asking spies to run the risks such exploits as these involved. Before retreating to Antietam, Lee had officers talking "carelessly" in Frederick, Maryland, mentioning Harrisburg and even Philadelphia, as if these were still rebel objectives. Before Stonewall Jackson left town, he inquired anxiously for a map of Chambersburg, Pennsylvania, which was on the way to Harrisburg—though Jackson had no intention of entering Pennsylvania at all.

"Deserters" were always entering the Union lines with astounding tales. The deserter, says the novelist Albion W. Tourgee, could be worth an army corps to the rebels. "He was ubiquitous, willing, and altogether inscrutable. Whether he told the truth or a lie, he was equally sure to deceive. He was sometimes a real deserter and sometimes a mock deserter. In either case he was sure to be loaded." It was a deserter who persuaded McClellan that Beauregard had been ordered west with fifteen regiments. Beauregard *had* been ordered west—all alone! Another reported a panic among Confederate troops at a time when, far from being in a panic, they were hoping to be attacked. Others reported discontent and poor rations. Johnston reported his men eager for battle, when that was anything but the truth. Secretary of War Stanton wanted to change plans for the next campaign because of fabrications by a "deserting" Confederate second lieutenant. It was not so easy to fool U. S. Grant. "I do not see how an officer of that rank comes to know so much of future plans," he told his timid superiors.

When the Pennsylvania 5th Cavalry was near Williamsburg, Virginia, in 1862, it received an average of one or two deserters a week. Many of them actually were deserters, but then a certain Edward Boyle appeared, explaining he was really a New Yorker who had been forced into the Confederate Army. Though at first put into the guardhouse, he was eventually allowed to join the regiment and was sent out with a reconnoissance company—which he promptly led into a Confederate trap. Then he reappeared, leading a Confederate attack upon the 5th Pennsylvania, being perfectly acquainted with its camp.

In a desperate situation on the evening of November 29, 1864, two Federal spies saved Major General John M. Schofield's Federal XXIII Corps from the annihilation of a large part of its force, by swiftly supplying the Confederate army commander, General John B. Hood, with false information and then delivering equally false orders to his troops. As a result, mystified rebels were ordered by their own officers not to fire, when they could have completely wiped out a helpless Federal column. Equally mystified, the Federals never understood why the enemy allowed them to pass within point-blank rifle range, unscathed.

Controversy has raged about this fantastic incident for a long time. General Hood and Major General John B. Cheatham, one of his division commanders, the two Confederate leaders whom the spies deceived, later told wildly conflicting stories. Nathan B. Forrest, equally deceived, never mentions the incident. A junior staff officer, conscience-stricken, feared later it was due to his failure to deliver an order. (It wasn't.)

The Confederates never guessed what had defeated them, nor did Schofield guess what had saved him. The contradictory reports that Hood and Cheatham later wrote, in happy ignorance of the completeness with which they had been fooled, were never corrected. By that time, one of the Union spies was dead, and the other wasn't talking. Neither were one or two Northern generals who knew the facts as they really were. (They might want to try that little trick again.)

The correct—or approximately correct—story, as it can now be pieced together from the accounts of all participants, is this:

In July of 1864, while Lee and Grant were battling at Richmond, Sherman advanced across Georgia to Atlanta, which he took September 2. Hood, after evacuating Atlanta, swung back into Tennessee and began to destroy Sherman's railroad supply line. Sherman, refusing to be diverted, cut loose from his communications and started on his march to the sea, November 16. But he sent Major General George H. Thomas, "the Rock of Chickamauga," to protect Nashville and as much of Tennessee as possible from Hood's forces and, in general, to keep Hood occupied.

Himself busy strengthening the defenses of Nashville, Thomas ordered Schofield, with his own XXIII Corps and with General David S. Stanley's IV Corps, to hold off Hood at Columbia, Tennessee, on the Duck River. When, however, the Confederates broke the Duck River line and came pouring into Schofield's rear, there was nothing to do but retreat along the Columbia–Spring Hill–Franklin–Nashville road. There were still a few Federal troops at Spring Hill, but the town itself was nearly empty when Forrest's Confederate cavalry approached it.

On the night of November 29–30, while the all-important road was filled with the crowded column of Schofield's retreating troops near Spring Hill, Cheatham's Confederates came down upon the flank. There was nothing whatever to stop them from shooting the blue column to pieces.

Into this advantageous situation rode Hood himself, strapped to his saddle—he had only one arm and one leg—but full of fighting spirit. As he saw the long thin column straggling past, he gave instant orders for Cheatham's I Corps to seize the turnpike on which the Yankees were marching. Colonel Henry Stone, a Union staff officer under Thomas, later declared that, if the rebels had resolutely thrust a single brigade across that road, they would have cut Schofield off completely. Cheatham's men had stumbled on a unique opportunity to win a resounding and easy victory.

Then what happened? Nothing whatever.

The Confederates closed in on the right flank of the blue column till one gray regiment was within 250 yards. Said a rebel soldier: "There was not even a skirmish line between us and the fleeing Federals on the pike, who were plainly visible. The Confederate pickets could hear the conversation of the passing Federals distinctly." No orders came. The Confederates simply went into bivouac.

Colonel Stone described the Confederate menace, as apprehensive Federals saw it from their own ranks: "The long line of Confederate camp-fires burned bright, and the men could be seen standing around them or sauntering about in groups. Now and then a few would come almost to the pike and fire at a passing Union squad, but without provoking a reply."

Confederate troops, astonished at being held back from the enemy's exposed flank, were still more astonished when they continued to be held back, hour after hour, for the rest of the night, within sight and sound of the long enemy column, marching quietly past.

The Federals moved safely to Spring Hill, reached Franklin on November 30, and later that day—having been given plenty of time to concentrate, reconnoiter, and deploy—defeated Hood completely. They then withdrew to Nashville, Hood limped on to the outskirts of the city, where Thomas was by this time completely ready for him. Again, Hood lost.

The leading spirit in the scheme that stopped Cheatham was Private J. D. Remington, Company I, 73rd Illinois Volunteers. Remington had already made six trips as a spy into the Confederate lines—three at Murfreesboro, Tennessee; two at New Hope, Georgia; and one at Atlanta. He was aided by a cousin, a captain in the Confederate Army, whose name Remington never revealed in print, who had long been a Union spy, reporting to Federal staff officers through two other secret agents, whose identities also remain unknown. This mystery man and the agents cooperating with him were probably all members of General Dodge's Federal spy network.

Rather late in the afternoon of November 29, his brigade commander, General Emerson Opdycke, ordered Remington to enter the Confederate lines, learn the enemy's strength, and collect any other information he could. Brigade headquarters had a Confederate captain's uniform, saber, revolver, and horse ready.

As he emerged on the Columbia–Spring Hill road, after riding some distance through the woods, Remington saw three horsemen: the Confederate generals Hood, Cheatham, and Patrick R. Cleburne, another of Hood's subordinates, with all three of whom he was acquainted. Pretending to come as a messenger from Forrest, he gave an entirely imaginary (but tactically reasonable) report of that general's movements. Remington was still riding with them when they came in sight of the exposed flank of the retreating Federals.

Hood gave Cheatham an attack order instantly, adding that Stewart's cavalry would cooperate. At the same time, he ordered the supposedly Confederate "Captain" Remington to ride back and bring Forrest's whole cavalry corps down on the Union column too. That meant annihilation, and Remington knew it.

"No one can imagine how I felt," he wrote in after years, "when I heard that Hood had two corps of his army [i.e., Cheatham's and Forrest's], while there was only one division of Federals."

Wondering what on earth he ought to do, Remington rode off as if to obey Hood's orders. By pure luck, he met his cousin, the other Federal spy, still posing as a Confederate captain. Together they concocted false orders to prevent the attack Hood had ordered. Then, riding to Brigadier General Otho French Strahl, one of Cleburne's subordinates, Remington persuaded him that Federals, probably imaginary, were in position to menace the general's flank.

Strahl took him to Major General John Calvin Brown, for whose benefit Remington invented a purely imaginary Federal corps. He himself had discovered these additional Federal troops, he told the alarmed and astonished Brown. They were, he said unblushingly, skillfully hidden in or near Spring Hill, and were supported by six masked batteries. (There really were a few Union troops in the town, whose presence, if Confederate scouts saw them, would strengthen this tale.)

Someone also carried false orders to Forrest—and it is easy to guess who that was. Hood was sure Forrest's cavalry was in position to block the Federal advance between Spring Hill and Franklin. When Brown finally did attack Spring Hill, he was upset to find that Forrest was not there to cover his right, as expected. Forrest's new "orders" had sent him to another part of the field.

Confirmation of these extraordinary tales is provided by a statement of Cleburne's adjutant. According to this officer, an unknown "Confederate" officer-courier—unknown, at least, to his victim—brought General Stewart a surprising order, just as he was putting his horsemen in position to block off the Federals. Hood had ordered him to take position across the pike, north of Spring Hill, and hold the Federals back, while Cheatham attacked at another point.

The new order, carried by the mysterious officer claiming to come from Hood, told Stewart he was on the wrong road and instructed him to take a quite different position. Stewart did not at the moment suspect espionage; but it all seemed queer, and he was dubious enough to ride back to see Hood. Hood informed him that original orders still stood.

By that time, it was so late that Stewart was told to bivouac for the night and move early in the morning. When morning came, it was too late—the Federals had reached safety. Someone sent Remington back to Cheatham, who took him to Hood. A proposed attack by Cleburne was hastily postponed. Even then, Hood and his staff command seem to have felt no suspicion, still believing that Remington was a genuine Confederate.

Hood did, however, ask, "How do you know there is a whole corps of Federals in Spring Hill?"

Remington glibly assured him that, after leaving Hood a little while before, to carry orders to Forrest (this Hood knew to be the truth), he had passed through the Federal lines and had personally observed the hidden corps. Remington says that Hood then halted the attack he had originally ordered. Hood himself, in his article on Spring Hill, emphasizes his effort to get Cheatham to attack and Cheatham's unaccountable failure to do so.

Cheatham, on the other hand, insists that it was Hood who held back; he himself was eager to attack. "I was never more astonished than when General Hood informed me that he had concluded to postpone that attack till daylight. The road was still open—orders to remain quiet until morning—and nothing to prevent the enemy from marching to Franklin," as they did. (This, of course, confirms Remington's story.)

As if to add to the contradiction of the two generals' narratives, one of Hood's staff officers long afterward confessed he had failed to deliver an attack order to Cheatham. But Cheatham does not say such an order failed to arrive. He says Hood explicitly *forbade* attack. One cannot help wondering whether Remington may not have interfered again.

Remington says that he now rode off a second time—ostensibly on his way back to Forrest. But that was merely for effect. Once safely out of sight, he went from one Confederate brigade to another. To each he delivered imaginary orders from Hood. They were to stay 400 yards from the pike on which the Federals were passing and not to fire unless the Federals attacked. (Remington knew well enough the Union forces were in no condition to attack.)

Remington and his "Confederate" cousin met at Hood's headquarters next day, the cousin having in the meantime contrived to supply further false information to the two cavalry leaders, Forrest and Stewart. His description of the road along which the Federals would continue to move sent the latter's horsemen completely astray.

Remington now brought Hood the information that Spring Hill was "all full of Yankees." In fact, Spring Hill was very lightly held —if, as late as noon of November thirtieth, there was more than a handful of Union troops anywhere near it. The Yankees were all hurrying to Franklin, but Hood was, by this time, so impressed with "Captain" Remington that the cousin heard him proposing to put the Union spy permanently on his own staff.

The two spies now fled to safety before their duplicity was discovered. The cousin was killed in the battle of Franklin, which began a few hours later. Remington, after "surrendering" to the Federals "as a deserting Confederate officer," asked to be taken to the nearest brigade headquarters, which, by good luck, turned out to be General Opdycke's. Opdycke sent the spy at once to division and corps headquarters and then to General Schofield himself.

The whole story is confusing. But that is not really surprising. The episode itself was meant to confuse Hood and his officers, and the two determined Union spies labored with all their might to make the confusion as complete as possible. The situation was not made any clearer when the leaders concerned, who never really knew what did happen, tried later to explain away their blunders.

The story of the spies is so remarkable that, inevitably, it has been questioned. S. A. Cunningham, of the 41st Tennessee, later editor of the *Confederate Veteran*, was skeptical of Remington's tale, even though he published it. But there is nothing really incredible in it, and it is the only explanation of the Confederates' inexplicable failure to attack. As Remington himself remarks, "To many who have not had experience as a spy it may seem impos-

sible to do the things that have been done by spies." In the nature
of things, it is frequently impossible to verify from other sources a
secret service agent's account of his own doings. But Remington is
an exception. His story is twice confirmed, though not so explicitly
as one could desire. Cheatham says he was amazed to receive
orders from Hood canceling the attack—almost exactly Remington's own story. Hood, who says he ordered the attack, never understood why his order was not delivered. Stewart was equally
amazed to receive orders from an unknown officer, also canceling
the attack. This corresponds with Remington's account of his own
and his cousin's doings.

It is also noteworthy that General Opdycke's brigade, which included Remington's regiment, the 73rd Illinois, was marching at the
head of the 2nd Division as it pulled out of Columbia at 8 A.M.,
November 29. It was, therefore, one of the first units to reach
Spring Hill. In other words, Remington *was* at the place he said
he was. He *was* there at the time he says. And he *was* thus entirely
able to do what he says he did.

Amazing as Remington's exploit was, it was no more extraordinary
than various similar deceptions. The Confederate Army had already played exactly the same trick on the Yankees at Chancellorsville. Stonewall made his famous flank march between 4 A.M.
and about 5 P.M., on May 2, 1863, and attacked about 6 P.M., only
about two hours before dark. All night the shattered Federals on
the right flank worked to strengthen a defensive line for the attack
they knew would come in the morning—though they did not yet
know Jackson had been mortally wounded.

About dawn, as the 1st Massachusetts and the 74th New York
Volunteers were preparing for the worst, a staff officer rode down
the line and ordered both regiments to withdraw to the Orange
Plank road and then to the rear. Somewhere near the Plank road
they met their divisional commander, General Hiram Gregory
Berry. Astonished to find his troops in retreat, the general demanded who had given such orders. The staff officer, who had not
withdrawn in time, was brought before him. In a fury, Berry seized
the shoulder of the offender's blue coat to tear off the shoulder
straps and in doing so, tore open the coat itself—and revealed a
gray uniform! The regiments reoccupied their positions in time to

stand off the Confederate attack that soon came. The spy's fate, though unknown, is not hard to guess.

On his long cavalry raid from Tennessee through Mississippi to Louisiana in April, 1863, the Union general, Benjamin H. Grierson, also tried planting false information to keep off a Confederate force that might have interfered with his march. Near Union Church, Mississippi, Grierson captured a prominent local citizen, whose name is now unknown. This magnate was courteously treated and given a room to himself. Next to it—and not by accident—was the room of General Grierson and his adjutant, ostensibly much occupied in discussing plans for their next move. Grierson finally announced his decision within hearing of his eavesdropping prisoner. He would continue his march to Natchez and thence across the state of Mississippi. The Confederate civilian, who was then allowed to escape, promptly carried word of the Union cavalry general's supposed plans to General Franklin Gardner, the local Confederate commander. That delighted officer at once prepared an ambush to trap Grierson at Natchez. To do this, he had to draw troops away from the line of march Grierson actually contemplated. Grierson, who had never had any intention of going anywhere near Natchez, marched on into Louisiana, nearly unopposed.

J. E. B. Stuart played the same game successfully as Sheridan's cavalrymen were approaching Richmond in May, 1864. He sent out a courier, with orders to let himself be captured with false orders in his possession. This is supposed to have saved Richmond for the time being. But it led to the fight at Yellow Tavern, in which Stuart himself was mortally wounded.

III

Where codes were known to be leaky, both sides sometimes used the flag signal stations to plant false information. None of the flag alphabets, even when ciphered, were very secure. The two signal services could often read each other's flag signals, even though ciphers were frequently changed; but the Confederates failed to break Union telegraph codes and ciphers. So far as is known, Union secret agents rarely had a chance to listen to Confederate telegraph signals, though the spy J. J. Kerbey, himself a telegraph operator, contrived to do so early in the war.

On August 31, 1864, Colonel Charles Marshall, Lee's military secretary, sent Ewell "the enemy's signal alphabet, as deciphered by some of our signal men here. We read their messages with facility," added Marshall, "and the general desires you to communicate the alphabet to all signal men operating north of James River, enjoining them to keep the fact of our knowledge of the alphabet secret. The enemy read our dispatches also, and you will please put your signal officers on their guard."

There was nothing new about this. The year before, as the siege of Vicksburg was about to commence, the Confederate Signal Service was able to send the whole Federal cryptographic system to Captain Maxwell T. Davidson, a Confederate signal officer there. From the signal station on Devil's Backbone, the rebel flagmen were able to read practically all Grant's messages. Captain Davidson does not seem to have thought this remarkable. "We always had the Federal alphabet," he said later, "and I suppose they had ours."

Captain Fitzgerald Ross, an officer of Hussars in the Imperial Austrian Army, accompanying Lee as a military observer, noted, "Sometimes they discover each other's alphabets"; but each side seems to have been quick to learn of such misfortunes. Thus, though the Federals broke the Confederate flag cipher just before Chancellorsville, the Confederates found it out almost at once and changed to a new one before any harm was done.

On one occasion a Federal signal came in, asking for the whereabouts of Generals Lee and Jackson. This was recognized at once as a Union plant and given a suitably false answer. Captain Ross, who mentions the incident, does not explain why a Federal station should have expected an answer at all. One may guess that this was a newly erected Union signal station pretending to be a new Southern station.

During the siege of Charleston in 1863, the Confederates were able to intercept and read flag signals between the cooperating land and naval forces of the Federals. When the latter prepared an attack on Battery Gregg, at Cumming's Point on Morris Island, the Confederates read signals describing the plan and were ready to concentrate the fire of seventy guns on the approaching boats. Infantry at Cumming's Point, knowing all about the attack before it started, also poured in a direct and deadly fire. In this case the secret Union cipher is said to have been sold to the Confederates by a Union naval officer. His price was $20,000 in gold.

While the siege of Richmond and Petersburg was in progress— and probably much earlier—the shrewd Lee knew perfectly well that the Union Signal Corps could read his flag messages. On August 25, a few days before Marshall's message to Ewell, Lee took advantage of his knowledge to feed the Yankees false information. He sent one message to Pickett, enclosing a second one to Beauregard. They went, not by flag signal—which the Federals might read—but by a secret courier. The first message contained instructions to send the second by flag signal to Beauregard. It further warned him not to be surprised by any answer Beauregard might send back, no matter how queer it might seem. Pickett was simply to disregard anything Beauregard might transmit. (It is plain, of course, that Beauregard had had a similar pair of messages.) Said Lee to Pickett, "An answer will be sent you by signals which will be unintelligible to you. Take no notice of it."

After the war, when all records were opened, it was discovered that Grant's signal men, falling into the trap, had carefully noted the false information Lee had prepared for them. Beauregard's false order (which Robert E. Lee had probably written himself) instructed Pickett, "Be prepared to blow up your mine at any time, as Hoke's two divisions are ordered to you. Pontoon bridges across the Potomac must be captured as soon as practicable."

The planted message was nicely calculated to frighten the Union command out of its wits. The Federals had set off their mine at "the Crater," outside Petersburg, a month earlier (July 30, 1864).

When Beauregard sent this order, neither he nor Pickett had the remotest intention of exploding a mine. Indeed—so far as is known —Pickett had no mine, anyhow. Moreover, Hoke did not have two divisions with which to go to Pickett's aid. All he had was one brigade, and he was not going to march anywhere. Neither he nor Pickett would even approach the pontoons over the Potomac, which were far beyond their reach. But it was all calculated to make the Federals' flesh creep, especially at a moment when

Union officers at some points on the front line were already listening anxiously for possible signs of mining beneath them.

Various Union generals had reported sounds of Confederate picks underground near their trenches. Some of these were genuine, made by men working on Hoke's mine. Others were imaginary. But Lee's hint drew attention away from Hoke's mine—which really did exist, though he could never make it explode—and started a small panic elsewhere, over mines that never had existed.

Early tried to trick Sheridan, then his opponent in the Shenandoah, with a similar deceptive message, only a few days before his Confederates made their surprise attack at Cedar Creek (October 19, 1864). On October 15, Sheridan had started for a conference in Washington. At nearly the same moment, Early was approaching a Confederate signal station, from which a Federal station was in plain sight, with its signal flag in motion. Early, noticing the Confederate signal officer taking down Federal messages, asked whether the Federals were able to read Confederate messages.

They had discovered the key to the signals formerly used, replied the signal officer. But a change had been made. The Federals could not as yet read the new Confederate cryptographic system.

Early at once saw a fine chance to use the old one. He wrote out an imaginary message from Longstreet. This was put into the old cryptography and sent by flag in full view of the Federal signal men.

In this message Longstreet—who was then at Richmond and knew nothing about these goings-on—was made to advise Early: "Be ready to move as soon as my forces join you, and we will crush Sheridan."

The message was meant to suggest that Longstreet had recovered from the wounds he had received in the Wilderness (May 6, 1864), had returned to active duty, and was now moving from Richmond to Early's support. It was a clever falsehood, because part of it was true. Longstreet really had recovered and really was about to return to active duty. If the Federals knew this, as they probably did, they would be all the more ready to believe Early's little fiction. They would also feel sure that Longstreet, a lieutenant general, would bring his entire army corps, which would certainly make Early strong enough to overwhelm Sheridan. This would also mean—or seem to mean—that Lee felt so strong, as compared with Grant, in front of Richmond, that he was willing to detach a very large force.

As Early himself said, in 1890, when it was safe to talk, "My object was to induce Sheridan to move back his troops." In fact, Longstreet did not resume corps command till October 19, and he did not move his corps anywhere. Lee kept him near Richmond for the rest of the war.

The Union signalmen, intercepting Early's message, sent it to General H. G. Wright, commanding VI Corps, whom Sheridan had left in temporary command. Wright had certain doubts, no matter how plausible the message sounded. Still, if there was even a trace of truth in it, it was an important indication of enemy intentions. True or false, this was something Sheridan ought to see at once, and Wright sent it after him. The messenger caught him at Front Royal, October 18, 1864.

Sheridan shared Wright's suspicions. Had Longstreet really sent such a message? The thing was possible. There was no use taking chances. Early was plainly up to something. Sheridan ordered Wright to prepare for attack at once, at the same time sending him additional cavalry.

From Rectortown, between Front Royal and Washington, Sheridan telegraphed ahead to General Halleck at the War Department, "I have no cipher clerk here. An intercepted signal dispatch would indicate Longstreet was marching to join Early with considerable force, and was not far off. Have you heard that any rebel force has been detached from Richmond?" (It is typical of slack Civil War security that a field army commander, in a possible crisis, had to send an important message in clear.) Halleck inquired of Grant, who at once replied that Longstreet's Corps was still opposing him at Richmond, where it had been for months.

To the anxiously watching Early, it soon became apparent that his trick was not working. The Union line was hot withdrawing, as he had hoped; but he prepared to attack at dawn, on October 19, all the same. While Sheridan, returning from Washington, was at Winchester on the night of October 18–19, Early's men were already creeping around the Federal left and rear at Cedar Creek.

There was no excuse for Wright's letting the Federals be surprised, as they were at Cedar Creek. The Longstreet–Early signal was an ingenious fraud. When revealed as a fraud, it should also have been a warning. It indicated that Early was planning mischief of some kind. General Wright, a careful man, did order a reconnoissance in force by a full brigade, but the brigade failed to find the wily Early, mainly because they looked for him where they thought he ought to be—which was not in the least the place where Early was.

In spite of that Federal error, the Confederates were accurately located as they were moving into position a little later on the Federal eastern (left) flank. Alvin Stearns and Dominic Fannin, two of Sheridan's specially trusted secret agents, reconnoitering in Confederate uniform, spotted them exactly. A third secret agent, reconnoitering the Moorefield–Romney area in West Virginia, found everything quiet there, which showed clearly the whole attack was coming in the east. However, the officer to whom the secret agents reported, in Sheridan's absence, would not believe them because their information did not agree with what the brigade reconnoissance had shown. In fact, Early's men had moved up secretly, only after the brigade had withdrawn.

The result was the Union defeat at Cedar Creek, a battle lost by this foolish refusal to believe accurate intelligence. But for "Sheridan's Ride," there would have been a complete defeat. At Winchester on his way back from Washington, Sheridan heard the firing as the second day of battle began, made a wild dash to the field, rallied the troops, and saved the day. During a lull in the battle, he at last received positive information that—as he had always suspected—Longstreet was still at Richmond. The Federals had never had any reason to fear that Early was being reinforced.

IV

Telegraph lines gave a little more security than flag signals. At least they could not be read, and perhaps deciphered, by anyone with field glasses. But, though telegraphic codes and ciphers were never broken, it was often easy for the enemy to cut in and listen to the flow of orders and reports sent in clear. There were a good many such messages, since neither side had many cryptographers. This made it possible for hostile telegraphers to tap the Federal wires and send false Federal information and orders.

During the second week of July, 1862, Union telegraphers in Memphis experienced a vague feeling that something was wrong. Just why they felt this, surviving reports do not state; nor do they explain why trouble-shooters did not go down the line at once and see what was happening. The Memphis operators did, at least, notify the telegraph superintendent, and they also warned Union operators in Corinth.

Otherwise, the telegraph clicked away as usual until, on July 17, a total stranger broke abruptly into the flow of messages with an exclamation of "Oh, pshaw!" Then the startled Union operators heard another interruption: "Hurrah for Jeff Davis." The triumphant rebel stayed on the line long enough to reveal that he had been listening for four days, having cut in with a pocket instrument. A Memphis operator recognized the telegraphic style as that of an operator named Ed Saville. The Federal operators, aghast, remembered that a number of important messages had gone over the wires unciphered in the last four days, including data on the exact strength of local Union forces at Memphis and other posts. Saville dropped off the line and vanished.

Far bolder than this was a telegraphic scheme proposed by D. F. S. Ways, another rebel operator, who wanted to connect "all wires leading out of Baltimore to the various cities" with a secret wire leading to Confederate headquarters. Ways thought he could make this connection within twenty-four hours. This would have been wire tapping on a scale greater than anything dreamed of, even in modern times; but there is no evidence that the proposal was ever carried out.

J. E. B. Stuart, on his raid immediately after Christmas, 1862, captured the town of Burke's Station on the Orange & Alexandria Railroad, not many miles from Washington. Replacing the Union operator with his own, he was able to read all General Heintzelman's orders to Fairfax Station and Fairfax Court House, ordering troops out to intercept the raiders. Once he knew what the Federals were going to do, Stuart had no trouble evading them. But Stuart could never quite control his sense of humor. This was the occasion when he sent his famous telegram to the U.S. Quartermaster General in Washington, complaining of the bad quality of the mules he was capturing from the U.S. Army. Confederates enjoyed the joke—but it alerted the Federals.

Most telegraphers learn to recognize the individual style, "fist," or touch each operator unconsciously acquires in sending. In World War I, British wireless operators learned to recognize the style of individual operators on German naval vessels and could thus locate each ship. In World War II, American operators located Japanese ships in the same way. One of the methods of deception the Japanese Navy used before Pearl Harbor was to put all the regular operators ashore and keep them sending there, while the invading fleet—with new operators aboard—was really hundreds of miles away, en route to Hawaii, in radio silence. Civil War operators could also recognize the "fist" of an individual operator; but for some reason Union telegraphers were often slow to discover that a new Confederate operator had taken over the key.

The Confederate Army did a good deal more wire tapping than their opponents, one reason, no doubt, being that there were more Federal wires to tap. Rebel operators—by listening quietly on a Union line, then slyly insinuating false orders or false information of their own into the flow of Union telegrams—could sometimes send Union forces scurrying off in the wrong direction. Sometimes the Federals, discovering the trick in time, only pretended to be fooled. Thus, when the Union XVI Corps at Memphis found in late March of 1864 that Forrest's raiding cavalry had tapped the wire at Paducah, the staff made sure Forrest had every chance to hear Sherman issue genuine orders that sent the Union 4th Division to Savannah, Tennessee. Then, sure that Forrest would hurry to Savannah to cut off the isolated 4th Division, the XVI Corps command sent Grierson's cavalry hastily and secretly to reinforce it. Forrest met an overwhelming force he had not in the least expected. He wriggled out of the trap, but it was a narrow escape.

One of the most dangerous Confederate feats of this sort was the tapping of the Union telegraph line between Grant's headquarters and Washington, on which the Confederate operator, Charles A. Gaston, listened in for more than two months. Lee is said to have ordered this wire tap in mid-July of 1864, so that Gaston was listening during part of August, all of September, and part of October.

Gaston and the detachment protecting him were guided by Roger A. Pryor, a former Confederate brigadier, who, when he had to give up his brigade because of legal changes, enlisted as a private in Fitzhugh Lee's cavalry. Pryor was an ideal guide, since he had roamed and hunted over this country from boyhood. Undetected, he led Gaston and his guards, special troops known as Reide's Scouts, through, or around, the Union siege lines and into a woods not far from the house of a certain Dr. Richards, near the town of Surrey, east of Petersburg.

The whole group settled down in the woods, the scouts disguised as wood choppers, ostentatiously chopping down trees whenever there was any chance of discovery, but spending most of their time on guard.

Gaston had provided himself with a special insulator that would hold the two ends of a main line in place on the pole so as not to attract attention. A hastily erected Civil War telegraph line was strung on trees when possible, otherwise on hastily cut poles with the bark still on. Selecting one of these, Gaston ran a fine wire down it, under the bark, and then along the ground to a thicket of wild plums, where the instrument was installed, deep enough in the woods so that the clicking telegraph key would not be heard. The wire was carefully covered with dead leaves.

In this woodland retreat, Gaston settled down peacefully, never attempting to send messages himself but listening to everything Grant and the War Department had to say to each other. Guards were constantly alert on the edges of the woods, trying to be inconspicuous but trying even harder not to look mysterious. "If seen, they made the best of it, being careful not to appear unwilling to meet the discoverers."

Their scheme worked perfectly, A few casual passers-by did see the "wood cutters"; but in a day when wood was standard fuel, people were always cutting down trees. No one paid any attention. No one was at all suspicious. The guards had orders not to challenge, but merely to whistle, if they saw Federal troops approaching. The whistle was to be passed on, from guard to guard, till warning reached Gaston. This would have given him time to cut off his instrument and vanish, but it was never necessary.

On August 26, the Federals discovered another "rebel operator" on Grant's telegraph wire, near Cabin Point, east of Petersburg, but this man seems to have been trying to cut the line. Probably he had been sent out by some subordinate officer, who had not been informed of the more important wire tap.

The Army of the Potomac's intelligence service, headed by the extremely able Colonel George H. Sharpe, knew that a small rebel force was hanging about the telegraph line. Sharpe's men also knew that Pryor was in command. The colonel of an Ohio regiment even reported Pryor's position with approximate accuracy. He said the Confederates were somewhere near Swan's Point, which is immediately north of Surrey, and Pryor's men were only a little way outside the town. But the colonel apparently thought the instruders were merely trying to cut the wire, for he reported complacently, "The line, however, is still working." The last thing the Confederates wanted was to interfere with messages between Grant and Washington, so long as Gaston was listening to them.

The wire tappers were never caught, but, sad to say, their risks did the rebel cause very little good, since most dispatches were in cipher. Gaston dutifully sent copies of the cryptograms to Richmond, but no cryptanalyst there was skilled enough to crack the cipher, simple though it must have been.

17

SECRETS OF GETTYSBURG

Neither the Union nor the Confederate Army, as the Gettysburg campaign opened, had much cause for pride in its intelligence service. Union scouts and spies inexcusably failed to notice that Confederate strength on the Rappahannock front had suddenly been reduced from three corps to one. Not for several days did the Federals wake up to the fact that Robert E. Lee and the two missing army corps were marching swiftly around the Federal flank and would soon be in their rear, ready to assail Washington itself.

If the Federals had had this information in time, General Joseph Hooker could easily have let loose the whole Army of the Potomac on the weak third of the Confederate Army left by Lee to deceive him, and could then have turned west, in vast numerical superiority, to crush the other two thirds. Instead, the besotted general sat still, with his eyes tightly shut, until it was almost too late to save his own army. Lee was far up the Shenandoah Valley, and his II Corps was attacking the painfully surprised General Robert H. Milroy at Winchester—throwing that grieved and astonished man out of the town entirely—before the Federals realized where the great Confederate really was.

In this advance, Lee had one special advantage. The Confederates had recently broken the Union cipher and had been reading the secret messages of the Federals. General Thomas L. Kane, while a pneumonia patient in a Baltimore hospital, had in some mysterious way learned that the cipher had been broken and had sent word from his sickbed to General Meade, only a short time before the battle.

Confederate collection of secret information preparatory to Lee's advance was delayed by one ludicrous bit of misfortune. A secret courier named William Croft Hyslop, or Heslop, arrived in Richmond with a cipher message. Like most Confederate ciphers, it could be read only when one had the key word. This was a new cipher, with a new key word, which, to ensure complete secrecy, had been trusted to no one save the courier himself. But Hyslop, who had had a good deal on his mind during his dangerous and secret journey, had completely forgotten it by the time he reached Richmond!

Much annoyed, the disgusted authorities there locked him up in Castle Thunder, where, with limitless leisure to reflect, he finally managed to remember. When deciphered at last, the message was found to come from Confederate sympathizers in Baltimore. This group reported that it had two hundred armed men ready to join the Confederates on their northward march if Lee would only bring his army near the city—which, of course, he was never able to do. The forgetful Hyslop was not further employed as a courier but was put to smuggling drugs, at a time when couriers were needed.

A new Federal intelligence organization, which Hooker had set up after Burnside's shattering defeat at Fredericksburg (December 13, 1862), was not yet fully efficient. General Marsena R. Patrick and Colonel George H. Sharpe had organized it, most of the work being done by the colonel. But either its spies had not yet succeeded in infiltrating the Confederate Army on the Rappahannock·or it had not yet had time to build up an adequate system of secret communications. A few days later—once they had discovered Lee's troops approaching—Colonel Sharpe's spies began doing excellent work; but, by that time, it was almost too late.

After Lee had been located, one of Sharpe's particularly brilliant agents, John C. Babcock, kept the advancing rebel host under continual observation, moving with it as it approached the Potomac, crossed it, and moved on toward Pennsylvania. Other scouts and agents now began to report, as the men in gray drew nearer, until at last a steady stream of intelligence was flowing into Hooker's headquarters. But that was only after two magnificent chances of swift and easy victory had been lost for lack of timely intelligence.

The Confederate service was nearly as bad. Clumsily phrased, ambiguous orders from Lee's headquarters sent the impetuous Stuart dashing so far east of the main body of the Confederates that he could get no couriers back to Lee, who, for several critical days immediately before the battle, could get no information of the enemy at all. Again Captain Conrad, star secret agent in Washington, did not know where to find Stuart, though the clever spy for the second time had vital information which, if swiftly transmitted, would certainly have enabled the rebel cavalry to ride straight into Washington, unresisted.

Not until Longstreet's spy, James Harrison, arrived at headquarters from Washington, on June 28, 1863, only three days before the battle began on July 1, did Lee at last find out that the whole Federal Army was on the move. By that time, his own forces were widely scattered over central Pennsylvania, from Chambersburg to Harrisburg, while the whole Army of the Potomac, with General Meade as its new commander, was concentrating in his rear.

I

One touching incident marked Confederate espionage in Winchester, Virginia, just before the battle there, in which Milroy was driven out. Both sides had men out on reconnoissance, some in disguise, some in proper uniform. Major Harry Gilmor, reconnoitering ahead of the Confederate column, was on this occasion in gray, though he frequently did wear false Federal uniform, when it seemed advisable. On this occasion, even his legitimate uniform was a kind of disguise. Confederates would recognize him for the genuine Confederate he was; but Union intelligence agents would mistake him for a fellow spy, for he was also wearing the secret sign by which they identified themselves to each other.

The use of false uniform made it possible to conduct reconnoissance in areas a legitimate scout in proper uniform could never have entered; but it doubled a soldier's peril. He was certain to be hanged if detected. His own army would shoot him on sight, unless he had some secret way of indicating to friendly troops that his uniform was false—without at the same time revealing it to the enemy.

Many spies simply accepted the additional risks. There were, however, various devices to indicate true identity. Union soldiers near Kenesaw, Georgia, about the time of the battle of Kenesaw Mountain (June 27, 1864) were astonished to see a man in a blue Federal uniform rush through the Federal firing line and safely into the Confederate line. The Union soldiers fired on him, the Confederates did not. The man was carrying a tin pail in his hand, queer equipment for a battlefield. Too late the Union soldiers realized that the pail was "no doubt a signal for the Rebels to recognize him." Only then did they realize this must be "a spy who had dressed up in one of our stolen uniforms."

This interchange of uniforms led to so much confusion that genuine Confederate soldiers sometimes had trouble being recognized as such by zealous but suspicious Confederate civilians. Captain Elijah V. White found people near Lacey's Spring, in the Shenandoah, unwilling to accept him, gray uniform or not. They thought he was a Jessie Scout, "for their dress about as closely resembles one uniform as the other and the 'Jessie Scouts' of Frémont's hatching were plentiful in the Valley." Lieutenant Frank M. Myers finally persuaded the suspicious Southrons to examine the metal buttons on his uniform—after which everyone accepted Lije White's argument that "nobody but a Virginia soldier ever did wear a Virginia button."

The Jessie Scouts quickly developed various methods of recognizing each other. From their early days in the Shenandoah, they had used prearranged but natural-sounding conversations, the sort of thing espionage scandals have made familiar in recent times. Such a series of remarks was carefully planned:

"Good morning [or evening]."

"These are perilous times."

"Yes, but we are looking for better."

"To what shall we look?"

"To the red and white cord."

Artificial as this seems when written out, it was cleverly arranged to sound natural and casual at the beginning and to become more artificial as it proceeded. Thus no one could *accidentally* complete the identification. The remark about red and white cord made identification certain. No one would ever just happen to say that!

The Jessie Scouts, for the same purpose, added to the Confederate uniform "a white handkerchief, having a long end hanging down over the shoulder," which was not likely to be worn by a genuine Confederate but which would not arouse suspicion if noticed. This eventually became "the badge by which the 'Jessies' distinguished each other."

Though the meaning of the dangling white scarf was supposed to be a strictly guarded Federal secret, the assiduously inquisitive Harry Gilmor usually knew a good many things the Federals did not want him to know. That day, Major Gilmor had added it to his genuine Confederate uniform. Other Confederates wouldn't know what it meant. Disguised Federals, noting the kerchief, would think him a disguised Federal.

Scouting along the Berryville road, almost due east of Winchester, the major met another scout, also in Confederate gray—and also with a white scarf about his neck. Though the disguised Union spy was careful to keep a pistol in his hand, he saw Gilmor's scarf and did not fire. Instead, he rode up till their horses' heads were nearly touching. Gilmor, well aware that the man was an enemy, also approached as if he had no suspicions at all.

"Where are you going?" asked the Union soldier.

"Going into town," said Gilmor. Where did Gilmor belong? "To the same crowd you do—to Captain Purdy's scouts."

"Why," said the Federal, "I don't remember seeing you, though I haven't been detailed long myself."

"That is just my case," replied Gilmor, blandly.

The other man may have been mildly suspicious, or he may have been merely curious. At any rate he asked further questions, which may have been meant for traps. What regiment had Gilmor belonged to before Purdy's Scouts? Gilmor was ready for that query, too: Company F, 12th Pennsylvania, Captain Fenner commanding. Company, regiment, and officer's name were all correct.

Gilmor now asked a question himself. Noticing that the Federal was carrying handcuffs, he asked why he was carrying these "ruffles."

"There is a reb out at old Griffith's, and I am going after him," said the Union man.

"Let me look at them," said Gilmor. It was a natural enough request. Handcuffs were unusual—not standard military equipment.

The Federal, now convinced that the Confederate major was a Union man in disguise, bent over to release their fastening.

In that unguarded instant, Gilmor's saber flashed. The unlucky "Fed," unable to use either pistol or saber, tried to get through an open gate. Instead of taking him through, his horse clumsily pushed it shut, blocking escape. Gilmor mercilessly thrust again with his saber, and the genuine Jessie Scout fell dying. It was all over in a minute or two; but before he died, the victim paid his slayer—who was now trying to staunch the wound he had himself inflicted—a chivalrous compliment: "You sold me pretty well, but I don't blame you."

Gilmor gave him whiskey and water and "tried to save him, but my blade went too near the heart." Taking the man's horse and saddle, which were better than his own, Gilmor went on, leading his mount. Federals soon surprised him and killed the captured horse. But Gilmor saved his victim's fine saddle and carried the handcuffs as far as Gettysburg, where he gave them away.

With his own troops in Winchester and steadily moving farther north, Lee now knew all about Union forces in the Shenandoah. But after 1 A.M., June 25, when Stuart left Salem Court House on his raid through Maryland and Pennsylvania, the commander-in-chief was wholly in the dark so far as the rest of the Union Army was concerned. Lee had meant him to remain in touch with the main body of the Confederate Army. Perhaps because he momentarily expected Stuart's usually excellent intelligence reports to arrive, he failed to use in reconnoissance the considerable cavalry forces he still had left. He heard nothing whatever from Stuart until long after the fighting at Gettysburg had actually begun.

Stuart himself was handicapped by the simultaneous failure of his three best intelligence agents. Some time before he moved out of Salem Court House on June 25, 1863, he had sent John S. Mosby and Frank Stringfellow to reconnoiter ahead of the cavalry. Captain Conrad went back to Washington to continue supervising his permanent spy ring there. Longstreet's agent, Harrison, had also gone to Washington, though he and Conrad seem to have known nothing about each other.

Mosby had orders to reconnoiter northwest of Harpers Ferry. He spent a good deal of time among the Federals, invariably in a gray uniform, suitably covered with a nondescript waterproof, reporting regularly until June 23. Then he was sent out with orders to meet Stuart after the Cavalry Corps had crossed the Potomac but, like Conrad, could not find him. When Meade took over from Hooker, Mosby was constantly behind the Federal lines, but none of his information reached Lee before Gettysburg.

Stringfellow had the same misfortune. He had been sent to examine Potomac fords east of Harpers Ferry but ran into wandering Federals and barely escaped capture. He had made the mistake of calling at a house long occupied by friends, only to discover too late that it was now occupied by Union sympathizers. Escaping, he went to the home of a schoolmate, Joseph Hazslett, near Bull Run Mountain. Young Joseph was in the Confederate Army, but his parents gladly welcomed Stringfellow.

Meantime, Federal cavalry, alerted by Union sympathizers at the house he had first visited, were searching every dwelling, house by house. Before Stringfellow could get away, the Hazslett home was surrounded; but a quick-witted Negro maid, Josie, took him to the attic, where, from a window, a board protruded. On this, hidden by the roof of the porch, the fugitive lay, while Josie obligingly "helped" the searchers. Volubly, the Negro girl explained —though with a suitable vagueness. Yes, she had seen a man. At any rate she thought so. He had run off through the garden, or seemed to, though she wasn't quite sure. Once an officer held a lamp to the window, so that light fell on the porch roof and the lawn below. But Stringfellow, who was very slender, squeezed under the board and remained invisible in its shadow. He seems to have escaped in the same way several times, once by lying on an attic beam, once by hiding in an attic cubby hole.

Riding south to report to Stuart near Middleburg on June 12, Stringfellow was captured by Federal cavalry, who sent him to the Old Capitol Prison. Here he was grilled by relays of Pinkerton men and threatened with execution as a spy. He had been captured in his own Confederate uniform, which made him an ordinary prisoner of war. But the Federals, knowing of his previous espionage, proposed to hang him for that. This would have violated the ordinary rule that a secret agent who has returned to his own lines and resumed legitimate uniform cannot be executed.

The threat may have been a mere effort to extort information. At any rate, he was paroled June 25, sent south at once, and exchanged June 30 for a captain from Connecticut—too late to join Stuart, who at that time was skirmishing at Hanover, Pennsylvania, and would not reach Gettysburg until July 2.

Mosby's and Stringfellow's ill fortune also dogged Captain Conrad in Washington. When news of Stuart's approach reached him, Conrad saw at once that the Federal capital had been so stripped of its covering forces to reinforce Meade that it was nearly defenseless. It was easy to see "how pitifully weak were the forces which stood alone between the oncoming gray-backs and the White House." Here, for the second time, was a golden chance for Jeb to strike the Union a mortal blow—if Conrad could only get the intelligence to him in time. The spy had had exactly the same opportunity the year before. In 1863 as in 1862, before Gettysburg as before Second Manassas, the problem was communications. Exactly where, at the moment, could he find Stuart? By this time, Jeb must be somewhere near the District of Columbia. Captain Conrad mounted his horse and started out.

As he passed through the entrenchments protecting the Federal capital, the rebel spy could see that they were manned only by clerks, hastily brought from desks in government departments. Soft from civilian life, these men could not stand ten minutes against Stuart's hardy troopers.

Some distance beyond the defenses, Conrad met a Union courier, riding to Washington from Meade's headquarters. From him he learned that Meade had taken over command of the Army of the Potomac—news that Meade himself had not received till four o'clock that morning. Longstreet's spy Harrison was at that moment eagerly verifying the same information from Federal troops between Frederick, Maryland, and Chambersburg, Pennsylvania. News of the change in command had thus been picked up by two Confederate spies almost as soon as it happened.

Conrad knew it would take a good deal of luck to get his information even as far as Stuart's swiftly moving headquarters. There was no chance at all of reaching Lee—wherever in Pennsylvania he might be—in time. The "Doctors' Line" was still carrying dispatches, but it had to send its information from Washington through Richmond. Richmond would have to telegraph to some point in the Shenandoah, from which a series of flag signal stations would carry it up the valley. Then couriers would have to ride through Maryland and Pennsylvania, risking their lives every moment, to find Lee's headquarters. Even if the message finally got through, Lee himself could not possibly reach Washington in time to seize the city. Conrad's only hope was to get word immediately to Stuart, who had the only Confederate force big enough and also close enough.

Eventually Conrad met a second Union soldier. In view of all the excitement around Washington that day, a lone civilian toiling along the road for no apparent reason seemed queer, and the blue-clad trooper halted the rebel spy at pistol point.

Who was Conrad? A local farmer, nothing but a local farmer. Where was he going? To his farm near Rockville. Still doubtful, the Federal inquired about other matters only a local man could know. Conrad gave all the answers correctly—he *was* a local man. Convinced at last by this flood of perfectly accurate information, the suspicious soldier let him pass.

A little farther on, a third Union trooper, pointing a carbine, halted Conrad again. But this man, too, finding the civilian could answer any question about the locality, let him proceed.

The Union soldiers had good reason for their precautions. The road Conrad was traveling was a main Federal supply route,

and—though Conrad did not know it yet—a calamity had just be-
fallen the U.S. Quartermaster Corps on that very road.

Stuart's rebel horsemen had ridden into Rockville, Maryland,
some ten miles northwest of Washington, about noon. The town
was enveloped in Sabbath calm. The townspeople were friendly.
There was a school for girls in Rockville, and the girls—in their
Sunday best—were friendly, too.

John Esten Cooke—a future novelist of the worst mid-nineteenth
century style, then on Stuart's staff—has left a description of this
enjoyable episode. Cooke had pushed on, ahead of the advance
guard, and was riding along through the town, when he

> came suddenly upon a spectacle which was truly pleasing. This was a
> seminary for young ladies, with open windows, open doors—and doors
> and windows were full and running over with the fairest specimens of
> the gentler sex that eye ever beheld. . . . The beautiful girls in their
> fresh gaily coloured dresses, low necks, bare arms, and wilderness of
> braids and curls, were "off duty" for the moment, and burning with
> enthusiasm to welcome the Southernor; for Rockville, in radical par-
> lance, was a "vile secesh hole." Every eye flashed, every voice ex-
> claimed; every rosy lip laughed; every fair hand waved a handkerchief
> or a sheet of music (smuggled) with crossed Confederate flags upon
> the cover. The whole façade of the building was a tulip-bed of brilliant
> colours, more brilliant eyes, and joy and welcome!

Maybe not every damsel was quite the raving beauty the susceptible Cooke describes. To a soldier, after a few months of hard
campaigning, almost anything in skirts looks like Helen of Troy.
But, beautiful or not, these were rebel girls and they were demon-
strative.

As she saw Cooke ride up, one "beautiful girl of about sixteen
rushed forth from the portico, pirouetting and clapping her hands
in an ecstasy at the sight of the gray uniform, exclaiming, 'Oh! here
is one of General Stuart's Aides!'" Then Stuart himself appeared,
a magnificent horseman, always well mounted, always brilliantly
uniformed, never averse to feminine society, and at his back the
clattering column, every man a figure of romance.

Well, soldiers being soldiers, there was much enthusiasm in the
ranks. The column halted. Though one reluctant detachment had

to ride away to destroy the telegraph station, a large number of other horsemen stayed at the school, where they were soon having a delightful time. It is not improbable that the young ladies were soon having a delightful time, too.

But this agreeable pause in the grim business of war was interrupted. A scout clattered up to Stuart: a Federal wagon train was approaching, as yet unaware of the rebel cavalry—which Stuart had skillfully posted out of sight, amid the houses of Rockville. The guard of Federal cavalry escorting the train was very small.

The hidden rebels gazed in delight as the unsuspecting wagoners drew near. They hadn't had a chance like this for a long, long time. The train was eight miles long. There were 150, or perhaps 175, wagons, drawn by 900 mules. Said the colonel of the 9th Virginia, "The wagons were brand new, the mules fat and sleek, and the harness in use for the first time. Such a train we had never seen before and did not see again." The rebel horsemen held their breath. So, doubtless, did the watching schoolgirls. There may have been a few nervous giggles. Somewhere, not many miles away, the faithful Captain Conrad was toiling onward through Maryland heat with his all-important news.

The luckless Union team masters had almost reached the town before any of them noticed the gray horsemen. They fled—or tried to flee—while the gray cavaliers followed in a mad chase, with the famous scout and spy, Isaac S. (Ike) Curtis, among the leaders.

Now, it takes time to turn an eight-mile-long wagon train drawn by 900 more or less recalcitrant mules completely around and move it to the rear. Even when the mules *are* turned around, a team with a heavy wagon cannot outrun the finest cavalry in the world, riding some of the best mounts in the world, fighting for their country—and also with a bountiful supply of rations in plain sight! The mule-drawn teams had to move in file. A fast team could not pass a slow one. Worse still, some of the fleeing teamsters upset their wagons at turns in the narrow road. Worst of all, other mules behind piled up on the overturned wagons.

As the charge drove past one house, a woman ran out clapping her hands and calling, "Push on; you have nearly caught them!" But the Confederates did not really need encouragement.

The weak little Union escort was no match for all of Stuart's troopers and had no possible hope even of holding them off till the wagons could escape.

The Confederate troopers enjoyed themselves. So, it may be assumed, did the young ladies, who had a bird's-eye view of the entire skirmish. When it was over, Confederate horses feasted on Federal oats and corn, their riders on an abundance of crackers, bread, sugar, and hams, with whiskey enough to wash it all down. Whiskey was always welcome, but this was more welcome than usual. In crossing the Chesapeake & Ohio Canal, a little while before, the raiders had captured a canalboat loaded with spirits. To their intense disgust, Stuart ordered it all destroyed. Now, Providence had sent more whiskey; and, this time, all fluids disappeared before the general could give any orders.

The victors first looted, then burned, all wagons too badly damaged to take along, paroled most of their 400 prisoners, and rode on toward the Pennsylvania line, taking 125 undamaged wagons with them. The girls they left behind them must have had plenty to whisper about in the dormitory that night.

Conrad, some miles away, heard none of the sounds of combat. The wagon chase had not been very noisy: Stuart's troopers had used their sabers, and there was very little shooting. But Conrad soon did see a great deal of smoke, rising beyond the small hills ahead of him. Then, as he rode over the last crest, he suddenly saw "dozens of wagons being burned with all their contents and only one smoke-begrimed individual in sight," a solitary and badly frightened country lad.

Riding up to the fence on which the boy was sitting, almost in tears, the spy learned that Stuart's troopers had left him to keep the fires going, threatening that "if all were not destroyed on their return, they would split his head open." The lad was really in no danger of violence. Some trooper had uttered this blood-curdling threat to make sure the wagons burned completely. Stuart, who never covered the same ground twice when raiding, was well on his way to Pennsylvania by this time and had no intention of returning.

Conrad now knew by how narrow a margin he had missed the

general, but he also knew he had missed him completely. There was no hope of overtaking him in time, with news of Washington's defenseless state. The capital would not remain defenseless very long. The War Department was recalling troops. Union cavalry was coming in. On every hilltop the rebel spy began to see mounted men, scanning the countryside for the raiders.

After Gettysburg, when Stuart at last did receive Conrad's message, he remarked that if he had had that information in time, he "would have charged down Pennsylvania Avenue, if it had been his last charge." This one report of Conrad's might easily have won the Gettysburg campaign—perhaps the war—for the Confederates.

II

Only two other secret agents are known to have supplied the Confederates with intelligence about Union troop movements before Gettysburg, until Longstreet's remarkable spy, James Harrison, came in on June 28. One of these agents was Charles T. Cockey, who lived in, or somewhere near, Reisterstown, Maryland, some miles northwest of Baltimore. Cockey's house was a station on the Confederate line of communication out of Baltimore. He had provided Lee with information on McClellan's movements after Antietam. Whatever Cockey's information may have been on this occasion, it either was of minor value or else it never reached Lee, who himself said he had no information of Union troop movements until Harrison arrived.

The other agent was in York, Pennsylvania, probably a woman, certainly someone with a remarkable grasp of tactical intelligence, unknown then, even to General John B. Gordon, who received the information, and now unknown forever. On June 26, 1863, Gordon's infantry division reached York on the march to Wrightsville, some distance below Harrisburg, to seize a tactically important bridge across the mile-wide Susquehanna.

In peaceful, prosperous Pennsylvania, the rebels were an appalling spectacle. Gordon himself admits his men were "ill-clad and travel-stained," but to the startled people of the towns through which they passed, the invaders looked a great deal worse than that. Said a scandalized mathematician on the faculty of Gettysburg College: "Most of the men were exceedingly dirty, some ragged, some without shoes, and some surrounded by the skeleton of what was once an entire hat."

The unkempt column had created so much terror along the way that Gordon himself rode ahead into York, hoping to quiet the frightened townspeople with a short propaganda speech, before his troops arrived. He found everyone so completely on edge that, as he turned his dust-covered face toward them, a group of girls shrieked in alarm. Gordon spoke briefly, assuring them that the rebel host behind him consisted of "dust-covered but knightly men."

Then, as he turned his horse, a little girl of about twelve ran out of the crowd and handed him a large bouquet. A divisional commander on a long march can't very well carry a bouquet. But Gordon could only unsuspectingly accept the gift, not guessing what it contained, and ride on.

A surprise awaited him. Hidden among the flowers lay "a note in a delicate handwriting," which, like the posies, suggested a feminine source. The delicate handwriting gave exactly the information General Gordon needed, at the exact moment when he needed it most. It was a full report of the strength and position of the Union forces defending that all-important Susquehanna bridge at Wrightsville. The message was unsigned. But, says the astonished general, "it was so terse and explicit in its terms as to compel my confidence."

The unknown Pennsylvania Confederate—whoever she may have been—was a model secret agent. She correctly located the Union detachment protecting the bridgehead. She gave exact tactical information on the military geography of Wrightsville. There was a ridge near the town. A ravine led around the Federal left. By following it, Gordon could get on the enemy's flank, perhaps even into the enemy's rear.

Two days later, Gordon sat his horse on the very ridge the spy had described, eagerly surveying the terrain around Wrightsville through field glasses. It corresponded exactly with the terrain data in the note in the little girl's bouquet:

There, in full view before me, was the town, just as described, nestling on the banks of the Susquehanna. There was a blue line of soldiers guarding the approach, drawn up, as indicated, along an intervening ridge and across the pike. There was the long bridge spanning the Susquehanna and connecting the town with Columbia on the other bank. Most important of all, there was the deep gorge or ravine running off to the [Confederate] right and extending around the left flank of the Federal line and to the river below the bridge. Not an inaccurate detail in that note could be discovered. I did not hesitate, therefore, to adopt its suggestion of moving down the gorge in order to throw my command on the flank, or possibly in the rear of the Union troops and force them to a rapid retreat or surrender. The result of this movement vindicated the strategic wisdom of my unknown—and judging by the handwriting—woman correspondent, whose note was none the less martial because enclosed in roses, and whose evident genius for war, had occasion offered, might have made her a captain equal to Catherine [i.e., Catherine the Great].

No clue to the identity of this Confederate agent has ever been found, but there was at least one other agent in the vicinity. A Confederate cavalry captain, armed and in his own uniform, was caught a little while before dawn on July 2, floating about on a flatboat making soundings of a Susquehanna ford at Harrisburg. When searched, he was found to have a map of the river, with other fords already marked. Though fighting had already begun at Gettysburg, Lee may still have hoped for a victory complete enough to make possible his original plan of a deep invasion of Pennsylvania. Gordon's unknown informant was probably not a professional Confederate secret agent. Almost certainly she was one of the native Pennsylvania "Copperheads," or Confederate sympathizers, of whom there were a good many in some parts of the Susquehanna Valley. A little farther north along the river, in the mountains about Fishing Creek, in Columbia County, there was so much hostility to Lincoln's government that Federal troops had to be sent in to control the "Fishing Creek Confederacy."

III

At the very moment when Conrad was hunting in vain for Stuart, on June 28, another Confederate spy was working his way, in civilian clothing, directly through the Union Army to General Longstreet's headquarters at Chambersburg, Pennsylvania. This was Harrison, who had also been in Washington, though apparently he and Conrad knew nothing whatever about each other.

Though Harrison's last-minute warning to Robert E. Lee has been known for at least a century, his identity has to this day been a profound mystery; but it is a mystery that need never have existed, if anyone had troubled to follow the single clue that has been glaringly obvious for most of that period. Harrison was not even using a cover name. His name really was Harrison. He was a Shakespearean actor, who had been prominent on the American stage for years as the "juvenile tragedian"—James Harrison.

So far as his association with Longstreet is concerned, one might almost imagine that Harrison, the skilled actor, had set out intentionally to impersonate a hero of cheap fiction. He was, to the life, an example of the sinister secret agent beloved of sensational novelists—a bit raffish, willing to run hideous risks, adept at disguise, addicted to strong drink, yet a quick and keen observer. Though a commissioned officer of the Confederate Army, he was able to pass through the Union forces, from flank to flank, never detected, posing as a bona-fide civilian.

In February, five months before Gettysburg, Longstreet had been sent temporarily to southern Virginia and North Carolina, where a Federal attack seemed possible. One evening in the early spring of '63, according to his own account, as he was sitting in his tent, a slender, wiry stranger entered. He was wearing "a citizen's suit of dark material," and stood "about five feet eight, with hazel eyes, dark hair and complexion, and brown beard." Except for stooping shoulders—which Longstreet, the West Pointer, noted at once—he was "well formed and evidently a man of great activity."

He brought a letter of introduction from James A. Seddon, Confederate Secretary of War, who had long been involved in secret service. The fact that Harrison came directly from Seddon suggests that he had already been engaged in espionage; and his success in the mission on which Longstreet now sent him also suggests experience.

Harrison's talk with Longstreet cannot be. exactly dated, but it took place before the general returned to Lee's army in May, 1863. On his return journey, Longstreet had paused in Richmond for a chat with the Secretary of War; and it is possible Seddon then agreed to let him have the spy's services.

As Longstreet later remarked, Harrison "in his unpretending citizen's dress passed unmolested from right to left through the Federal army, visited Washington City, ate and drank with the Federal officers, and joined me at Chambersburg with information more accurate than a force of cavalry could have secured."

Longstreet does not say whether he was expecting the man, when he appeared at the I Corps commander's tent; and Moxley Sorrel, who came to know more of Harrison's mysterious doings than any other officer on Longstreet's staff, merely repeats that Seddon sent him as "a scout, more properly a spy." (Sorrel was one of the few men of the period careful to make that essential distinction.) Harrison, then "about thirty" (actually twenty-eight) was paid $150 monthly—necessarily in U.S. currency, since Confederate money would at once have betrayed him. Sorrel, who approved all requisitions on the quartermaster for this money each month, calls him "an extraordinary character" and adds, "His time seemed to be passed about equally within our lines and the enemy's"—more evidence of experience in espionage. The contacts that enable a man to do that are not built up in a day.

His skill and success were almost incredible. The man's reports stood up under every test. He always brought back "true information," says Sorrel, and "there was invariable confirmation of his reports afterwards." He seemed able to see everything, go everywhere, in Washington, "even through Stanton's War Office." Probably Harrison, like Conrad, had cooperative friends within the Federal government.

Inevitably, such success breeds suspicion. It was too much like a miracle. Harrison seemed too good to be true. Some of Longstreet's officers wondered, and the general himself was not without doubts. Sorrel reflected, "Such secret instruments give away as much as they bring and may be in touch with both sides."

As a general observation, this was certainly true. It is almost exactly what General Washington said in a similar situation. But it didn't apply to Harrison. The staff, says Sorrel, "could never discover that he sold anything against us; besides, we had means, and did verify his account of himself as coming from Mississippi"— which is a little odd, since Harrison was certainly born in Baltimore, November 1, 1834.

"He appears to have been a daring Southerner," Sorrel adds, "hating Yankees most bitterly, but loving their greenbacks, and fond of secret, perilous adventure." Sorrell's statement is not, however, quite fair to the spy. Such greenbacks as Harrison is known to have possessed had been given him by the Confederate Army, and he could not possibly have secured intelligence in Washington or in the Union Army without a plentiful supply of them.

Neither Longstreet nor Sorrel indicates whether he set off immediately after seeing Longstreet, or whether he was merely held in readiness. Longstreet says only that, as preparations for the invasion of Pennsylvania began, he sent for Harrison—a statement which shows he already knew all about him, knew exactly where to find him, and had therefore employed this expert agent on earlier missions. Sorrel's description of the payments in the quartermaster accounts sounds as if there were a good many of them— in which case Harrison must have done a great deal of spying for Longstreet. However fond the spy may have been of the U.S. Treasury's greenbacks, he preferred "hard" money, which would buy a great deal more; and Longstreet gave him "all the gold he thought he would need."

Longstreet was certainly convinced of Harrison's ability, for the instructions he now gave him were such as no ordinary agent could have carried out. He was to work his way through the Union lines, proceed to Washington, and stay there "until he was in possession of information which he knew would be of value to us." Sorrel says this meant Harrison was to stay "until the last part of June. Then he was to report to General Longstreet, it was hoped, with the amplest and most accurate information." And that is exactly what he did. It is noteworthy that Harrison was expected to bring, not send, his own report. He did so, without difficulty, when no other secret communication line could reach the advancing Confederates.

After receiving his instructions, Harrison asked a natural question: "Where shall I find you, General, to make this report?"

Longstreet was evasive. Harrison had done valuable service. Secretary Seddon had vouched for him. He seemed trustworthy. Still, to tell him where a corps commander expected to be at the end of June was equivalent to announcing Lee's plan for the invasion. Harrison probably *was* a loyal Confederate; but you never can tell about a secret agent; and—loyal or not—the man certainly would not reveal facts he did not know. "That," said Longstreet after the war, "was information I didn't care to impart to a man who was going directly to the Federal capital."

"With the army. I shall be sure to be with it," was all he was willing to tell Harrison. Though newspapers had been predicting Lee's march for weeks, the exact route the Confederates were going to take was still an important military secret. Besides, as Longstreet further told his spy, with what sounds like a note of asperity, "my command was large enough to be found without difficulty."

Longstreet's I Corps marched into the startled town of Chambersburg, Pennsylvania, on June 27, a week before the battle. On the night of June 28, while Lee and Longstreet were both in Chambersburg, a sentry halted a weary and bedraggled civilian, "filthy and ragged, showing some rough work and exposure." He seemed to have no business near the outpost line. It was Harrison.

He must have demanded to be taken at once to General Longstreet; but no officer of the guard is inclined to bother a corps commander with a fellow like that, especially late at night. Still, very high headquarters sometimes take a very keen interest in very queer people who show up mysteriously at the outposts at the oddest hours. Someone in the provost guard finally sent the shabby stranger to Longstreet's headquarters. Here—since no one ever cares to disturb a commanding general's slumbers—Lieutenant Colonel Sorrel was roused to receive the dubious fellow.

"I knew him instantly," says Sorrel, who at once woke his commander. There is no doubt about the date. Lee himself says that the scout arrived "on the night of the 28th."

To Longstreet, Harrison gave "the first complete account of the enemy since Hooker left our front"—in other words, the first intelligence in nearly two weeks. All of Harrison's news was fresh, "down to a day or two." Some of it had been collected that very day, for Harrison had continued to use his eyes and ears while passing through the Union Army. He thus learned, only a few hours later than Conrad, that Meade had replaced Hooker; and, though Conrad failed to transmit the information, Harrison contrived to bring it through the lines to Longstreet and Lee the very day Hooker was relieved. It was mere luck that the actor-spy was not recognized by someone who had seen him on the stage, but relatively few Civil War soldiers had ever entered a theater.

On June 27, Hooker had telegraphed President Lincoln an offer to resign his command. Lincoln accepted at once. An officer-courier from Washington woke Meade with news of his appointment at 4 A.M., June 28, and Hooker was on his way to Baltimore a few hours later. Harrison may have had news of the relief before he left Washington and even before the unfortunate general himself, as he almost certainly had a pipeline into the War Department.

In Washington, Harrison had spent the gold Longstreet had given him, freely and to good purpose. He made the rounds of the numerous saloons in the capital, drinking with Union Army officers, working his way into their confidence. Probably not one of these blundering fellows realized he was talking carelessly—certainly not that he was talking to an enemy agent. Probably not one of them told Harrison anything of great importance in itself. But a good agent can piece together many small bits of apparently insignificant information, to produce a "big picture." Harrison heard enough, says Longstreet, to gain "a pretty good idea of the general movements of the Federal Army and the preparation to give us battle." He learned also that the Federals were moving north (not south against Richmond, as some Confederates had feared). "The moment he heard Hooker had started across the Potomac," says Longstreet, "he set out to find me."

Before the spy reached Frederick, Maryland, he began to meet Federal troops. His plan of operation thereafter was to "walk at night and stop during the day in the neighborhood of the troops," from whose casual talk he could not fail to learn a good deal. He was thus able to report on Union troops at Frederick and a Union corps whose exact position he did not know, though he was sure it was in the vicinity.

As soon as Longstreet heard of Harrison's report, he sent him to Lee, in charge of Major John W. Fairfax.

"What do you think of Harrison?" Lee asked the major.

"General Lee, I do not think much of any scout [i.e., spy]," replied Fairfax, "but General Longstreet thinks a good deal of Harrison."

"I do not know what to do," replied Lee. "I cannot hear from General Stuart, the eyes of the Army. You can take Harrison back."

This conversation—written down in 1896, thirty-three years later—is not altogether clear. It probably took place privately, after Lee's talk with the scout. Lee is reported to have expressed the same doubt in the same words, but he did talk with Harrison, acted on his information, and thereby saved his army.

Lee had been uneasy because he had heard nothing from Stuart between June 25 and 28. He had no idea where Hooker's army (now Meade's, though the Confederates did not know it yet) might be; and loyal Unionist Pennsylvanians were telling him nothing. Meade, more fortunate, had—at eleven o'clock that morning, a few hours after assuming command—received a detailed report on the Confederates and their movements from "Thomas McCammon a good man, from Hagerstown," who had suddenly appeared at Union headquarters.

All Lee knew was that the Federals had not attacked him; and he began to fear that they were not following him at all, but were striking south toward Richmond to do some invading themselves. They could march into the Confederate capital, now nearly defenseless, if they wanted to. They could also move into the Shenandoah Valley and cut his ammunition supply line.

Actually—though only Meade knew it—the armies were by that time not very far apart. The Confederates were northeast and northwest of Gettysburg, spread out over Pennsylvania as far as the Susquehanna. The rebels were still moving north, with Meade coming in behind them. Both armies were feeling for each other more or less blindly, in spite of Meade's better information. Lee had no real idea of exact Federal movements. An improvised Federal secret service, observing Lee's troops around Chambersburg, Pennsylvania, could report only by sending secret couriers, on foot and on horse, to Harrisburg, whence information could be telegraphed to Washington and might perhaps be sent on to Meade.

Late on June 28, before Harrison was brought to him, Lee had sent out orders for a march farther north next day. With Confederate troops already on the Susquehanna and no sign as yet of a Federal attack, he might be able to push his invasion much farther into Pennsylvania. Under these field orders, Ewell, with II Corps, was to advance from Carlisle to Harrisburg and support the rebel cavalry already nearly there. Hill, with III Corps, was to leave his position four miles east of Chambersburg, cross the river below Harrisburg, and cut the Pennsylvania Railroad. Longstreet, with I Corps, was to move forward to support him.

Then Colonel Fairfax brought Harrison to Lee's tent. Lee talked with the spy at some length. Sorrel says, "The general heard him with great composure and minuteness." Lee's aide-de-camp, Colonel Marshall, says that some time after 10 P.M. on June 28, he was told to report to Lee. "I found him sitting in his tent with a man in citizen's dress, whom I did not know to be a soldier, but who, General Lee informed me, was a scout of General Longstreet's, who had just been brought to him."

Harrison's news revealed an entirely new tactical situation. As a Federal enlisted man noted in his diary, Lee "had no idea that the 'Army of the Potomac' could get so far north in so short time."

Rarely, if ever, has the commander of a field army—on the basis of a single spy's report—changed his plans so swiftly and so completely as Lee now changed his. The information reached his headquarters barely in time to save him. Without it, he would have continued to march straight ahead, across the Susquehanna and into eastern Pennsylvania. An engineer captain had already been sent ahead to reconnoiter the defenses of Harrisburg, where Ewell hoped to cross the river with II Corps.

Lee would then have been caught with his troops divided, his supply lines cut, and most of his cavalry far away, while Meade came down on his unprotected rear. If Meade had been able to concentrate against the Confederates while their divisions were still widely scattered, he would have ended the war in an afternoon

—particularly as Grant was at that very moment blasting the line of the Mississippi open at Vicksburg, where Pemberton would surrender July 3, 1863, the day when the failure of Pickett's charge ended Lee's hope of victory at Gettysburg.

Luckily for the rebels, the Union Army was scattered, too. There was still time for the gray invaders to concentrate before the Federals could take them in the rear.

Under Lee's new, last-minute orders, Longstreet's I Corps would not march north on the morning of June 29, 1863, as Lee had originally planned. It would stay at Chambersburg that day, then move on down the Cashtown road to Gettysburg. Hill's III Corps would move east of South Mountain, toward Cashtown— that is, toward Gettysburg, which lies just beyond—on the morning of the twenty-ninth. It would not march for the Susquehanna, as originally planned. Ewell's II Corps, already approaching the Susquehanna, south of Carlisle, had already received orders to cross the river and seize Harrisburg. It was now ordered to pull back toward Cashtown. Except for Stuart's missing cavalry, the Army of Northern Virginia would then be concentrated for battle.

Conrad's information on the defenseless state of the capital might easily have made it possible for Lee to end the Civil War with a Southern victory in July, 1863. The capture of Washington— and probably of President Lincoln—would have been a fearful blow to the Union cause. Harrison's intelligence, vital though it was, could not have won the war. It did not win even the Battle of Gettysburg. But it did save Lee from being surprised with his forces hopelessly scattered and from being defeated in detail. It thus postponed the collapse of the Confederacy for two more years.

IV

Before the four days' fight began, Harrison contributed one more useful bit of espionage, after which he faded gently out of the picture, as a good spy should. (Later, when Longstreet wanted him again, he had vanished on some mysterious errand.) Lee still had no clear idea what Federal forces were in Gettysburg itself, and not even Harrison could tell him. Rather surprisingly, on his journey to Chambersburg, the spy seems to have avoided Gettysburg, the tactical point where all roads centered. Probably he had taken a direct route, cross-country, to avoid main-traveled ways.

Harrison, however, was perfectly willing to enter Gettysburg and find out, and he probably spent a day on this mission. The town had been empty of all troops when Gordon's Confederate cavalry arrived for a one-night bivouac on June 24; but two regiments of Federals had come in on the twenty-eighth, though A. P. Hill on June 30 reported to Lee that there were no Federal troops then in Gettysburg.

Hill was probably wrong, for on July 1 Colonel Fremantle noted in his diary: "A spy who was with us insisted upon there being 'a pretty tidy bunch of *blue-bellies* in or near Gettysburg,' and he declared that he was in their society three days ago." This can only mean Harrison, who had, of course, been with Federal troops all day June 27 and most of the twenty-eighth, after leaving Washington. Though he does not seem to have entered Gettysburg until June 30, or early on July 1, before combat began, he had been near enough to have a fair idea of troop locations. By a curious coincidence, Sergeant Joseph E. McCabe, soon to become one of the ablest of the Union spies, was in Gettysburg about this time. The two highly skilled agents probably passed close to each other, without the slightest suspicion on either side.

When Lee's retreat from Gettysburg began, there was nothing for Harrison to do but jog along with the withdrawing rebels. The Confederates at the moment had no need of further information of the Union Army's position and capabilities—they knew both all too well. Harrison simply "trotted along from day to day."

Thus far, no one in the Confederate Army seems to have had any more idea who Harrison was than the soldiers of the Union Army —or the American historians of the last hundred years. Then, about the end of August, he was given leave to go to Richmond. Before he went, he made a remark to Colonel Moxley Sorrel, of Longstreet's staff, that has made it possible to identify him.

"Colonel," he said, "if by any chance you should be in Richmond next week, I hope you will take in the theater one evening."

Sorrel was surprised. He had had no idea of going to Richmond. Idly he asked, "What is the attraction?"

"Myself," said Harrison. "I have made a bet of fifty greenbacks [i.e., U.S., not Confederate currency] that I play Cassius success-fully."

"Are you an actor?"

"No," said Harrison (untruthfully), "but I can play."

Sorrel, though a trusted member of Longstreet's staff, had no idea that plans were afoot to send I Corps, swiftly and secretly by rail, to fight at Chickamauga. Longstreet had been discussing the plan with Secretary of War Seddon since the middle of August, but he did not at first mention it to Lee; and certainly what he did not mention to the commanding general and the trusted Sorrel he also kept secret from the rest of the staff. Not until September 6, 1863, did Lee order his quartermaster to get transportation ready for the first large rail movement of troops in military history.

But, though the staff knew nothing till the last minute, Harrison knew all about the proposed move, long in advance. As Sorrel remarked later, "Harrison knew everything"—in this case undoubtedly through Secretary of War Seddon, who had originally sent the spy to Longstreet.

Sorrel soon found how accurate Harrison's knowledge was. A week later, the colonel was in Richmond with Longstreet and his troops, on their way to Tennessee. He was given a seat in a friend's box for a production of *Othello* in the New Richmond Theatre. To his amazement, Harrison appeared—Sorrel says in the role of "Cassius."

Sorrel was slightly confused. Cassius is a part in *Julius Caesar*. There is no doubt the play Sorrel saw was *Othello*, since, in the book he subsequently published, he mentions both Othello and Desdemona. One would suppose, therefore, that Harrison was playing Cassio. But Sorrel may have been mistaken even in that. Though no playbills or programs of the performance can now be found, an advertisement in the *Richmond Examiner* for September 10, 1863, announces a production of *Othello* in the New Richmond Theatre. One character is mentioned: "Iago. . . . By an officer of the army, first appearance."

Since Harrison was already a veteran of the stage, this probably means his first appearance as Iago. The theater was still advertising him as its juvenile tragedian three months later. This was certainly Longstreet's secret agent, since there was no other actor named Harrison in the company. Surviving playbills of May 1 and 3, 1865, show that he was a member of the regular stock company two years later and that he played the ghost of Henry VI in *Richard III*, May 3, 1865. His full stage name, which he also used in private life, was James Harrison. Army officers refer to him only as "Harrison."

The production Colonel Sorrel saw was hardly an artistic success. An advertisement announced that the piece had been "cast with care," but evidently not with quite enough care. If we can trust Sorrel, "'Othello' was in drink, 'Cassius' [sic] was really quite far gone, and even 'Desdemona' was under more than one suspicion that evening."

Somewhat startled, Sorrel made a few inquiries. Harrison, he found, was both drinking and gambling. He had probably been doing both most of his life; but now he was in the intelligence service, where that kind of thing can be dangerous. Longstreet listened to Sorrel's report, then ordered Harrison paid off and sent back to the Secretary of War, from whom he had come.

Given so obvious a clue to the spy's identity as Moxley Sorrel's account of his performance in *Othello*, it is strange there has been so much mystery about him. Even Dr. Douglas Southall Freeman, dean of Civil War writers, remarks that Harrison's career might be of great interest, "if it could be traced." But no man is easier to trace than an actor, who necessarily lives in the full blaze of publicity, and Harrison was already a well-known actor and manager.

He was born in Baltimore, November 1, 1834, and is said to have made his stage debut at the Old Museum there, September 8, 1852, with Joseph Jefferson as stage manager. This may be an error, for the *Baltimore Sun* of that date notes a performance of "the sterling comedy of Wild Oats" and a farce, "The Face of My Friend Jack," at the Museum that night, with no mention of either Harrison or Jefferson. Both of them, however, were obscure young men at the time.

Thereafter, however, Harrison rose rapidly. He went to the Old Richmond Theatre, where Sorrel saw him a few years later, in juvenile and light comedy roles, then, as leading man, to Joseph Foster's Pittsburgh Theatre in 1855–56, and, in 1856–57, to the Holliday

Theatre, Baltimore, managed by John Ford, who later managed Ford's Theatre, Washington, where Lincoln was assassinated. After this engagement, he cast his lot with the Confederacy and probably soon began to undertake secret missions, since Secretary Seddon felt free to recommend him as an agent. That would explain why his military record cannot now be traced.

Sorrel, watching him in Richmond, at once recognized the professional touch. "His acting was as if he had regularly strutted the boards for a stock company"—which was, of course, exactly what he had been doing for years.

A little more than two months after the notable production of *Othello* in which Harrison had acted, before the fighting at Chickamauga was over, in November, 1863, Longstreet found it had been a mistake to dismiss the actor spy so abruptly. He needed him again, but Sorrel's "careful efforts" to find him failed. It is hard to see why, unless Seddon had sent him on a short secret mission, for Harrison was "acting and stage manager" at the Petersburg Theatre, near Richmond, during the early part of 1864. Still there as late as May, he was rejoining the Richmond Theatre before June 11, 1864.

After the war, Harrison returned to the stage, where he had a long and successful career. It was also a somewhat varied career. He was, for instance, one of the producers of *Ten Nights in a Barroom* and once remarked that he had played every male lead in Shakespeare except Macbeth, a role to which he felt himself unequal. Apparently because of improvidence, he ended his life in poverty and had to be assisted by the Actors' Fund in his old age. He went to live in Louisville about 1904 and died in the City Hospital there, February 22, 1913. The old spy died game, true to the traditions of the intelligence service. His obituaries describe his achievements in the theater and mention his services as a Confederate officer—but there is not a word about his secret service, about which apparently he had revealed nothing.

18

THE SPIES AND
THE BEEFSTEAK RAID

Not all the trouble started at the desk of an unknown junior officer of the Quartermaster Corps in Washington. But that misguided individual—whoever he may have been—certainly helped it on, albeit with the very best intentions. The quartermaster, a well-meaning soul, was arranging a large shipment of beef cattle to the Army of the Potomac in the late summer of 1864. General Grant was building up a herd of 3,000 head at Coggins Point, on the James River, near Richmond. Like every other Federal, the quartermaster officer by this time knew the danger of rebel raids only too well. Meaning it all for the best, eager to protect the army's steers, he telegraphed Army of the Potomac headquarters, outside Richmond, to make sure a strong guard would receive the cattle at Coggins Point.

The well-meaning quartermaster failed, however, to take the one precaution most needed. He didn't encipher his telegram. Perhaps that harried officer was too busy. Perhaps no cipher clerk was available. Perhaps he just forgot. Anyhow, he didn't.

The fact remains that suddenly, in his lair among the wild plums, Charles Gaston, the Confederate telegraphic eavesdropper, heard the wearisome flow of unintelligible Federal cipher turn into something he could read. It was the careless quartermaster's message. And gladsome news it was. Beef cattle? The hungry Confederates, hiding in the woods around the wild plum thicket, pricked up their ears. This would have to go to General Lee at once.

I

Gaston's report must certainly have cheered the commander and his staff immensely, for the Confederate Army was on very short rations at the moment—shorter even than usual. But, even though it came straight from General Grant's special wire, Gaston's report wasn't news at Confederate headquarters, by any means. That remarkable spy, George D. Shadburne, supported by that astonishing group, the Iron Scouts—a name said to have been bestowed by admiring Yankees—had already begun to get ideas about General Grant's herd. Gaston's report was only useful confirmation.

Some days earlier, Sergeant Shadburne and another scout, John S. Elliott, had been prowling by night through the Federal Army. They had heard cattle lowing—a good many cattle.

"Elliott," said Shadburne, "what do you reckon that means?"

Elliott said it sounded to him like a whole herd of beef cattle, but morning was approaching and they could not linger. They withdrew a half mile to the enemy's picket lines, passed through them, walked a mile to their tethered horses, and then rode several miles to safety in a special hidden camp. During the rest of the day, except when they were sleeping, they discussed those cattle. That evening, Shadburne, with a friend named Merchant, and Elliott, with a scout nicknamed Sneak—doubtless in recognition of his skill—set off in opposite directions to find out exactly where the cattle were and how many herds there were. It was agreed that a "tomtit" whistle would be a recognition signal, should they meet.

Elliott and his companion—whom he designates only by his nickname, Sneak—could find no cattle till very late that night, when they finally learned that the herd they were looking for had been driven two miles west, toward Petersburg. In the darkness, they had to feel the earth for hoofprints and at first could not tell which way the herd was headed. Eventually they found a patch of soft earth, with hoofprints all pointing in the same direction. When they came upon the cattle at last, they approached close enough to disturb a few steers, but without attracting attention from the guards, and started home after making an estimate of 800 to 1,000 head. (This was before the Quartermaster Corps had sent in its new herd.)

On the way, they passed an isolated house with one brilliantly lighted room. "Here is our chance to take a Yankee officer or two with us," murmured Sneak, hopefully, but they decided to avoid causing alarm—steers were more valuable than prisoners.

Eventually they met Shadburne and Merchant, who had found another herd. Shadburne went off to prepare a report for Major General Wade Hampton, who took over command of the Cavalry Corps after Stuart's death. Elliott and one or two friends spent their time dragging the James River with long poles weighted with iron at the end, hoping to find and cut the cable carrying Grant's telegraph line to the other bank—an effort that failed.

Shadburne returned with orders from Hampton to watch the cattle while Lee reached a decision, and the scouts entered the Federal lines night after night, for two weeks, to make sure they knew all about that enormous supply of fresh beef.

Aided by the Iron Scouts, Shadburne kept an eye on those steers for several days. He was probably sending regular reports to Hampton, but only one, dated September 5, 1864, survives. This tells exactly where Grant's quartermasters were keeping the potential steaks that hungry Confederates craved: "At Coggins' Point are 5,000 beeves, attended by 120 men and 30 citizens without arms."

The report also told Hampton exactly how to get there; what trouble might be expected; and where to look out for Yankees. It warned there would be delay if the Union forces burned down "Frog Hole Bridge." The Federals *did* burn down a bridge or two; but Hampton, thus forewarned, was fully prepared to get his cavalry across. Shadburne's report made only one mistake. It located the Federal XVIII Corps correctly but gave it the wrong number.

Shadburne had sent this particular report by a trusted assistant, Sergeant J. Dickerson (Dick) Hogan, 2nd South Carolina Cavalry, a talented young secret service agent, then in his late teens; but he himself remained behind in observation. This is said to have been one of the occasions when Shadburne moved about City Point, near Grant's headquarters, in feminine garb—an exploit made no easier by his height of six feet two inches. On September 8, three days after hearing from Shadburne, Hampton sent Lee his plan for raiding the herd. One day later, Lee approved it.

On September 12, Shadburne reported to Hampton in person. His men had captured a Union courier with a message stating that Grant would leave his headquarters on September 14. (He actually left City Point on his way to visit Sheridan at Halltown, near Harpers Ferry, on the fifteenth.) Thus the Confederates knew, two or three days before the Federal commander-in-chief started, that he would be at a convenient distance when their raid began.

Meantime, south of Ebenezer Church, on the Jerusalem Plank road, "old Captain Belches" was waiting to guide the raiders behind the main Union positions. The Confederate spies had really surpassed themselves. Rare is the general with such full and accurate information as Hampton possessed when, at 3 A.M. on September 14, 1864, he ordered his advance guard forward. At dawn on the sixteenth, the rebel cavalry rode down on the Union pickets, scattered them, forced them back, killed some herdsmen, and drove off the entire beef supply of the Army of the Potomac.

According to official Union figures, the triumphant rebels had captured 2,486 head—all beef cattle except one milch cow whose presence in the herd no one has ever explained. On the way back, a little girl named Margaret Donnan asked for the cow.

That raised a problem. General William Mahone, universally known as "Little Billy," was a gallant soldier, but he had a ticklish digestion. To make sure of a fresh milk supply, he habitually had a cow driven along with his division headquarters (Robert E. Lee carried a hen); and, at the time of the raid, General Mahone's cow was going dry. The Confederate cattle thieves couldn't give little Margaret the only cow they had. That fortunate animal was destined to provide General Mahone with milk, instead of providing the rest of the troops with beefsteak. They did, however, give Margaret a steer that seemed too exhausted to be driven farther but could quickly be nursed back to health on a farm.

Having thus made a little girl happy, the triumphant raiders drove their herd on to make the Army of Northern Virginia happy, too—though it is said the Cavalry Corps insisted on having the first steaks themselves.

No doubt the cattle, after being driven a long distance at full speed, with Union cavalry in hot pursuit, did not provide the choicest cuts of prime beef. But the Confederate Army, half starved as usual, feasted mightily and rejoiced in what was at once dubbed "the Beefsteak Raid." It was not long before there was so much meat in the rebel ration that Confederate pickets were shouting offers across the front lines to the Federal pickets to exchange captured U.S. Army beef for small luxuries from the Federal sutlers. Other Confederates merely bellowed across the line: "Good fit beef over here; come over and get some."

When news of the Beefsteak Raid reached Richmond, an exultant newspaper hastened to consult a Loudoun County grazier. Noting that the Federal quartermasters bought only the largest beeves, the cattleman estimated an average of 800 pounds weight. He multiplied 800 pounds by the number of the herd (2,486 head) and announced that Hampton had brought back 1,988,800— or nearly two million—pounds of beefsteak. This, he thought, would be enough to feed 1,000 soldiers for 2,000 days; 10,000 soldiers for 200 days; or 50,000 soldiers for four days.

The grazier was estimating an issue of one pound per man per day; but he quite forgot that, even if a steer does weigh 800 pounds, you can't eat the whole steer. Modern experts, however, say the estimate is about right if you issue a ration of considerably less than a pound per man per day. The Department of Agriculture says 2,486 cattle would feed the estimated number of troops if you issued only a third of a pound per day, but even this would be "a good basis for a diet, providing other nutrients were available." Not many nutrients were available in the Confederate Army at the moment (Lee had reported on August 22 that all corn supplies were exhausted); and all that beef certainly helped. John S. Elliott, the scout who had assisted Shadburne in locating the steers to begin with, says simply that there was enough beef to last Lee's whole army for three weeks.

Viewing the ruin the raiders had left behind, Captain Nathaniel

Richardson, who had been in charge of General Grant's herd, was disconsolate. The attack, he wrote, "unless led by some one very familiar with the topography of the country and the different roads, could not have been so suddenly and successfully executed."

Captain Richardson was right. Several rebels knew topography, roads, and nearly everything the Federals were doing, because for a long time they had been practically living with the Federal Army. However much the erring quartermaster in Washington may have helped, the Beefsteak Raid was also due to Sergeant George D. Shadburne and a few of his friends.

II

Shadburne spent a large part of the war within the Union lines, usually wearing a neat blue uniform, though occasionally he wore skirts. Rarely, if ever, did he enter the enemy lines in his own gray or butternut uniform. He was alleged by admiring colleagues to possess two pairs of ears and extra eyes at the back of his head. Assisting him was an almost equally skilled group, Sergeant Hogan, Sergeant Joe McCalla, 1st South Carolina Cavalry, a certain "Dolph" Kennedy, and Hugh Henderson Scott, 1st South Carolina Cavalry. Shadburne and his friends—and there were a good many others—were now operating from two secret base camps well inside the Federal picket lines, in territory that the misguided Yankee invaders imagined they could control. Both camps were in the country drained by the Blackwater River—so badly drained, however, that the area was usually called the Blackwater Swamp, a wild tangle of bogs and thickets, almost impassable except to people who knew it well. In other words, to Shadburne and Co.— and certain charming and helpful young ladies.

The largest camp was a permanent base for Confederate scouts and spies, at times perhaps as many as a hundred. Here the Confederates were so secure that they seem to have given up gray uniforms almost entirely, living permanently in the uniform of the enemy. The false uniforms were a great advantage. In the fastnesses of the swamp, there was little chance of being caught and hanged for wearing them; and any genuine Yankee scout, wandering into a rebel lair, would imagine himself among friends—

until it was too late. The rebel spies were so completely and comfortably established that they kept with them a Confederate army medical officer, Dr. Tom Thistle.

There were probably a good many small camps scattered through the swamp, but the only one now known was "at Mrs. Tatum's," also in the Blackwater area. This was not placed in close proximity to the Tatum home but safely hidden near it. Union soldiers, who frequently paused at the house (Mrs. Tatum's daughter Molly was very attractive), would have been suspicious if they had found a shelter for thirteen men and twenty-six horses in a spot so remote, even if the men did wear Union blue and even if the horses were branded "U.S."

Eventually, while a party of scouts were breakfasting at Mrs. Tatum's, the inevitable happened. A Negro girl ran in shrieking, "Here is the Yankees!" Looking out, the Confederates could see Union soldiers in the orchard and others hitching their horses in the garden. They killed seven or eight, then ran for their own horses. Shadburne was captured, and immediately afterward there were several shots. Convinced that these meant the end of Shadburne, his companions were amazed to find, a minute or two later, that the resourceful fellow had escaped. The Federals had, however, seized their horses, and the disconsolate rebels had to limp ahead on foot, till they could raid a Union camp for remounts. Long after the war, Scott, talking to a casual stranger, found he was the Union officer involved in this skirmish.

From these secret bases, Shadburne, Hogan, and the others carried out frequent guerrilla raids, some enjoyable horse-stealing, some illicit purchasing in U.S. Army canteens, a great deal of astonishing espionage, and a little sabotage. It was evidently this group who, a month before the Beefsteak Raid, aided the Confederate secret service in blowing up an ammunition barge (or perhaps two barges at once) on the James River, at a spot so close to Grant's headquarters that flying fragments killed a headquarters orderly and wounded an aide-de-camp and a few soldiers. There were about 3,000 barrels of gunpowder, plus explosive shells, canister, and grapeshot. Grant was sputtering angrily over the telegraph to Halleck within five minutes of the explosion: "Every part of the yard used as my headquarters is filled with splinters and fragments of shell."

It was eventually learned that a Confederate agent had smuggled in the time bomb that touched everything off. But no one could understand how he knew where the barges were or how he escaped detection. It is reasonably certain that Shadburne and his friends could have answered both questions.

The explosion was managed by John Maxwell, of the secret service, with a certain R. K. Dillard as guide. The Confederate secret service was not devoted to the collection of secret information or the protection of high officials. It was a special organization engaged in developing new and secret weapons. One of these was its so-called "horological torpedo"—in other words, a time bomb. Learning that Grant was landing stores at City Point, Maxwell crept past the Federal pickets on hands and knees, carrying one of these contrivances, which he smuggled into ammunition waiting to be unloaded. Maxwell does not specifically mention any help from the spies hidden in the Blackwater Swamp; but he certainly received their aid if he needed it—and it is hard to believe he did not need a good deal. The bomb contained twelve pounds of powder, which Maxwell thought did $4,000,000 worth of damage. Though he himself was unharmed, Dillard was a minor casualty, being shocked and deafened.

Shadburne and his friends were so much a part of the hostile army that they became regular customers of the canteens run by Union sutlers. They carried back to their own army many of the luxuries that Confederate soldiers, penned up in Richmond and Petersburg, could not get, besides purchasing at the Union canteens various small comforts for themselves—and possibly for appreciative maidens in the rebel capital.

It was not unusual for spies elsewhere to make similar purchases in the Union lines for friends in the Confederacy who could not shop for themselves. Before Grant's advance began, one intrepid fellow, operating north of the Rappahannock in the midst of the Union Army, thoughtfully did some shopping for Mrs. Robert E. Lee—and sent the package safely to her husband's headquarters. Two soldiers in Buford's division, then with Forrest's cavalry, were sent into Memphis for intelligence, in the late summer or very early fall of 1864. As they could get only one blue uniform, Scott donned civilian clothing and was promptly invited to enlist by a Federal major. The disguised Confederate demurred, saying he would enlist for a short time only.

"We are not enlisting short-term men now, it's for the war," replied the recruiting officer. This was very helpful. It was one of the details the spies had come to learn. Enemy recruiting reveals enemy strength. Long-service troops mean combat effectiveness.

Hiring a hack, the pair toured various camps to make sure no Federal raid was in preparation—meantime buying books, music, and candy for various rebel damsels. These they sent out of Memphis by an elderly civilian, a friend they could trust, after which they returned to Forrest with the information he needed for his raids on Athens, Alabama; Pulaski, Tennessee; and Thompson's Station, Tennessee, in late September, 1864.

Not content with patronizing Federal sutlers, one or two spies in Shadburne's group (apparently including Shadburne himself) went into business as Federal sutlers themselves. To appreciative Yankee soldiers, at suitable prices, they supplied small pies made by Virginia cooks in local Virginia farm kitchens. It was profitable —and, besides, a pie salesman could go almost anywhere in the Union Army, suspected of nothing more serious than the desire to turn an honest penny.

Union soldiers were so hungry for pie that a sutler could sell 650 a day, but the kind of pie the sutlers sold is described by a disgusted army surgeon as "putrid animal food." Sutlers' pies are also described as "villanous," and a despairing army musician says they tasted like "rancid lard and sour apples." They were, he adds, "moist and indigestible below, tough and indestructible above, with untold horrors between." Small wonder a rebel spy, suitably disguised, was a welcome visitor, if he was selling fresh, Southern, farm-cooked pastry!

III

Shadburne and his assistants received a more or less steady flow of information from at least two (and probably from several) charming but deadly Confederate maidens. The most helpful was Molly Tatum, who lived with her mother in a house in the part of the Blackwater Swamp within Grant's lines, below Petersburg. Molly was able to pick up a good deal of information from sundry Federal admirers ready to relieve the rigors of war by pleasant chats with a delightful girl. She had no difficulty getting her swains to talk freely, since the befuddled Yankees supposed the Tatums to be "a truly loyal household"!

Among Molly's numerous Northern admirers was one of the cowherds taking care of Grant's beef. Shadburne, who knew Molly well, certainly picked up a good deal of useful information about the herd, which the infatuated youth had let slip to her.

Other local girls were equally cooperative. There was, for instance, Carrie Gray (about whom nothing else is known) who constantly passed information to the Confederates. Just after the fight at the Tatum farm, Carrie, from within her home, heard her dog bark. That, she knew, meant the approach of Southern spies. It was a most unsuitable time for Southern youths to come calling, for Carrie was entertaining three Yankee visitors. In some way, she was able to warn her new visitors in time, adding a bit of useful information: There were seventeen mounted Yankees two miles down the road.

Leaving the three Federals to enjoy their visit to Carrie, the Confederates made a surprise attack on the larger group, killing nine men and capturing all the horses. But retribution overtook them at once: Union troops appeared, recapturing ten horses and also capturing Dr. Thistle, the only Confederate surgeon in Blackwater Swamp.

There are references also to a helpful blonde, aged nineteen, who may have been either Molly or Carrie, since there is no record of the complexions and coloring of these rebel girls. Or the fair-haired and helpful lady may have been a third ardently Confederate maiden. Several references to "the girl on the Lawyer's Road" in Blackwater Swamp, which appear in *Official Records*, are probably to Molly.

Quick-witted damsels often used extraordinary methods to save secret agents. A certain Bill Mikler, while visiting a friendly home in Prince William County, found the house was surrounded with

Yankees. He took refuge upstairs in the bedding. But that was sure to be searched. Somehow or other the Yankees must be diverted. Downstairs, one of the daughters of the house immediately had a "hard fit." Suspicious men in blue uniforms entered to find the "hard fit" getting harder every minute, while the afflicted patient's sisters were devoutly praying over and vigorously rubbing her. That ended the search. Unwilling to intrude upon a domestic crisis, the gallant Yankees departed. (It is perhaps just as well no medical officer was present to note the patient's symptoms.)

Federal intelligence, knowing perfectly well what was going on, never had adequate evidence against any of the girls. Although the Union men knew Shadburne's name and knew exactly what he was doing, nobody knew what he looked like and therefore nobody could catch him. Every man on the Federal picket line also knew there was a guerrilla base somewhere near—much nearer than it ought to be. This opinion was confirmed September 15, 1864, when a Confederate deserter, seeking refuge in the Union lines, reported a hundred mounted scouts and "a Louisiana company called McCullough rangers," all hiding in the swamps near City Point. This meant Shadburne's group, since the Blackwater area begins only a few miles south of City Point.

Probably there were several such hidden camps, for a Federal order of September 12, 1864, employs a suggestive plural. It tells General A. V. Kautz to clean out "the nests of guerrillas in front of you." One day before that, John C. Babcock, a skilled Union agent, had warned, "A regularly organized band of scouts under a Lieutenant Reed, rendezvous in Black Hole [sic] Swamp."

19

SPYING IN THE WILDERNESS

Grant's advance in early May, 1864, which began the Battle of the Wilderness and led on to Spottsylvania, Cold Harbor, the siege of Richmond and Petersburg—and eventually to Appomattox—was no surprise at all to Robert E. Lee. His spies had been telling him for weeks exactly what was coming—had, indeed, been keeping him so well informed that even his own officers wondered at the exactness of his information.

"How General Lee finds out Grant's intention I cannot imagine," wrote Captain Charles Minor Blackford to his wife, when the Battle of the Wilderness was over, "but, as soon as Grant commenced to move, Lee commenced also, though, in some instances, as much as twenty miles apart; yet when Grant formed his new line, there was Lee in front of him as surely as if they had moved by concerted action."

Captain Blackford was writing in early June of 1864, after he had seen the great Confederate work his seeming miracle three times in a single month—in the Wilderness, May 4; at Spottsylvania, May 7; at Cold Harbor, May 30. He and Lee's other officers (except the chosen few who shared the secret) could not guess how their commander did it. All they knew was that he had an uncanny way of discovering exactly where Grant was going—and getting there first.

In fact, it was the perfection of his espionage and other intelligence that enabled Lee to hold off Grant's superior army so long. His forces were so small that his only hope was to concentrate at exactly the right spot at exactly the right time. It was hard enough to hold off the Army of the Potomac, at best. If Lee ever concentrated at the wrong spot, he would never get another chance.

I

Except that it was a main part of their duty to keep silent, two groups of men and women could have explained it all very easily. One was the network of secret agents and couriers operating in Washington and the North. The other was a specially chosen group of Confederate scouts and spies operating at the front, along Grant's lines and deep within them. The Confederate intelligence service in the North, with its intricate network, crisscrossing what remained of the Union all the way from Richmond to Canada, could give Lee long-range warning of what was coming. But this strategic intelligence was often several days, sometimes a week or more old. If Federal detectives caught the couriers, or if alert sentries stopped them at the picket lines, the information never arrived at all.

In any case, all such intelligence had to be supplemented by last-minute tactical intelligence gathered in the field, by experienced scouts and secret agents sent out by local commands and moving continually back and forth in the Federal rear areas. Especially valuable among these sources were Sergeant Ike Curtis, Sergeant Dick Hogan, Hugh Henderson Scott, Stringfellow, Shadburne, and Channing M. Smith, Company H ("the Black Horse"), 4th Virginia Cavalry, which was also Stringfellow's regiment.

Though Smith must have done a great deal of scouting and spying earlier in the war, nothing is to be learned of these adventures. One finds him in the records for the first time in the period immediately preceding the Wilderness campaign.

Channing M. Smith had his own way of doing things. Though he practically lived with the Union Army, he "disliked entering the enemy's lines alone, either by day or night," and his commanding officer, realizing the man's value, let him have his own way. Smith usually took along his "regular guide," a certain M. B. Chewning, though he had other aides when Chewning was engaged in other duties.

Chewning was Smith's companion on the gratifying occasion when they laid violent hands upon an elaborate luncheon, meant for Union officers of high rank and consisting of delicacies long unknown to the Confederate Army. The Confederates' suspicions had been roused when they saw three Federal cavalry horses tethered in front of a house in the country. Their hopes also were roused when, as they approached, three Union soldiers emerged, bearing large baskets. Taken by surprise and handicapped by their burdens, the Yankees were easily compelled to carry the baskets to a safe and secluded spot. Here Smith and Chewning, examining their loot under an oak by a small stream at a safe distance from the enemy, were delighted to find a large pan of hot baked potatoes, hot white rolls, cold tongue, strawberry jelly, cheese, and a bottle of whiskey. There was even silverware and a plated drinking cup. As can well be imagined, none of these blessings ever reached the Federal officers for whom they had originally been destined.

Also engaged in independent reconnoissance of his own, in or out of disguise, was Lieutenant Colonel John S. Mosby, who made the Federals so much trouble that it has been suggested the mere effort to track him down was in itself enough to delay Grant's advance. Certainly the Union commander had a marked postwar admiration for the Southern guerrilla and spy and did everything he could to secure financial help for him when hostilities ended. Channing Smith was at times under Mosby's command, though at other times he reported to Stuart.

The probability that Lee would soon find himself facing a new opponent, Ulysses S. Grant—who had hitherto commanded only in the West—seems to have been hinted in military intelligence reaching the Army of Northern Virginia as early as mid-February, 1864. This was about a month before Grant was promoted lieutenant general (March 9) and made commander-in-chief (March 11). Stringfellow is said to have picked up part of this information while dancing—disguised as a young girl—with Union officers.

Confederate spies in the North began sending warnings to both Lee and Davis, telling exactly what the new Union commander-in-chief was going to do, long before troop movements of any sort began. One remarkable and very early report on Grant's exact intentions is dated March 24, 1864. The information had been secured less than two weeks after Grant became commander-in-chief. It was one of the most valuable bits of intelligence the Confederates had secured since Mrs. Greenhow's early successes; but unhappily it was intercepted on April 12, 1864, when Federal detectives arrested Miss Sallie Pollock, not yet eighteen, of Cumberland, Maryland. Sallie had long been making secret journeys down the Shenandoah Valley to Staunton, Virginia, fording the Potomac on horseback, bewitching any pickets she happened to meet, and finding shelter in the homes of relatives along the way. She had come under suspicion earlier, had been arrested twice, had always talked her way to freedom. This was the first time the Federals had been able to catch her with incriminating evidence.

Scandalized Union detectives found in her possession two copies of the same letter, one for Lee, one for Davis. The fact that, though these were dated March 24, Sallie still had them when arrested, nearly three weeks later, suggests that the Confederate secret couriers had been very slow and cautious in working their way southward through the Northern states. But no matter how slow transmission may have been, the letters—if they had ever been delivered—would have warned the Confederates a month or more in advance of exactly what was going to happen:

> The Army of the Potomac will be under the immediate command of Major Gen'l Grant—when the grand movement is made—They will move upon Richmond in three columns, one from North Carolina under Butler—one from East Tennessee commanded by Hooker—the Potomac Army will advance by way of Gordonsville—
>
> This information is reliable to a fault, the Army of the Potomac will number One Hundred Thousand men—the Army of North Carolina

will number Seventy Five Thousand—all details will be forwarded soon. Pro-Bono-Publico.

Not all of this really was "reliable to a fault," however—at least not by the time the Federals got it. Grant was no longer a major general. He had been promoted lieutenant general a fortnight earlier. Moreover, Meade, not Grant, was in command of the Army of the Potomac; but, when it moved into the Wilderness, Grant *was* with it and *was* in supreme command. The Army of the Potomac *did* have 100,000 men—or at least 99,400.

There *was* a converging attack by Butler's army, though not with 75,000 men. Hooker, it is true, did not attack from Tennessee. But even that part of the advance information, though it contained a good deal of error, was partly true. Hooker had for some time commanded XI Corps and XII Corps. Though Hooker himself did not come east to fight, these troops did. But they did not join Grant, they joined Sherman. And, by Grant's own order, they fought on the march through Georgia, not in the Wilderness.

II

The Confederate spies kept the Army of the Potomac under careful observation all through the winter of 1863–64, with more or less help from sympathizers within the Union lines. One winter night Shadburne and some of his men roused a Confederate girl sympathizer at Fairfax Court House, which had been occupied by the Federals for years. She guided them to her brother's house three miles away, through the darkness. Here they secured information on a Federal force at Centreville and the movement of Federal wagon trains. As this helpful damsel is described as a blonde, aged eighteen, she may have been Antonia Ford, who was then still living at Fairfax Court House. There is no doubt that she had continued spying for Mosby and probably for other Confederates, like Shadburne, until she was finally arrested in March, 1863. After this success, Shadburne also managed to work his way into Centreville, for further observation of the Yankees.

The spies maintained a continuous watch over the Orange &

Alexandria Railroad, running southwest from the vicinity of Washington through the country where the coming battles would be fought. Movement of troops and supplies along this line was an essential element of information, which the Confederates from time to time secured through various agents. Hugh Henderson Scott was one of the spies watching it in February, 1864, probably under the direction of Sergeant Hogan. As early as March 8, 1864, General Wade Hampton was able to pass on to Lee and Stuart news brought in by Shadburne which showed the Federals were beginning to move troops south.

At about the same time, Channing M. Smith rode through Meade's artillery park, then went on to the headquarters of V Corps, where he sat for some time with his hand on the staff of the headquarters flag, hoping for a chance (which never came) to pull it down and make off with it. On this same reconnoissance, he also visited Meade's own headquarters, where he contrived to steal a small flag, which he triumphantly presented to General Lee. (A Confederate officer remarked that Smith returned to the Confederate lines "tired, hungry and sleepy." No wonder!)

At least once during this period, Stringfellow donned Federal uniform, posing as an officer in a regiment known to be at a safe distance on the extreme Federal right. Thus arrayed and responding gracefully to salutes, he penetrated to the headquarters of VI Corps, ascertaining strength, position, and the intentions of the commander. The story that he also dined with General John Sedgwick, though dubious, is not entirely incredible.

In mid-February, Shadburne, assisted by Hogan, led a detail of three mounted men and five or six infantry to a point near Brentsville, only about thirty-five miles from Washington. Here they settled down in a very secret, semipermanent camp, just outside the town, and devoted themselves to continuous observation of what the Federals were doing. On St. Valentine's Day, Scott and two others breakfasted in the village itself, within three or four hundred yards of Union cavalry. When they had finished, they withdrew calmly to the "blind or ambuscade we had on a hill," returning in due course to their own lines to report what they had learned.

Most of this midwinter reconnoissance amounted to little more than keeping the Yankees under observation and making sure that no immediate moves were in contemplation. But in early April, Shadburne was able to report that the whole Army of the Potomac had been paid on Tuesday, March 1. That might indicate an impending movement, especially as Shadburne also reported that all troops were *ready* to move (though they did not actually do so for another two months). He added that Kilpatrick's cavalry, which had returned in early April from raiding Richmond, had set off on another march, carrying three days' rations. They had already passed "Sheppard's" and were now near "Madden's"—both eviently farms used as landmarks by the Confederates. Shadburne suggests that Kilpatrick was on his way to Ely's Ford. This seems to have been merely a routine cavalry movement, probably in preparation for reconnoissance when the advance into the Wilderness began. Shadburne added that the Federal II Corps was on the same road. Gregg's 2nd Cavalry Division had reached the front March 3, 1864. The Federal command had sent sutlers and women to the rear. For the time being, Robert E. Lee hardly needed any more information than the inimitable Shadburne had packed into this one report.

On April 10, Smith was able to confirm Shadburne's report with additional facts. Not only had the Federal command sent sutlers, traders, and other non-military personnel to the rear; it had also ordered all baggage back to Washington.

Smith was, however, a little premature in reporting the persistent and false story that XI and XII Corps had already been ordered to join Grant. This was common gossip among civilians in Culpeper and Fauquier counties. Sallie Pollock's message—the one captured by Federals, so that Lee never received it—had hinted at the same thing when it predicted that Hooker, whose forces in Tennessee included both corps, would join Grant in the attack on Lee. It was alarming news for the Confederates; but queries to General Johnston and Longstreet soon brought word that both corps were still in the West. It was, however, useful for the Confederates to know that the Federals were contemplating such a troop movement.

III

Two other Confederate secret agents, deep within the Union lines, were also reporting in early April. There is not much doubt (though no absolute proof) that these men were Stringfellow and Mosby. On April 10, Stuart addressed a note "To Capt. Stringfellow, war-path," in which he said, "I have just heard, though Col. Mosby, that the enemy is carrying troops every night from Culpeper towards Alexandria. You must find out the truth."

Stringfellow probably went to Alexandria at once, since he had many sources of information in the town, where he had already carried out numerous espionage missions. Alexandria was the home of his future wife, and he knew many of the people. Presumably he was the Confederate spy who, at this time, "had communications with persons inside the town every day," whose report suggested that there would be a Federal advance on the Rapidan "as soon as the weather is settled." He had noted that all white troops had been withdrawn from trenches around Alexandria and sent to the Army of the Potomac, their places being taken by Negro troops.

This is perhaps the occasion when Stringfellow indulged in one of his most whimsical exploits. He suspended his secret labors long enough to visit the theater among the Yankees in Alexandria and see a topical drama devoted to the career of his friend Mosby. It was entitled *The Guerrilla; or, Mosby in Five Hundred Sutlerwagons.* When he rejoined the Confederate ranks, Stringfellow brought with him copies of the play, one of which he presented to Mosby himself.

The other spy in this incompletely identified pair was probably Mosby, who had been living with the Federals in Culpeper County, where he could keep a close eye on Grant's headquarters at Culpeper Court House. This agent, whoever he was, also picked up the recurrent and alarming rumor about the Union XI and XII Corps, which continued to worry the Confederate staff until the very beginning of the Wilderness Campaign—in which neither corps ever appeared!

Stringfellow's secret reconnoissance during this period very nearly cost him his life. Arrayed in a pair of Union officer's trousers, a Confederate gray jacket, and a Union overcoat—thus presenting the outward appearance of a Union soldier—he was leading a small band of prowlers, hoping to capture Federal dispatches and pick up a few prisoners.

While his men were under cover, somewhat to his rear, String-fellow himself captured a Federal courier, who, seeing the Confederate spy's blue overcoat, had expected no trouble. Calling one of his men, Stringfellow sent him to the rear with the prisoner—and also with orders to bring up the whole detachment. Unfortunately, the guard paused—as guards in charge of prisoners of war are only too likely to do—to "go through that Yank" in the hope of loot. This proved a pursuit so engrossing that he failed to get String-fellow's horsemen moving forward promptly.

While anxiously waiting for them, Stringfellow encountered two more Union cavalrymen, soon reinforced by a third and a fourth. They had seen him halt the Union courier and were naturally suspicious. Approaching quietly, all four suddenly sur-rounded the Confederate spy and covered him with their pistols. The somewhat heated conversation that ensued has been set down by one of Stringfellow's companions, who was not far to the rear when it was taking place and who certainly heard it repeated a few minutes later. The dialogue has the stilted quality of mid-nineteenth-century reporting, but it is certainly accurate in essentials.

"What does all this mean?" demanded Stringfellow, with a suit-able show of indignation. "Are you bushwhackers?"

"No, sir."

"If you are not bushwhackers or guerrillas, why do you capture a United States soldier in his own lines? You must know me. Do you not belong to General Gregg's Cavalry?"

"Yes, we do."

"Well, don't you remember seeing me at headquarters?"

So persuasive was Stringfellow's tone that three of them promptly did remember seeing him there. They may even have been right. Stringfellow was quite bold enough to penetrate a hostile di-visional headquarters. When the sergeant swore he had never seen him, at headquarters or anywhere else, Stringfellow himself as-sumed an air of appropriate skepticism.

"Boys, it is very easy for you to deny being bushwhackers; it is

easy for you to get into our lines with our uniform coats on, but
let me see your pants."

Thus far, no uniform had been visible on either side except
blue overcoats and high cavalry boots. The genuine Union men
threw back the skirts of their overcoats and displayed regulation
trousers.

"Now," they said, "let us see yours."

This was exactly what the spy had been hoping for. Carefully
keeping his gray jacket covered, he revealed U.S. Army trousers—
plus the stripe of a commissioned officer. The Yankees stared at it;
Stringfellow's tone became very authoritative indeed.

"You see you have insulted an officer."

The three privates wanted to let him go. But the sergeant was
a confirmed skeptic.

"There is something wrong about him," he insisted.

Expecting to hear his own cavalry arriving at any moment,
Stringfellow took a bold tone.

"Come right on with me to headquarters and I will have satisfaction before I am done with you."

He turned resolutely toward the Union outposts, refusing to
give up his arms, waited for a good chance, then suddenly announced he was a Southern soldier, demanded surrender, and
began firing. The Yankee bullets missed. Stringfellow's second shot
hit the sergeant, his own men came to his aid at last, a hesitant
force of Yankees appeared, and there was a lively skirmish, the
wounded Yankee sergeant—a persevering fellow—taking a shot at
Stringfellow whenever he had the chance. Eventually, the Confederates fell back, carrying the sergeant with them. A penitent Stringfellow paid his prisoner's expenses at a Richmond hotel.

Stringfellow had had a similar escape the year before, when
his superb knowledge of the Union Army had enabled him to talk
his way out of impending arrest. He met a Federal cavalry detachment which demanded his surrender. This time, he was wearing a
Federal overcoat over a gray uniform.

"Surrender?" said the spy. "What do you mean?"

"We mean that you are a guerrilla and you are our prisoner,"
said the Yankees.

Stringfellow explained that he belonged to the 1st New Jersey. "Who is in command?"

"Major Janaway."

"Right. Who commands the brigade?"

"Colonel Taylor."

"Right again. Where is it stationed?"

"In the edge of Warrenton."

"Yes—and who commands the division?"

As usual, Stringfellow knew the right moment at which to assume a tone of irritation.

"My friend, I am tired of your questions. The First New Jersey is in Taylor's Brigade, Gregg's Division, and Pleasanton commands the whole."

"He's all right, boys, let him go."

The Confederate spy rode peacefully forward on whatever nefarious mission concerned him at the moment. But one can understand why he told John Esten Cooke, the novelist, then on Stuart's staff, that he never went out on an espionage mission without expecting it to be his last.

In late March and early April, 1864, while occupied in the all-important Confederate espionage before the Federal advance into the Wilderness, Stringfellow and Channing M. Smith were exposed to needless danger by an egregious piece of folly in which General Stuart and Governor William Smith, of Virginia, were equally guilty. Stuart foolishly let the governor into the secret of the two men's undercover exploits. Governor Smith, dangerously ignorant of security requirements, allowed some of their adventures to reach the press.

Lee, when he heard of the leak, was sufficiently alarmed to rebuke Stuart, though in his usual tactful way. "I consider the lives of Stringfellow and Channing Smith and others greatly jeopardized. They will be watched for, and if caught, hardly dealt by. You had better recall them and replace them by others." The general's final suggestion was not very practical. Nobody could possibly replace these two men, who simply had to shoulder the extra risk. By pure good luck, the incredible blunder of the general and the governor did no harm.

IV

In the last week of March, 1864, a report published in Northern newspapers the week before alarmed Robert E. Lee. Since the Confederate spies were usually able to deliver Northern newspapers to the Army of Northern Virginia soon after publication, Lee probably saw the story on March 25 or 26. Certainly he was taking steps to verify it on the twenty-eighth. One account said Burnside was "collecting his corps at Annapolis." Another Annapolis report said, "There will be at least fifty thousand troops here in the course of a few weeks." One regiment was already there, two more were on the way, the rest would arrive in a few weeks—as in fact they did. Burnside would lead these men on a "second expedition." There was a further tale (entirely false) that Burnside now had under his command both his own IX Corps and Hancock's II Corps. Such strengthening of his force might be serious, for the Union general had three ways of making trouble from Annapolis: He could raid the Confederate coast, as he had done before. He could support Butler in an attack up the James against Richmond. Or he could (as he did) march overland to reinforce Grant.

Lee read this in the *Philadelphia Inquirer* and the *Washington Daily Morning Chronicle*, but it also appeared in the *National Intelligencer*, and doubtless in many other papers.

It was not hard for Lee to make sure part of this was wrong. Hancock and II Corps had long been right in front of him, and it required very little reconnoissance to show that they were still there. But where were Burnside and his IX Corps? Were they really at Annapolis? If these troops had been moved east, there was no doubt where the new Federal commander-in-chief meant to make his main effort. A query went off on March 28, 1864, to Longstreet in Tennessee, on whose front IX Corps had long been stationed. Longstreet replied that Burnside and IX Corps didn't seem to be there any more. Toward the end of March, when Burnside's preparations at Annapolis were being first suspected, an unidentified and badly misinformed spy who had been visiting Washington and Baltimore reported that IX Corps was still somewhere in the West. This at least seemed to be confirmed by statements in the *New York Times* and *Washington Chronicle* that Burnside had been in Cincinnati March 24, preparing to defend Kentucky. Though all this was quite wrong, it was confusing to Lee—so very confusing that the Federals may have been deliberately "planting" the misleading reports to deceive him.

By this time the Confederates had begun to think that Burnside really was at Annapolis, or soon would be, but they had no hard information. Someone had to find out, and President Jefferson Davis himself now took a hand. He personally instructed Stuart's chaplain spy, Captain Conrad, to discover exactly what Burnside meant to do. Was he really preparing to support Grant? Or was he preparing for another raid on the Confederate coast, like his North Carolina raid of 1862? For once, enemy intentions would be easy to ascertain: If the Federal general was really thinking of an amphibious operation, he could not possibly conceal the inevitable concentration of shipping. Conrad was probably also told to find out what he could about Burnside's new Negro division, about which Confederate intelligence was very curious indeed.

Donning civilian clothes, the captain rode up the Shenandoah and entered Washington again, relying on "full facial decorations of over a year's growth" to conceal his identity. He still had his mysterious friend in the War Department, but this clerk-spy was now finding it difficult to procure information. "Three years of war had taught Stanton to be more discreet." Papers in the War Department were now so carefully restricted that the clerk-spy could give no information about Burnside, and neither could anyone else.

A single night of vigorous inquiry sufficed to show Conrad he would have to go to Annapolis and see for himself. In his civilian clothing, he would be dangerously conspicuous about the camps —the first sentry he met would certainly stop him. But Captain Conrad knew what to do about that. Nothing simpler! He would don his old Federal chaplain's uniform. After all, he really was a chaplain—though, unfortunately, in the wrong army.

Conrad went back to the permanent Eagle's Nest intelligence base along the Potomac to get the uniform, incidentally seizing the opportunity to cut his whiskers, so as to give his face "a more clerical cast." That is, he reduced the year's growth of beard and shaved off his mustache, but he retained luxuriant side whiskers.

However handicapped he may have been by the tighter Federal security measures, Conrad's secret agent in the War Department was nevertheless able to get his friend into the camp at Annapolis by forging a letter of introduction from a Union officer of impressive rank. The Union man, entirely loyal, never suspected how his name had been misused, but the spy within the War Department knew enough about him to make the forgery sound entirely authentic.

Armed with this useful document and arrayed in his chaplain's uniform, Conrad entered Burnside's camp at Annapolis and began to move about among the troops with complete freedom.

A stroll along the waterfront showed at once that Burnside was not going to attempt another coastal landing like that in North Carolina in 1862. There were not nearly enough ships. Chats with the troops confirmed his observations. Conrad had no trouble getting the incautious Negro recruits to talk freely with a clergyman. They were positive they would join Grant in Virginia.

Conrad was thus able to report "that Burnside contemplated no sea attack but would re-enforce Grant's left." (Burnside actually did enter the Battle of the Wilderness on the night of May 5–6, on the left of Grant's center, though not on his extreme left flank.)

Having sent his preliminary report, Conrad lingered in Washington long enough to see Burnside's column enter the city. This was confirmation of his report. It could mean only that IX Corps was on its way to the Army of the Potomac. Conrad slipped quietly out of the Federal capital to report personally at Lee's headquarters. Soon there was still more confirmation. A day or two later, on April 28, while Lee was telegraphing Longstreet to ascertain Burnside's whereabouts, Mosby's prowlings in search of information for Stuart took him within a mile of Centreville, Virginia. Some of Burnside's troops were passing through the town, and Mosby's horsemen picked up a few Federal prisoners. These men assured him that IX Corps had left no troops except convalescents in Annapolis. This news went on at once to Lee, who telegraphed it to Davis on April 30.

Stringfellow had also supplied confirmation on April 28, the

very day when General Lee was anxiously inquiring of Longstreet as to Burnside's whereabouts. The information was probably
rather late in reaching army headquarters, but that was no fault
of Stringfellow's.

The trouble was, some staff officer in Fitzhugh Lee's headquarters, through which the message came, was careless enough to give
the name of the spy responsible for the report as "Franklin." That
made a good deal of difference when the telegram reached Stuart.
If it came from Stringfellow, it would be as reliable as military
intelligence would ever be. If it came from some unknown individual named "Franklin," it would have to be given a very low rat-
ing indeed. There was no secret agent named "Franklin" in the
service; but Stringfellow's full name—by which no one is ever
known to have called him—was Benjamin Franklin Stringfellow,
as we have seen.

From Fredericksburg, without even troubling to encipher, Fitzhugh Lee telegraphed Stuart that "one of your scouts Franklin just
from Md near Washington" was reporting that Burnside with
23,000 troops, 7,000 of whom were Negroes, had marched through
Washington on the twenty-fifth and had passed near Alexandria.
The report was especially valuable because it also confirmed at
last the fact that XI and XII Corps, about which Lee had been so
much disturbed, had not been sent to Virginia at all.

Stuart realized at once that this report really was Stringfellow's
and therefore reliable. In forwarding it to Lee, he added an unsigned note:

Gen'l
    This must be Stringfellow.

After the war, Stringfellow himself printed the report as his own.

General Lee wrote President Davis at once. The general felt
certain this report really did come from Stringfellow. If so, that
conscientious spy must have "good grounds for his assertion." If
Conrad, Mosby, and Stringfellow all reported movement of IX
Corps from Annapolis toward the Rappahannock front, the thing
simply had to be true. It meant that one more army corps was
being put into the line against the Army of Northern Virginia.
On the other hand, it was now fairly clear that XI and XII Corps

would not be with Grant's army. At this time, Lee also decided that VIII Corps, under General Lew Wallace, would not be brought against him. Previous reports do not mention it, and Lee does not seem ever to have been seriously worried about it.

V

It would, of course, have been an advantage to the Confederates if Pro-Bono-Publico's information on enemy intentions had reached the Army of Northern Virginia promptly, instead of being picked up by Federal detectives when they captured Sallie Pollock. At best, however, this information would not have arrived until mid-April; and, even without it, Lee, by combining the various bits of intelligence that did reach him, was able to make surprisingly accurate estimates of the situation in early April, changing them as required when new reports came in.

Grant's appointment as lieutenant general and commander-in-chief was at once announced in the press, but the question remained whether his headquarters would be with the western forces or with the Army of the Potomac. The main blow would probably fall wherever Grant was, though even on that point Lee still had doubts. Grant had visited Brandy Station and the Army of the Potomac, March 10, immediately on his appointment, but had returned at once to Washington and had then gone west. As late as March 25, Lee still doubted "that the first important effort will be directed against Richmond." No troops seemed to be coming east to join Meade over the Baltimore & Ohio, which Lee had "ordered to be closely watched." He rather thought the first attacks would be in the west "against Genl Johnston or Genl Longstreet, most probably the former." Even when a scout reported that Grant had visited the Army of the Potomac again on the twenty-fourth, Lee was unconvinced that the attack would come in the East. He regarded Grant as very wily, quite capable of appearing personally here and there, just to fool the Confederates.

Lee soon began to change his mind. By March 30, he knew—only a few days after Grant's return—that the new commander-in-chief was again with the Army of the Potomac and that the Yankee soldiers expected to have him with them permanently. "From the reports of our scouts," said Lee, "the impression prevails in that army that he will operate it in the coming campaign." By April 5, he had decided that probably "Grant with a large force is to move against Richmond." By April 7, so much information had come in that he began to concentrate troops to meet "the approaching storm, which will apparently burst on Virginia." A few days later, on April 12, uncertain how long his Confederates could keep the Yankees away from Richmond, he warned the Secretary of War that "an investment of Richmond is one of the possibilities for which we should be prepared."

Spies' reports continued to confirm this view. Two agents, one on each side of the Orange & Alexandria, on April 6 reported "great activity" on that railroad. These agents, Lee noted, were not in communication with each other, and their reports were mutually confirmatory. The spies thought the troops now moving in were recruits and soldiers returning from furlough: "Their clothes are too new & overcoats of too deep a blue for old troops." That was worth remembering. If these men were recruits, they would be less formidable in combat than veterans.

By April 13, Lee regarded it as reasonably certain that Grant would begin his advance with only three corps, but he was still uneasy about Burnside's IX Corps and does not seem to have considered the probability that Grant would also use Sheridan's Cavalry Corps. He was by no means certain what additional forces Grant might receive. At the moment, he estimated his opponent's force as 75,000 men, but expected it to reach 100,000 before the advance began. He probably did not anticipate the forces that actually marched against him—four infantry and one cavalry corps, with 118,700 men.

By the end of April, Lee was expecting attack at any time. He could be sure that he would face Meade's Army of the Potomac, with three corps—II Corps (Hancock), V Corps (Warren), and VI Corps (Sedgwick). Thanks to Conrad and Mosby, he now knew that these troops would be supported by IX Corps (Burnside), though he may not have realized that IX Corps would not be under Meade's orders but directly under Grant's.

This awkward arrangement was due to Grant's effort to be tactful. Burnside ranked Meade as a Regular officer on the old Army

List. He had also commanded the Army of the Potomac (very badly) himself. It would be awkward to serve under Meade, his junior, in the army he had himself once commanded. But, since Grant, as lieutenant general, now ranked both of them, it would be natural for Burnside to take orders from him; and, as commander-in-chief, Grant could easily coordinate their movements.

On April 30, about seventy-two hours before the Battle of the Wilderness began, Lee sent his son, General Custis Lee, in Richmond, a remarkable accurate estimate of the whole situation, which shows how completely successful the rebel spies had been:

> The reports of scouts all indicate large preparations on the part of the enemy and a state of readiness for action. The Ninth Corps is reported to be encamped (or rather was on the 27th) on the Orange & Alexandria Railroad, between Fairfax Court House and Alexandria.
>
> This is corroboration of information sent the President yesterday, but there may be some mistakes as to the fact or number of corps. All their troops north of the Rappahannock have been moved south, their guards called in, &c. The garrisons, provost guards, &c., in Northern cities have been brought forward and replaced by State troops. A battalion of heavy artillery is said to have recently arrived in Culpeper, numbering 3,000.
>
> I presume these are the men stated in their papers to have been drawn from the forts in New York Harbor. I wish we could make corresponding preparations.

Lee's estimate of the situation was much assisted by the view from Clark's Mountain, near Rapidan Station, immediately south of the Union lines, whence he could look directly into the Federal camps, across practically all of Culpeper County. Clark's Mountain had been his observation post for personal reconnoissance on various occasions, ever since 1862. When Lee climbed it for the last time, May 2, 1864, immediately before Grant's advance began, he could examine Union troop concentrations, conveniently spread out before his eyes, as if on a staff school instructor's sand table. They were distributed about as he had expected. Grant's own maps could have told Lee little more than his spies and his personal reconnoissance.

Looking down on all the bustling military activity below, the Confederate commander made one last prediction: The Federals would cross the Rapidan at Germanna and Ely's Fords. Thirty-six hours later, they were doing exactly that.

VI

Fortunately, Channing Smith wrote two articles describing his exploits among General Grant's troops and near Grant's own headquarters, as the advance into the Wilderness began. And Colonel John Scott, who, as a captain, had commanded the Black Horse Troop in Stuart's cavalry and who had been somewhere near when Smith came in with his report, also wrote an account, which corresponds exactly with Smith's.

How often Smith had been in and out of the Federal camps during the spring of 1864, there is no telling; but he was certainly wandering about in Grant's army, very much as he pleased, in the first two or three days of 1864. With him were three picked men—R. H. Lewis, James Hansborough, and an unnamed "Member of the Fourth Virginia Cavalry" who may have been Stringfellow or may have been Smith's specially valued guide, M. B. Chewning.

It was not hard for the spies to see what Grant was planning. Three army corps could not possibly conceal their preparations for movement from observers moving freely about their entire area. Smith says that, on the night of May 3–4, 1864, he was certain of Grant's intended march some hours before the troops actually moved out, in the very early morning of May 4. Though the spies had probably not had time to send the exact D day and H hour to Lee, they had certainly been able to make extremely accurate predictions and were about to observe the actual movement of the army in time to bring Lee up-to-the-minute observations.

Grant stayed at his headquarters at Culpeper Court House till the whole army was in motion, then set out in person. Scarcely had he departed when Smith and the others also started south to take this last-minute information to Lee. They reached the headquarters at Culpeper just after Grant himself had left, but soon overtook him. It would be interesting to hear what Grant would have said had he known that these stars of the Confederate intelligence service were his traveling companions. Or what else he might have said had he known that Sergeant Shadburne could mobilize twenty

Confederates for intelligence missions behind the Union lines, whenever he thought it desirable. Grant later expressed himself with much vigor on the whole subject of careless Federal security.

Though on this mission the Confederates were wearing their own uniform, they moved with perfect freedom in the darkness. No one stopped or questioned them. Probably the only reason they could do this was that they traveled the main roads only after dark and, in daylight, moved only in the thick woods characteristic of this region. They did, however, have conversations with Union troops in daylight. On these occasions, they were certainly wearing raincoats of some kind over their uniforms, though Smith does not specifically say so. Scott, who was behind the Confederate line at this time or reconnoitering immediately ahead of it, says specifically that "they were all clad in Confederate gray."

It was somewhere near Stevensburg, Virginia—southwest of Culpeper, between that town and the Wilderness—that the two Confederate agents caught up with the Union commander-in-chief, whose presence meant a continual flow of staff officers, scouts, and messengers. The rebels prudently took refuge in the home of a sympathizer, where they stayed out of sight till it grew dark. It was dangerous, but there was a good chance of valuable information. Besides, it would have been even more dangerous to proceed by daylight.

The spies waited till ten o'clock at night, May 4, before starting out again, and darkness stood their friend. Before reaching Germanna Ford—which the Federals were using to cross the Rapidan, exactly as Lee had predicted—they encountered a courier from Grant's own headquarters. Seeing mounted men in uniform, the color of which he did not notice in the darkness, the man paused to ask the way to General Charles Devens's cavalry command. It was too good a chance to miss. The Confederates amused themselves by misleading the poor fellow with "such directions as would furnish him employment for the rest of the night."

When Smith, in turn, asked for "headquarters news," the trusting Union courier supplied useful information. A report from Gregg's advance cavalry had just reached Grant. Gregg reported he had thus far seen no rebels. He intended to press on south with his

2nd Cavalry Division in the morning—another bit of news for Robert E. Lee.

The Confederates crossed the Rapidan on pontoons specially laid for Grant's forces, "their way being lit up by a brilliant white light on the south side." The light was near headquarters and had probably been put up for Grant's own convenience. All things considered, the Union Army had been extremely helpful.

Thus far, everything had gone well; but they soon reached a large fire, around which Union troops were gathered. Here they were asked to identify themselves. Probably their gray uniforms were visible in the firelight, but Smith's explanation was accepted: "One of General Stahl's scouts with a detail, on our way to the front."

His gray uniform, worn by a supposed Federal scout, did not surprise anybody. Union soldiers on espionage missions were sometimes rash enough to appear at Union headquarters still in the enemy's uniform. Sheridan's scouts wore it when riding with Sheridan himself, among Union troops.

It was characteristic of Channing M. Smith that, when questioned, he had instantly ready on the tip of his tongue, a plausible cover story with the name of a real Union general. The officer Smith called "Stahl" was General Julius Stahel. As he commanded a cavalry division, he was certain to be sending out a good many scouts, some of whom were certain to be in false uniform. Besides, Stahel was at the moment in West Virginia, not on the Rapidan. Hence no one could make inconvenient inquiries. Yet the story was credible enough. Grant had been drawing troops from the west. Stahel might already have joined the Army of the Potomac or might have sent scouts ahead, while marching to join it.

A little farther on, the rebels encountered a group of Union horsemen.

"What cavalry is that?" someone called from the darkness.

"Jeb Stuart's for all you know," yelled Smith—and rode on undisturbed. Everyone appreciated the joke. It never occurred to the Union troopers that these really were Jeb Stuart's horsemen in their own gray uniforms. (He was a truthful man, was Channing M. Smith—whenever the truth was at all useful.)

Toward daylight, Hansborough, who knew the country, pointed out the direction in which Lee's headquarters ought to lie. It was high time they were reporting all they had seen, and they turned in that direction, passing through Sedgwick's VI Corps just as the drums began to beat and the men began packing knapsacks and raking up their fires. Hurrying to get out of this dangerous neighborhood before the rising sun revealed their uniforms, they were suddenly halted by a sentry's challenge.

Again Smith was equal to the occasion. To the usual "Halt! Who comes there?" he replied casually:

"One of General Meade's aides with my escort. Is this General Sedgwick's outpost?"

"Yes, sir."

"Who commands this outpost?" asked the Confederate.

"Major Forbes." It was always useful to have the names of outpost officers, and Smith tried for a little more information.

"Can you tell me how far in advance I will find General Gregg?"

"No, sir."

"Good night. Forward, escort."

Pushing quickly ahead, they emerged on the Orange Plank Road near Parker's store, which was soon to be the scene of bitter fighting. Now safely through the Federal infantry pickets, they would still have to work their way through Gregg's alert cavalry, somewhere ahead. They would have to be extremely alert themselves and—after a day and a night of constant riding and reconnoissance —they were very tired. Lee would have to wait a few hours for his information. They tied their horses in the woods about a hundred yards from the Plank Road and lay down on the ground for a little sleep.

About seven in the morning, waking at the sound of clattering hoofs, they saw through the trees a large cavalry force moving on the road. Hastily mounting, they trailed the column, keeping far enough away to avoid its flankers, who soon came into sight. Presently they heard pistol fire, as the Federals encountered Confederate pickets; then heavier fire. As they watched the Federals retreat, they saw Rosser's Confederate cavalry in pursuit. Knowing now that they were safe within Confederate lines, they galloped another three miles, found Robert E. Lee, and reported.

Smith probably brought Lee his first hard intelligence of the Federal forward movement, but there is some doubt as to the exact hour when the information reached him. At any rate, the general was able to telegraph Jefferson Davis from Orange Court House that Grant had struck his tents and was moving toward Germanna and Ely's Fords, though the hour of the telegram is doubtful. In view of the Confederate enciphered flag signals that his own signalmen had been able to break, Grant thought Lee must have learned "at a very early hour" on May 4 that the Federal Army was moving and knew by 1 P.M. that it would come by Germanna Ford—but Lee had guessed that before the Yankees even started.

Lee soon knew a great deal more, from some secret agent who may or may not have been Smith. Whoever this man was, he had a line directly into Union headquarters. On May 5, Grant gave oral orders to Colonel W. R. Rowley, "night officer" at headquarters. Three days later he "read in a Richmond paper a verbatim report of these instructions." (When Butler, moving up the James River toward Richmond, reported to Grant—also on May 5—Lee knew all about it by the twelfth, though, by the standards the Confederate spies had by this time established, that was pretty slow work.)

The only reason for attributing this coup to Smith is that Lee sent him back into Grant's lines on the night of May 5, just before all this happened. Tired as he was, Smith had remained with his own army only a few hours. Lee, giving him no time for rest, sent him out again at once. Instead of Richard H. Lewis, who had in the meantime been wounded, he took two orderlies from Stuart's headquarters, with whom he rode toward Chancellorsville, where Stonewall Jackson had been shot almost exactly a year before (May 2, 1863). Judging by the ease with which they moved about, all three were in disguise of some kind.

About ten o'clock that night, halted by a Union sentry, Smith identified himself as an officer of Stoneman's Union cavalry, "on my way back to report" after reconnoissance. The sentry passed him and, on request, supplied the Confederate with the name of the local commander, General Wilson. In other words, the 3rd Cavalry Division held this part of Grant's line. General Lee would be glad to learn that! Nothing so useful as a really accurate enemy Order of Battle.

Always thorough in verification, Smith rode on to Major General James Harrison Wilson's own tent, observed the general "sitting at a table in his tent, busily engaged in writing, the fly in front being drawn back," reflected how easy it would be to kill him "but how useless it would be to do so," rode about chatting with anyone likely to have information, then heard a large column "moving out on Todd's Tavern road."

By this he undoubtedly meant what is usually called the "Brock Road," leading just behind the Federal front toward Todd's Tavern. What he heard was almost certainly the beginning of Grant's move around the Confederate right to Spottsylvania, which Lee, fully informed by his scouts and spies, anticipated and blocked.

Pausing only to steal the best horse they could see at Wilson's headquarters, Smith and his companions started back across the road where the Federals were marching. When, reaching the outpost at which they had entered, the party were challenged, Smith rode boldly up to the sentry and asked if the man he had relieved had not told him about the "Union" reconnoissance party. The sentry was properly respectful.

"Yes, it is all right—but what are you going to do with that led horse?"

"Why, sometimes we get one shot," said Smith glibly, "and it is well enough to provide against emergencies."

Both the emergency and the shot came sooner than he had expected. As they passed through a small woods, expecting no trouble, there was a sudden volley immediately in front of them. Whether it was fired by concealed Federals or concealed Confederates they never discovered, nor did they pause to find out. In the confusion, their stolen horse broke loose, but followed the other horses and was easily picked up again.

As the night of May 6, 1864, drew on, fighting in the Wilderness slowly died down. No special reconnoissance or espionage seems to have been attempted that night or the next day. Lieutenant Colonel Charles S. Venable, of Lee's staff, says only that, after the first three days of the Wilderness, "the quiet on the 7th told Lee that Grant would move around on his left"—i.e., around the Confederate right. Lee did reach that conclusion eventually, but probably not at first. Grant always believed that he had fooled his great opponent into thinking the Union forces would now retreat. That was what they had always done before. Lee, Grant believed, saw the Federal wagon trains moving and "interpreted this as a semi-retreat of the Army of the Potomac to Fredericksburg."

In this, Grant was partly right—Lee had indeed toyed with the idea of driving the Yankees straight back across the Rapidan; but his intelligence service soon set him straight. During the afternoon of the seventh, Stuart's cavalry patrols reported that Grant's baggage trains were moving; and after dark the Confederates could hear columns of troops moving, too. Stuart's troopers were certainly alert enough to discover before very long that the movement was east and southwest—toward Spottsylvania, not to the rear.

But the obvious way to make sure at once was to send Channing Smith into the Union Army again. Soon the spy was riding over the ghastly battlefield where the Federal attack on Lee's cavalry had been repulsed. En route, he saw a Federal colonel, lying badly wounded on the ground. The spy paused, found some litter bearers, and sent the officer to safety. This humane act nearly cost the Confederate spy his life. A little later, while hobnobbing, in disguise, with Yankees, he heard someone mention this very colonel as killed. For once, Channing Smith did not think quite fast enough.

"No," he exclaimed, "he was only desperately wounded, for I saw——" At the last moment he realized he was not in the uniform of that regiment and had no reason for being in that part of the field. He changed his sentence just in time: "——saw one of his regiment, who said he was only badly wounded."

VII

While Grant was moving his forces eastward and while Channing Smith and his friends were moving quietly about among the Union troops, two other Confederate reconnoissance groups were also operating deep in Federal terrain. One of these was led by Sergeant C. P. Curtis, a scout for Fitzhugh Lee; the other by Ike Curtis, scout for W. H. F. ("Rooney") Lee. The adventures and achievements of the first group are unknown; the second left one record—short but sufficient.

Ike Curtis and the man with him, one Tapscott, paused for supper at the home of a certain Granville Kelly, not far from Kelly's Ford on the Rappahannock, far to the north of the fighting. What observations of the Federal rear they may have made, no one knows—probably a good many. But they brought off one coup that justified the whole reconnoissance, when they fell in with a group of three correspondents, two for the *New York Herald,* one for the *Tribune.*

The journalists had with them three mailbags containing a good many papers, among them letters from Grant to Lincoln, which the rebels joyously seized. There were also long casualty lists and combat reports, exactly the kind of information the Confederates needed.

This was on May 7, 1864. Late that same day, Lee began to move troops southeast along roads parallel to the front. Longstreet was at Spottsylvania, ready for the Yankee advance, at 8 A.M. on May 8. Lee had been able to place I Corps at the right spot because of the mass of information his spies had given him. Whether the contents of the mailbags reached him in time to confirm the other intelligence that influenced his decision remains unknown, but Ike Curtis's haul was much appreciated. The more newsworthy contents of the mailbags were being exultantly reprinted by Richmond newspapers a few days later.

After the days of stubborn fighting at Spottsylvania, Grant still had made no real progress. He knew he would have to move again. Lee knew it, too, again analyzing enemy capabilities—and even enemy intentions—with uncanny skill and absolute precision.

Channing M. Smith was sent back into the Union Army for more reconnoissance—in or out of uniform—in the Spottsylvania–Chancellorsville area. The record of what he did in the few days after the Wilderness is not complete; but he did so much that by May 11 he was worn out and, after getting back through the Confederate lines, lay down to snatch a little sleep, while the battle still raged.

On May 11, Grant wrote his famous dispatch to Halleck in Washington. He meant to "fight it out on this line if it takes all summer." And on that day, at Yellow Tavern, on the edge of Richmond, one of Sheridan's troopers killed General J. E. B. Stuart. After that tragedy, Smith seems to have reported chiefly to Lee.

Smith was roused before midnight on the eleventh by orders from General Lee himself. He was to "go into the enemy lines and report such information as I could of their position, etc., just as soon as possible." Lee had good reason for sending his weary secret agent back into action. He had refused his flanks and thus for a time delayed combat, but that night, May 12, the powerful Union forces were converging on his center, soon to be known as the "Bloody Angle."

With Fred Moore, of Aldie, Loudoun County, who had brought the orders, Smith set out at once. The two entered the Union line on, or beyond, its left (eastern) flank, near Fredericksburg, and rode up the Plank Road toward Salem Church, through the flood of traffic that always moves in the rear of a moving army—orderlies, staff officers, messengers, ambulances, and one extremely indignant chaplain. The rebels had fired upon this holy man, who was furious: "My uniform should have protected me." The two Confederate spies paused in their espionage to offer consolation to the Federal man of God. Probably the rebels had been firing at such long range they had not been able to see he was a chaplain, they assured him.

Pushing on, they soon found that Grant was extending his left toward Massaponax Church. The road was crawling with ammunition wagons, supply wagons, ambulances, and—this was interesting!—fresh troops coming in from Washington via Grant's base at Fredericksburg.

"We then went among them," says Smith (which shows plainly that the pair were in disguise), "and soon ascertained the direction they were moving in and the different commands of the Army of the Potomac engaged." It was easy to identify the various corps by the colored cloth patches—precursors of modern divisional shoulder patches—which the Union Army had introduced.

No one seems to have disturbed the rebel spies, who wandered calmly about, observing Union forces to their hearts' content.

When Smith felt sure they had all the information they needed, he "told Moore we would get back to General Lee as soon as possible."

All would have been well if, at this point, Moore had not proposed pushing their luck one degree too far. His own horse was nearly worn out. Smith, too, needed a remount. The Federals had plenty of horses. Why not wait long enough to steal two? Regarding his own broken-down nag, Channing Smith agreed.

The spies' troubles started when they tried to cross the Plank Road again, on their combined return journey and horse-stealing expedition. However complete their disguises may have been, they were not eager to have them closely examined. The Plank Road was now so crowded with Grant's passing forces that they had to lurk out of sight in the woods beside it for a long time, till a break in the flood of military traffic left the road empty, save for a well-mounted major and his orderly. Here, at last, were the two horses they wanted.

Drawing their pistols, Smith and Moore rode out, yelling a demand for surrender. The outraged major had time to fire one shot at Smith—a miss. Smith shot the officer, but Moore, trying to shoot the orderly, hit the major's horse. No one knows what became of the orderly and *his* horse after that, because fifty men of the 13th New Jersey Cavalry suddenly rounded a bend in the road, a hundred yards away, saw what was happening, and came pounding down the road. The two Confederates reached the woods just in time. They found concealment—but they also found about twenty Union infantrymen. These men had foolishly stacked arms without posting a sentry and, without their muskets, were helpless. It was easy for the two armed Confederates to drive them off, but they knew the Yankee fugitives would spread the alarm.

At this extremely inopportune moment, a Union artilleryman came along. This inconvenient prisoner, whom the Confederates didn't in the least want, was a new problem. They could not bring themselves to slaughter a helpless man in cold blood. Neither could they release him, since, in some way Smith does not explain, he had discovered they were Confederates. Smith finally told the man they would kill him if he revealed what they really were, but they would set him free when they reached a place where they themselves were safe.

The three were riding amicably along a narrow back road, when they suddenly met a Union officer and twenty men, with drawn pistols. At the officer's "Who are you?" Channing Smith's courage for once gave way. He himself says he was "so badly scared I couldn't speak." Fortunately, the prisoner kept silent.

Equally fortunately, Moore kept his head. In an instant the quick-witted fellow was improvising a highly plausible story. They had been with a squad guarding ambulances to Fredericksburg. On their return journey, they had ridden into the country for milk —as soldiers were always doing. Completely deceived, the Yankee replied, "You men had better get back to the Plank Road as soon as possible. A major has just been killed, and I am looking for the party who killed him."

A few minutes later, another party of Federals stopped them, but these were unsuspicious. They only wanted to know if they had seen traces of the rebels who had killed the major. Smith and Moore said they hadn't. Indeed, they were appropriately shocked at the news. Presently they had to ride, with their prisoner, through a third party of Federals. After that, there were no more difficulties. Ever a man of his word, Smith released his prisoner, though he kept the man's horse.

Early in the morning of May 12, he was reporting to Lee. The first wave of Federals began their assault at dawn. No general in history ever had more completely up-to-the-minute combat intelligence. Smith and Moore had been riding among the enemy only a few hours before the attack.

VIII

As the third week of May began, Lee was badly in need of information that would show what the Federals were going to do next. But by May 16, after a little more than a week, he began to suspect that Grant would again try to envelop the Confederate right flank. This was exactly what Grant did order a few days later.

Much of the intelligence that led to Lee's correct conclusion reached him this time through other Confederate commanders. How much of it also reached him through the spies is not clear, for there is a gap in all their narratives at this period. Smith, Curtis, Stringfellow, Shadburne, and the others were certainly active, but there is no real clue to what they were doing.

In addition to information from other commanders and whatever intelligence the usual spies brought in, Lee also wanted information from the front line itself, and brigade commanders were told to send out patrols to listen with special care for the sound of moving troops.

Innumerable such local patrols must have gone out, but full record of only one has survived. This was entrusted to Sergeant Berry Benson, Company H, 1st South Carolina Volunteers, McGowan's Brigade, who had volunteered for this dangerous duty. Benson hoped to gain the information General Lee wanted by venturing into the enemy's share of the narrow stretch of No Man's Land between the armies—but no farther. There, listening in the darkness, he might be able to hear the sound of marching feet, the clatter of equipment, the hum of soldiers' talk, rattling combat wagons, and clattering hoofs.

Would that do? he asked the captain who gave him his orders at brigade headquarters. Perhaps not, said the officer.

"If you can't get the information *outside*, you must go *inside*." Furthermore, the brigade wanted that report within two hours.

Benson decided he could do it. A countryman, used to the outdoors, ought to be able to slip between outposts in the night. After that, he thought, he could move about the Federal camps without undue trouble. He was in Confederate uniform, but it was dark, and he was wearing a nondescript topcoat. He wasn't sure how he would get back—if he did get back—especially within two hours. Some way would probably present itself.

With two other volunteers, Benson approached the Federal outposts in the night of May 16, hoping to establish a listening post. He observed an approved tactical principle for infantry patrols, having his men follow at a distance sufficient for get-away in case of trouble. (It is extraordinary how much like a 1914–18 night patrol Benson's own account makes this Civil War adventure sound.)

The trio worked their way close to the Federals in safety. Benson, some distance in advance, ventured closer still—too close. An alert sentry challenged but fortunately did not fire. Benson surrendered at once. This looked like a good chance to enter the enemy's line. Being—strictly in line of duty—a liar of genuine talent, Benson had decided in the beginning that, if caught, he would pose as a Federal scout, who was wearing rebel uniform only as a disguise. He was "trusting to the chance of their letting me go into camp without further questions—an exceedingly slim chance, I knew, but I knew there were fools in the army as well as elsewhere."

Knowing that his statement could be quickly tested if he pretended to come from a neighboring Federal unit, Benson was careful to identify himself as a member of a Yankee brigade he knew to be in a distant part of the Federal line of battle. Although the Federals could check that, too, it would take some hours. In the meantime, he had a chance—just a bare chance—of getting away alive with the information General Lee wanted.

Benson had, however, fallen into the hands of experienced old soldiers, who knew all about rebel tricks. He had also failed to realize how completely Southern his accent was. There were, to be sure, Southern men in the Northern armies, but they were mostly from the border states, where Northern and Southern accents tend to approach each other. Benson's South Carolina speech was unmistakable. So completely Southern an accent required explanation; and, though Benson lied like a hero, no amount of explanation did very much good.

He presently found himself facing a highly skeptical Federal brigadier, who forced him to admit that he was, in fact, a Confederate soldier. Quick-witted to the end, however, even after his mission had failed, Benson still saw a chance to deceive the enemy and seized it at once.

How were Confederate rations these days? his captor inquired. Excellent, Benson assured him, mendaciously. The brigadier didn't believe it. Benson took a piece of bread from his pocket and invited his interrogator to sample it. When the brigadier tested it, he agreed with Benson. It *was* excellent bread.

And no wonder! Benson had traded three days' rations for a

single loaf, a fact he didn't mention—thereby planting at least one item of false information in the enemy's mind.

Later that night he escaped, encountered Federal cavalry, avoided them, then encountered Federal infantry he could not avoid, and was again captured. There was some talk of hanging him for espionage. True, he was in the proper uniform of his own army. But he had pretended to be a Federal spy. Some guardhouse lawyer evolved the extraordinary idea that this in itself constituted espionage. But the idea that a Confederate soldier could be convicted of espionage in a Confederate uniform was so obviously ridiculous that it was soon brushed aside. The alleged spy lived to write down all his adventures—but Robert E. Lee got no information from Berry Benson that night.

Benson's failure did not matter too much, for—whatever the other spies may have been doing—Captain Conrad was still keeping a close eye on the War Department.

On May 17, just after Benson had fallen into enemy hands, the captain sent a wire from Milford Depot, Virginia, to Major William Norris, head of the Confederate War Department's espionage service: "A special messenger left Washington yesterday for General Grant's headquarters, with instructions to him to hold his present position at all costs, and he should be re-enforced by 60,000 men immediately. The plan is to call out the militia to do garrison duty all over the North and send the volunteers to the army. If time is allowed them, this will be done." Conrad's telegram was sent on to Jefferson Davis, who certainly passed it along to Lee.

Conrad himself can hardly have left his post to send the message from Milford. It probably passed down the courier line, through Eagle's Nest, and so to Milford and the Confederate telegraph. If Conrad was right, this promise of enormous reinforcements (which the Confederacy could not possibly match) may have encouraged Grant in the exceedingly bold move he was about to make.

20

THE LAST MONTHS

When fighting ceased at Cold Harbor (June 1–3, 1864), something seems to have gone wrong with Confederate intelligence.
After the spectacular failure of his last assault—which, in later
years, he always regretted—Grant held his ground until the middle of June, then, with most of his army, simply vanished. Reconnoitering Confederates could not find them. For once—as the West
Point Department of Military Art has remarked officially—"Grant
had done the near-impossible and completely outwitted Lee." During the night of June 12–13, he had silently withdrawn the Army of
the Potomac. Confederate scouts and spies could not find 100,000
Union troops.

This, Lee thought at first, did not greatly matter, for he felt sure
Grant was merely making another of those marches around the
Confederate flank that he had tried in the Wilderness and had tried
again at Spottsylvania. Federal cavalry suddenly became very active at New Market, on Lee's right flank and almost in his rear,
thus apparently confirming Lee's idea. Grant and the infantry, he
felt sure, might be expected to appear at any moment. Moving to

the right, as they had done before, the Confederates would prepare to block the Yankees off from New Market.

I

Grant was, indeed, trying another envelopment, but much bolder than any he had tried before. He was moving away from Lee's front entirely, preparing to cross the James River, leave Lee behind, and bring his full force down on Beauregard, isolated in front of Petersburg—while Lee and the whole Army of Northern Virginia sat waiting for Yankees, where no Yankees were ever going to come.

One Federal corps went in small vessels down the York River, through Hampton Roads, and up the James, almost to Petersburg, where it confronted Beauregard on the night of June 14–15. Another marched to the James River and was ferried across that same night. Army engineers began building a 2,100-foot bridge across the James, beginning at 4 P.M. and finishing at midnight, so that Grant's supporting corps began marching across by the time the first two had begun to arrive.

Lee was handicapped by lack of cavalry. Hampton's and Fitzhugh Lee's divisions were absent in pursuit of Sheridan, who had suddenly moved his horsemen toward the Valley. This meant there were not enough for vigorous reconnoissance and not enough to concentrate quickly on the south bank of the James to oppose the crossing Federals. Grant also had the good fortune to be moving through a part of Virginia where there were few country roads. The road net consisted of a few very large quadrilaterals. Hence Grant could screen his force by posting strong forces at a few crossroads. So far as surviving records show, practically no information came in through the espionage system.

The absence of Hampton's and Fitzhugh Lee's sorely needed cavalry divisions was due to the misplaced efficiency of a handful of Confederate spies. But for them, Hampton and Fitzhugh Lee would probably have been available on the James to delay Grants' crossing. The rebel espionage had been clever. But it was a little too clever—it spoiled everything!

Toward the end of the first week in June, 1864, while the two armies still confronted each other at Cold Harbor, Grant evolved a plan to have Sheridan lead his cavalry west toward Charlottesville, while General David Hunter, commanding Union forces in the Shenandoah Valley, moved east. Uniting at Charlottesville, they were to march back toward Richmond along the Virginia Central Railroad, tearing up the tracks as they went. They would thus destroy a vital Confederate supply line and would also draw Confederate cavalry away from the James River.

Sheridan received his orders June 6 and moved out June 7. Though they do not seem to have found Grant's other forces, Shadburne, Hogan, Wallace Miller, Lieutenant Bob Shriver, Walker Russell, Phil Hutchison, and others reported to Generals Wade Hampton and M. C. Butler that a large force of Yankee horsemen had moved northward from behind Grant's lines, then still at Cold Harbor, and were crossing the Pamunkey.

This information was confirmed at once. At about the moment Sheridan was starting, it occurred to Hugh Henderson Scott that it was about time to steal some more Federal horses. With this laudable purpose—and nothing else—in mind, he and Dolph Kennedy rode, in complete tranquillity, straight through the Union Army, till they reached the northern bend of the North Anna. By the time they got there, Sheridan had already passed the Pamunkey, where Shadburne had earlier reported him. Farther upstream from that point, the North Anna branches off, almost due northwest. Sheridan's cavalry would have to cross it as they turned westward.

Scott, Kennedy, and Sheridan reached the North Anna at just about the same time. The Federals had laid a pontoon bridge over the river, and the cavalry were already crossing. It was an ideal moment for observation. The whole force had to pass—practically in review—before the two Confederate spies. All Scott and Kennedy needed to do was count the flags, which revealed the number of regiments, count the artillery, and probably also note the length of time it took the column to pass. They were able to report Sheridan's new location, note the direction of his march, and give an accurate report of his strength, all from firsthand observation.

To their own enemy strength report, they were able to add a strength estimate given them by a local female spy, whose name

remains unknown. She was one more of those remarkably useful
Southern ladies who were always on hand when facts about the
Yankees were needed. From this talented amateur, the professional spies learned that Sheridan had ten thousand men. She also
reported—probably from chats with incautious Federal officers—
that the column was heading toward the Shenandoah.

All her information was correct, though the last bit was somewhat misleading. Sheridan *was* heading *toward* the Shenandoah,
but he didn't mean to go there. He meant to halt in Charlottesville. However, her report that the men were carrying six days'
rations gave a fair idea of the length of the proposed march.

The date and place of this espionage can be accurately fixed.
The spies reported they had watched Sheridan crossing the North
Anna. Sheridan crossed that river at Carpenter's Ford on June 7,
1864.

Scott sent Kennedy back to report this vital information directly to Hampton, who must have received it about the same time
as Shadburne's report. Scott hung about Sheridan's advancing
column for another day, to make sure which way it was going,
then himself reported to Hampton, who hurried him back at once to
continue surveillance of Sheridan.

Shadburne's, Scott's, and Kennedy's observation of Sheridan was
now confirmed by Captain Thomas N. Conrad, who at the moment was not spying in Washington but was engaged in legitimate
scouting along the front. Conrad had the luck to meet an unarmed
mulatto in Federal uniform. The man, who had been a servant of
General Thomas L. Rosser, one of Hampton's brigade commanders,
had "just escaped from Sheridan's headquarters." He described the
prospective raid and named the points through which the Union
column would pass. Conrad took him at once to Rosser, who
"knew when and where he was captured and all about him." After
interrogation, Rosser sent him on to Hampton, who thus had the
same information from four known and trustworthy sources.

The bugles sounded "Boots and Saddles" June 9, and Hampton
began a forced march west, pausing only to graze the horses from
noon till two o'clock every afternoon and from midnight till two
o'clock every night.

Being now well aware exactly what the Yankees meant to do,

the Confederates moved swiftly to the right place. On June 11, Sheridan found Hampton's gray cavalry squarely across his path at Louisa Court House, with Butler's cavalry a mile to the rear at Trevilian Station. On the twelfth, Sheridan limped back to Grant in defeat. Early, meantime, had beaten Hunter in the Shenandoah. The Federals had thus suffered two tactical defeats, but Grant's main strategic purpose was accomplished: There had been no Confederate cavalry to interfere with Grant's swift bridging and crossing of the James River, which made possible the siege of Richmond—which led on to Appomattox.

Scott, after spying on Sheridan all the way to Louisa Court House, returned with more information for Hampton, after a fight with a few Yankees, who were probably a security detachment of some kind. But—however brilliantly it had dealt with Sheridan —Confederate intelligence failed to warn in time of Grant's fateful movement across the James. It had allowed the Confederate cavalry to be decoyed away from the James River when it was most needed.

II

Shadburne practically duplicated the feat of Scott and Kennedy about six weeks later, toward the end of July or perhaps during the first few days of August. On August 1, 1864, Grant ordered Sheridan to Washington for consultation at the War Department and thence to the Shenandoah to assume command. Though Grant did everything in his power to maintain secrecy, the Confederate spies sniffed this out, almost as soon as the Union commander-in-chief gave the order.

Shadburne and one of his men, Jack Shoolbred, both in blue uniforms, were off to investigate at once. Indeed, it is said they were looking into the matter as early as July, before Sheridan had even started.

On their way into the Union lines they made one of their usual pauses to see what information Molly Tatum might have for them. At her mother's cabin, they found two other men also in blue uniforms. They were not surprised; Molly encouraged Federal admirers for the information they let slip. Shadburne and Shoolbred were disconcerted this time, however, because they were not sure whether these were genuine Union men or disguised Confederates like themselves; and there was no chance to take Molly aside without rousing suspicion. In the end, all four blue uniforms sat down to table together. Only then did Molly, waiting on them, have a chance to signal silently, from behind the other pair, that the strangers really were Yankees. That settled it. They shot it out right at the breakfast table, the result being an appalling mess and two corpses that had to be secretly and instantly disposed of, lest retribution fall upon the Tatums. The scene of battle was cleared up so carefully that, though other Federals continued to call, no one in the Northern army ever did find out what had become of the missing men.

It is by no means clear how much information this desperate reconnoissance produced. Even the date is by no means certain. It may have been ordered before Sheridan set out to take command in the Shenandoah Valley, in an effort to learn in advance what he was likely to do there. Or it may have been timed after Sheridan's departure to see what changes Grant might make when Sheridan had gone. As for the date, it can only be said that Shadburne was certainly engaged in this mission in the late summer or the fall of '64.

Shadburne, also watching General Gouverneur K. Warren's troops, was soon able to warn Hampton that Warren would move sometime in December to raid the Weldon Railroad, an important supply line running due north from the Carolinas through Petersburg to Richmond. Warren had already raided this line at Globe Tavern, a few miles south of Petersburg, in August, 1864. Shadburne was able to tell Hampton that the raid now contemplated would strike south across the North Carolina border and try to break the rail line at Weldon, North Carolina. He also knew that Warren's V Corps would be reinforced by Gregg's 2nd Cavalry Division, but he did not know that General Gershom Mott's 3rd Division of II Corps would also be in the column.

With this exception, Shadburne's information was completely accurate. Warren swept south on December 7. He did not quite reach the town of Weldon, but came within a few miles of it and succeeded in devastating forty miles of track, in spite of Shadburne's warning.

Though General Warren did not know it, Shadburne was traveling with him. After warning Hampton, he had calmly ridden to the Union rear, past Warren's advancing troops, until he reached the end of the Union column. Here he assembled twenty of the Iron Scouts, whose lurking places he knew, and with this little force—all of whom must have been in Federal uniform—he set off in pursuit of Warren's reinforced army corps.

It is pleasing to report that such valor was not without reward. Hanging resolutely on Warren's rear, Shadburne captured a large quantity of applejack—a fluid very acceptable in the bitter December cold. He is also said to have secured a quart of peach brandy, simply by asking for it at a country house—though to do that he must, in some way, have identified himself as a rebel.

Working with Shadburne was Private Isaac S. (Ike) Curtis, 9th Virginia Cavalry, who had for some months been assigned to reconnoissance for General W. H. F. (Rooney) Lee, son of the commanding general, commanding one of Hampton's divisions. When Warren made his move, the two Confederates amused themselves by riding, in blue uniforms, through his column, snarling "Close up!" to all stragglers, with a suitable air of authority.

Hampton, meantime, having received the scouts' warnings, marched all through the night of December 7–8 and in the morning confronted Warren's troops at Bellefield. Though they could not keep Warren from destroying the railroad, the Confederates were able to force him to retreat on the eighth.

Despite all his risks, Shadburne was never captured till the very end of the war, in March, 1865. He escaped at once and, in the days before Appomattox, was again scouting about Grant's headquarters, though no one knows exactly what he was doing.

After these espionage exploits, the record temporarily fails. There are no more spy adventures till the siege of Richmond was ending and the last, desperate, bloody weeks of the Civil War began. During the siege, two newsboys, venturing across the lines with local newspapers, were accused of espionage but do not seem to have been punished.

This is not to say that Confederate espionage ceased, only that the spies' adventures were not recorded. There is no doubt that the intelligence agents of both sides were hard at work till the very end. Two Union spies, captured and court-martialed a few days before Appomattox, were under death sentence when Lee surrendered. The surrender saved their lives.

III

No Confederate spies seem to have been under death sentence in Federal prisons at the time of the Appomattox surrender; but one spy, who had had an incredible escape the year before, was again a prisoner. This was Private (later the Reverend) J. T. Mann, a practically indestructible Confederate, who had been wounded in the hand and neck at Gaines's Mills, June 27, 1862; had had his hip and thigh broken at Gettysburg, a year later; and had then survived a wholly illegal hanging by a mob of Federal soldiers, April 4, 1864. In spite of all this, he was back with the Confederate Army and fighting until he was captured, unhurt for once, in the attack on Federal Fort Stedman, near Petersburg, 1865. This time, being an ordinary prisoner of war, he was merely jailed and, after the war ended, released May 28, 1865.

Soon after being wounded at Gettysburg, Mann had been promoted captain, assigned to espionage, provided with a forged proclamation offering $50 for his own arrest as a deserter, given an expired furlough (also forged), which he was supposed to have overstayed (thus making himself a deserter), and ordered to go into the U.S. Navy Yard at Pensacola and into Fort Pickens, to collect any available information. He entered the Federal lines near Fort Barrancas, opposite Fort Pickens, on the coast southwest of Pensacola, and soon formed a warm friendship with a sergeant in Company B, 7th Vermont Volunteers.

Mann was soon able to report to General D. H. Maury, Confederate commander on the Gulf Coast, that a U.S. Army paymaster would visit Fort Barrancas, carrying enough cash to pay "all troops in New Orleans and on the Mississippi River and the men on the gunboat fleets." Since the Confederate Army was always short of funds, Maury took prompt measures to seize that cash. Mann was told that a force of Confederates would approach Fort Barrancas and would signal its readiness with a single pistol shot. When he heard the shot, Mann was to set fire to the powder magazine. (The signal was badly chosen, since a pistol shot might be heard almost any time.)

On the night of the proposed raid, Mann was up late, drinking with his friend, the Vermont sergeant, and seized an opportunity during the evening to turn his friend's watch ahead secretly, by nearly two hours. When the spy left the sergeant's tent about eleven o'clock, the unsuspecting Yankee thought it was nearly one in the morning, an impression that may have been helped by the wine. Mann had ready a ball of twine steeped in turpentine.

Almost at once he heard a pistol shot, approached the magazine, lighted the ball, and tossed it toward the magazine—then saw a Union sentry not fifteen feet away. The soldier snatched up the flaming ball and tossed it at Mann, fired, and missed him. There was no sign of the Confederate attack Maury had promised. The general had canceled it without informing his spy, and someone else had fired a pistol—as might have been expected.

Mann fled, found shelter in the house of a devoted Confederate for three days, tried to escape on the fourth night, but was captured and taken back to the fort.

An infuriated mob of Union soldiers, well aware most of them would have been killed or blown to bits if the spy's plan had succeeded, seized him and, without waiting for a court-martial, prepared to lynch him. Throwing a rope over a projecting beam, they hauled him up before anyone noticed that his feet were only an inch or two off the ground so that he could give himself a little support with his toes. The mob dug a hole in the earth under him and then stood about to watch him die. His neck had not been broken by the usual drop and he was slowly strangling to death, a sensation he later described: first intense pain like "a steam boiler ready to explode," then relief from pain and a strange light, then imaginary music of harps and many voices. (Mann was, after all, a devout and orthodox Baptist.

At the last moment, his friend, the sergeant, intervened. The soldiers cut him down and resuscitated him, the resulting sensations being "just as painful as those I experienced when being hanged." He was court-martialed but acquitted of trying to destroy the magazine, because the sentry swore (correctly) that he had seen him throw his fireball at 11:30 P.M., while the Vermont sergeant swore (falsely but sincerely) that he and the spy had been drinking together till nearly one in the morning! No one seems to have realized that Mann was a Confederate soldier in disguise.

He returned to the Confederate Army, only to be captured again, though this time as an ordinary prisoner of war. He seems to have been the last Confederate spy to escape death on the gallows. No one seems even to have thought of executing Captain Conrad, when he was caught in late April or early May.

Other spies were active to the very end. The capture of their leader and the tragic deaths of men like Jobe and Davis did not damp the ardor of Coleman's Scouts. There is a story that one S. Disheroon, chief of scouts for Wheeler, took over after Shaw had been captured. If so, his service was very brief and it is almost impossible to find out anything about him. Whatever Disheroon may have done, there is no doubt that Alexander Greig, or Gregg, one of Shaw's best agents, became head of Coleman's Scouts almost at once. He was careful to keep on signing all reports with Shaw's usual pseudonym, "E. Colman," so that if documents were captured, the Federals would not guess there had been a change. They never did.

Shaw was exchanged February 16, 1865, and Sergeant Richard B. Anderson saw him at General Joseph Wheeler's headquarters in Georgia, April 9, 1865, the day of Lee's surrender; but General Joseph E. Johnston would not surrender until April 26, and Gregg's agents remained grimly at work. When Bragg gave up his command and there was no more need of Confederate espionage in Tennessee, they operated for Johnston around Sherman's army, and "all the way from Dalton to Atlanta, Johnston knew Sherman's every plan." Said the veteran Sergeant Anderson, "When old Joe Johnston laid down his sword, I was still on old Sherman's rear counting his regiments and his artillery."

Even now, Mosby and his men were not quite ready to give up the Lost Cause. A few days after Appomattox, Robert E. Lee, worn out and disheartened, went out for one of those night walks through the Richmond streets that he loved to take. He paused at the house of General R. H. Chilton. Though it was completely dark, he knocked at the door, probably thinking, in that time of privation, the family was saving candles—as in fact they were.

When the Chiltons found that it was Lee, they brought him in and lit a candle. Channing Smith stood before him. He had come as a messenger from Mosby, still at large, still in command of his rangers, still full of fight, still loyal to the Lost Cause. It had been no trouble for Smith—merely like old times—to work his way secretly into a Richmond held by the Yankees, with a message for General Lee. But the scout's eyes filled with tears as he saw him, "now pale and wan with the sorrow of blighted hopes."

Mosby had sent Channing Smith to ask for orders. Ought Mosby and his men fight on? They were quite capable of doing it. Or must they surrender, too?

"Give my regards to Colonel Mosby," said Lee, the ever-scrupulous, "and tell him that I am under parole and cannot for that reason give him any advice."

Since the general could not give an order, Channing Smith asked for personal advice. "But, General, what must I do?"

"Channing," said his old commander-in-chief, "go home, all you boys who fought along with me, and help build up the shattered fortunes of our old state."

ACKNOWLEDGMENTS

Work upon a book of the present sort, extending over more than ten years, inevitably requires the help of librarians, archivists, naval and military personnel, and fellow students, in numbers greater than anyone can possibly list. Hence, to my regret, I can name here only a few of the innumerable friends who have generously assisted me. To all my requests there has been but one rebuff—by a rather churlish schoolmaster who invited me to travel several hundred miles to discuss a Confederate spy he had known personally, and then refused to discuss anything at all when I arrived!

I must specially acknowledge the kindness of Colonel Howard V. Canan, U.S.A., Ret., who allowed me to examine his voluminous collection of intelligence materials compiled with the thoroughness of a scholar and the precision characteristic of the Corps of Engineers. Rear Admiral E. M. Eller, U.S.N., Ret., until recently Chief of Naval History, supplied badly needed aid in critical moments.

The debt to librarians is enormous, as usual. I have been greatly aided in securing obscure books by the late Miss Margaret H. Woodruff and by Mrs. Michael J. McCarthy, former librarians of the Ansonia Library; by Mrs. Mabelle W. Cummings, the present librarian; and by Mrs. Alton W. Mabry, Jr., librarian of the Seymour Public Library. Though I have had endless aid from many members of the New York Public Library staff, I owe a special debt to Robert W. Hill, former Keeper of Manuscripts; to Gerald G. McDonald, Chief and Curator of Special Collections who is now also Keeper of Manuscripts; to Paul R. Rugen, First Assistant; to Miss Jean R. McNiece, Research Librarian of the Manuscript Division; and to Leon Weidman, First Assistant in the American History Room. In the National Archives I have had much cordial assistance but have relied principally on Mr. Elmer O. Parker, Assistant Director, Old Military Records, and Mrs. Sara D. Jackson, his former assistant.

In the complex mass of obscure material relating to espionage in Tennessee, I should have been helpless but for many years of continuous aid from Mrs. Margaret Parsley, former Reference Librarian of the Tennessee State Library, and Miss Kendall J. Craig, her successor.

Other librarians and archivists to whom I am indebted include James W. Patton, Director of the Southern Historical Collection, and Mrs. Carolyn A. Wallace, Manuscript Curator, both of the University of North Carolina Library; Pierre Brunet, Assistant Dominion Archivist, Public Archives of Canada; James M. Day, Director of Texas State Archives; Miss Virginia Gray, Assistant Curator of the Manuscript Department, Duke University Library; David C. Mearns, Chief of the Manuscript Division, Library of Congress; John Mullane, Head of the History and Literature Department, Cincinnati Public Library; Howson W. Cole, Curator of Manuscripts, James A. Fleming, Curator of Printed Books, William E. Rachal, Editor, and N. E. Warringer, Building Superintendent, all of the Virginia Historical Society; William J. Van Schreeven, Archivist, and his staff at the Virginia State Library; and Miss M. Patricia Carey, Headquarters Librarian, Fairfax County Library.

In special problems, I have had the assistance of the following:

Betty Duvall and her journey: E. L. Inabinett, Director of the South Caroliniana Library; Miss Connie G. Griffith, Manuscript Librarian, Tulane University; Walter Pilkington, Librarian of Hamilton College; Colonel Catesby ap Catesby Jones, U.S.A., Ret., whose ancestors knew Betty; Harry Wright Newman, leading authority on the Duvall family; and Mrs. Ishbel Ross, who collected some family legends.

George A. Ellsworth: Professor James A. Carpenter, Mississippi State University, owner of the original manuscript of Ellsworth's diary, who had the passages bearing on the present study copied for me; Warren A. Reeder of Hammond, Indiana, who supplied information from his personal collection; Cecil Holland of the *Washington Star*, who lent his copy of the Ready diary; and Major Eugene P. Reynolds, A.U.S., Ret., of the AGO, Kentucky National Guard.

Antonia Ford: J. Willard Roosevelt of New York, who allowed me to see the family portraits of Antonia Ford, his remarkable great-grandmother; and Eppa Hunton, Jr., of Richmond, Virginia, long distinguished as a Civil War authority, whose family were friends and neighbors of the Fords for many years.

West Virginia spies: Charles Shetler, Curator, and Miss Joan M. Ellis, Assistant Curator, of the West Virginia Collection; Miss Charlotte Bailey, Librarian, and Miss Elizabeth Sloan, of the Clarksburg Public Library.

Senator Wilson and Mrs. Greenhow: Stephen T. Riley, Director, and Malcolm Freiberg, Editor, of the Massachusetts Historical Society.

Russian Fleet in New York: Dr. Samuel Flagg Bemis, Sterling Professor Emeritus of Diplomatic History and Inter-American Relations at Yale.

Frank Stringfellow: Dr. Stringfellow Barr and Mr. James Barr, who, as admiring grandsons, were well acquainted with Stringfellow; Robert E. Stocking, Alderman Library, University of Virginia; and Miss Ellen Coolidge, Alexandria Library.

Charles T. Cockey: Wade Chrismer, Bel Air, Maryland.

Maryland spies: Dr. Gardner P. Foley, University of Maryland; Mr. John D. Kilbourne, Librarian, Maryland Historical Society; Miss Elizabeth C. Litsinger, Head of the Maryland Department, and Miss Martha Ann Peters, Enoch Pratt Free Library, Baltimore, Maryland.

James Harrison: Dr. Ford E. Curtis, University of Pittsburgh; Mrs. Dorothy Thomas Cullen, Curator and Librarian, Miss Mabel C. Weaks, former Archivist, and Miss Evelyn R. Dale, Assistant Curator, all of the Filson Club; Miss Hester Rich and Miss Eleanor M. Lynn, Enoch Pratt Free Library; Miss Celeste Ashley, Theater Librarian, Stanford University; and Miss Helen D. Willard, Curator, Theater Collection, Harvard College Library.

False Uniform: Mrs. Linda P. Newman, Assistant Archivist, Indiana State Library.

Francis Hawks Govan as Grant's prisoner: Frank P. Govan, Sewanee, Tennessee; Mrs. Carl Black, Research Assistant, Mississippi Department of Archives and History; and Mrs. Lois E. Jones, Arkansas History Commission.

David O. Dodd: Mrs. Marion Jelkes, Reference Librarian, Little

Rock Public Library; Mrs. Frances M. Bowles, Arkansas History Commission; Edwin Vaulx Boles, Pine Bluff, Arkansas.

Sam Davis and Coleman's Scouts: Professors Robert Womack and Homer Pittard, of Middle Tennessee State College, and Mrs. Pittard. Both Professor Womack and Mrs. Pittard sent material from their own collections, and I have been greatly assisted by two truly remarkable theses by both Professor and Mrs. Pittard. Mrs. Frances H. Stadler, Archivist of the Missouri Historical Society, supplied manuscript sources. Mrs. Mary R. Baird, Regent of the Sam Davis Memorial Association, also supplied material.

Captain Conrad: President Gilbert Malcolm and Charles Coleman Sellers, Librarian Emeritus, of Dickinson College; Miss Josephine Wingfield, Librarian of the Jones Memorial Library, Lynchburg, Virginia; Miss Lucy Lee, Associate Librarian at Virginia Polytechnic Institute.

NOTES

Reference numbers are to page and paragraph, an incomplete paragraph at the top of a page being reckoned as the first paragraph. Thus the number "25.1" indicates the first paragraph (or partial paragraph) on page 25. In the same way, "25.2" indicates the second paragraph, "25.4–5" the fourth and fifth paragraphs, on page 25. "25–26" indicates pages 25 and 26.

Besides the ordinary abbreviations for states, the following abbreviations are used:

AAG: Assistant Adjutant General
AG: Adjutant General
AGO: Adjutant General's Office
ALS: Autograph letter, signed
B&L: *Battles and Leaders of the Civil War*
Canan MSS.: MS. Note File of Col. Howard V. Canan, U.S.A., Ret.
Cav. Journ.: The Cavalry Journal
CMH: Confederate Military History
CSA: Confederate States of America
CV: The Confederate Veteran
C/W: Civil War
C/W Dict.: Mark M. Boatner, *Civil War Dictionary*
DAB: Dictionary of American Biography
Diss.: Ph.D. dissertation
f: folio
GO: General Orders
Grant Mem.: Personal Memoirs of U. S. Grant
HCL: Harvard College Library
HEH: Henry E. Huntington Library
H/S: Historical Society
Ia. Hist. & Arch.: Iowa Department of History and Archives, Des Moines
IG: Inspector General
IGO: Inspector General's Office

JAGO: Judge Advocate General's Office
JB: Author's Collection
LC: Library of Congress
MoHS: Missouri Historical Society
MOLLUS: Military Order, Loyal Legion of the U.S.
N&Q: Notes and Queries
NA: National Archives
NC: University of North Carolina Library
NG: National Guard
NYHS: New York Historical Society
NYPL: New York Public Library
NYT: *New York Times*
OR: Official Records of the War of the Rebellion
PL: Public Library
pt.: "part"—used in citations of OR
PWT: *Philadelphia Weekly Times*. File in the Philadelphia Free Library
    and a nearly complete scrapbook in the Richardson Collection, HEH
RG: Record Group, National Archives
S/L: State Library
SHS: State Historical Society
SHSP: Southern Historical Society Papers
SHSWis: State Historical Society of Wisconsin
SO: Special Orders
s.v.: under the word
USMA: United States Military Academy, West Point
UVaLib: Library, University of Virginia
VaArch: Virginia State Archives
VaHS: Virginia State Historical Society
WD: War Department
Yale: Yale University Library

2.4. "Dr. Freese" (Jacob R. Freese): *Secrets of the late Rebellion.*
The hotel named and the employee who arranged for the room did exist,
according to a Washington directory of the period.

2.5. James Morris Morgan: *Recollections of a rebel reefer* (1917),
pp. 33–35; case of Alexander M. Flowers, *Richmond Daily Dispatch,*
Aug. 19, 1861.

4.1. Joseph Holt to *National Intelligencer,* Mar. 6, 1861. See also Jacob
Thompson to Lincoln, resigning, Jan. 8, 1861. Copies in Holt Papers,
HEH.

5.4. Elizabeth Todd Grimes: "Six months in the White House," *Journ.
Ill. H/S,* 19:57 (1927). Mrs. Grimes was a relative of Mrs. Lincoln's,

who lived with the Lincoln family for some time. See also Lamar Williams: "Rose O'Neal Greenhowe [sic]," M. A. Thesis, Univ. of Ala., 1942; Mark M. Boatner: *C/W Dict.* (1959), p. 90; Rose O'Neal Greenhow: *My imprisonment* (1863), p. 78.

6.1. Holt to *National Intelligencer*, Mar. 6, 1861 (typed copy in Holt Papers, HEH); Fitz-John Porter: "Curtin's early war trials," in W. H. Egle (ed.): *Andrew Gregg Curtin* (1895), pp. 334–335. See also *National Intelligencer*, Mar. 25, 1861.

6.3. Confed. Records, NA, Acts of Congress, Apr. 19, 1862, I Cong. CSA, Statute 38. See also in NA, AIGO—GO–40, May 29, 1862; SO 177, July 31, 1862; SO 60, Jan. 27, 1865; SO 285, Dec. 1, 1864; Confederate States WD, Orders, Vol. IV, 1864, E. 545, C. 69S, p. 299; OR, ser. 3, vol. 1, p. 577; ser. 1, vol. 18, p. 1095; Walter Lord (ed.): *Fremantle's Diary* (1956), pp. 158–162.

7.3. *DAB*, V, 217; West Point Alumni List, No. 1057; Cullum, No. 1057; W. J. Marrini: *Annual Reunion Assn., Grads. USMA*, 1896; C. A. Evans: *Confed. Mil. Hist.* (1899), III, 618–619; L. C. Tyler: *Encyc. Va. Biog.*; Service Record, NA, RG 94; Johnson Hagood: *Memories of the War of Secession* (1910), pp. 112–113; *B&L*, I, 197, 211–219; Jordan Papers, NA, RG 48.

8.2. Elizabeth Lindsay Lomax: *Old Washington diary* (1943), p. 161; *Nashville Banner*, Jan. 13, 1913. This article was checked before publication by Captain Webb himself.

8.3. *Nashville Dispatch*, Aug. 1, 1863; Lancaster Papers, NA, RG 109.

10.4. The original letters are in NA, RG 59.

11.4. Greenhow: *My imprisonment* (1863), pp. 35–37; Ishbel Ross: *Rebel Rose* (1954), p. 121; Harnett T. Kane: *Spies for the blue and the gray* (1954), pp. 43, 62.

12.3. Greenhow, *op. cit.*, p. 38. This was probably Anson O. Doolittle, the Senator's son. See Doolittle folder, Ford MSS. Coll., NYPL. The clerks were H. J. and J. R. Doolittle. See Senate Misc. Doc. 66, 37th Cong., 2nd Sess., p. 57; 3rd Sess., Misc. Doc. 11, pp. 4, 11, 16, 30, 40, 58.

12.5. Greenhow, *op. cit.*, p. 38.

16.3. J. J. Kerbey: *Boy spy in Dixie* (1897), pp. 110–114.

17.2. Imboden's first account is in *Century Mag.*, 30:281 (1885). His later account in *B&L*, I, 111–114, is somewhat more accurate. Lt. Jones's account is in *B&L*, I, 125-n. See also *C/W Dict.* s.v. "Harper's Ferry."

17.4. *B&L*, I, 197. On Beauregard's information, see skeptical comment by Duff G. Read: "Beauregard in history," *PWT*, Dec. 20, 1884.

20.3. Greenhow, *op. cit.*, p. 15; Kane, *op. cit.*, p. 15; *Harper's*, 124:564 (1912); Louis A. Sigaud: "Mrs. Greenhow and the rebel spy ring," *Md. Hist. Mag.*, 41:173–198 (1946); Jordan to Benjamin, Oct. 29, 1861,

OR, ser. 1, vol. 5, p. 928. Callahan held this clerkship from Dec. 5, 1859, to Apr., 1862. See Senate Misc. Docs., 36th Cong., 2nd Sess., pp. 7, 13, 47; 37th Cong., 2nd Sess., pp. 7, 57; 3rd Sess., pp. 9, 18, 30, 40, 51.

20.4. On Beauregard's remark, see OR, ser. 1, vol. 51, pt. 2, pp. 688–689. Beauregard's account is in Kane and Ross and in Hamilton Basso: *Beauregard*; in Doris Faber: *Rose Greenhow* (1967); and in Nash K. Burger: *Rose O'Neale [sic] Greenhow (1967)*. Belle Boyd: *Belle Boyd in camp and prison* (1865), I, 919–922, mentions this episode. Not one of these writers gives any source. In fact, the original source, Bonham's letter to Beauregard, has been lost. It was originally in the Beauregard Papers, now at Tulane, but disappeared before the papers were deposited there. Fortunately, Professor M. L. Bonham, grandson of the general, had made a copy for future use in a biography of the General that he hoped to write. This copy is now in the Bonham Papers in the South Caroliniana Library, Columbia, S.C. There are xerox copies at Tulane and in the author's collection.

21.2. Greenhow, *op. cit.*, p. 15. See also Edwin C. Fishel: "Mythology of C/W intelligence," *C/W History*, 10:349–353 (1964).

22. Beauregard reports the incident in OR, ser. 1, vol. 51, pt. 2, pp. 688–689, and Bonham gave a much fuller account in his letter, now lost, written to Beauregard in 1877 (see note under 20.4). There is some reference to Betty's adventure in Sigaud, *loc. cit.*; Boyd, *op. cit.*, I, 92–95; and Mrs. Burton Harrison's *Recollections grave and gay* (1911), pp. 53–54. On the message, see William G. Beymer: *On hazardous service* (1912), p. 182; K. P. Williams: *Lincoln finds a general* (1950), I, 394. On Mrs. Greenhow's cipher, see Jordan to Benjamin, OR, ser. 1, vol. 5, pp. 928–929; Harry Wright Newman: *Mareen Duvall of Middle Plantation* (1952). The Tulane University MS. Collection has a folder on Betty Duvall.

23.2. Washington directories give Mrs. Greenhow's address as 398 Sixteenth Street. Allan Pinkerton: *Spy of the Rebellion* (1886), p. 253, places the house "at the corner of Thirteenth and I Streets." On Donellan, see Appointments File, Applications, Dept. of Interior, NA, RG 48, and Donellan's personal file in Rebellion Records, NA. There are some biographical data on Donellan in the Keokuk (Iowa) PL. See also OR, ser. 2, vol. 2, pp. 572, 865, 1308–1312.

That Donellan was the messenger is established by Jordan to Hqrs. Army of the Potomac (an early Confederate designation of Beauregard's forces), Jan. 8, 1862. Beauregard added an enthusiastic postscript as to the value of Donellan's services. See Jordan Papers, NA, RG 48, Appointments Division, Interior Dept., Applications file, U.S. Land Office,

Nebraska City. See also Confederate Records, Compiled Service Records, G. Donellan, RG 109. Beauregard confirms the arrival of the message on July 16, 1861, in OR, ser. 1, vol. 51, pt. 2, pp. 688–689.

23.7–24.1. On Jordan's answer, see Beymer, *op. cit.*, pp. 182–183, and *Harper's*, 124:564 (1912). Mrs. Greenhow's own text differs slightly, but she was writing in England, probably without documents. Beymer may have secured this version from Rose, who later supplied him with information. Cf. Greenhow, *op. cit.*, p. 12. Mr. Beymer's notes cannot now be found, though many of his MSS. are in Los Angeles.

On the whole Greenhow story, see also Louis A. Sigaud: "Mrs. Greenhow and the rebel spy ring," *Md. Hist. Mag.*, 41:173–198 (1946).

24.4. Greenhow, *op. cit.*, p. 16; Beymer, *op. cit.*, pp. 181–183. On Burke and his later career in Confederate military intelligence, see Chapter 6, "J. E. B. Stuart's Secret Agents," Part 1.

24.5. Maude Merchant: "A Virginia heroine," *CV*, 7:156 (1899); Kane, *op. cit.*, pp. 169–175. The father of Eppa Hunton, Jr., who had known Antonia's son, Joseph Willard, was asked by the Willard family to collect all available information about Antonia Ford. He did so but failed to keep a copy of his letter, the original of which cannot now be found. The two men had known each other when the elder Hunton was practicing law in Warrenton and later, when both families lived in the same block in Richmond.

25.6. For documents relating to this episode in Antonia Ford's life, see NA, RG 94.

26.2. WD Comm. State Prisoners, Mar. 22, 1862, ff. 41–48; Mar. 26, ff. 1–6. NA, RG 94, AGO Records.

27.3. J. J. Kerbey: *Boy spy in Dixie* (1897), pp. 59–84.

29.3. Greenhow, *op. cit.*, pp. 17–18.

29.5. On Mrs. Greenhow's assistants, see Ben Perley Poore: *Perley's reminiscences* (1886), II, 110–114; index to OR, ser. 2, vol. 2; WD Comm. State Prisoners, NA, RG 94, AGO Records; Sigaud: *op. cit.*, pp. 173–175; Greenhow, *op. cit.*; Ross, *op. cit.*

30.3. OR, ser. 2, pp. 865, 868, 876, 880. On the later use of the Doctors' Line, see Chapter 3, "The Greenhow Ring after Bull Run."

31.1. Hunter McGuire in William Couper: *One hundred years at V.M.I.* (1939), IV, 66; E. P. Alexander: *Military memoirs* (1907), p. 42; Burke Davis: *They called him Stonewall* (1954), p. 152; *B&L*, I, 224.

32.2. Beymer is wrong (*Harper's*, 124:573–574 [1912]) in supposing Mrs. Greenhow's description of these papers to be the only one. A report of her hearing is available in the WD Commission's report, ff. 1–31.

F. 31 shows that she was still sending reports from the Old Capitol Prison, "through our under-ground."

33.1–3. Proc. Comm. relating to State Prisoners, 1862. Greenhow hearing, Box 2. Gaps in the torn documents are indicated by asterisks.

34.7. Allan Pinkerton: *Spy of the Rebellion* (1886), pp. 250–253. On Betty Duvall (Mrs. Walter Webb), see Harry Wright Newman: *Mareen Duvall of Middle Plantation* (1952), pp. 339–340. Mr. Newman secured information through a niece and a grandnephew.

35. Pinkerton, *op. cit.*, pp. 156–157, 252–253; OR, ser. 1, vol. 2, p. 588; ser. 2, vol. 2, p. 588.

36.3. Greenhow, *op. cit.*, p. 38; Pinkerton, *op. cit.*, pp. 252–264; Kane, *op. cit.*, Chapter II; Ross, *op. cit.*, pp. 136–137; WD Commission, NA, RG 94, AGO Records. The detective Pryce Lewis, who was with Pinkerton, gives a dramatic account in his diary in the Shoen MSS., now owned by the Canton (NY) H/S, in the Archives of St. Lawrence Univ.

37.7. Pinkerton, *op. cit.*, pp. 255–260. Mrs. Greenhow gives an erroneous account, partly, no doubt, from a malicious desire to ridicule Pinkerton. See Greenhow, *op. cit.*, pp. 66–67.

39.5. Pinkerton, *op. cit.*, pp. 257, 267–268. See also NA, RG 94— RA60, WD AGO, 4461, A.C., P. 1893, dated Dec. 15, 1893, Mrs. Elwood's pension application. On Elwood's appointment as Provost Marshal, see GO 16, Hqrs. Washington, May 4, 1861.

40.3. Kane, *op. cit.*, p. 45; Greenhow, *op. cit.*, p. 57.

40.4. Pinkerton, *op. cit.*, pp. 268–269; OR, ser. 2, vol. 2, pp. 1307–1321.

41.2. Greenhow, *op. cit.*, p. 39.

43.2. Ross, *op. cit.*, p. 136, quoting Mrs. Morris's "diary." Stanton, of course, did not become Secretary of War until 1862. There is no Morris diary, but the Library of Congress has a MS. entitled "Memories," which Mrs. Martha Wright Morris read before the Tuesday Afternoon Club of Glendale, Calif., on June 28, 1916, a discovery I owe to the extraordinary research and extreme kindness of Prof. and Mrs. William Matthews, of the Univ. of California. This paper describes the incident.

44.2. Boyd's *Washington Directory* gives the number of Mrs. Greenhow's home, as does OR, ser. 2, vol. 2, p. 566. Pinkerton, *op. cit.*, p. 253 places the house at the corner of Thirteenth and I Streets. The Directory shows that Senator Henry Wilson lived at Eighth Street and Pennsylvania Avenue, not far away.

46.4. See cover cartoon in *Vanity Fair*, vol. IV, Sept. 28, 1861; Kane, *op. cit.*, pp. 46–47; Ross, *op. cit.*, p. 144; Beymer, *op. cit.*, p. 190. Beymer secured the daughter's own account of this episode some years later, but his notes cannot now be found. See also *Harper's, loc. cit.*

48.4. OR, ser. 2, vol. 2, p. 569. For Rennehan's imprisonment, see pp. 152, 237.

51.1. Ben Perley Poore: *Perley's reminiscences* (1886), II, 110–114; OR, ser. 2, vol. 2, pp. 237, 295; Ross, *op. cit.*, p. 168; Greenhow, *op. cit.*, pp. 106–107.

51.3. Wheeling *Daily Intelligencer*, Oct. 8, 9, Nov. 9, 1861 (file at UWVa); OR, ser. 2, vol. 2, pp. 152, 190–191, 237, 306; Frank Moore: *Rebellion record* (1861–65), IV, 39–40; Poore, *op. cit.*, II, 111–112. The girl's name is given as Ella in the newspaper and as Ellie in OR.

52.2. Melville O. Briney: "Captain Bligh, 'toughest fly-cop in the country,'" *Louisville Times*, Jan. 23, 1958; obituary, *ibid.*, Mar. 1, 1890.

54.1. *Phila. Press*, Jan. 19, 1862; Greenhow, *op. cit.*, pp. 206–207.

54.2. OR, ser. 2, vol. 2, pp. 564–565.

55.3. Jordan to Benjamin, Oct. 28, 1861. OR, ser. 2, vol. 2, pp. 264–265.

56.2. F. L. Sarmiento: *Life of Pauline Cushman* (1890); *DAB*, V, 4–45; NA, WD Records, WC 362644; *San Francisco Chronicle*, Dec. 3–7, 1893; *Call*, same dates; Kane, *op. cit.*, pp. 177–191; *Pasadena Playhouse News*, Apr. 21, 1936, pp. 6, 10, 14; Kane, *op. cit.*, pp. 177–191. On Jane Ferguson, court-martial papers, NA, RG 153, JAGO Papers; *Louisville Daily Democrat*, June 24, 1864; *Nashville Dispatch*, same date.

56.3. Greenhow, *op. cit.*, pp. 92–93.

57.3. Greenhow Papers, NA, RG 109, Nos. 745, 9090–1861Y; Greenhow, *op. cit.*, pp. 110–112; Shelby Foote: *Civil War* (1958), I, 227–230; OR, ser. 2, vol. 2, pp. 567, 573, 1282; Ross, *op. cit.*, p. 170.

59.1. Greenhow, *op. cit.*, pp. 97–98, and, on Averell, pp. 72, 91–92. Averell's own account of his first secret mission was written for him by David H. Strother in *PWT*, Jan. 18, 1879. There were four, perhaps five, men named Samuel Applegate in the Union Army.

59.4. On Mrs. Hassler, see OR, ser. 2, vol. 2, p. 295; Greenhow, *op. cit.*, pp. 106–107.

59.5. *NYT*, Jan. 19, 1862: *Phila. Press*, Jan. 20, 21, 1862; *Vanity Fair*, Sept. 28, 1861, cover cartoon; Greenhow, *op. cit.*, pp. 202–209.

60.1. Thomas A. Jones: *J. Wilkes Booth* (1893), p. 21; OR, ser. 2, vol. 2, pp. 857–881; see also pp. 152, 237, 271, 277.

60.4. OR, ser. 2, vol. 2, pp. 259–260, 270, 309–310; WD Comm. on State Prisoners, ff. 32–36, NA, RG 94.

61.3. OR, ser. 1, vol. 5, pp. 968–979. Original is in NA, RG 109, Rebel Archives.

62.1. Portraits of Antonia Ford (Mrs. Joseph Willard) are now in the possession of her descendants, Mr. Willard Roosevelt and Mrs. Antonia Ford Palfrey, of New York. One, probably made in early youth, shows definitely blond coloring. Others show light hair of indeterminate color.

62.4. Jeanne Rust: "Portrait of Laura," *Va. Cavalcade*, 12:38–39 (1962–63). There is a collection of newspaper clippings and other memorabilia in possession of Mr. William Holbrook, Fairfax, Va. This includes the album and watch chain given her by Stuart.

63.6. John Scott: *Partisan life with Col. John S. Mosby* (1867), pp. 30–32; Rust, *loc. cit.*; Roberdeau Wallace: "Anecdotes and little family stories," MS. in Fairfax County (Va.) Library.

64.3. Charles E. Taylor: "Signal and secret service of the Confederate States," *NC Booklets*, vol. II, no. 11 (1903), p. 18; T. C. De Leon: *Four years in rebel capitals* (1890), p. 286.

65.5. WD Comm. on State Prisoners, Mar. 21, 1862, ff. 52, 58–59, NA, RG 94.

67.1. Thomas N. Conrad: *Rebel scout* (1904), pp. 143–153. Conrad's strong religious interests are shown in the record of his college reading, preserved in the MS. Circulation Record, Belles Lettres Literary Society, Dickinson College Library. The student diary of Horatio King, also at Dickinson, shows that Conrad was cast to play Lady Capulet in a Dramatic Association production in Jan., 1857, and that his favorite expression of approval was "bully riptum."

68.2–3. Thomas N. Conrad: *Confederate spy* (ca. 1895), p. 7. Another arrest is noted in *Washington Star*, Aug. 4, 1862.

69.3. Letter of Sept. 30, 1863; Conrad Papers, NA, RG 109.

70.3. Conrad: *Confederate spy* (ca. 1895), p. 11; *Rebel scout* (1904), pp. 68–70; *PWT*, May 7, 1887.

72.4. For some reason, Conrad uses the absurdly transparent name "Nillard's" in his first book. He gives the correct name in *Rebel scout*. He gives the room number as 45 in his first book and 35 in his second. The hotel registers for this period have disappeared.

73.3. Conrad: *Confederate spy* (ca. 1895), pp. 26, 31–32.

75–76. OR, ser. 1, vol. 11, pt. 1, p. 914; ser. 2, vol. 4, p. 579, also pp. 40–41, 313–314, 579; *Nashville Dispatch*, June 21, 1862, quoting *Chicago Times*. Lt. Washington's papers are in NA, RG 109. He is not to be confused with Col. John Washington, of Lee's staff, who had been killed in 1861. See Lee to Mrs. Lee, Sept. 17, 1861, in Clifford Dowdey and Louis H. Manarin: *Wartime papers of Robert E. Lee* (1961), No. 77, pp. 73–76, 139.

77.1. Dowdey and Manarin, *op. cit.* (1861), no. 242, p. 237.

77.3. Allen C. Clark: "General John Peter Van Ness," *Columbia H/S Records*, 22:125–204 (1919); H. Paul Caemmerer: *Manual on the origin and development of Washington* (1939), p. 177; Caemmerer: *Washington the national capital* (1932), p. 262.

77–78. For Stringfellow's reconnaissance at this time, see Chapter 6, "J. E. B. Stuart's Secret Agents," Part 2.

78–79. Conrad: *Rebel scout* (1904), pp. 73–74. On the situation just before Gettysburg, see Chapter 17, "Secrets of Gettysburg."

79–80. H. B. Smith: *Between the lines* (1911), pp. 88–91.

80.2. Gardner P. Foley: "Adalbert Volck, dentist and artist," *Dental Radiography and Photography* (Eastman Kodak Co.), 35:86–89 (1962); obituary, *Baltimore Sun*, Mar. 27, 1862, Apr. 22, 1934, Oct. 19, 1958; Muriel Dobbin: "Old fashioned valentines," *Baltimore Sun* (Family Section), Feb. 14, 1864; "A Southern artist in the Civil War," *Am. Heritage*, 9:117–120 (1958); Forest H. Sweet: *Autograph letters*, Catalogue No. 98 (1947); *DAB*, XIX, 288; Van Dyk MacBride: "Lincoln caricatures, eight etchings by Dr. Adalbert H. Volck," *Lincoln Herald*, 56:23–43, (1954); "Sketches from the Civil War in America," London: 1862, reprinted in *Mag. Hist. with Notes and Queries*, Extra No. 60 (1917).

80.4. Longstreet's statement in his account of Fredericksburg. See also Edward J. Stackpole: *Fredericksburg Campaign* (1957), p. 71.

80–81. Conrad: *Rebel scout* (1904), pp. 75–76; *CV*, 17:236–237 (1909); Ella Lonn: *Foreigners in the Confederacy* (1940), pp. 248, 265. Dr. Passmore's service record is in NA, RG 94, and also in Va. State Archives.

81–82. House Judiciary Committee in *Congressional Globe*, 1861–62; Ben Perley Poore: *Perley's reminiscences* (1886), II, 142–143; Edward Bates's Diary in Ann. Rept. Am. Hist. Assn., 4:341 (1930); Carl Sandburg: *Abraham Lincoln, the War Years* (1926–39), II, 250–251, 255 (wrongly giving the name as James K. Watt); "A.M." (Mrs. Augusta Morris) to Col. B-T Johnson, Feb. 19, 1862, in OR, ser. 2, vol. 2, p. 1350; Ruth Painter Randall: *Mary Lincoln* (1953), pp. 254–255, 303. Watt was summoned by the House Judiciary Committee on Feb. 10, 1862, answered questions, and was released on Feb. 14. The White House dismissed him that month. See also Records Sec., Interior, Lrs. from Comrs. of Pub. Bldgs., NA, RG 48.

82.6. Conrad: *Confederate spy* (ca. 1895), pp. 38–41.

84.4. *Ibid.*, pp. 48–49; Field and staff muster roll, 3rd Va. Cav., also regimental records for May and June, 1864, NA, RG 109.

84–85. Conrad, *op. cit.*, pp. 37, 50–59; see Chapter 17, "Secrets of Gettysburg," and Chapter 19, "Spying in the Wilderness." On Federal chaplains' uniforms, see Frederic Denison: "Chaplain's experience." *RI Soldiers and Sailors H/S, Personal Narratives*, 4th ser., no. 20, p. 187.

86. The present owner of the spurs is J. E. B. Stuart, III, of Manhasset, L.I. On Dr. Philpot, see *Nashville Dispatch*, Nov. 20, 1862, quoting a Richmond correspondent who cannot now be traced. Stuart to Parran, Dec. 5, 1862, and to Payne, Apr. 6, 1863, both MS. letters at Duke Univ.

87.1–3. H. B. Smith: *Between the lines* (1911), pp. 61–62. The report on Langley is in Baker-Turner Papers, NA, RG 94. He is there said to have been a native of Winchester, Va. Smith gives Emmerich's address as South Gay Street; but Baltimore directories of 1860, 1864, and 1865–66 give his business address as 18 South Street, and his home as 324 West Lombard Street in 1860 and as 657 West Lombard Street thereafter. There is no indication he ever lived on South Gay Street. Smith probably confused it with South Street. In 1860, Langley was living at the National Hotel, Camden Street, three blocks south and about five blocks east of Emmerich. Copies of directories in Enoch Pratt Free Library, Baltimore.

87.4. Smith, *op. cit.*, p. 22. Gen. Lew Wallace, in his autobiography, says the smuggler was "a woman of high standing socially" (p. 687), but Lt. Smith says the General was mistaken. On Confederate smuggling from Baltimore, see S. P. Bates: *Hist. Pa. Vols.* (1869), I, 546.

88. The most important source for Stringfellow is a long MS. addressed to Jefferson Davis in UVaLib. While Stringfellow lectured widely on his adventures, the newspaper reports are so incompetent that most give no facts at all.

89. Boyle Papers, in Turner-Baker Papers, NA, RG 94, File No. 1588; OR, ser. 2, vol. 5, p. 355; ser. 1, vol. 27, pt. 2, p. 512; *National Republican* (Washington), Jan. 22, 1863, p. 3, and Jan. 24, p. 2; *Nashville Dispatch*, Jan. 27, 1863, under Washington dateline of the 24th. There is a file of the *Republican* in LC, and a file of the *Dispatch* in Tenn. H/S. Neither man appears in existing lists of Stuart's officers.

90.3–4. R. Shepard Brown: *Stringfellow of the Fourth* (1960), pp. 11–12. Brown's report is obviously based on family legend. As Stringfellow was a serious-minded cleric, and as he frequently discussed his adventures in espionage, the legend has more than usual evidential value.

90.5. The convention adopted an ordinance of secession on Apr. 17, but this had to be ratified by a referendum on May 23. The popular vote was 96,750 to 32,134 for secession, the "no" votes coming mainly from the western counties, which are now West Virginia. See OR, ser. 1, vol. 3, p. 387; J. F. Rhodes: *Hist. C/W* (1917), p. 24.

91.1. On the activity of Confederate agents in Alexandria, see witnesses before WD Comm. on State Prisoners, *passim.* NA, RG 94, AGO Records.

91.2. Evidence for Stringfellow's Arlington espionage is mostly plausible guesswork by R. Shepard Brown, *op. cit.*, pp. 21–35. Stringfellow told his grandniece, Miss Esther M. Green, of Alexandria, about his share in the

battle. See Brown, *op. cit.*, p. 295, note 19. The MS. of a book Stringfellow had begun to write was destroyed by fire.

91.3. W. W. Blackford: *War years with Jeb Stuart* (1945), pp. 91–
202. Blackford does not name all the scouts and agents Stuart employed
at this time or a little later. Probably he did not even know their names.
He mentions Farley's death (p. 216), his rank at that time being captain.
See also John Esten Cooke: *Wearing of the gray* (1959), pp. 130–140.
Lee to Stuart, Apr. 23, 1864, H. B. McClellan MSS. Quotes in Douglas
S. Freeman: *Lee*, III, 239. The McClellan MSS. are partly in Chicago,
partly in Biarritz. Freeman's copies are in LC. John Esten Cooke: "Right
at Fredericksburg," *PWT*, Apr. 26, 1879.

91–92. Anon.: "Capture of the Confederate scout," *Southern Bivouac*,
2:271–272 (1884).

93–96. Report of Silas Colgrove, 27th Inf., OR, ser. 1, vol. 21, pp. 7–8;
vol. 5, pp. 494, 1085; vol. 12, pt. 1, p. 417; pt. 2, pp. 121, 727; vol. 11,
pt. 1, p. 573, 1038–1039, 1041; pt. 2, p. 422. NA records show he
enlisted in Co. B, 1st Va. Cav., July 2, 1861, and was commissioned
lieutenant on or about Apr. 3, 1861, advancing through grades to colonel.
There is also a service record in Va. Archives. See also "Story of Redmond Burke," *Jefferson* (W. Va.) *Co. Hist. Mag.* 22:40–43 (1956); John
W. Thomason: *Jeb Stuart* (1930), p. 348; Virgil Carrington Jones: *Gray
ghosts and rebel raiders* (1956), p. 133; *Shepherdstown* (W. Va.)
Register, June 7, 1934; M. K. Bushong: *Hist. Jefferson Co., W. Va.*
(1941), p. 162.

93.1. *CV*, 7:268–269 (1899). On the third Burke, see *PWT*, May 7,
1881.

94.1. Hamilton's Crossing is not on many war maps. It can be found
in the SE corner of the map in *B&L*, III, 74, and in S. P. Bates: *Hist.
Pa. Vols.* (1871), II, 865. W. R. Hanleiter, of Griffin, Ga., in *CV*, 5:28
(1897). This cannot have been Redmond Burke, who was then dead.

94–95. U. R. Brooks: *Butler and his cavalry* (1909), p. 235.

95.2. Lamar Fontaine: *My life and lectures* (1908), pp. 206–207;
Beymer, *op. cit.*, pp. 113–115.

95.3. *CV*, 7:268–269 (1899). According to this account, Burke was
captured in Philadelphia and leaped from the train at High Bridge, N.Y.,
on the way to Washington! The geographical difficulty of this is obvious.
He may, however, have been taken to New York for interrogation and
started on the way to Washington. He might then have jumped at High
Bridge, N.Y. High Bridge, N.J., is not on the route to Washington. For
further data on Burke, see Muster Rolls, CSA, Texas Arch., also roster
of the Confederate Home and Executive Record Book, 1863–65 (MS.),
p. 380.

95–96. For duplication of Stringfellow's and Burke's exploits, see John Esten Cooke: *Wearing of the gray* (1959), pp. 486, 489. On the adventure with the Federal prisoner, see *CV*, 5:12 (1897).

96–97. E. P. Alexander: *Military memoirs* (1907), pp. 54–56; SHSP, 16:95 (1888). On Bryan's subsequent capture, see WD Comm. on State Prisoners, Mar. 28, 1862, NA, RG 94, AGO Records. See also Edward S. Gregory: "Confederate Signal Corps," *PWT*, Feb. 22, 1879; David J. Marshall: "Confederate Army's Signal Corps," in Max L. Marshall: *Story of the U.S. Army Signal Corps* (1965), pp. 63–76.

98–99. The Baltimore directories for 1858–59, 1860, and 1865 give an Edward Delcher, "huckster," at 132 North Bond Street. No trace can be found of Dr. Jethro Morris, John Delcher, or Harley Delcher.

100.1. WD Comm. on State Prisoners, *loc. cit.*, Greenhow hearing.

100.5. Brown, *op. cit.*, p. 139; K. P. Williams: *Lincoln finds a general* (1950), I, 13; Margaret Leech: *Reveille in Washington* (1941), p. 135; Greenhow, *op. cit.*, p. 129.

102.6. Stuart's report on Cold Harbor, OR, ser. 1, vol. 11, pt. 2, p. 522.

104.1. Lamar Fontaine: *My life and lectures* (1908), pp. 130, 137; OR, ser. 1, vol. 12, pt. 2, p. 490. On Mosby's release, see OR, ser. 2, vol. 4, p. 442. See also Willard Glazier: *Three years in the Federal cavalry* (1847), p. 73; N. D. Preston: *Hist. 9th NY Cav.* (1892), p. 616; Virgil Carrington Jones: *Gray ghosts and rebel raiders* (1956), pp. 100–102.

104.3. John Stewart Bryan: *Joseph Bryan, his time, his family, his friends* (1939), p. 113. Copy in NYPL.

104.4. Cooke, *op. cit.*, p. 105, says: "It is probable the battle of Cedar Run, where General Pope was defeated, was fought by Jackson in consequence of this information." Cooke was on Jackson's staff at this time.

106.1. Lenoir Chambers: *Stonewall Jackson* (1959), II, 117; Cooke, *op. cit.*, p. 105.

106. This incident appears in various reports of Stringfellow's lectures and in *CV*, 11:518 (1903). James Dudley Peavey: *Confederate scout* (Pamphlet, 1956), p. 54. See also R. Shepard Brown: *Stringfellow of the Fourth* (1960), p. 260. This correspondence does not appear in OR or in C. Dowdey and L. Manarin: *Wartime papers of R. E. Lee* (1961).

107. On the raid, see OR, ser. 1, vol. 12, pt. 2, p. 731; Heros von Borcke: *Memoirs*, I, 124; Blackford, MS. Memoirs, p. 143; Freeman: *Lee's Lts.*, II, 70–71; *Lee*, II, 286–287; Brown, *op. cit.*, pp. 160–162; H. B. McClellan: *Life and campaigns*, pp. 94–95. On the importance of the information, see Peavey, *op. cit.*, pp. 45–46; A. L. Long: "Gen. Pope in the Valley," *PWT*, Apr. 12, 1879; W. A. Spicer: "High school boys of the Tenth R. I. Regt.," *RI Soldiers and Sailors H/S: Personal Narratives*, 2nd ser., no. 13, pp. 46–47.

109.2. Peavey, *op. cit.*, pp. 22 ff. Undated interview in *Richmond Dispatch*: Emma Stringfellow Scrapbook, MS. 1—St—864a, in VaHS.

110.2. Interview, *loc. cit.*, Emma Stringfellow Scrapbook, VaHS. The name Arundel may, of course, be another of the pseudonyms Stringfellow employed. It has not been possible to trace such a family as he describes.

111.2. Peavey, *op. cit.*, pp. 24–27.

112.1. The blanket version is in Peavey, *op. cit.*, pp. 25–26. For another version, see Brown, *op. cit.*, pp. 176–177.

113.3–5. Peavey, *op. cit.*, pp. 48–49.

114.1. *CV*, 15:261 (1907).

115.1. On Stringfellow's adventures in the Gettysburg campaign, see Chapter 17, "Secrets of Gettysburg." The date of his capture is fixed by prison records. See NA, RG 98, Records of U.S. Army Commands, Dept. of Washington, vol. 309 (Old Book 792), no. 183; Old Capitol Records, RG 109, WD Coll. of Confed. Records, Roll 26, Sheet 13; H. B. Mc-Clellan: "Scout life in the Confederacy," *PWT*, May 19, 1879.

116.2–4. This story is reported by Brown and Peavey and is part of the family tradition. It is not nearly so incredible as it sounds today. Numerous spies on both sides did the same thing.

116.4. Brown, *op. cit.*, pp. 234–235; Cooke, *op. cit.*, p. 474, mentions this copy.

116.6. Statement of Mr. Stringfellow Barr, the spy's grandson, after personal examination. Conversation of Stringfellow with R. W. D. Taylor, retired master of Woodberry Forest School, who knew Stringfellow as the school chaplain. See also Brown, *op. cit.*, p. 298.

117. Letter to J. M. Feeley from his son, Co. G, 9th Pa. Reserves, V Corps. Feeley sent a copy of the letter to *PWT*, which printed it on Oct. 20, 1877. Neither NA nor the Pa. AGO Archive has any trace of Feeley.

118.1–2. John Esten Cooke, who talked with Stringfellow about his adventures not long after this one, tells the story in his "Virginia Partisans," *PWT*, Oct. 29, 1881. See also the issues of May 19, July 14, Oct. 20, 1877, and clippings in the H. B. McClellan Scrapbook, I:34–36, VaHS. Cooke, Channing Smith, and McClellan all knew Stringfellow and accepted his version of this episode.

118.3. OR, ser. 1, vol. 33, pp. 15–16; James J. Williamson: *Mosby's raiders* (1909), pp. 410–419; John W. Munson: *Reminiscences of a Mosby guerrilla* (1906), pp. 241–242; Emma Stringfellow scrapbook, VaHS., MS. 1—St—864a.

118–119. Mr. James Barr, of Charlottesville, Va., grandson of String-fellow, says there was a Marsten family in Culpeper County about this time. Culpeper marriage records show the name Marsten once and Marston once, in the latter eighteenth century. Culpeper Will Book C records the will of James Marshall, mentioning "Dr. Marsden" in 1783. Personal Property Tax Lists, 1862–1863, list Kitty A. Masten. Land Tax Lists, 1860–1863, list James Masten. These are in the Virginia State Library. The letter "r" disappears easily in the South, so that Masten may equal Marsten.

119.2. Spencer to Miller, July 30, 1863. Dodge Papers, III, 4670, Iowa H/S, Des Moines.

119.3. Alice Ready Journal, Vol. IV, Apr. 30, 1862. Original in Southern Collection, NC. Typed copy in possession of Cecil Holland, *Washington Star*.

119.5. Emma Stringfellow scrapbook, VaHS, MS. 1—ST—864a.

120.3. William F. Fox: *Regimental losses* (1898), p. 81.

121.2–4. Brown, *op. cit.* The story is pieced together from statements of people who had either known Stringfellow or had heard him lecture. The date of Grant's appointment and the movement of IX Corps to some degree confirm the oral tradition.

121.5–6. The late Prof. William E. Dodd is the "W.E.D." who wrote the Stringfellow article in the *DAB*, according to Mr. Stringfellow Barr, who provided some of the facts. By editorial inadvertence, the identity of "W.E.D." was omitted from this volume. On Captain Frank Battle, see Chapter 11, "Secrets in Tennessee." On girls in uniform, see WD Comm. on State Prisoners, Mar. 28, 1862, f. 56, NA, RG 94 and the cases of Kate Brien, *Nashville Dispatch*, July 30, 1864, and of Jane Ferguson, p. 56 of the present book.

122.1. This incident also comes from family tradition, hence ultimately from Stringfellow himself. For other incidents that make it entirely credible, see *Grant Mem.*, II, 42–43, 145; Emmet Crozier: *Yankee Reporters* (1956), p. 392.

122–123. Compiled Service Records, NA, RG 94; Pension File WC 337/765, RG 15 B; Hist. & Roster, Md. Vols. War 1861–1865, I, 106, 418, 645 (Md. Hall of Records, Annapolis).

130.1. J. M. Gould: *Hist. 1st–10th–29th Maine Regt.* (1871), p. 109.

130.3. *Natl. Intelligencer*, Mar. 16, 1863. On Strother, see Walter A. Clark: *Four years under the Stars and Bars* (1900), pp. 23, 52–53; *CV*, 5:168 (1897). *Va. Republican*, Nov. 4, 1861. No copy of this issue can now be found, but it is given as a source in F. B. Voegel's chronology of the Civil War in that area, as published in the *Martinsburg News*,

Mar. 18, 1937. See also Lester J. Capon: *Bibliog. Va. Newspapers,* 1921–1935.

131.1. *Photographic history of the Civil War* (1911), VIII, 287; J. B. Jones: *Rebel war clerk's diary* (1866), p. 17; Canan MS. I, 107.

131.2. F. B. Voegel, *loc. cit.*; John J. Rivers: "Heroines of the Shenandoah Valley," *CV,* 8:482–496 (1911).

131.4. On Jackson's spies, see Alexander B. Boteler: "Stonewall Jackson's discontent," *PWT,* June 2, 1879; William Walter Edwards: "Turner Ashby, beau sabreur," *Cav. Journ.* 3:148 (1922).

132.2. B&L, I, 124.

132–133. "*E. J. Allen*" [i.e., Pinkerton] to Stanton, June 25, 1862, NA, RG 94, AGO, Turner-Baker Papers, 3751: Wolcott to Scott, July 18, 1862, NA, RG 94, AGO Records; OR, ser. 1, vol. 12, pt. 3, p. 878; Freeman: *Lee's Lts.* (1944), I, 350.

133.3. E. K. B. to W. H. Winder, July 28, 1861. WD Comm. on State Prisoners, Apr. 24, 1862, ff. 33–34, NA, RG 94.

134.1. G. F. Henderson: *Stonewall Jackson* (1897), I, 296; L. Chambers: *Stonewall Jackson* (1959), II, 19; Allen Tate: *Stonewall Jackson* (1928), pp. 163–164.

134.3. Jedediah Hotchkiss, MS. Diary; Freeman: *Lee's Lts.,* I, 414–415.

134.5. *United Daughters of the Confederacy Mag.,* 17:10 (1954).

135.1. J. B. Jones: *Rebel war clerk's diary* (1866), I, 135; Walter Taylor: *Four years with General Lee* (1878), p. 43.

136.1. See Chap. 5, "J. E. B. Stuart's Secret Agents," Part 1.

137.1. On Union troop movements, see *Harper's,* 34:188–191 (1887); Averell, *loc. cit.*; *PWT,* Dec. 24, 1880, and Apr. 26, 1884, especially letters from E. V. Smalley and W. Allen; J. H. Simpson: *Battle of Kernstown.*

137.2. Lucy R. Buck Diary (mimeograph), LC.

137.4. Weather studies, based on old diaries, made by William H. Runge, Curator of Rare Books, UVaLib; Allen Tate: *Stonewall Jackson* (1928), p. 129.

142.2. James J. Williamson: *Prison life in the Old Capitol* (1911), p. 52-n; Louis J. Sigaud: *Belle Boyd* (1944), p. 3. See also Walter A. Clark: *Four years under the Stars and Bars* (1900), pp. 50–54.

142.5. The AP dispatch is in *NYT,* May 31, 1862, and, of course, other newspapers.

144.6. *Belle Boyd in camp and prison* (1865), I, 58–59. Quotations are from Belle Boyd's own first edition, but the reader should consult the valuable annotations in a new edition by Curtis Carroll Davis (NY: Yoseloff, 1968).

144.7. Clark, *op. cit.*, p. 51.

145. AGO Records, Pa. National Guard. See also file in NA; Samuel P. Bates: *Hist. Pa. Vols.* (1869), I, 76; Sigaud, *op. cit.*, p. 15. Belle Boyd herself says she killed the man. Walter A. Clark (*op. cit.*, pp. 51–52) says "neither of her shots hit their mark," but this is mere hearsay. On Martin's burial, see *American Union*, an army newspaper, July 9, 1861, copies in SHSWis and NYHS.

146.1. Ophie D. Smith: *Old Oxford houses* (1911), p. 54; *West Tenn. Hist. Papers*, 9:95 (1955).

146.3. Perry L. Rainwater: "C/W letters of Cordelia Scales," *Journ. Miss. Hist.*, 1:169–181 (1939).

146.4. On Alice Ready, see her Journal, now at Duke University. In Cecil Holland's typed transcript, this entry is in vol. VI, p. 63, May 5, 1862. See also vol. V, p. 60, Apr. 30, 1862. B. L. Ridley: *Battles and sketches* (1906), pp. 492–500.

147–148. Wm. F. Evans: *Hist. Berkeley Co.* (1928), pp. 184–185; OR, ser. 2, vol. 2, p. 159; vol. 5, pp. 978, 979; *Calendar Va. State Papers*, XI, 380–381, 466; Thomas A. Ashby: *Valley campaigns* (1914), pp. 73–74; K. P. Williams: *Lincoln finds a general* (1950), I, 82–83, 303, 403; "A Virginian: Personal recollections of the war," *Harper's*, 33:1–25 (1866). Author identified by Williams as General David Hunter Strother. On the other two spies, see J. J. Kerbey: *Boy spy in Dixie* (1897). Where Kerby's narrative can be checked, it is completely accurate. Mr. Robert W. Waitt, former head of the Richmond Civil War Commission, has examined his references to the topography of the city and found them invariably correct.

149.2. Bates, *op. cit.*, I, 49; Sigaud, *op. cit.*, p. 20.

149.3. Cornelia McDonald: *Diary* (1934), pp. 163–164.

149.4–5. Belle Boyd, *op. cit.*, I, 75. On Eliza's biography, see Curtis Carroll Davis's edition of Belle Boyd's autobiography, *passim*.

150.2. OR, ser. 2, vol. 51, pt. 2, p. 599; Sigaud, *op. cit.*, p. 65.

152. The conversation is recorded by Belle Boyd herself in *Belle Boyd in camp and prison* (1865), I, 85.

153. Strasburg correspondent of the *NY Tribune*. Reprinted in *Nashville Dispatch*, June 25, 1862.

154. *Tribune* and *Dispatch*, as above. There were seven stars in the "Stars and Bars," national flag of the Confederacy. They commemorated the seven states that had already seceded when the flag was first raised, Mar. 4, 1861. No other stars were added when other states joined them. The familiar battle flag with the St. Andrew's cross, designed by Beauregard, however, received a new star for each new state. This is the only Confederate flag most people know anything about. See Milo

M. Quaife: *Hist. of the U.S. Flag* (1961); M. M. Boatner, *C/W Dict.* (1959), p. 284; *CMH*, XII, 369.

155.1. Heitman, I, 587; OR, ser. 1, vol. 12, pt. 1, pp. 690, 697; Sigaud, *op. cit.*, pp. 60–61. See also index and the captain's personnel record in NA.

155.2. Thomas A. Ashby: *Valley campaigns* (1914), p. 139; Sigaud, *op. cit.*, p. 60. The mysterious German officer was not Heros von Borcke, of Stuart's staff, who was wounded in June, 1863, about a year later.

155.3. Belle Boyd, *op. cit.*, I, 104–105; Sigaud, *op. cit.*, pp. 60–62; Kane, *op. cit.*, p. 137.

156.1. Cecil D. Eby, Jr. (ed.): *Virginia Yankee in the Civil War: Diaries of David Hunter Strother* (1961), May 19, 1862, p. 37. Sigaud, a veteran staff officer, believes the May 14–15 date is correct. See Sigaud, *op. cit.*, pp. 33, 35, and Belle Boyd, *op. cit.*, I, 105.

157–158. Boyd, *op. cit.*, I, 105–111; Kane, *op. cit.*, pp. 137–138; Sigaud, *op. cit.*, pp. 33–37.

160.1. On Lt. Col. Denny's career, see page 178. See also Henry Kyd Douglas: *I rode with Stonewall* (1940), pp. 62–63; Freeman: *Lee's Lts.*, I, 412–413; Sigaud: "William Boyd Compton," *Lincoln Herald*, 67: 23–24 (1965).

161.5. Boyd, *op. cit.*, I, 11; Lucy R. Buck Diary, May 21, 1862 (LC).

162–164. John M. Gould: *Hist. 1st, 10th, 29th Maine Regt.* (1871), pp. 56–57; Boyd, *op. cit.*, I, 116, 121; *NYT*, May 31, 1867.

166. J. Cutler Andrews: *North reports the C/W* (1955), p. 255.

167–170. Boyd, *op. cit.*, I, 122–136; Douglas, *op. cit.*, pp. 50–53; *Toledo Daily Blade*, Feb. 22, 1886; Richard Taylor: *Destruction and reconstruction* (1897), pp. 57–58. There is a late account of this episode, which adds no new details, in John S. Robson: *How a one-legged rebel lives* (n.d.). There is nothing about Belle in the 1876 edition, but the story does appear in a still later edition, probably of the 1880's. It appears to be based on Taylor. The Buck Diary account is dated May 23, 1862, but Miss Buck was a little mixed in dates. Wednesday was May 21, two days before the battle. On Clark, see Boyd, *op. cit.*, I, 132; Sigaud, *op. cit.*, p. 57; OR, ser. 1, vol. 12, pt. 1, p. 558; *NY Herald*, June 10, 14, 1862.

170–171. Harry Gilmor: *Four years in the saddle* (1866), pp. 77–78. Sigaud, *op. cit.*, p. 129, agrees with me on this date.

172. Thomas A. Ashby, *loc. cit.*; Walter A. Clark, *op. cit.*, p. 54; N. T. Colby: "Old Capitol Prison," *PWT* clipping in H. B. McClellan Scrapbook, I, 45, VaHS.

173–174. John D. Imboden: "Averill's celebrated raid," *PWT*, May 15, 1880; OR, ser. 1, vol. 53, p. 1324; vol. 33, p. 1324.

175. OR, ser. 1, vol. 21, pp. 6–7; M. K. Bushong: *Hist. Jefferson Co., W. Va.*, p. 162; William N. McDonald: *Hist. Laurel Brigade* (1907), p. 465; George Baylor: *Bull Run to Bull Run* (1900), pp. 121–122. In OR, ser. 1, vol. 12, pt. 2, p. 747, "Leopold" is commended for gallantry in action. The court-martial record is NA, RG 153, File MM, No. 232. Both the names Andrew Laypole and Isidore Leopold are used; but, as the regiment is noted, there is no doubt they refer to the same man. Sentence was confirmed by GO 3, Hqrs. Middle Dept., Jan. 9, 1863. Laypole's first capture is recorded Oct. 24, 1862, in the diary of an unidentified Confederate sympathizer. This originally appeared in the Shepherdstown (W.Va.) *Register*, Apr. 23, 1925, and was reprinted in *The Reporter*, June 7, 1934.

176–177. Gordon Court-martial record, NA, RG 153, MM 1332, Box 106; *Nashville Dispatch*, Nov. 21, 1863. Haymond Maxwell: *Story of Sycamore* (1938). There is no pagination in this book, but these facts are on what should be p. 21. See also Wheeling *Daily Intelligencer*, Nov. 14, 1863; H. B. Smith: *Between the lines* (1911), pp. 55–56; GO Fort McHenry, Nov. 19, 1863, in pursuance of GO 54 and 56, Hqrs. Middle Dept., VIII Corps, Oct. 26 and Nov. 2, 1863, also GO 22, 2nd Separate Bde., Defences of Baltimore, Nov. 19, 1863; Mrs. Gordon to Bennett, Aug. 22, Sept. 25, 1864; William F. Steuart, Jr., to same, Jan. 26, 1864, both in MSS. Coll., W. Va. University. A letter in this collection signed W. F. Gordon, Jr., is, of course, not from the captain himself.

178–179. Compton to Davis, Nov. 10, 1862, NA, Rebel Archives. Compton court-martial record, NA, RG 153, JAGO; Rockingham (Va.) *Register*, Jan. 20, 1893; OR, ser. 2, vol. 5, p. 747. There is a file of the *Register* at Madison College, Harrisonburg, Va. See also George Baylor: *Bull Run to Bull Run* (1900), p. 121; Louis A. Sigaud: "William Boyd Compton, Belle Boyd's cousin," *Lincoln Herald*, 67:22 (1965).

180. R. W. Grizzard: "A close call," *CV*, 26:524 (1918). I have made Sheridan a present of the correct spelling of the name "Haman." See also *CV*, 10:412 (1902); Baylor, *op. cit.*, pp. 121–122.

183–184. M. A. M'Laugherty: "Revelations on Andrews 'the Raider,'" *CV*, 16:23–24 (1908); *CV*, 17:217–219 (1909). The names of Morgan's helpers are given.

184.2–3. Williamson Papers, quoted in Cecil F. Holland: *Morgan and his raiders* (1942), pp. 71–72. The Williamson Papers are in the possession of Mrs. Charles Ready Williamson, Lebanon, Tenn. See also the Alice Ready Diary (MS.), now in Duke University Library.

184.5. Under Regulations, only the coat was gray. Actually, as shown by soldiers' letters and by wartime uniforms displayed in various museums, gray trousers were common. Lee, however, refers in domestic correspondence to his own blue trousers. See *Confed. Army Regs.*, 1862, Article 47, Para. 1484. This is repeated in the 1864 Regulations. See also Plate 72, Atlas of OR, and Bell I. Wiley: *Life of Johnny Reb* (1943), p. 11.

185.2. On Morgan's exploit, see *Shelbyville News*, April 8, 1862, quoted in *Nashville Dispatch*, May 20, 1862.

185–186. Leeland Hathaway: *Soldiering with Morgan*, no folio number, photostat in Univ. of Kentucky Library. The original MS., formerly in possession of Miss Carrie Lee Hathaway, Lexington, is now owned by Miss Alice Apperson Young, Apperson Heights, Mt. Sterling, Ky.

186–187. CV, 19:382–383 (1911), 25:565 (1917), also pamphlet by Isaac Marker: *Why President Lincoln spared three lives*; Baylor, *op. cit.*, pp. 291–292; Leeland Hathaway MS.

187.2. William Witherspoon: *Reminiscences of a scout, spy, soldier* (1910), reprinted in R. S. Henry: *As they saw Forrest* (1956), pp. 74–85.

187–188. U. R. Brooks: *Butler and his cavalry* (1909), pp. 399–402, 411, 417–418; OR, ser. 1, vol. 46, pt. 1, p. 543; F. B. McDowell: "Hampton's splendid scouts," clipping from an unidentified newspaper in Julian Shakespeare Harris Papers, Southern Hist. Coll., NC.

188.4. Since this incident involved both Mrs. Grant and the General, it can be dated fairly closely. Both were in Holly Springs in Nov., 1862. The General departed, expecting to return, and leaving his sword, which he rarely wore, with Mrs. Grant, who was captured in Van Dorn's raid of Dec. 20. Grant returned after the raid but moved his headquarters to Grand Junction on Jan. 10, 1863. See *Grant Mem.* I, 427, 432, 438.

189. Data and dialogue from a sworn statement by the Hon. William L. Ward, Sr., Representative from Lee County in the Arkansas Legislature. Mr. Ward, who was Govan's son-in-law, was sure these are "the exact words as told to me by Captain Govan." See also CV, 40:90–91 (1932); 33:20 (1925). Tennessee and National Archives show that Govan was in Co. B, 17th Mississippi Infantry, in 1861, transferred to the Army of the West on July 17, 1862, and eventually became an officer on a kinsman's staff in Arkansas.

189–190. Frank Battle: "Entering the Union lines in a petticoat," CV, 7:79 (1899); 15:347 (1907).

190.2–3. Leland Jordan: "Civil War at Triune, Tennessee," pp. 31–34. MS. in collection of Professor Robert Womack, Middle Tennessee State College; copy in NYPL.

190–191. Bromfield L. Ridley: *Battles and sketches* (1906), pp. 506–507; Jordan, *op. cit.*

191.3–6. Thomas Frank Gailor: *Some memories* (1937), p. 15.

196.3. Bromfield L. Ridley: "One of Morgan's scouts," *CV*, 5:76–77 (1897). The author had the accuracy of this account checked by Sgt. Seth Corley and "the First Lieutenant of Company F, Ward's Regiment, John Morgan's Cavalry." See also Ridley: *Battles and sketches* (1906).

196–197. G. W. Duncan: "How General Morgan captured Hartsville," *CV*, 8:431–432 (1900); Cecil F. Holland: *Morgan and his raiders* (1942), pp. 167–169. See also Morgan to Cooper, Aug. 22, 1862, in Hartsville *Vidette*, Aug. 24, 1862; Leeland Hathaway: *Soldiering with Morgan* (MS.), no folio number; William D. Bickham: *Rosecrans' campaign with the XIV Army Corps* (1863), pp. 93–94.

197.5. *Chicago Evening Journal*, May 22, 1862, quoted in *NY Herald*, May 28, 1862, and *Nashville Dispatch*, June 3, 1862. Mrs. Nancy Irwin appears to have been a wealthy widow, as the 1860 census lists her real property at $25,000 and her personal property at $68,500. The daughters were 21, 18, and 16 when the census was taken and, of course, two years older in 1862, the time of this incident. There were two younger daughters not mentioned in the newspaper accounts. On the sons, see *CV*, 17:565 (1909) and 22:220 (1914).

199–200. John W. Headley: *Confederate operations in Canada and New York* (1906), p. 444; Mabel Baxter Pittard: *Coleman's Scouts*, Middle Tennessee State College M. A. Thesis, 1953, p. 30; *CV*, 29:26 (1931); Whipple to Milroy, Apr., 1865, NA, RG 109; Leland Jordan, *loc. cit.* On Fort Negley, see William D. Bickham: *Rosecrans' campaign with the XIV Army Corps* (1863), p. 81.

200–201. Family data on the Pattersons from Mrs. Gertrude M. Parsley, former reference librarian in the Tennessee S/L. Dr. Everand-Mead Patterson's name is variously given. The form here used is from W. W. Clayton: *Hist. Davidson Co.* (1880), for which the Patterson family undoubtedly provided the facts. See also "Operations of the secret scouts," *Nashville Banner* (n.d.), clipping in the Sam Davis scrapbook, Tenn. H/S.

201–204. This incident is described in the papers of Richard H. Adams, now in the possession of his granddaughter, Mrs. Robert D. Fitting, Midland, Texas. Though Adams kept a diary, he left Dec. 24, 1862, blank, probably because he did not wish to risk capture with such a record in his pocket. At some undetermined time, probably after the war, he wrote out the story and gave the date. Both MSS. are in Mrs. Fitting's possession, and she has generously copied her grandfather's MS. for me.

206. See Chapter 11, "Secrets in Tennessee." On Dr. Patterson, see Clayton, *op. cit.* There is further information in M. Pittard, *op. cit.*, f. 77 ff.: W. M. Hamil: *Sam Davis* (Griffin, Ga., ca. 1911); *CMH* (1899),

VIII, 440; *CV*, 5:556 (1897); 9:271 (1901); 16:522 (1905); 39:127, 169 (1931). Mrs. Gertrude M. Parsley, former reference librarian at the Tennessee S/L, supplied local detail.

206–207. Shaw Papers. Misc. Unit, "Bragg's Scouts," formerly Rebel Archives, Letters Received A & IGO, NA, RG 94; *Nashville Banner*, May 27, 1929; Sam Davis scrapbook, Tenn. H/S; M. B. Pittard, *op. cit.*, f. 270; *CV*, 6:69 (1898). James D. Porter is certainly wrong in believing that Shaw had a hundred agents. See M. B. Pittard, *op. cit.*, f. 12. The account of the group in Mrs. T. P. O'Connor's *My beloved South* (1913) is highly sentimental and largely inaccurate.

207.4. Anderson was First Sergeant of the Reserve Company, Beat No. 4, Navarro County, 19th Brigade, Texas Military. He became a private in Co. F, Maul's Legion, in 1862. There is no mention of secret service in his military papers, a silence usual in Civil War (though not in Revolutionary War) records. See NA, Index to Compiled Service Records of Confederate Soldiers; also microfilm of same in Texas State Archives. This is based on Muster Rolls. See also Roster of Confederate Home, Texas State Archives, and R. B. Anderson: "Secret Service in the Army of the Tennessee," *CV*, 21:344–345 (1913).

208. On Mrs. Lee and Mrs. Beauregard, see *Nashville Dispatch*, June 4 and 21, 1862. On Mrs. Grant, see Victor M. Rose: *Ross's Texas Brigade* (1881), p. 87; Olga R. Pruitt: *It happened here, true stories of Holly Springs*; J. M. Deupree: "Capture of Holly Springs," *Miss H/S*, 4:58; Edwin C. Bearse: *Decision in Mississippi* (1962), p. 92. On the enormous stock of supplies in Holly Springs, see *Nashville Dispatch*, Jan. 23, 1863.

209.1–2. On Jobe, Smith, and Shaw, see M. B. Pittard, *op. cit.*, especially quotations from the now lost "Tribute of respect to the dead." For General Dodge's comment, see J. T. Perkins: *Trails, rails and war* (1929), p. 117. See also Alf. H. Douglas, E. M. Patterson, William B. Robinson, Tom M. Joplin: "Career of Coleman's Scouts," *CV*, 6:69 (1898). Since Patterson and Douglas are among the authors, the facts must be authentic. It is a pity they did not tell more of their personal adventures.

209.3. *CV*, 3:202 (1895).

210.1. *CV*, 21:344–345 (1913); M. B. Pittard, *op. cit.*, pp. 82–83. Chickamauga was fought Sept. 19–20. The information was received the Monday after the battle, i.e., Sept. 21.

211.1. *CV*, 16:522–529 (1908); Adams MS., in possession of Mrs. Robert D. Fitting, Midland, Texas.

211.3. *CV*, 3:202 (1895); 17:52 (1909).

212.1. M. B. Pittard, *op. cit.*, pp. 73–80. Identification of the "safe

houses" is by Clyde Schuler, grandson of Squire Schuler, who passed
on to Mrs. Pittard the family traditions.

212.3. Fremantle Diary, ed. Walter Lord (1956), p. 94; OR, ser. 1,
vols. 24 and 25 *passim.* Original telegrams in Miss. Dept. Archives and
Hist.: Tenn. S/L and Archives, Box 15, No. 5; Box 17, No. 11, C/W
MSS.

213.3. John Fitch: *Army of the Cumberland* (1864), pp. 346–356,
499–500. T. Woods Sterrett: *Sterrett genealogy* (1930), p. 82, says that
Truesdail died in St. Louis in 1886. His signature in Fitch, *op. cit.*,
shows that he spelled his name as here given.

214.2. Major Ranney cannot be traced, but the shoemaker Zeulzschel
appears in a Nashville directory.

214–215. On Capt. Bligh, see Louisville *Courier-Journal*, Mar. 2, 1890;
Louisville *Times*, Jan. 23, 1858, which prints an article by Melville O.
Briney (Mrs. Russell Briney), "Captain Bligh, 'toughest fly-cop in the
country.' " On Ella M. Poole, see Chapter 4, "Ladies in Jail."

215. Fitch, *op. cit.*, pp. 534–539; James C. Burt: "Widow and the
scoundrel," *Nashville Tennesseean Mag.*, Mar. 31, 1957; Fitch to Wiles,
Jan. 13, 1863, and other Judd Papers, NA, RG 153, JAGO.

217.2. Though Sam Davis's age is given as 19, he was born on Dec. 6,
1842, and was aged 21 years, 1 month, and 21 days when hanged on
Nov. 26, 1863. See M. B. Pittard, *op. cit.*, pp. 37, 43; W. J. McMurray,
Hist. 20th Tenn. (1904), pp. 429–431; Leland Jordan, "Civil War at
Triune," MS. in possession of Prof. Robert Womack, Middle Tennessee
State College, ff. 21–23, copy in NYPL; C. C. Henderson: *Story of
Murfreesboro* (1921), pp. 81–82; H. F. Jobe: "D. S. Jobe, fellow scout
of Sam Davis," *CV*, 1:373 (1893).

218.2. Matlock MS. in Tenn. H/S. Its facts are largely reproduced
in *CV*, 13:168–169 (1905); Deering J. Roberts: *Hist. 20th Tenn.* (1904),
pp. 426–428; Alumni Records, Univ. of Tennessee.

220–221. *CV*, 13:169 (1905); 17:276–279 (1909), the latter containing statements made to the Rev. N. W. Baptist. See also Surby,
op. cit., pp. 360–362; SO 19, U.S. Forces, Nashville, Oct. 21, 1862. See
Nashville Dispatch, Oct. 30, 1862.

221.6. P. N. Matlock: "Sam Davis and others visit Nashville," *CV*,
13:168–169 (1905); Matlock Memoir (MS.), Acc. No. 1448, Box 14–3,
and Military Record, Box 3–11, MS. Division, Tenn. S/L and Archives.

222.3. *CV*, 15:458 (1907); 17:167 (1909); J. R. Perkins: *Trails,
rails and war* (1929), pp. 115–117.

223.2. See Shaw to McKinstry, Nov. 19, 1863, in Davis court-martial
record, Dodge Papers, Iowa Dept. Hist. & Arch., which indicates that

Samuel Roberts was the messenger. Davis, on his return journey, probably passed Roberts.

223.3. A. L. Sharp: "Some recollections of Sam Davis," *CV*, 19:580–581 (1911).

223.5. The date is fixed by Davis's own testimony in the court-martial testimony. See Dodge Papers, *loc. cit.*

223–224. "E. Colman" [sic] to McKinstry, Nov. 19, 1863, the letter captured with Davis and now in the court-martial record; letter of Mrs. Frances Stephenson, Columbia, Tenn., to Mrs. Pittard, *op. cit.*, pp. 46, 90; *Nashville Banner*, May 30, 1937.

224.2. Newman Cayce: "Was on scout with Sam Davis," *CV*, 10:350–351 (1902). See also *ibid.*, p. 289.

224.4. Cayce, *loc. cit.*

225–226. Anon.: "Sam Davis's sister-in-law," *CV*, 4:36–37 (1896); interview with Kate Patterson, unidentified clipping of Nov. 26, 1926, in Sam Davis Scrapbook, Tenn. S/L. Local topographical data from Mrs. Gertrude L. Parsley, former state librarian. Davis is said to have arrived on Sunday, Nov. 13, but Sunday fell on the 15th that year.

226.2. *CV*, 16:522–528 (1908); Perkins, *op. cit.*, pp. 115, 117.

226.3. *CV*, 16:522–528, 530, 613 (1908); Davis court-martial record, in the Dodge Papers.

226.4. The memorandum book is mentioned by Colonel J. B. Killebrew, Tennessee Commissioner of Agriculture, who rode about the country a few years after the war, collecting all the facts he could about Sam Davis. See E. L. Drake: *Annals of the Army of Tennessee* (1878), p. 345, also his article, "Giles County," in *Nashville Union and American*, July 4, 1871 (file in Tenn. S/L). See also the court-martial evidence, in the Dodge Papers.

227.1. Interview with Mrs. Kate Patterson Kyle, unidentified newspaper, Nov. 26, 1926, Sam Davis Scrapbook, Tenn. S/L.

228. *CV*, 4:36–37 (1896); 5:556–577 (1897); 7:538–542 (1897).

228.4. These facts did not become known until 1909 (and even then obscurely), because Robert English insisted that they be kept a complete secret until his death. Alfred H. Douglas, who helped Shaw select the group and was himself an active agent present in the rendezvous at the English farm that night, says the papers were stolen by a Negro, who took them to English, who gave them to Davis. See Killebrew and Drake, *op. cit.* See also C. W. Tyler: *The Scout* (1911), Appendix; *CV*, 17:167 (1909); 5:556 (1897). Killebrew also printed his article in the *Nashville Union and American*, July 4, 1872, only nine years after Davis's execution. There is further information in Homer Peyton Pittard: "Legends and stories of the Civil War in Rutherford County," M.A.

Thesis, George Peabody College, Nashville, 1940; Mabel Baxter Pittard, *loc. cit.*; *CV*, 6:69 (1898). James D. Porter, in *CMH* (1898), VIII, 440–441, says that the papers were given to, or stolen by, the slave Houston English and then given to Davis. There is also information in B. L. Ridley, *op. cit.*, p. 272. Ridley had been a schoolmate of Sam Davis's.

229.1. On the druggist, see Lebanon (Tenn.) *Democrat*, Aug. 8, 1928; Sam Davis scrapbook in Tenn. S/L.

229.2. The Carter story comes from Lumsden's neighbor, "Uncle Joe" Smith, a Confederate veteran, who appears to have kept the secret until he was 88. Mrs. Carter's maiden name was Sarah Ewing. She was successively married to Boyd McNairy Sims, Joseph W. Carter, and John C. Gant. See Edythe Johns Rucker Whitley: *Sam Davis* (1947), quoting *Nashville Banner*, Mar. 13, 1932, and article by Christine Sadler.

229.3. *CV*, 20:488 (1912), quoting Franklin correspondent of the *Nashville Banner*.

229.4. Ridley, *op. cit.*, p. 509.

230.2. L. O. Naron in R. O. Surby: *Grierson's raids* (1865), p. 256; N. W. Baptist: "More history of Sam Davis," *CV*, 17:105 (1909); Joshua Brown in *CV*, 17:186 (1909).

231.3. *CV*, 17:52 (1909). See Naron's statements in Surby, *op. cit.*, pp. 360–362.

232.2. Testimony of Farrar and King, court-martial record, Dodge Papers, Ia. Dept. Hist. and Arch.

233.5. Original in Dodge Papers. The signature is undoubtedly "Colman," but the organization is invariably referred to as "Coleman's Scouts." The report is in Ridley, *op. cit.*, but it has been expanded and "improved." The text here is from the original.

234.4. On the 66th Illinois, see Frederick H. Dyer: *Compendium of the War of the Rebellion* (1959), III, 1076, 1329.

236.1. J. B. Killebrew: "Hanging of Sam Davis," in Drake, *op. cit.* See also his article in *Nashville Union and American*, July 4, 1871.

236.5. M. B. Pittard, *loc. cit.*; Ridley, *loc. cit.*; *CV*, 3:202 (1895); 9:271 (1901); 17:186 (1909).

237.1. The official file on Shaw's imprisonment dates his capture as Nov. 24, 1863, but Shaw himself, in the same file, gives the date as Nov. 22. See NA, RG 94, Confed. Staff File, H. B. Shaw. See also *CV*, 4:437 (1896); M. B. Pittard, *loc. cit.*, p. 21. On Tom J. Brown, see *CV*, 15:273 (1907).

237.3. Some time after the war, Randall settled in Covington, Tenn., where he told this story to the Rev. N. W. Baptist, who printed it in *CV*, 17:185 (1909).

238.4. L. H. Naron: "Questioning of Sam Davis," MS. Coll., Box 15,

No. 8, Tenn. S/L (Archive on Sam Davis). See also Box 8, No. 38; Box 20, No. 2; and F. 23–6.

239.3. Hamill, *op. cit.*, pp. 16–17.

239.4. CV, 19:27 (1911); Ridley, *op. cit.*, pp. 261–262. CV, 10:25 (1902); 9:27 (1911); 17:186 (1909); Ridley, *loc. cit.* Location of the overcoat by Mrs. J. D. Hale, Sam Davis Memorial Assoc. *Cincinnati Commercial*, Dec. 8, 1863.

240–241. These are two separate offers. The first was by a certain "Captain Conn," whose full name is not given. The second was by Naron. See CV, 10:205 (1902) and Joshua Brown: "Heroic death of Sam Davis," CV, 3:181–184 (1894). L. W. Forgrave, drummer boy at the execution, gave an interview to the *Nashville Tennesseean* on Jan. 12, 1928. Several contemporary accounts give essentially identical versions of Davis's words. On the Davis monument, see CV, 3:240, 257–258, 370–373 (1894). Captain Conn is named in CV, 3:149 (1894). See also reprint of the *Pulaski Chanticleer* (army newspaper), Dec. 2, 1863, reprinted in Hamill, *op. cit.*; CV, 5:182–183 (1897). Emory University has a copy of Hamill's book.

241.6. Surby, *op. cit.*, p. 357. CV, 5:202 (1897); 15:458 (1907); 17:375 (1909). CV, 5:202 (1897); 19:27 (1911). The Rev. A. W. Bill, 66th Illinois, heard various men make this remark. Surby, *op. cit.*, pp. 357–358; news story signed "Young America" in *Cincinnati Commercial*, Dec. 8, 1863; *Cincinnati Daily Gazette*, same date.

241–242. Mary McEwen's home in 1863 was Rockville, Ind., but she spent much time visiting relatives in Davenport, Iowa. See McEwen Papers, Mo. H/S. See ALS, Thomas Gahagan and Charles Oatman to Mary McEwen, from Pulaski, Dec. 7, 20, 1863, McEwen Papers; diary of James C. Harwood, Co. C, 64th Illinois, in Tenn. S/L. Two entries are photographically reproduced in the Memorial Assoc. pamphlet, *Home of Sam Davis*. An interesting source is Swarts to "Brother," from Pulaski, Nov. 27, 1863. This is in the collection of Thomas R. Hooper, Maryville, Mo., who has generously provided a copy. The Illinois (Army) National Guard AGO has the military record of Thomas Edward Swarts, Co. F, 66th Illinois, which is also in NA, RG 94, AGO Records.

242. The story of Shaw's tears is in M. B. Pittard, *op. cit.*, pp. 22–23.

243–244. Leland Jordan: *Civil War at Triune, Tenn.*, pp. 21–23, MS. in possession of Prof. Robert Womack, Middle Tennessee State College; M. B. Pittard, *loc. cit.*, Chapter II; Ridley, *op. cit.*, pp. 503–509; W. J. McMurry, *Hist. 20th Tenn. Vol. Inf.* (1904), pp. 429–431; C. C. Henderson: *Story of Murfreesboro* (1929), pp. 81–82; H. F. Jobe: "D. S. Jobe, fellow scout of Sam Davis," CV, 1:373 (1893). The name of Jobe's first host is sometimes given as Noss, instead of Moss.

245.1. Sergeant Temple's service record and grave registration record are in AGO, Ohio (Army) National Guard. The statement about the yells of the torturers is from Jordan, *op. cit.*, p. 22. Colonel Jordan's mother was living in the vicinity at this time.

245.2. Statement of Mrs. J. T. McCarty, Abilene, Texas, a niece of Jobe, Oct. 28, 1938, quoted in M. B. Pittard, *op. cit.*, pp. 48–53. Miss Jeannette King, Murfreesboro, heard in her youth the story that "his body was thrown into a deep sink hole," but Mrs. McCarty's story represents what the family knows. On DeWitt Smith, see M. B. Pittard, *op. cit.*, pp. 61–65.

245.3. Samuel [Boyer] Davis: *Escape of a Confederate officer from prison* (1890). Copy in LC.

246.6. "Master" was a naval rank corresponding to lieutenant, junior grade. Officers in the Navy for wartime service only were called "acting," as were those temporarily promoted.

246–247. Davis, *op. cit.*, pp. 44–45; James D. Horan: *Confederate agent* (1954), pp. 154–165, 255–264; Isaac Markers: "Last days of John Yeats Beall," *CV*, 30:426–428 (1922); court-martial papers of John Yeats Beall, NA, RG 153, JAGO; *Ohio Soldier*, 14:49 (1898); *CV*, 19:128, 343 (1911); "A leaf from history," report of Jacob Thompson to Confederate Secretary of State, Dec. 3, 1864 (Yale). The only complete file of *Ohio Soldier* is in Western Reserve H/S, Cleveland. The official record of Beall's court-martial is in NA, RG 153, NN 3513.

248. The same conversation is reported, with slightly different wording, in Lewis H. Bond: "Capture and trial of a Confederate spy," Ohio Commandery, MOLLUS, Feb. 2, 1897. The dialogue here is from the court-martial records, NA, RG 153, NN 3453, Box 1172.

249. OR, ser. 2, vol. 46, pt. 2, pp. 58–59. David D. Anderson: "Robbery or warfare?" NW Ohio Quarterly, 32:46–50 (1900).

250. The official record, GO No. 4, Hqrs. Northern Department, Cincinnati, Ohio, Jan. 26, 1865, is reprinted in Davis, *op. cit.*, pp. 56–59. His release is AGO, WD, Dec. 4, 1865, to C.O., Fort Warren, Boston, endorsed Fort Warren, Dec. 7, 1865.

252.9. I, 44–63 (1934); Mrs. W. H. Walkup: "A Confederate hero," *CV*, 39:292–294 (1931); Edwin Vaulx Boles in *Arkansas Democrat*, Jan. 16, 1955. Both state definitely that General Fagan did tell Dodd to bring back intelligence. The late Dallas T. Herndon questions this, both in his collection of "Letters of David O. Dodd," *Ark. Hist. Rev.*, 1:44–64 (1934), and in his undated pamphlet, "Memorial to Arkansas' boy hero, David O. Dodd." Herndon was secretary of the Arkansas historical commission. The court-martial record, including two pathetic braids of girls' hair, is in NA, RG 153, JAGO, Box 1006. See also *CV*,

30:477 (1922), and a news story by V. C. Meadow in *Little Rock Democrat*, Jan. 9, 1864, reprinted by B. L. Ridley: *Battles and sketches* (1900), pp. 277–278.

253–254. Boles, *loc. cit.* Mr. Boles received his information from Frank Tomlinson's daughter-in-law, a lady of historical interests, then in her eighties, who had had every opportunity to secure firsthand information. (Letter to author, Feb. 16, 1962.)

254.2. Mrs. Mary Brantly, formerly Miss Mary Swindle, of Little Rock, dictated this statement at the request of Dr. S. Smith Stewart (or Steward), of Little Rock. Dr. Stewart, much interested in the Dodd story, also searched the files of the *Little Rock Democrat* until he found the news story of Jan. 9, 1864, published the day after the execution. This was by V. C. Meadow, editor and publisher, which is reprinted by Ridley, *op. cit.*, pp. 275–276. Dr. Stewart also found a scrapbook owned by Capt. W. M. Watkins, of Little Rock, which contained an article from a Memphis newspaper, n.d., but published soon after the tragedy. This is quoted by Ridley, and also in *CV*, 13:550 (1905).

254–255. Statement of Durand Whipple, Mary Swindle Whipple's son, which is said at one time to have been "at the Old State House at Little Rock." The document cannot now be found.

255.3. Court-martial record, NA, RG 153, NN 1429, JAGO, Box 1006.

255–256. Small-scale modern maps do not show the road details, but they are clearly described in the testimony of Sgt. Frederick Micher, Co. B, 1st Missouri Cav., at Dodd's court-martial.

257.4. Transcript of the court-martial record gives the name as Clouny, but this is corrected by Herndon, *op. cit.*

258.3. *CV*, 17:409, 498, 591 (1909); 10:353 (1910); 13:550 (1905); 30:477 (1922); 39:292–294 (1931).

259.3. Authority for the parade in the spy's honor is a statement of Tomlinson's daughter-in-law to Mr. Edwin Vaulx Boles.

259.4. E. S. Dodd was in Co. D, 8th Texas Cav. (Terry's Texas Rangers). See AGO Records, Archives Division, Texas S/L.

260.3. Sam R. Watkins: *Co. Aytch* (Jackson, Tenn.: McCowat Mercer Co., 1952), pp. 107–108. Copy in Tennessee S/L.

262.4. *Grant Mem.*, I, 379–380; Thomas L. Snead: "With Price east of the Mississippi," *B&L*, II, 720; John S. Mosby: *Stuart's cavalry in the Gettysburg campaign* (1907), p. 21; Canan MSS., XI, 7.

263.2. *Nashville Dispatch*, May 21, 1862, quoting *Cincinnati Gazette*. On Union use of dummy artillery, see S. P. Bates: *Pa. Vols.* (1869), II, 137.

263.6. Comte de Paris: *Hist. of the Civil War in America* (1876), II, 406; Fletcher Pratt: *Ordeal by fire* (1935), pp. 138–139. Basil Brown

Shaw, a Confederate veteran living in Corinth, used to tell stories of a girl spy living there who attended a party at Fort Ord while an attack was impending and then sent information to the Confederates, but he left no written record.

263–264. A Confederate deserter who claimed to have given Halleck his first intimation of Beauregard's retreat was probably only boasting. See J. D. Bond (or Boyd), record of arrest, NA, RG 94, Turner-Baker Papers, Turner File, No. 565.

264. Roll of Co. A, 2nd Cav., Ky. Vols., CSA, in AGO, Ky. (Army) NG; Ellsworth Papers, NA, RG 94; Ellsworth MS., f. 7; Allan Keller: *Morgan's raid* (1961), p. 46.

264.2. Hamilton Basso: *Beauregard, the great Creole* (1933), pp. 193–196; Ellsworth MS. ff. 6–7. Near the end of the war, Ellsworth became Morgan's chief telegrapher (*ibid.*) The most important source for Ellsworth's doings is his own MS. of reminiscences, here referred to as the "Ellsworth MS.," now in possession of Prof. James A. Carpenter, Miss. State Univ.

265. Ellsworth's report to Capt. R. A. Alstort, AAG in Morgan's command, appeared in *Southern Confederacy* for July 30, 1862. This was reprinted in *Nashville Dispatch*, Sept. 10, 1862. It is the basis for an article by George I. Kitman: "Raid by telegraph," *Ohio Soldier*, 3:326, May 24, 1890. (File in Western Reserve H/S.) See also W. N. Mercer: "Organizing a Signal Corps," *CV*, 7:549–551 (1899); Anon.: "Gen. Morgan's telegraph operator," *CV*, 6:174 (1898); Bromfield L. Ridley: *Battles and sketches* (1906), pp. 117–130; "Col. John H. Morgan's late Kentucky expedition. By one of Morgan's men," *Knoxville Register*, Aug. 10, 1909; *Nashville Dispatch*, Aug. 26, 1862. There is a file of the *Knoxville Journal* in the Western Reserve H/S Library. A Union version of these stories, mentioning the same incidents and the same individuals, is in W. R. Plum: *Military telegraphy in the Civil War* (1882). The Leeland Hathaway MS. (photostat in the University of Kentucky Library) gives a spirited account of the lives of Morgan's raiders, thus providing background for Ellsworth's adventures. There is a special folder of Ellsworth material in the Kentucky H/S. See also Richard H. Collins: "C/W annals of Kentucky," Filson Club *History Quarterly*, 35:242–246, 275–278 (1961).

265–266. Dee Alexander Brown: *Bold cavaliers* (1959), p. 80; *CV*, 8:35–36 (1900); Ellsworth MS., f. 14; Cecil F. Holland: *Morgan and his raiders* (1942), p. 119.

266.5. Ellsworth MS., f. 13; Plum, *op. cit.*, p. 194. The telegram places Morgan "between Scottsville and Gallatin." There is no Scottsville in Tennessee, but Scott's Hill is some distance southwest of Gallatin.

267. Ellsworth MS., ff. 17–18. Some accounts suggest that Ellsworth
cut in before reaching Lebanon and that he already knew "B" was the
call letter for that station. Ellsworth's own account, here cited, shows
that this was not the case. The telegraphic conversation is not reported
by Ellsworth in his printed accounts and seems to have come from his
own retained copies of the telegrams. Plum accepts these as accurate,
perhaps because he had Union originals. See *CV*, 6:164 (1898); *Knoxville Journal*, Aug. 3, 1862; *Louisville Journal*, Aug. 12, 1862; *Nashville
Dispatch*, Aug. 26, 1863.

268–269. This question is mentioned by Plum, *op. cit.*, I, 195. The
rest is from the *Nashville Dispatch*, though Plum also records it. See
also *CV, loc. cit.*, and George I. Kitmer: "Raid by telegraph," *Ohio
Soldier*, 3:326 (May 24, 1890). The text of the conversation may be
taken as in general accurate, since operators often wrote out messages,
though not necessarily these purely personal chats. Plum and Ellsworth
usually agree in their stories, probably because both had file copies.

272.5–6. Information from Mrs. Frances Leslie McKean, a Gano
descendant, Georgetown, Ky.

274.2. Plum, *op. cit.*, I, 199, says "Ellsworth's claims [of success at
Somerset and Crab Orchard] are doubtless entirely fictitious." But this
can hardly be accepted. Doubtless Ellsworth's achievements lost nothing
in the telling; but many of his claims are confirmed, some of them by
Plum himself. Besides, Ellsworth had so many real triumphs that he had
no need to invent fictitious successes.

274.5. Ferdinand Foch: *Memoirs* (1931), pp. 476–477.

276.2. Plum, *op. cit.*, I, 189–200. On Somerset, see Ellsworth MS.,
f. 44, and "One of Morgan's men," *loc. cit.*

277.3–4. See Holland, *op. cit.*, pp. 78–83. Aug. 10 is the accepted
date for the raid. Ellsworth, f. 47, gives it as Aug. 11. Ellsworth also
gives the captain's name as "de Shea," but Tennessee military records
give it as "Desha."

278.2. Morgan's report, dated Hartsville, Tenn., Aug. 15, 1862; *Mobile
Register*, Sept. 2, 1862, reprinted in *Nashville Dispatch*, Oct. 1, 1862;
L. S. Ferrell in *CV*, 450 (1900). There is a spirited account in Holland,
op. cit., pp. 136–144, 157. See also *The Vidette* (Hartsville, Tenn.),
Aug. 17, 1862. This is "printed and published by 'Morgan's Brigade.'"
There is a file in Tenn. S/L.

280–281. The telegraphic dialogue is recorded partly in the Ellsworth
MS., ff. 46–56, and partly in *CV, loc. cit.* I have retained Ellsworth's
own text and punctuation, except that I have made him a present of a
few question marks when needed. Brooks describes his own experience
in *CV*, 6:12–13 (1898).

282.3. *Baltimore American,* Jan. 6, 1863. This gives the date of the incident as "Friday of last week"—in other words, Jan. 2, 1863, when Morgan was gone. This is probably an error resulting from careless copying of an exchange, for the preceding Friday, Dec. 26, 1862.

282.5. Ellsworth MS., ff. 77–86. Ellsworth MS., ff. 96–100; *CV,* 6:174 (1898); Plum, *op. cit.*

283.6. Ellsworth MS., f. 99, says forty or fifty soldiers. *CV, loc. cit.,* gives the number as thirteen.

284.5. Plum, *op. cit.,* II, 57; Ellsworth MS., ff. 99–100. Plum was an operator in this area at that time and knew Atwater. I have corrected his error in giving Ellsworth's first name as "John."

285–286. Ellsworth MS., f. 155. Ellsworth's capture is recorded in AGO Records, Ky. (Army) NG.

287.4. Charles T. Loehr. *War hist. of the old 1st Va. Inf.* (1884), pp. 26–27; James Longstreet: *From Manassas to Gettysburg* (1960), pp. 163, 662.

288. Lt. Col. S. I. Keith had just been killed, and in his place, Tanner, then a captain, was to be promoted to lieutenant colonel next day (Oct. 9, 1862). At the moment of his conversation with Polk he was in acting regimental command. See R. V. Marshall: *Hist. sketch 22nd Regt. Ind. Vols.* (1877), p. 24; OR, ser. 1, vol. 16, pt. 1, p. 1080. For similar incidents, see C. A. Heckman: "General Butler's failure," *PWT,* Mar. 2, 1888; S. P. Bates: *Hist. Pa. Vols.* (1869), I, 391, 142–143, 391; *RI Soldiers and Sailors* H/S, *Personal Narr.,* 7th ser. No. 3, pp. 9–23; Ann Sophia Stevens: *Pictorial Hist. of the war for the Union* (1866), I, 463–464; *CV,* 15:258 (1907).

The most trustworthy account of this episode is in the Fremantle Diary (ed. Walter Lord, 1956), pp. 132–133. Fremantle had this story directly from Polk, while the war was in progress. It is substantially confirmed by a note in *Southern Bivouac,* 2:403 (1884) and by W. N. Mercer Otey: "Organizing a Signal Corps," *CV,* 7:549–551 (1899). Fremantle's version is repeated in Stanley F. Horn: *Army of Tenn.* (1941), p. 185.

288–289. Major Cotter was an officer of the first Ohio Vol. Light Arty., later promoted colonel and placed in command of the regiment. His capture is reported in the *Nashville Dispatch,* Oct. 23, 1862. Since the newspaper notes that Cotter had by that time returned to Nashville on parole, he probably supplied the facts himself. See muster rolls of his regiment in AGO Records, Ohio (Army) NG, Division of Soldiers' Claims, Veterans' Affairs. "General McCook" was probably Gen. Alexander McDowell McCook, commanding I Corps at Perryville. However, the fighting McCooks of Ohio were a numerous breed, seventeen of whom were in service. Cotter may have been serving under Brig. Gen. Edward

Moody McCook, commanding the 1st Brigade, Cavalry Division, in Sept. and Oct., 1862, the period during which Perryville was fought. See *C/W Dict.*, s.v. "McCook."

289–290. *Ohio Soldiers,* 3:326, May 24, 1890. Cf. S. P. Bates: *Hist. Pa. Vols.* (1869), I, 418; II, 288, 632.

290–291. Theo F. Klutz: "Boy who saved Richmond," *CV,* 6:213–214 (1898); John W. Moore: *Roster of NY Troops,* II, 179–180; Wood enlisted on May 12, 1861, from Yadkin County, N.C., in Co. B, 21st NC. In 1862 this became the 9th Bn. Sharpshooters. There is a typewritten copy of the Klutz article, perhaps the author's original, in the NC Dept. of Archives.

291–292. John W. Dyer: *Reminiscences* (1898), pp. 140–141. No other source gives this tale, but as Dyer was present he is to be regarded as correct in essentials. He does say that Sherman was trying to envelop the Confederate left. In fact, Sherman was trying to envelop the Confederate right with his own left.

292.3. W. G. Beymer: *On hazardous service* (1912), pp. 118–119; W. A. Spicer: *Colonel H. H. Young* (1910), p. 42; Martin H. Jacoby: *Campaign life* (1882), pp. 39–40.

292.5. John Esten Cooke: "Virginia partizan," *PWT,* Oct. 29, 1881. See Chapter 17, "Secrets of Gettysburg," on the use of oilskins as disguise.

293. OR, ser. 1, vol. 7, p. 571; vol. 10, pt. 1, p. 773; pt. 2, pp. 2, 55, 225, 230. On Grant, see ser. 1, vol. 33, p. 1022; vol. 26, pt. 2, p. 319; Albion W. Tourgee: *Story of a Thousand* (1896), p. 213. There are many such stories in Canan MSS. VI, 9; XIV, 3; XX, 8, 12. See also K. P. Williams, *op. cit.,* III, 337.

294–295. T. Hennessy: "Edward Boyle, the spy," *PWT,* Oct. 9, 1880.

295.6. F. Shepard: "At Spring Hill and Franklin again," *CV,* 24:138–139 (1916); statement of Capt. P. H. Coleman, 1st Florida Inf. in John A. Wyeth: *That devil Forrest* (1959), p. 479. Capt. Coleman was in charge of these pickets. See also C. E. Merrill: "Battle of Franklin," *PWT,* May 17, 1879.

295–296. Henry Stone: "Repelling Hood's invasion of Tennessee," *B&L,* IV, 448.

296.2. W. W. Gist: "Other side at Franklin," *CV,* 24:13–14 (1916). See later comment by E. Shepard, *ibid.,* pp. 138–139.

296.4. J. D. Remington: "Cause of Hood's failure at Spring Hill," *CV,* 21:569–571 (1913). Remington's veracity is attacked in a later number, but the attack is followed by some surprising confirmation.

297.5. W. J. McMurray: *Hist. 20th Tenn. Vol. Inf.* (1904), pp. 334–335.

298.5. *B&L,* IV, 430–431. Hood himself states that the road was left open for the Union troops. He made this statement in a paper read at the Opera House, Louisville, on Dec. 1, 1881. See *Courier-Journal*, Dec. 4, 1881. This is repeated in Murray, *op. cit.*, pp. 333, 338. See also J. W. A. Wright: "Hood's Nashville campaign," *PWT*, Nov. 15, 1884.

299–300. *B&L*, IV, 438.

300.3. E. Shepard: "At Spring Hill and Franklin again," *CV*, 24:138–139 (1916). This is a comment on W. W. Gist: "Other side at Franklin," *ibid.*, pp. 13–16. Cf. Remington's "Hood's failure at Spring Hill," *CV*, 22:58–60 (1914). General John B. Hood: *Advance and retreat*, describes troop movements exactly as Remington does. Part of Hood's book appears in *B&L*, IV, 425–437. However, J. P. Young, in "Remington and General Hood at Spring Hill," *CV*, 22:126–128 (1914), denounces Remington as a "rank impostor." See also "Remington and Spring Hill," *CV*, 22:234–235 (1914). The fact that Remington is not mentioned by Hood proves nothing. Hood never knew Remington's identity. Besides, no general likes to tell how badly he has been duped. Remington's brigade *was* where he says it was when he says it was—in a favorable position for his exploit.

Authorities do not agree on the exact hour of Jackson's attack at Chancellorsville. The hours here are from Vincent J. Esposito (ed.): *West Point Atlas* (1959), Map 87.

300–301. W. C. De Zouche: "Gray under the blue," *PWT*, Scrapbook, Richardson Collection, HEH. F. E. Garnett: "Scenes at Chancellorsville," *ibid.*, Dec. 27, 1884. See also regimental histories.

301.2. Grierson's own account is in his MS., "Lights and shadows of life" (1892), ff. 417–418, in Ill. H/S. On the false orders at Yellow Tavern, see *CV*, 33:179 (1925).

302.1. OR, ser. 1, vol. 42, pt. 2, p. 1210. On J. J. Kerbey, see his *Boy spy in Dixie* (1897), pp. 110 ff.

302.3. E. L. Drake: *Annals of the Army of Tenn.* (1878), I, 147–148. On Captain Ross, see Fitzgerald Ross: *Visit to the cities and camps of the Confederate States* (1865), pp. 100–101. See also Anon.: "Scraps from a signal station," *Ohio Soldier*, 2:822 (1888); Edward S. Gregory: "Confederate signal corps," *PWT*, Feb. 22, 1879. For Hooker's distrust of cipher, see J. W. Brown: *Signal Corps, U.S.A.* (1896), pp. 348–355.

302–303. For other examples of interception, see J. W. Brown: *Signal Corps*, p. 526, and Charles E. Taylor: "Signal and secret service of the Confederate States," NC Booklets, vol. 2, no. 11 (1903), p. 12.

303–304. For the false signals, see OR, ser. 1, vol. 42, pp. 468, 1202; for Hoke's brigade, p. 1218; for his mine, p. 1205; for the other mines, pp. 50–59, 63–64, 68, 71, 1160, 1163. The Confederate order of battle, cited above, gives Hoke only a brigade. However, Federal intelligence was crediting him with a division.

304.2–3. This was either the station at Three Top Mountain or the station at Round Top. Round Top was not, of course, the famous hill near Gettysburg. Lee to Early, Aug. 31, 1864. Lee's Letterbooks, Va. H/S; OR, ser. 1, vol. 43, pt. 2, pp. 1009–1010.

304.5. Early told this story in a letter of Nov. 6, 1890, reproduced in Richard S. Irwin: *XIX Army Corps*, pp. 407–410. See also Virgil Carrington Jones: *Gray ghosts and rebel raiders* (1956), pp. 314, 410.

304–305. Longstreet to Irwin, Nov. 6, 1890, reprinted in Irwin, *op. cit.*, p. 407. On Longstreet's sick leave, see *C/W Dict.*, s.v. "Longstreet."

305.5. George A. Forsyth: *Thrilling days in army life* (1900), pp. 130–135. V. C. Jones: *Gray ghosts and rebel raiders* (1956), p. 314; Irwin, *op. cit.*, pp. 407–409, quoting a letter from Early to the author, *C/W Dict.*, p. 134.

306–307. *Nashville Dispatch*, quoting *NYT* under Memphis dateline of July 28, 1862.

307.4. Turner-Baker Papers, NA, RG 94, No. 3137.

308.3. Hurlbut to Grierson, Mar. 31, 1864, Grierson Papers. Ill. Hist. Library. On the raid, see John A. Wyeth: *That devil Forrest* (1959), pp. 304–305. Grierson's own MS. autobiography, contained in the Papers, is the best authority.

309–310. OR, ser. 1, vol. 42, pt. 2, pp. 1233–1236; Mrs. Roger A. Pryor: *Reminiscences of war and peace* (1904), p. 288; *My Day* (1909), pp. 206–207; John Emmett O'Brien: *Telegraphing in battle* (1910), pp. 151–152; *C/W Dict.*, p. 674. Edward Boykin: *Beefsteak raid* (1960), p. 162, gives the July date. The other dates, though not explicitly stated, are implied in W. R. Plum: *Military telegraph*, II, 264–265, the main source for this episode. The scheme began after the fight at Reams's Station (Aug. 25, 1864), lasted about six weeks, and was over before Pryor was captured, Nov. 27, 1864. The most valuable message was taken from the Federal wire "about the 12th of September."

310.2. OR, ser. 1, vol. 42, pt. 2, pp. 72, 542; Boykin, *op. cit.*, pp. 163–164, suggests that this was another eavesdropper.

312.3–4. Turner-Baker Papers, NA, RG 94, no. 3339.

314.3. *Cincinnati Commercial*, July 8, 1864, under a July 2 dateline showing that the incident took place "yesterday," i.e., July 1. There is a file in Cincinnati PL.

314.4. Frank M. Myers: *The Comanches* (1956), p. 56.

314–315. John W. Wayland: *Twenty-five chapters on the Shenandoah Valley* (1957), p. 398.

315–316. Gilmor records this episode, including the dialogue, in his

Four years in the saddle (1866), pp. 87–88. One typographical error is silently corrected in the passage here quoted. Official records of the Pennsylvania (Army) NG confirm Gilmor's identification of Capt. Fenner's command.

317–318. John S. Mosby: "General Stuart at Gettysburg," *PWT*, Dec. 15, 1877. See also his letter, "Reply to General Pleasanton," in *PWT*, Apr. 13, 1878; Virgil Carrington Jones: *Gray ghosts and rebel raiders* (1956), p. 67; E. P. Alexander: *Military memoirs* (1907), p. 379. There is a report of one of these escapes in *PWT*, Feb. 17, 1883.

318.2–3. Miss Esther Green, Stringfellow's grandniece, remembers hearing him say that he had been exchanged for a "Connecticut volunteer captain." For his capture and exchange, see service record, NA, RG 109, WD Coll., CSA records; Old Capitol Prison Records. It is sometimes said that Stringfellow was captured near New Baltimore, while following Stuart, after the Cavalry Corps had left Salem. The records here cited show this is impossible. See also Freeman: *Lee's Lts.*, III, 60–62.

318.4. Thomas Norton Conrad: *Confederate spy* (ca. 1895), pp. 52, 189. For Stuart's comment, see p. 54.

321–323. G. W. Beale: *Lieutenant of Cavalry* (1918), p. 112; R. L. T. Beale: *Hist. 9th Va. Cav.* (1899), pp. 79–81; H. B. McClellan: "South Carolinian's gallant service," *PWT*, Aug. 17, 1878; T. S. Garnett: "Cavalry service with General Stuart," *ibid.*, Feb. 8, 1879; Freeman: *Lee's Lts.*, III, 66; OR, ser. 1, vol. 27, pt. 2, p. 694; pt. 3, pp. 63–64; Edwin B. Coddington: *Gettysburg campaign* (1969), pp. 198–199.

323.3. Cockey made the mistake of talking to a disguised Federal officer. See H. B. Smith: *Between the lines* (1911), pp. 89–90.

323–325. On the appearance of Gordon's command, see John B. Gordon: *Reminiscences* (1904), p. 142; M. Jacobs: *Notes on the rebel invasion and Battle of Gettysburg* (1864), p. 11. On Wrightsville, see Gordon, *op. cit.*, pp. 143–144, and S. P. Bates: *Hist. Pa. Vols.* (1871), V, 122.

326. Mosby refers rather contemptuously to Longstreet and Harrison in *Belford's Monthly*, 8:159 (1891). In his book on *Stuart's cavalry in the Gettysburg campaign* (1908), he actually denies there was any such scout as Harrison—an obvious error. For minor references to Harrison, see E. P. Alexander: *Military memoirs* (1907), p. 379; R. H. McKim: *Soldier's recollections* (1910), pp. 257–258; John B. Hood: *Advance and retreat* (1880), p. 55. For Longstreet's own account, see his *Manassas to Appomattox* (1896), pp. 327–328, and *Annals of War*, p. 416. Cf. Freeman: *Lee's Lts.* (1944), III, 48–49, 226–227.

327–328. C. Moxley Sorrel: *Recollections of a Confederate staff officer*

(1905), pp. 156–157; *Louisville Times*, Feb. 22, 1913, p. 11; Louisville *Courier-Journal*, Feb. 22, 1913, p. 3.

329. On the date of Harrison's arrival, see Dowdey and Manarin: *Wartime papers of R. E. Lee* (1961), p. 574. On Longstreet's asperity, see B&L, III, 249–250.

331. On McCammon, see OR, ser. 2, vol. 27, pt. 1, p. 65. For a general picture of Harrison's arrival, see the Fairfax MSS., owned by Mrs. Eugenia Tennant Fairfax, Richmond, Va., described by Freeman: *Lee's Lts.*, III, 600–601 and 49–n. Some of these MSS. have been on loan. See also Longstreet: "Campaign of Gettysburg." *PWT*, Nov. 3, 1879; Sir F. Maurice (ed.): *Aide-de-Camp of Lee* (1927), pp. 219–221; Freeman: *Lee*, III, 61; A. A. Long: "Lee and his corps commanders," *PWT*, Vol. II of the Scrapbook in the Richardson Collection, HEH.

332.3. Sorrel, *op. cit.*, p. 161. General A. A. Long, Lee's military secretary, says that Lee learned the Federals had reached Frederick on the night of June 28, and that "this important information was brought by a member of Hood's Texas brigade." This may have meant Harrison, who cannot be identified among the numerous men of the same name in the National Archives. Sorrel says that Harrison was a Mississippian, but Mississippi AGO records have no trace of him. See A. A. Long: "Lee in Pennsylvania," *PWT*, Nov. 1, 1884. The contemptuous view of scouts is attributed both to Fairfax and to Lee himself. But see *B&L*, III, 271; F. Maurice: "Lincoln as a strategist," *Forum*, 75:161–169 (1926), also his *R. E. Lee the soldier* (1926), pp. 202–203.

333.5. R. H. McKim: *Soldier's recollections* (1910), p. 167.

334.2. John S. Mosby: *Stuart's cavalry in the Gettysburg campaign* (1907), pp. 92–93; M. Jacobs: *Notes on the rebel invasion* (1864), p. 15.

334.8. *Fremantle Diary* (ed. Walter Lord, 1956), p. 202.

335–336. *Richmond Examiner*, Sept. 10, 1863; *Southern Punch*, Dec. 5, 1863, p. 1. Both playbills are in the Harvard Theatre Collection. See also G. C. D. Odell: *Annals of the New York stage* (1927–1929), s.v. "Harrison."

336–337. Obituaries in Louisville *Times*, Feb. 22, 1913; *Courier*, Feb. 23, 1913; *Herald*, Feb. 23, 1913; *Dramatic Mirror*, 69:11 (1913); death certificate in Vital Records, Dept. of Health, Frankfort, Ky.; Edward G. Fletcher: *Records and history of theatrical activities in Pittsburgh, Pa., from their beginnings to 1861*, Harvard Diss., 1931; Pittsburgh Programs, MS. in Pennsylvania Room, Carnegie Library, No. r, 792/P67. As Baltimore did not preserve birth records before 1875, there is no birth certificate. The death certificate is in File 4684, No. 619, Registration District 550, Primary Registration District No. 2275, in Vital Records, Dept. of Health, Frankfort, Ky. The Actors' Fund unfortunately destroyed all its Harrison papers and preserves only an index card, showing that they once existed. There is a clipping folder in the Theatre Collection, NYPL. Innumerable Confederate officers named James Harrison are listed in NA. Louisville Directories show Harrison living at 606 West Walnut Street, where he died, as early as 1904. In 1906 he is described as a "solicitor." After that, no profession is stated. There are brief references in *Southern Illustrated News*, 3:160, June 11, 1864, and in Sylvia G. L. Dannett: "And the show went on . . . in the Confederacy," *Maryland Hist. Mag.*, 61:118 (1966).

338. Coggins Point is near Garysville, Va. It is not on many maps, but it does appear on the Gilmer Survey of Prince George County (1863), in VaHS.

339. John Emmet O'Brien: *Telegraphing in battle* (1910), p. 152; John S. Elliott: "Scouts with Wade Hampton," *PWT*, May 3, 1884. "Tomtit" is a southern name for the tufted titmouse (*Parus bicolor*) and the black-crested titmouse (*Parus atricristatus*). See *Audubon Bird Guide* (1949), pp. 92–93 and index.

340. OR, ser. 1, vol. 42, rt. 2, pp. 1235–1236, 1242; U. R. Brooks: *Butler and his cavalry* (1909), p. 308; Edward Boykin: *Beefsteak raid* (1926), pp. 195–196; Richard Lykes: "Hampton's cavalry raid." *Military Affairs*, 27:1–20 (1957), also his articles in *United Daughters of the Confederacy Mag.*, 17:11, 28, 30 (Mar.); 38–39 (Apr.); 34, 35, 38, 42 (May), 1954; John Esten Cooke: "General Wade Hampton and his cavalry," *PWT*, Feb. 21, 1880; "Hampton's Virginia campaigns," *ibid.*, Apr. 10, 1880; John F. Baer: "Cavalry armies compared," *ibid.*, Mar. 20, 1880; Thomas L. Rosser: "Rosser and his men," *ibid.*, Apr. 19, 1884. Mr. Boykin derived a good deal of his information from a local antiquary, now deceased, who had long collected local information. While this is not a source one would choose, it is now the only source there is.

341–342. Joseph Mills Hanson: "Rustling Yankee beefsteaks," Richmond *Times-Dispatch*, Section IV, p. 4, Aug. 1, 8, 1943. Margaret Donnan lived on into the 1940's, so that Mr. Hanson could get firsthand information.

Captured Federal reports give the herd as 2,486 head. Hasty estimates in other reports vary a little. See OR, ser. 1, vol. 42, pt. 1, pp. 853, 865, 877, 888, 891, 892. There are other references to the raid in this volume. See also Boykin: *Beefsteak raid* (1926), *passim*; Brooks: *op. cit.*, pp. 308–314; F. W. Myer: *The Comanches* (1956), pp. 330–331; George Baylor: *Bull Run to Manassas* (1900), pp. 243–247; *Nashville Dispatch*, Sept. 24, 1864; *NY Commercial*, Sept. 14, 1864; Anon.: "Great cattle raid of 1864," perhaps written by Shadburne, in Julian Shakespeare Harris Papers, Southern Historical Collection, NC;

John Emmet O'Brien: *Telegraphing in battle* (1910), p. 153; Richard W. Lykes: "Hampton's great beef raid," *C/W Times*, 5:4–13 (1967).
342. Edward Alfred Pollard: *Early life, campaigns and public services of Robert E. Lee* (1871), p. 743; Richard Lykes: "Hampton's cattle raid," *Military Affairs*, 21:19 (1957); estimates of S. G. Davis, Swift & Co., Miss Peg Swanson, Armour & Co., P. A. Putnam, Department of Agriculture; John Esten Cooke: "General Wade Hampton and his cavalry," *PWT*, Feb. 21, 1880.
343. OR, ser. 1, vol. 42, pt. 1, p. 946; obituary of Hogan in Atkins (Ark.) *Chronicle*, Jan. 28, 1923; *Biog. and Hist. Mem. of Ark.* (1891), p. 234; *Centennial Hist. Ark.* (1922), II, 1022. Hogan moved to Arkansas in 1888. The Pope County Pension Records list him as No. 25493 (1915).
344.2. There is a reference to "Mrs. Tatum's house" at "Despotona" in a typed copy of Hugh Henderson Scott's personal narrative, with MS. corrections, possibly by Scott himself, in the U. R. Brooks Papers at NC. A map accompanying the Official Records makes this somewhat clearer. "Despotona" is "Disputanta." A house marked "Tatam" is south of Disputanta.
344.3. Scott MSS., ff. 4–5.
344.4. OR, ser. 1, vol. 42, pt. 2, pp. 94–95; Charles Porter: "City Point explosion," *PWT*, Oct. 30, 1880; Morris Schaff: "Explosion at City Point," MOLLUS, II, 477–485. See also C/W Papers of the State of Mass., II, and Philip Van Doren Stern: *Secret missions of the Civil War* (1959), pp. 230–235.
345.3. OR, ser. 1, vol. 42, pt. 1, 954–956; vol. 46, pt. 3, p. 1250; Horace Porter: *Campaigning with Grant* (1908), p. 274.
346.1–3. Henry Hord: "Scouting about Memphis," *CV*, 20:207–208 (1912); John A. Wyeth: *That devil Forrest* (1959), pp. 424–447; Ewell Hord, said to be identical with Henry Hord and therefore one of the spies, was a private in Co. D, 3rd Mounted Ky. Vols. (Confederate). See Hord Memoir (MS.), Box 13–8, acc. no. 1617, in Tenn. S/L.
346.5. Charles William Bardeen: *Little fifer's war diary* (1910), p. 47; *Military Affairs*, 21:175–177 (1957); Stipp to Wilson, *Congressional Globe*, 37th Cong., 2nd Sess., p. 538, cf. p. 33–n; Edward L. Wells: *Hampton and his cavalry* (1890), p. 305; John W. Munson: *Reminiscence of a Mosby guerrilla* (1906), pp. 208–215.
347.1. Wells, *op. cit.*; Scott MS., f. 8; Brooks, *op. cit.*, pp. 105–106.
347.5. Brooks, *op. cit.*, pp. 41–43, 140; OR, ser. 1, vol. 42, pt. 2, pp. 785–786, 803–804. Cf. pp. 810, 827, 933.
349. Charles Minor Blackford: *Letters from Lee's army* (ed. Susan Leigh Blackford, 1947), p. 254, June 10, 1864.

351.3. Stuart to General "Chelton" (i.e., Chilton), Aug. 31, 1863, on Smith's promotion. See also *PWT*, May 24, 1879. On Grant and Mosby, see Virgil Carrington Jones: *Ranger Mosby* (1944), pp. 260, 273–274, 295, 301, 309. On Grant, see Chapter 6, "J. E. B. Stuart's Secret Agents," Part 2. Press reports show that Grant was formally handed his new commission on Mar. 9, 1864, though it was dated Mar. 10.

352. Pollock court-martial, NA, RG 153, JAGO, CM—LL—1968; also RG 94, JAGO, CM—LL—1968.

353.2. Vincent J. Esposito (ed.): *West Point Atlas* (1959), Map No. 120; *C/W Dict.*, pp. 194, 409.

353.4. Portraits of Antonia Ford courteously shown me by her great-grandson, Willard Roosevelt, show rather sandy hair that might be called blond. A third, however, probably painted rather earlier, shows blond hair. There is a caricature of her in *Harper's Weekly*, 7:211 (Apr. 4, 1863). See Shadburne's statement of Aug. 7, 1910, in U. R. Brooks: *Stories of the Confederacy* (1912), pp. 41–43. On Miss Ford's arrest, see Edward Bates's Diary and *Washington Star*, Mar. 18, 1863, also Garrett Laidlaw: *Willard's of Washington* (1954), pp. 74–76.

354. Hugh Henderson Scott: "Story of a scout told in his own way." In U. R. Brooks: *Butler and his cavalry* (1909), p. 96. On Scott, see also AGO Records, SC (Army) National Guard.

354.3. J. Marshall Crawford: *Mosby and his men* (1867), pp. 152–153.

355.1. Woodford B. Hackley: *Little Fork rangers* (1927), pp. 56–58, LC, NYPL. On movement of sutlers and women, see OR, ser. 1, vol. 33, p. 201.

355.3. Dowdey and Manarin: *op. cit.*, pp. 691–692, 694.

356. Benjamin Franklin Stringfellow: *War reminiscences* (n.d.), p. 3. This is a pamphlet about his lectures. Copies in LC and HEH.

357–358. William M. Dame: "Frank Stringfellow," *PWT*, Feb. 18, 1887. Clipping preserved in Stringfellow Scrapbook (kept by Mrs. Stringfellow), now in Virginia H/S. The Rev. Mr. Dame was in Stringfellow's party. He does not date the episode, but the presence of Stringfellow and Gregg's Cavalry Division near the Orange & Alexandria, at the same time, points clearly to the spring of '64. I have not quoted all the dialogue and have added two question marks to the text. The Rev. Mr. Dame was a private in Anderson's Company, Virginia Light Artillery (1st Company, Richmond Howitzers). See also John Scott: "Scout life with the Black Horse," *PWT*, May 24, 1879. See also John Esten Cooke in *PWT*, Oct. 29, 1881.

359. Lee to Stuart, Apr. 23, 1864, in H. B. McClellan MSS., quoted in Freeman: *Lee's Lts.*, III, 239. The McClellan MSS. are partly in Chicago and partly in Biarritz. Copies made for Freeman are with his papers in LC.

360.1. *National Intelligencer*, Mar. 23, 1864; *Philadelphia Inquirer*, Mar. 22, 1864; *Daily Morning Chronicle*, Mar. 24, 1864. Files of the Chronicle for this period are very rare, but the Newberry Library, Chicago, has a copy of this issue.

360.3. On Lee's query, see Dowdey and Manarin, *op. cit.*, pp. 685–691, and, for Longstreet's reply, p. 692. See also p. 420. Conrad reports his exploits in his own two books.

363–364. OR, ser. 1, vol. 33, p. 1326; Dowdey and Manarin, *op. cit.*, pp. 707–708. Stringfellow's pamphlet, *War Reminiscences*, shows that he did send the telegram. Its text also appears in *Kentucky Leader* (Lexington, Ky.), Aug. 23, 1892.

365–366. Dowdey and Manarin, *op. cit.*, pp. 692–699; *Grant Mem.*, II, 116–118. Grant was able to keep his own troops largely in the dark over his own intentions. See the MS. diary of Private Austin A. Carr (now in HEH), for April and early May, 1863. On strength estimates, see Esposito: *West Point Atlas*, Map 120.

366. Dowdey and Manarin, *op. cit.*, p. 707; J. William Jones: *Life and Letters* (1906), p. 305.

366–367. B&L, IV, 118; Freeman: Lee, III, 267–268; CMH, III, 431; OR, ser. 1, vol. 56, pt. 1, p. 1070; pt. 2, 942–943.

367–368. *Grant Mem.*, II, 177; John Scott: "Scout life with the Black Horse," *PWT*, May 24, 1879.

368. Channing Smith: "In deadly peril," *CV*, 30:222–223 (1922); W. B. Hackley: *Little Fork rangers*, pp. 56–58; John Scott: "Chapters of heretofore unwritten history," *PWT*, May 24, 1879.

369. Scott records the conversation and the events immediately following.

372–373. Scott, *loc. cit.*; *West Point Atlas*, Map 125, A-B; B&L, IV, 242; *Grant Mem.*, II, 211.

374. Channing M. Smith: "In deadly peril," *CV*, 30:222–223 (1922); Emmet Crozier: *Yankee reporters* (1956), p. 391; A. Fontaine Rose: "A good haul," *CV*, 17:223 (1909). On "Ike" Curtis, see U. R. Brooks: "Memories of battles," *CV*, 22:408 (1914); *Butler and his cavalry* (1909), p. 90; and service record in NA.

378–380. Barry Benson Papers, ff. 173–184, in Southern History Collection, NC. See also Susan Wilson Benson: *Barry Benson's Journal* (1862), Chapter IV.

384. Conrad: *Rebel scout* (1904), pp. 109–110. Rosser in *PWT*,

Apr. 19, 1884, says that the Negro reached the pickets and asked for Rosser himself.

385–387. Edward Boykin: *Beefsteak raid* (1960), pp. 148–151.

388–389. Mann told his story to the *Pensacola Journal.* This has been reprinted as a pamphlet, "A spy in the service of the Confederacy" (NYPL).

390. R. B. Anderson: "Secret service in the Army of the Tennessee," *CV,* 31:344–345 (1913). See also 3:202 (1905) and Mabel Baxter Pittard, *op. cit.,* pp. 28–29. On Disheroon and Gregg, 3:202–203 (1895); 8:57 (1900); 31:344–345 (1913). On Shaw's imprisonment, see NA, RG 109, Confederate staff file, H. B. Shaw.

391. *CV,* 35:327 (1927); Freeman: *Lee,* IV, 191–192.

INDEX